A MISPLACED MASSACRE

A MISPLACED MASSACRE

*Struggling over the Memory
of Sand Creek*

Ari Kelman

HARVARD UNIVERSITY PRESS
Cambridge, Massachusetts, and London, England

First Harvard University Press paperback edition, 2015

Fifth Printing

Publication of this book has been supported through the generous provisions of the Maurice and Lula Bradley Smith Memorial Fund.

Library of Congress Cataloging-in-Publication Data
Kelman, Ari, 1968–
A misplaced massacre : struggling over the memory of Sand Creek / Ari Kelman.
p.   cm.
Includes bibliographical references and index.
ISBN 978-0-674-04585-9 (cloth : alk. paper)
ISBN 978-0-674-50378-6 (pbk.)
1. Sand Creek Massacre, Colo., 1864.   2. Cheyenne Indians—Wars, 1864.
3. Chivington, John M. (John Milton), 1821–1894.   4. United States. Army.
Colorado Cavalry Regiment, 3rd (1864)—History.   5. United States. Army.
Colorado Cavalry Regiment, 1st (1862–1865)—History.   I. Title.
E83.863.K45   2012
978.8004'97353—dc23   2012012122

CONTENTS

Maps and Illustrations

PREFACE

I first became aware of Sand Creek more than two decades ago, while reading a letter written by an enlistee in the Iron Brigade, the unit that suffered the highest rate of casualties in the Union Army. At the time, I was looking through sources for my undergraduate thesis in one of the Wisconsin Historical Society's reading rooms, and I hoped that the tattered pages spread out before me would reveal what had motivated volunteer troops to fight with such ferocious courage during the Civil War. I never adequately answered that question, but I still remember details of the document: written in a shaky hand, the words filled with remorse that caught me off guard, the paper cracked and yellowed with age. Looking back, the note must have been composed sometime in 1865 as its author, a farm boy from Indiana, bemoaned an event that had taken place the previous year, a slaughter he labeled "Chivington's massacre." The passage caught my attention because the soldier seemed to think that an explosion of violence on the borderlands, a faraway "massacre," somehow diminished the integrity of his own service. More than a little confused, and with no Internet search engines at my disposal—truly, those were benighted times—I approached one of my mentors and asked for help. Who was Chivington? What was this mysterious episode? I found out that Sand Creek was actually part of the Indian Wars and not related to the Civil War at all. Alas, another wasted day in the archives—or so I recall thinking.

Fifteen years later, having read more about Sand Creek while in graduate school, I moved to Colorado, where I taught history and discovered that the massacre can be hard to escape. Thoroughfares that crisscross urban areas along the Front Range, a chapel on the campus of the university where I worked, a lonely town in the middle of the state's Eastern Plains, a snow-capped mountain looming over the city of Denver—all these and more bear the names of Sand Creek's sponsors and perpetrators. It seemed that by the end of the twentieth century, though most Coloradans no longer celebrated the massacre, they were still haunted by that chapter of their history. After learning that the National Park Service, partnered with descendants of Sand Creek's victims and survivors, hoped to commemorate the violence, I began following that project closely. I attended public hearings, met with the principals in the memorialization process, and decided to write a book about how various groups of people have recalled the massacre very differently—from its aftermath in late 1864 through the opening of the Sand Creek Massacre National Historic Site in 2007. I learned that the massacre has always been hotly contested, a vivid example of the truism that collective remembrance both shapes and is bound by contemporary politics. You hold in your hands the result of my efforts: a study of the collision of history and memory, of past and present, at Sand Creek.

As I began doing the research for this book, I realized that I would have to move beyond archival records and consult oral histories as well. As a result, I conducted well over a hundred interviews that eventually produced in excess of 3,500 pages of transcribed text. By the time this volume appears in print, copies of those transcriptions and the original taped conversations will be available as part of the National Park Service's Sand Creek Massacre National Historic Site collection, housed within the Western Archaeological and Conservation Center in Tucson, Arizona. It probably goes without saying that as a participant-observer, I became part of the memorialization process that I documented. Nevertheless, I do not appear as a character in these pages. I made the decision to remain in the background because although I relate this story, it is not in any meaningful way mine, and the people who can legitimately claim it as their own are far more interesting than I am. After making that choice, I then adopted a nontraditional architecture for this book. Rather than proceeding neatly in chronological order, the events that I recount here often moved in fits and starts, as the past impinged on the present. To make this point, I use the central narrative of the historic site's creation as the book's spine; I flesh out that tale with flashbacks to the era of the massacre and various moments when people struggled over Sand Creek's memory.

Those struggles taught me that I misunderstood the massacre when I first learned about it as an undergraduate pondering an especially beguiling primary source. From the perspective of the soldier whose letter I read, a young veteran gazing west from the trenches outside Richmond, Virginia, Sand Creek looked like an abomination and an aberration, a fit of frontier brutality that threatened to diminish glorious achievements hard won during a terrible but ultimately just war. As this book will demonstrate, by reversing that frame of reference, we can see that for Native people gazing east from the banks of Sand Creek, the Civil War looked like a war of empire, a contest to control expansion into the West, rather than a war of liberation. The massacre, then, should be recalled as part of both the Civil War and the Indian Wars, a bloody link between interrelated chapters of the nation's history.

A project like this rests upon the work of dedicated archivists and librarians. I owe a great debt to the outstanding staff members at the Bancroft Library at the University of California, Berkeley; the Beinecke Rare Book and Manuscript Library at Yale University; the Buffalo Bill Historical Center; the Colorado Historical Society; the Colorado State Archives; the Denver Public Library's Western History and Genealogy Collections; the Huntington Library; the Library of Congress; the Montana State Archives and Libraries; the National Archives and Records Administration in Washington, DC; the National Archives and Records Administration, Great Lakes Region; the National Museum of the American Indian; the National Park Service, Intermountain Region; the National Park Service, Western Archaeological and Conservation Center; the New York Public Library; the Office of Interlibrary Loan and the Special Collections at the University of California, Davis's Shields Library; the Oklahoma Historical Society; the Oklahoma State Archives and Records Management; the Special Collections at Colorado College's Tutt Library; the Special Collections at the University of Colorado Library; the Special Collections at the University of Denver's Penrose Library; the Western History Collections at the University of Oklahoma; and the Wyoming State Archives.

I also could not have written this book without the help of the following individuals: Emily Albu, Thomas Andrews, Herman Bennett, Joe Big Medicine, Larry Borowsky, Chuck Bowen, Sheri Bowen, Ray Brady, Steve Brady, Barbara Braided Hair, Otto Braided Hair, Rod Brown, Ben Nighthorse Campbell, Tom Carr, Steve Chestnut, Jon Christensen, Susan Collins, Colleen Cometsevah, Laird Cometsevah, Adina Davidson, Josh Davidson, Mark Davidson, Rachel Davidson, Bill Dawson, Bill Deverell, John Donohue, James Doyle, Jim Druck, Susan Ferber, Conrad Fischer, Karen Fisher, Homer Flute, Scott Forsythe, Janet Frederick, Rick Frost, Norma Gorneau, Andy Graybill, Jerry Greene, Chuck Grench, David Halaas, Ellen Hartigan-O'Connor, Steve Hillard, Don Hughes, Andrew Isenberg, Ruthanna Jacobs, Karl Jacoby, Rod Johnson, Sasha Jovanovic, Abbey Kapelovitz, Len Kapelovitz, Anna Kelman, Sam Kelman, Andrew Kinney, Kevin Kruse, Gregg Kvistad, Thomas LeBien, Jacob Lee, Randy Lewis, Patty Limerick, Ed Linenthal, Modupe Lobode, Lisa Materson, Kathleen McDermott, Kyme McGaw, Sally McKee, Greg Michno, Craig Moore, Jennifer Morgan, Zach Morgan, Kathy Olmsted, Lorena Oropeza, Josh Piker, Miles Powell, Eric Rauchway, Mildred Red Cherries, Bob Reinhardt, Andres Resendez, Myra Rich, Ben Ridgely, Gail Ridgely, Alexa Roberts, Joe Rosen, Jerry Russell, Susan Schulten, Philip Schwartzberg, Doug Scott, Nancy Scott-Jackson, David Shneer, Robert Simpson, Judy Smith, Cathy Spude, Ellen Stroud, Barbara Sutteer, Paul Sutter, Ingrid Tague, Alan Taylor, Pam Tindall, Cecilia Tsu, Chuck Walker, Clarence Walker, Louis Warren, Lysa Wegman-French, Christine Whitacre, Richard White, Cynthia Young, Charles Zakhem, and Karl Zimmerman.

The people listed above were incredibly generous with their time, and I thank them for their efforts on my behalf. They agreed to be interviewed, shared knowledge of the memorialization process in other ways, read part or all of my manuscript in draft, prepared elements of this book, provided me with a meal to eat or a bed in which to sleep while I did my research, or, in some cases, all the above. Their contributions have made this book better in more ways than I can count. The errors that remain are my responsibility alone.

Additionally, I am grateful to a number of organizations that provided the financial support that allowed me to complete this project: the Colorado State Historical Fund; the Huntington Library; the

National Endowment for the Humanities; the University of Denver Division of Arts, Humanities, and Social Sciences; and the Office of Research and the Division of Social Sciences at the University of California, Davis.

Finally, I dedicate this book to my best friend, Lesley, and my children, Jacob and Ben.

A Misplaced Massacre

I

A Perfect Mob

Mixed emotions transformed the ceremony into equal parts celebration and memorial service. On April 28, 2007, the National Park Service (NPS) opened the gates to its 391st unit, the Sand Creek Massacre National Historic Site. Hundreds of people gathered at a killing field tucked into the southeastern corner of Colorado. The hallowed ground sits near Eads, population 567, in Kiowa County, which, when the wind whips from the west, is within spitting distance of Kansas. In many ways Eads is typical of small towns scattered across the Great Plains: derelict historic structures line its wide main street; its fiercely proud residents love their community while worrying over its future; and a fragile agricultural economy threatens to blow away in the next drought. The massacre site, located twenty miles northeast of town, sits on a rolling prairie, a place transformed by seasons. From late summer till winter's end, it remains a palette of browns, grays, and dusty greens: windswept soil, dry shrubs, and naked cottonwoods. In early spring through the coming of autumn, though, colors explode. Verdant buffalo and grama grasses, interspersed with orange, red, and purple wildflowers, blanket the sandy earth, and an azure sky stretches to the distant horizon. That vivid quilt had not yet draped itself over the landscape on the day of the historic site's opening. The trees lining the creek bottom were just beginning to leaf out; it looked like the NPS had made a bulk buy of olive-drab scenery at a local army-navy surplus store.[1]

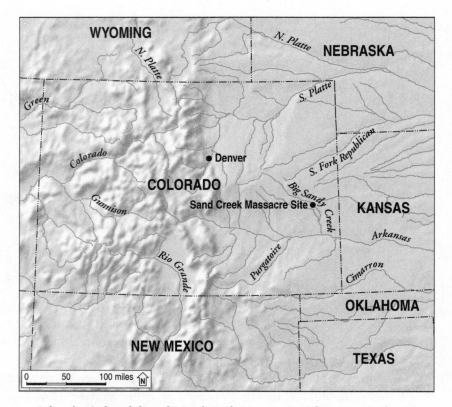

Colorado. (*Adapted from the Sand Creek Massacre Special Resource Study, U.S. Dept. of the Interior, National Park Service.*)

The site's austere beauty suited the proceedings. A Northern Arapaho drum group opened the ceremony, playing a veterans' song as a color guard carried American and NPS flags to positions flanking the dais. A Southern Cheyenne chief named Gordon Yellowman offered an opening prayer, while other dignitaries thumbed through notes for speeches that would stretch across more than three hours. After Yellowman finished, tribal chairmen, chiefs, spiritual leaders, U.S. senators, members of Congress, governors, NPS officials, and politicians from the surrounding community mourned the dead and lauded the process that had brought the diverse crowd together. The speakers shared, some implicitly, some explicitly, their visions for what the historic site could accomplish. Save for a few exceptions, they struck an optimistic pose: protecting the Sand Creek site not only honored the memory of the people killed at the massacre, promising long-deferred "healing" for the affected tribes, but also offered a blueprint for future cooperation between Native American peoples and federal authorities. Collective remembrance, if situated in a sacred place, could seal a historical rift, cut by violence, that yawned between cultures.[2]

Memorials are shaped by politics. Contemporary concerns inflect how history is recalled at such places, as people engaged in the process of memorialization envision their projects with eyes cast toward the present and future as well as the past. This is especially true for federally sponsored historic sites, because government officials have long viewed public commemoration as a kind of patriotic alchemy, a way to conjure unity from divisiveness through appeals to Americans' shared sense of history. This impulse may have been best expressed on March 4, 1861, when Abraham Lincoln responded to secessionists, then shredding the national fabric, with his first inaugural address. In the speech's final sentence, Lincoln implored Southerners to heed the "mystic chords of memory, stretching from every battlefield and patriot grave to every living heart and hearthstone all over this broad land." Those chords, he promised, would once again "swell the chorus of the Union" when "touched . . . by the better angels of our nature." At historic sites scattered across the United States, including the shrine devoted to President Lincoln that opened in Washington, DC, in 1922, sentiments like these, evincing an abiding faith in the nationalizing power of public memory, have been carved into stone. These monuments ostensibly serve the nation's interests by linking its disparate peoples and, simultaneously, legitimating the authority of the federal government. Out of common memories, the theory goes, Americans have forged a common identity—even, Lincoln believed, as they broke into warring camps.[3]

Nowhere is this supposedly truer than at historic battlegrounds. At Lexington and Concord, Fort Mackinac and Chalmette, Petersburg and Shiloh, the Little Bighorn and Pearl Harbor, battlefield memorials recall the deeds of American history's patriots, warriors who died so that the nation might live. In preserving these sites, later generations have struggled to sustain the lessons of bygone eras, connecting past and present through memory. Conservators seemingly believe that blood-soaked ground is ideally suited to this kind of didacticism, not only because of the events that transpired there but also because the landscape appears permanent, unchanging through the years, and thus capable of trapping history in amber. By walking across a wooden bridge in Boston's exurbs, slogging through a Louisiana wetland, scaling a rocky promontory overlooking the straits connecting Lakes Michigan and Huron, descending trenches cut deep into the ground in Virginia and Tennessee, reading a list of soldiers' names carved into a granite marker looming over a Montana prairie, or gazing at drops of oil bubbling up from the depths of the Pacific Ocean off the coast of Oahu, visitors to these sites are encouraged to stand tall against long odds, to remain steadfast in the face of privation, to rally round the flag, to practice eternal vigilance against unexpected perils, and to venerate sacred soil. Even as turbulent changes shake American society, history's insights will remain accessible at such places. And the act of remembering, no matter how painful, will strengthen the foundation upon which the nation is built.[4]

Sand Creek, most speakers at the site's opening ceremony suggested, could play this role by encouraging supplicants to set aside their disagreements in service of healing. The justification for collective remembrance in the United States in recent years has often rested on a similar assumption: that memorialization has palliative qualities. From the Murrah Building in Oklahoma City to the National September 11 Memorial in Manhattan, memorial planners have secured public support for their initiatives by promising comfort to stricken communities and the nation at large. That Sand Creek would be the first unit within the National Park System to label an event in which federal troops killed Native Americans a "massacre" promised to deepen its utility. By remembering the dead and pondering the nation's history of racial violence, site visitors would fuel cultural pluralism's ultimate triumph over prejudice, brokering a rapprochement between long-standing enemies. At the same time, visiting the memorial landscape would exculpate the perpetrators' heirs, because of their willingness to mourn while admitting their forebears' guilt in a tragedy. This utopian vision suffused most of the speeches at the opening ceremony, typifying their authors' hopes for the historic site.[5]

But dissenting voices, ringing with skepticism born at Sand Creek and hardened during the tortuous process of memorializing the massacre, questioned this promise of easy diversity. These critics understood that for most of American history, whites had systematically written Native people out of the national narrative, more commonly forgetting than remembering them. For instance, most historic sites that recount the sweep of westward expansion adopt the perspective of white settlers. Given the celebratory vector of American memory projects more broadly, this is not especially surprising. In fact, few nations— the cases of South Africa and Germany are notable counterexamples— spend much time and energy remembering their sins alongside their heroic exploits. As a result, when memorials in the United States discuss Native Americans at all, they typically use them as benchmarks for national progress, as objects rather than subjects. These monuments often prop up frontier mythologies, celebrating, with imperialist rhetoric, the conquest of the American West and the dispossession of its indigenous inhabitants. Adding insult to injury, these sites regularly cast Native people as uncivilized by suggesting that they have no history of their own, that they are exclusively a people of memory. Until recently, even the NPS's historic sites typically framed the Plains Indian Wars using the words of Robert Utley, a renowned scholar and one-time NPS chief historian, who labeled the violence a "clash of cultures." Utley's phrase obscured responsibility for that conflict.[6]

Hoping to shift that context, many of the Native people who helped to create the Sand Creek historic site rejected what they saw as a hollow offer of painless healing and quick reconciliation at the opening ceremony. Concerned that the memorial might be a stalking horse for an older assimilationist project—the U.S. government's long-standing effort to strip tribal peoples of their distinctive identities—these skeptics instead portrayed the site as an emblem of self-determination. They understood that controlling the interpretative apparatus at a national public space, distant from the Mall in Washington, DC, but still wielding the weight of federal authority, offered them an opportunity to define insiders and outsiders. Consequently, they had fought for years to steer the commemorative process, struggling over nomenclature by insisting that the memorial be called the Sand Creek *Massacre* National Historic Site. They had turned next to narration, demanding that the site tell the massacre story from a Native perspective, featuring Cheyenne and Arapaho voices informed by indigenous knowledge. Finally, they had seized the chance to root their heritage in southeastern Colorado's landscape, reclaiming a piece of what once had been their homeland. As tribal traditionalists, they worried that modernity had besieged their way of life. They believed that the memorial would help them preserve their cultural practices, securing their future by venerating the past. For these activists, the site would serve tribal rather than federal interests.[7]

Other participants at the opening ceremony expressed suspicions about the memorial for a host of additional reasons: because the federal government remained unpopular on southeastern Colorado's plains, particularly when it insinuated itself into local land-use disputes; because of the perceived taint of political correctness hovering over what some onlookers viewed as an unnecessary reinterpretation of Colorado's history; and because of a gnawing sense that including the word "massacre" in the site's name indicted the U.S. Army. In the wake of the 9/11 attacks, with the nation embroiled in two controversial wars, some observers worried that a memorial questioning the military's rectitude flirted with anti-Americanism.[8]

Kiowa County commissioner Donald Oswald served as a greeter when he spoke first at the opening ceremony. He did not mention the massacre at all, instead expressing his hope that visitors would enjoy themselves during their stay and consider returning to the area in the future. That the memorial recalled one of the great injustices in Western history stood beside the point for Oswald; he saw the site as an engine of economic growth. His remarks made sense in context. Some of his constituents had misgivings about the historic site. Their home was unusually stable, and they liked it that way. County residents often were born, raised, and died on a single piece of land. They knew their neighbors the way many Americans know their families. As Rod Brown, another county commissioner, noted, "Nobody has to use turn signals in Eads, because everybody knows where everybody else is going." Seven in ten people residing in Kiowa County at the time had lived there for more than five years, a figure nearly 20 percent higher than for the rest of the state. The prospect of becoming a "gateway community," hosting thousands of heritage tourists annually, thus threatened the county's sense of itself as a quiet place, distant from the churn of urban life. Many local people also worried about tethering themselves to a service economy. They were used to being relatively independent, one of the virtues they saw in their agricultural way of life. The historic site, a sacrifice on the altar of commerce, seemed like a devil's bargain, then. It would force change on a place fond of stasis. As Janet Frederick, head of the Kiowa County Economic Development Corporation, suggested, "there is always that fear of the unknown. It's very comfortable here without any surprises." But something had to give; crisis heralded compromise.[9]

Over the previous five years, as Colorado's population had boomed by more than a tenth—an echo of the previous decade's even more explosive growth—Kiowa County had experienced an exodus. Approximately 15 percent of its residents had left, usually for the promise of one of the cities, including Albuquerque, Colorado Springs, Denver, Fort Collins, and Cheyenne, sprawling up and down the Front Range. Mirroring trends found throughout the nation's beleaguered small towns, young people especially had fled, leaving behind a rapidly aging population. Something like one in ten Coloradans were senior citizens when the Sand Creek site opened, compared to almost a quarter of Kiowa County's residents. So when Commissioner Oswald addressed the crowd gathered at the site's opening, he understood that if his community was not yet dying, it surely was on life support. The memorial offered a last-ditch chance to ensure that the county would have a future—even as it struggled to preserve its past.[10]

Still, some Kiowa County residents fretted about advertising that federal troops had perpetrated a "massacre" in their backyard. Janet Frederick, the site's most committed local booster, explained, "people get a little defensive," worrying that "they're going to be looked at as the bad guys." At the same time, she regretted that some of her neighbors found it easier "to see the cavalry and Colonel Chivington [who commanded the soldiers at Sand Creek] as more like us than the tribes are." Frederick understood the effect of demographics: Eads was 98 percent white. She also knew that the historical bonds linking Kiowa County's twenty-first-century residents to the violent dispossession of the Native Americans who previously had lived there could become suffocating. Few local people took pride in their relationship with John Chivington. But as Frederick allowed, some of them nevertheless recognized him as closer kin to them than the Cheyennes and Arapahos that his men had slaughtered in 1864.

Above all, Frederick's participation in the public remembrance of Sand Creek had taught her about the difficulty of trying to reconcile seemingly incommensurable historical narratives. For throughout the memorialization process, competing perspectives on the massacre appeared, like restless ghosts from the past, both informing and constraining the contemporary struggle to recall the violence.[11]

Three massacre stories in particular still loomed over the historic site when it opened: the first from John Chivington, an enthusiastic perpetrator; the second from Silas Soule, a reluctant witness; and the third from George Bent, a victim and survivor of the ordeal. Read together, their tales suggest that so much uncertainty shrouds Sand Creek that seeking an unchallenged story of the massacre may not be merely futile, but also counterproductive. Instead, the mayhem can best be understood by sifting through conflicting, often hazy, accounts of the past. In part, discrepancies in the historical record can be ascribed to the so-called fog of war. Scenes of violence, especially mass violence, are notorious for breeding unreliable and often irreconcilable testimony. But in the case of Chivington's, Soule's, and Bent's Sand Creek stories, their disagreements stemmed not only from the havoc they all experienced but also from the politics of memory surrounding the points they disputed: What caused the bloodshed? Could it have been avoided? Who should be held accountable for what happened? And was Sand Creek a glorious battle or a hideous massacre? Such questions raised thornier issues still: about the racial identities and gender ideologies that structured an emerging multicultural society in the West; about the interplay of politics and violence on the American borderlands; and, finally, about the righteousness of continental expansion and the bloody wars—both the Civil and the Indian—spawned by that process.[12]

Chivington, Soule, and Bent understood the stakes when they clashed over Sand Creek's memory. And even if they could not know for certain that their dispute would reverberate across the years, they crafted and recrafted their stories, hoping to win adherents in a contest they suspected would have lasting implications. The nation, they recognized, had recently fractured over the fate of its western territories, over the question of whether federal authorities would allow slavery to root itself in that soil. The country's future, they believed, would unfold in the same region, as white settlement stretched from the continent's interior to the Pacific coast. Because Sand Creek took place as the Civil

War raged, and because the massacre catalyzed the Indian Wars that followed, it seemed likely to be read by future generations as a pivotal chapter in the American story. Chivington, who believed that Sand Creek had been a noble and necessary part of winning the West, wanted the episode written into the national narrative as a glorious battle. Soule, who worried that the massacre would cast a pall over the preservation of the Union and westward expansion, hoped it could be forgotten. Bent agreed with Chivington: Sand Creek should be remembered by future generations. But he saw the violence as a tragedy in Cheyenne history, an ugly and violent outgrowth of the ongoing removal of the Plains Tribes. The struggle over how and even whether Sand Creek should be recalled would echo at the massacre site more than a century later.[13]

For his part, Chivington used the gallons of blood spilled along Sand Creek to depict a masterstroke. Late on November 29, 1864, with corpses still cooling on the ground, he passed along glad tidings to his superior, General Samuel Curtis, commander of the U.S. Army's Department of Kansas. Exhausted by the day's fighting, Chivington wrote: "at daylight this morning [we] attacked [a] Cheyenne village of 130 lodges, from 900 to 1,000 warriors strong." The fight had gone well, he bragged. His men had killed several chiefs, as well as "between 400 and 500 other Indians." After memorializing his fallen troops—"9 killed, 38 wounded. All died nobly."—Chivington justified the attack. Pointing to depredations allegedly committed earlier that year by the Native people his men had defeated at Sand Creek, he related tales designed to inflame observers familiar with the unfolding Anglo settlement of the Plains: "found a white man's scalp, not more than three days' old, in one of the lodges." In sum, Chivington's men had whipped "savages" guilty of desecrating white bodies, an outrage that demanded a quick reprisal administered by a sure hand. Sand Creek, in this view, was a job well done.[14]

Chivington seemed to understand in that moment that he stood at a crossroads. A Methodist minister, committed abolitionist, and stalwart Union man, he had preached Christ's gospel on the Plains before arriving in Colorado Territory four years earlier, ready to spread the Good Word to heathen gold seekers prospecting in the foothills west of Denver. Stories, perhaps apocryphal, circulated in the ranks about an episode from before the war, when the "Fighting Parson" had faced down a pro-slavery mob in Kansas. Coolly placing twin revolvers on the pulpit beside his text, he had delivered a rousing sermon. A bull of a man—Chivington weighed more than two hundred pounds, towered six feet four inches tall, and possessed a booming baritone that sounded like it could overawe artillery on the battlefield—he rejected a chaplaincy early in the Civil War and instead volunteered to fight. Commissioned a major in the 1st Colorado Regiment, he earned fame in March 1862, when he led his men on a complex maneuver at the Battle of Glorieta Pass in New Mexico, cutting off an invading force of Confederates from their supply lines. But after his superiors promoted him to colonel, the ambitious Chivington's military career stalled. He hoped to become a U.S. senator after the war, and Sand Creek presented him with a final chance to make his mark.[15]

After informing Curtis of his exploits, Chivington found energy later in the day for other important matters: public relations. He composed a second note, to editors at Denver newspapers. Although the men of the 3rd Colorado Regiment had enlisted months earlier expecting to fight Indians, they had mostly loafed around the city instead, winning only reputations for ignoring bar tabs. Onlookers taunted the soldiers for their inactivity, labeling the outfit the "Bloodless Third." Chivington's Sand Creek story responded to these slurs by celebrating the significance of the violence. Grander in the second telling than the first, what had been an "engagement" became "one of the most bloody battles ever fought on these plains." His men, he related, had attacked "one of the most powerful villages of the Cheyenne Nation." The result represented "almost an entire annihilation of the entire tribe." Perhaps concerned that he appeared to be gloating over fresh corpses, he then addressed "those gentlemen who are opposed to fighting these red scoundrels," concluding, as in his earlier note, by referencing abominations supposedly committed by the fallen enemy: "I was shown by [my] chief surgeon the scalp of a white man taken from the lodge of one of the chiefs, which could not have been more than two or three days taken, and I could mention many more things to show how these Indians that have been drawing Government rations . . . are and have been acting." The recovered remains again attested to the hostility and depravity of the vanquished Indians.[16]

Two weeks later, his perspective apparently sharpened by rest, Chivington wrote a more complete report to General Curtis. The colonel explained that on November 24, the 3rd Regiment, along with part of the 1st Regiment, had arrived at Fort Lyon, in southeastern Colorado, where they had collected more men and artillery, including at least "two howitzers." Four days after that, he recalled, the column had marched northeast throughout the night until, "at daylight on 29th November striking Sand Creek, about forty miles from Fort Lyon." There, the campaign "discovered an Indian village of 130 lodges, comprised of Black Kettle's band of Cheyennes and eight lodges of Arapahos with Left Hand." Chivington divided his troops and ordered an assault. Although the attack surprised the Indians, they "rallied" before "form[ing] a line of battle across the creek, about three-fourths of a mile above the village, stubbornly contesting every inch of ground." A running engagement ensued. "The Indians," facing heavy fire from infantry, mounted cavalry, and artillery, gradually "fell back from one position to another" across approximately "five miles." Eventually, though, Black Kettle's and Left Hand's people "abandoned all resistance and dispersed in all directions."[17]

In this telling, Sand Creek had been a terrible and glorious battle. As Chivington remembered it, his men, agents of an ascendant civilization sweeping inexorably across the Plains, had squared off against savages, the Cheyennes and Arapahos, guilty of countless crimes against white settlers in recent months. The fighting at Sand Creek had been so brutal, the Native warriors there so committed to their doomed struggle, that the soldiers had taken "no prisoners." Instead, Chivington's men had left between "500 and 600 Indians dead upon the ground . . . and all their lodges destroyed." The contents of those dwellings "had served to supply the command with an abundance of trophies, comprising the paraphernalia of Indian warfare and life." Leaving aside ethnographic curiosity, Chivington instead underscored the brutality of the clash, celebrating the soldiers who had given their lives during the fight, the two men who had since succumbed to their wounds, and the thirty-eight others who had been hurt. The living and the dead, he proclaimed, had "sustained the reputation of our Colorado troops for bravery and effectiveness." Again, Sand Creek had been a struggle between the forces of darkness and light. A new day, Chivington suggested, would dawn in its wake.[18]

At the close of his second dispatch to Curtis, Chivington alluded to a brewing controversy surrounding the violence. "I cannot conclude," he sniffed, "without saying that the conduct of Capt. Silas Soule, Company D, First Cavalry of Colorado, was at least ill-advised, he saying that he thanked God that he had killed no Indians . . . proving him more in sympathy with those Indians than with the whites." At Sand Creek, Soule had refused to commit his troops to the fight and had later raised questions about the violence. He suggested that the bloodshed had not been a triumph, as Chivington and his loyalists insisted, but a tragedy: a massacre of peaceful Indians. Tamping down these charges, Chivington reiterated to Curtis his earlier claims about the collective guilt of the Native people at Sand Creek: "The evidence is most conclusive that these Indians are the worst that have infested the routes on the Platte and Arkansas Rivers." Again pointing to the mutilation of white bodies, Chivington this time multiplied the proof recovered at Sand Creek. Not just one scalp, as he had previously mentioned, but "several," hacked from "white men and women," were "found in their lodges." Based on these grisly remains, he concluded, "the evidence was clear that no lick was struck amiss."[19]

As the final days of 1864 ticked down toward the new year, several disgruntled officers from the 1st and 3rd Regiments began openly questioning the veracity of Chivington's account. With the nation hopeful that the Civil War might soon end, newspapers in New York and Washington ran articles about atrocities recently committed on the frontier by soldiers who reportedly had slaughtered defenseless Indians. On December 29, the Denver press broke the story locally but with a different spin: enemies of the West and of Colonel Chivington were conspiring to tarnish the reputation of the heroes of Sand Creek. Then, early in January, officials in Congress and the War Department concluded that the allegations necessitated investigating Sand Creek. As this tide of recriminations rose around him in early 1865, Chivington treaded water. He allowed his former subordinates and editors at several Denver papers to mount spirited defenses of his good name and leadership. But when the first of what eventually would be three inquiries opened in the following months, Chivington testified on his own behalf.[20]

In April 1865, the colonel offered federal investigators his fullest recounting of the massacre. Across more than seven single-spaced pages, he answered nineteen pointed questions. He provided information ranging from autobiographical tidbits to his impression of the intentions of the Native Americans killed at Sand Creek. He recalled that the previous November his men, approximately five hundred soldiers, had attacked more than a thousand Cheyennes and Arapahos, of whom "about seven hundred were warriors." Responding to a drumbeat of allegations that these Indians had actually been peaceful, he noted the "unusual number of males" in the camp, hinting at their dark aims: perhaps so many men had gathered there because "the war chiefs of both nations were assembled . . . for some special purpose." Coloradans, Chivington went on, had feared that a vast confederation of Indians was scheming at the time to obliterate settlers on the Plains. Were these Native people part of that unholy alliance? Chivington could not say for certain. But, he explained, the warriors in this camp had prepared in advance for violence, belying later claims that they had been friendly. "Many of the Indians," he noted, "were armed with rifles and many with revolvers." And they had fortified the ground. "They had excavated trenches under the bank of Sand Creek," he seethed, taking "shelter in these trenches as soon as the attack was made, and from thence resist[ing] the advance of my troops." The Colorado volunteers had fought not with innocents, Chivington asserted, but with well-armed warriors, combat-hardened hostiles ready for a pitched battle.[21]

Pressed by examiners on whether his troops had violated the rules of civilized warfare, killing women, children, and the elderly and plundering the enemy's camp for valuables, Chivington first dodged the question and then dug in, maintaining that Sand Creek had been a legitimate engagement. Although he could not "state positively the number of women and children killed," he insisted, "from all I could learn, I arrived at the conclusion that but few . . . had been slain." As for allegations that his subordinates had ignored the regulations governing the handling of property seized from the enemy, Chivington demurred, insisting that his men had properly disposed of the goods they had taken from the field. Anyway, he concluded with a rhetorical wave, the "trinkets taken at the Indian camp were of no value. The soldiers retained a few of these as trophies; the remainder with the Indian lodges were destroyed."[22]

Chivington next explained why he had attacked the particular Indians at Sand Creek, bands that dismayed critics noted had been arrayed under peace chiefs like Black Kettle and Little Raven. Questioning this conventional wisdom, Chivington claimed again that the Cheyennes and Arapahos had actually been hostile. But when asked for specifics—"Give in detail the names of all Indians so believed to be hostile, with the dates and places of their hostile acts, so far as you may be able to do so."—he instead offered a composite sketch of savages who for years had menaced settlers on the Plains. "When a tribe of Indians is at war with the whites," he lectured, "it is impossible to determine what party or band of the tribe or the name of the Indian or Indians belonging to the tribe so at war are guilty of the acts of hostility." Having stripped Native people of their individuality, suggesting that any given Indian was neither any better nor any worse than the next, Chivington still concluded of the Cheyennes and Arapahos at Sand Creek, "they were of the same tribes with those who had murdered many persons and destroyed much valuable property on the Platte and Arkansas rivers during the previous spring, summer and fall." This damning fact, he insisted, "was beyond a doubt."[23]

With that established, Chivington admitted that he, along with John Evans, Colorado's territorial governor at the time, had parleyed the previous September with Black Kettle and several other chiefs outside of Denver at Camp Weld. The Cheyenne and Arapaho leaders had left that gathering convinced that they had forged an agreement guaranteeing their people's safety if they camped near Fort Lyon. Unfortunately, Chivington continued, the Indians had not fulfilled their obligations. They had never handed over the livestock and hostages their people had taken during recent raids. And, he added, General Curtis had later insisted that "there could be no peace without his consent." So although Major Edward Wynkoop, formerly Fort Lyon's commander, had "promise[d]" Black Kettle's people "the protection of our flag," Chivington said that Wynkoop had been cashiered for exceeding his authority in doing so. Curtis had replaced Wynkoop with Major Scott Anthony, who, when Chivington arrived at Fort Lyon the night before Sand

Creek, had informed the colonel that the Native people camped nearby "were hostile."[24]

Chivington buttressed that contention by underscoring the essential fiendishness of all Indians, appealing to white racial solidarity, and invoking gender ideologies—the sanctity of white femininity—that structured Anglo-American society. "I had no means of ascertaining what were the names of the Indians who had committed these outrages," he stated, "other than the declarations of the Indians themselves, and the character of Indians in the western country for truth and veracity, like their respect for the chastity of women who may become prisoners in their hands, is not of that order which is calculated to inspire confidence in what they may say." Indians, he suggested, were interchangeable and inscrutable. Apparently drawing on the pseudoscience of the day—the work of theorists like Samuel Morton, who, based on measurements of skulls, argued against a single creation, positing instead "polygenesis," the notion that people of different races were members of different species—Chivington reckoned that even reputedly friendly Indians, peace chiefs like Black Kettle, would ultimately revert to form. Subtle differences between individuals or bands must finally pale before the overweening power of immutable racial stock, he believed. As any self-respecting frontiersman knew, Indians were all alike: liars, kidnappers, rapists. And blood would out.[25]

Chivington then replayed his trump card: more evidence of atrocities committed on white bodies. Nearly half a year after the fact, the single scalp that he had originally reported had multiplied into "the scalps of nineteen (19) white persons." If those bloody remains did not justify the attack, then he pointed to "a child captured at the camp ornamented with six white women's scalps." "These scalps must have been taken by these Indians or furnished to them for their gratification and amusement by some of their brethren, who," he spat sarcastically, "were in amity with the whites."[26]

When federal investigators offered Chivington an opportunity to enter additional exculpatory material into the record, he seized the chance to provide a history lesson, waving the bloody shirt by placing Sand Creek in the context of the Civil War. "Since August 1863" he "had been in possession of the most conclusive evidence of an alliance, for the purposes of hostility against the whites, of the Sioux, Cheyennes, Arapahos, Comanche river, and Apache Indians." This conspiracy of hostile tribes, he reminded his audience, had fomented their plan against a backdrop of disunion: "Rebel emissaries were long since sent among the Indians to incite them against the whites." With the Cherokees already allied with the Confederacy, Westerners had to guard against more Indian trouble. In Colorado, he continued, George Bent (misidentified as "Gerry Bent"), son of borderlands trade tycoon William Bent and Owl Woman, his Cheyenne wife, had served as the South's agent. Bent had promised the Cheyennes that with "the Great Father at Washington having all he could do to fight his children at the south, they could now regain their country." In this way, Chivington made the Native people killed at Sand Creek enemies not just of whites in Colorado Territory but of the Union more broadly, the bloodletting not just a triumph in the Indian Wars but of the Civil War.[27]

President Lincoln had just been reelected and General Sherman was still marching to the sea when the Colorado soldiers descended on Sand Creek. And when Chivington submitted his detailed account of the attack to federal investigators, General Lee had not yet surrendered at Appomattox Court House. The fate of the nation, including its western territories, still hung in the balance. But with the war nearly over, the Thirteenth Amendment (then awaiting ratification by the states) apparently had settled the question that had sparked the conflict in the first place: whether slavery would spread west. Men like Chivington believed that they deserved credit for the outcome. Abolitionists and nationalists, they had migrated to the territories in the 1850s in part so that the region might remain free soil. And many of them had, when the war started, enlisted to fight for the Union. In spring 1865, these loyal Republicans looked back over the road to disunion and the war itself and decided that the federal government owed them fair recompense for their patriotic sacrifices: the West should be theirs. But then it turned out that, blinkered by a relentless focus on the future of African American slavery, earlier debates over how best to settle the region had often ignored the complicating presence of the Native peoples already living there.[28]

Chivington's testimony, a regional document with national implications, emerged out of that silence. Before the Civil War, most observers

had assumed that Indians, crippled by inferior racial stock, would van-
ish when faced with white settlers. Events like Sand Creek clouded
such visions. The transition from savagery to civilization would apparently be bloodier. Chivington, hinting that the federal officials investigating Sand Creek possessed effete eastern sensibilities misplaced in
the rough-and-tumble West, explained that his troops had understood
the real problem. Unlike their civilian minders in Washington, DC, the
men of the 3rd Regiment had recognized that if they mollycoddled the
Plains Tribes, the nation would be denied its Manifest Destiny. They
had removed an obstacle from the path of onrushing white settlement
as surely as a farmer might clear a stone before the plow in his fields.
Coloradans owed them a debt. The Union owed them a debt. And every
settler who shouted "Westward ho!" in the years after Sand Creek would
owe them a debt. He and his men, Chivington contended, had served as
the shock troops of expansion, beginning an American revival on the
frontier.[29]

Turning away from the war, Chivington narrowed his gaze, from the
national to the local, and telescoped his time horizon, from the more
distant to the recent past. He offered as a final rationale for Sand Creek
mute testimony from silent witnesses: the desecrated bodies of still more
white victims of Indian depredations. In June 1864, he recalled, Native
people had "brutally murdered and scalped" the Hungate family: a
father, mother, and two girls living near Denver. On the borderlands,
where cross-cultural interactions often spawned anxieties about the
threat of racial decay, the loss of Ellen Hungate and her daughters, white
females who served as a fragile community's keepers of virtue, threatened the social order. Chivington suggested that following the Hungate
murders, fear among settlers had escalated into desperation, and that
desperation had, by fall 1864, quickened into an ironclad conviction that
reprisals were not merely justified but necessary. The Hungates' remains
demanded retribution. At Sand Creek, Chivington said, his troops had
meted out punishment appropriate to the Cheyennes' and Arapahos'
crimes.[30]

Chivington remained unrepentant for the rest of his life. In 1883, for
instance, the Pike's Peak Pioneers of '58, a heritage organization devoted to commemorating the first generation of white settlers on the
Front Range, celebrated the twenty-fifth anniversary of their members'

arrival in the region. They invited Chivington to deliver the keynote address at their gala banquet. Intimidating even in his dotage, he opened his remarks by asking, "Was Sand Creek a massacre?" He answered by pointing to the Civil War context: "If it [Sand Creek] was [a massacre], we had massacres almost without number during the late rebellion." Next, he sneered in his detractors' voice, "But were not these Indians peaceable?" Ignoring the ongoing Indian Wars, he claimed that Sand Creek had pacified the region's Native peoples: "for almost nineteen years . . . none of them have been so troublesome as they were before." Finally, he returned to the mutilated bodies of settlers. As ever, these remains—not just ever more but ever more broken as Chivington's story changed over time—floated free of history, a chronicle of the misunderstandings that so often traveled back and forth across cultural lines, leading to bloodshed on the borderlands. From a single scalp originally, he now raged about "scalps of white men, women, and children, several of which they had not had time to dry and tan since taken" and an "Indian blanket . . . fringed with white women's scalps." He said, "These and more were taken from . . . the *battle-field* of Sand Creek." Having recovered such persuasive evidence, the original question answered itself: "Peaceable!" he taunted, in a righteous fury, "I stand by Sand Creek!" He would have been enraged to learn that federal authorities planned, more than a century later, to memorialize the violence as a massacre rather than a battle.[31]

Returning to 2007, after Commissioner Oswald finished speaking at the massacre site's opening ceremony, Bill Ritter, Colorado's governor, marched to the microphone. Distancing himself from anything like Chivington's combative tone, Ritter offered an all-things-to-all-people speech. He focused on a safe message of healing through memorialization, extolling the resilience of Native people, and spoon-feeding his audience rhetorical pabulum by calling on Coloradans to "teach our children so that we never forget." Rather than demanding that the assembled crowd confront the massacre's grim details, Ritter suggested that they should remember the image of comity constructed at the ceremony, which, he suggested, abjured Chivington's Sand Creek story by demonstrating that Native Americans and whites had finally "found a way to live in peace without conflict." The audience, in other words,

A view of the Sand Creek Massacre site. This photograph, taken from the dry creek bed, shows what is known as the monument overlook in the middle distance to the right. Atop that rise sits a small historical marker inscribed with the words "Sand Creek Battle Ground." *(Photo by Tom Carr.)*

should appreciate the Sand Creek site not for its challenging content but for its upbeat process.[32]

Ritter's sunny remarks suggested that he had no idea how painful commemorating Sand Creek had been, how, rather than improving federal-tribal relations, creating the memorial had laid bare two centuries of conflict between the U.S. government and the Cheyennes and Arapahos. As it had during the era of the Civil War and the Indian Wars, a struggle over control of the landscape had ignited modern disputes. Sometime late in the nineteenth century or early in the twentieth,

Coloradans had misplaced the massacre. Many local people still knew approximately where the slaughter had taken place, but they were no longer able to point with certainty to its precise location. The relevant tribes, though, believed that they had never lost Sand Creek. Their spiritual leaders, relying on oral histories and maps produced by George Bent, had performed rituals at the site across the years, maintaining a connection between past and present through their stewardship of the land. As a result, when they created the historic site, the Arapaho and Cheyenne participants in the memorialization process had hoped to embed their perceptions of tribal history in southeastern Colorado's sandy soil. NPS officials, however, had insisted that as a precondition of memorialization they must first "find Sand Creek." And when the NPS's site search relied on methods and reached conclusions that three of the four affected tribes had rejected, the outraged Arapahos and Cheyennes believed that the NPS had dispossessed them of their memories while threatening their cultural sovereignty. The ensuing conflict recapitulated rather than atoned for past abuses, as federal officials dismissed Native perspectives on the geography and cartography of a tribal tragedy. Ritter's view of the massacre site ignored this history.[33]

For the next speaker, NPS director Mary Bomar, the memorial evinced her organization's commitment to diversity. The NPS is a huge agency, usually perceived as a stalwart defender of the natural world because of the magnificent parks it oversees, but the NPS is also the country's largest historic preservation organization. In that role, the NPS acts as the United States' anthropologist, archeologist, and historian. Bomar, wearing her full dress uniform, including the iconic flat hat, embraced this responsibility, outlining a view at once ambitious and pluralistic for her agency: national narrator. "The public looks upon the National Park Service almost as a metaphor for America itself," she explained. "The Park Service," therefore, has to "ensure that the American story is told faithfully, completely, and accurately." That story is often "noble," she continued, as at units like Liberty Island, but it can also be "shameful and sad." Regardless, "in an age of growing diversity," Bomar suggested, "the Service must continually ask whether the way we tell stories has meaning for *all* of our citizens." Reconciling the triumphs and tragedies of the nation's past and reaching out to all corners in American society could best happen in "special places that unite us all"—places like Sand Creek.[34]

Senator Sam Brownback of Kansas followed Bomar to the dais, offering a quiet jeremiad. A farmer's son, Brownback had announced his candidacy for the Republican presidential nomination two months earlier. But at Sand Creek he projected the image of a supplicant searching for absolution, rather than an office seeker campaigning for votes. He had spent the morning prior to the ceremony walking among the Cheyenne people camped in the creek bottom, listening to their stories of the massacre. His speech suggested that the experience had moved him. "The spilling of innocent blood here is a gross sin that pollutes the land," he suggested, "and we must acknowledge it and repent of it." Brownback then admitted the federal government's complicity throughout much of U.S. history in the murder and dispossession of Native peoples, before adding, "there's healing needed in federal and tribal relations, healing that must precede true peace." Brownback concluded with a plea for compassion: "As a U.S. senator from a Plains state, I deeply apologize, and I'll work to right this wrong. I humbly ask the Native Americans here, and their leaders in particular, to forgive us." He walked from the podium, eyes cast downward, showered by thunderous applause.[35]

Marilyn Musgrave, eastern Colorado's congressional representative, spoke next. Reaching out to constituents embittered by the NPS's decision to label Sand Creek a "massacre" rather than a "battle," she insisted: "when we look at our history, we never want to rewrite it." Musgrave hinted that revisionists at the Sand Creek memorial had bowed to political correctness when they had chosen to mute the note of triumphalism common at most national historic sites. Then she struck a conciliatory tone. Years earlier, Musgrave, a staunch conservative like Brownback, had been pilloried in the local press for ignoring her home district, including the then-uncertain fate of the Sand Creek site, and instead focusing on the high-profile national debate over gay marriage. To answer her critics, Musgrave relied in her speech, as Brownback had in his, on a rhetoric of Christian redemption. But instead of apologizing for her own or her nation's sins, she congratulated the audience (and herself) for mourning the dead: "We're doing what good people do.

We're remembering the wrongs. We're regretting. We're repenting." She implied that penitents could shed the sins of history simply by visiting the memorial.[36]

The past would not be laid to rest so easily. Silas Soule's struggles with guilt and redemption—individual, collective, national—still shrouded the memorial at its opening gala. Soule, who at Sand Creek refused to order the men he commanded to fire, worried afterward that the attack could only be called a massacre. By early December 1864, news of Soule's and other officers' concerns about Sand Creek had reached Denver. And less than a week later, a critic, perhaps Soule himself, suggested that "Chivington ought to be prosecuted." Reaching out to their contacts in the abolitionist network back east, including Senator Charles Sumner and Secretary of War Edwin Stanton, Soule and his confidantes began spreading word of the slaughter.[37]

On December 14, just two weeks after Sand Creek, Soule poured his emotions out onto the pages of a letter he wrote to his friend and former commander, Edward "Ned" Wynkoop. At the time, Soule was only twenty-six years old. Handsome and headstrong, he had arrived in Colorado four years earlier, part of a wave of argonauts eager to find fortune in the gold fields west of Denver. Prior to that, Soule had lived in Kansas. His family settled near Lawrence in 1854 with the New England Emigrant Aid Society, an organization of free-soilers devoted to ensuring that Kansas would remain untainted by slavery as it moved toward statehood. In time, Soule earned a reputation as an abolitionist Jayhawker. He became acquainted with John Brown and squared off with pro-slavery border ruffians. Eventually, though, he left Bleeding Kansas for Colorado. And shortly after he arrived there, the Civil War started. Soule answered the call to arms, joining the 1st Colorado Regiment. By 1864, he had moved up in the ranks. On the eve of Sand Creek, he wore a captain's epaulettes and commanded Company D.[38]

Sitting in the cold at Fort Lyon, Soule fumed as he recalled Chivington's treachery. He remembered that when the 3rd Colorado volunteers had first arrived at the fort on their way to Sand Creek, the colonel had placed "pickets around the Post, allowing no one to pass." With access to the garrison barred, Chivington "declared [his] intention to massacre the friendly Indians camped on Sand Creek." An outraged Soule approached his fellow officers, telling them that "any man who would take part in the murder, knowing the circumstances as we did"—Soule, like Wynkoop, thought that Black Kettle's and Left Hand's people were peaceful and under the protection of Fort Lyon's troops—"was a low lived cowardly son of a bitch." When he heard about this dissension in the ranks, Chivington apparently threatened Soule's life. But Soule stuck to his guns. He approached the fort's new commander, Major Scott Anthony, and told him that he "would not take part in [the] intended murder" of the Indians at Sand Creek. But if the Colorado volunteers instead targeted "any fighting Indians," Soule would prove his race loyalties by going "as far as any of them." Reassured by Anthony that Chivington planned to do just that, Soule joined a march that ended on the banks of Sand Creek.[39]

Soule later recalled, "we arrived at Black Kettle's and Left Hand's Camp, at day light." After Chivington's men opened fire without warning, a soldier from the 1st Colorado and an interpreter trading in the camp "ran out with white flags," signaling that the Indians were peaceful. The troops "paid no attention." "Hundreds of women and children were coming towards us," Soule remembered, "getting on their knees for mercy." Major Anthony responded by shouting, "Kill the sons of bitches." A horrified Soule related in his letter to Wynkoop that he had "refused to fire." Instead, after taking his company across the creek, away from the melee, Soule watched, appalled, as artillery barraged the Native people: "Batteries were firing into them and you can form some idea of the slaughter." "When the Indians found that there was no hope for them they went for the Creek, and buried themselves in Sand and got under the banks." Here, Soule offered a different view of the fortifications that Chivington often cited as definitive proof that he had attacked a village overflowing with hostile Indians itching for a fight.[40]

In his note to Wynkoop, Soule also tried to undermine Chivington's efforts to bathe Sand Creek in the reflected glory of the Civil War. He wrote that the Colorado volunteers had been less heroic than harried, more craven than courageous: "There was no organization among our troops, they were a perfect mob." Such a charge revealed that Chivington had lost control of his men, deflating his grandiose claims of outstanding leadership. Soule's phrasing also called to mind more than a decade of sectional violence in his old home, Kansas, where first proslavery border ruffians and later guerrilla warriors led by William

Quantrill had repeatedly laid waste to the town of Lawrence and other free-soil strongholds. These were mobs, most observers in the Union agreed, groups of violent thugs who had lashed out at virtuous pioneers, much as the men of the 3rd Colorado Regiment, Soule insinuated, had lashed out at peaceful Cheyenne and Arapaho people.[41]

Soule further undercut Chivington's assertions of Sand Creek's legitimacy by depicting what seemed to him a topsy-turvy world of civilized Indians and savage whites. He did this by answering every mangled white corpse that Chivington toted out to justify the violence with counterexamples of Native bodies desecrated by soldiers. Chivington's men, Soule noted, had especially disgraced themselves and their commander by visiting unspeakable cruelties on Cheyenne and Arapaho women and young people. "It was hard to see little children on their knees . . . having their brains beat out by men professing to be civilized," he wrote, and also, "squaws' snatches were cut out for trophies." In another case, he remembered that a "woman was cut open, and a child taken out of her, and scalped." And in still another instance, a mother and her children, Soule recalled, had waited "on their knees, begging for their lives, of a dozen soldiers, within ten feet of them all firing." The frantic woman finally "took a knife and cut the throats of both children, and then killed herself." Men suffered too. Among the defiled corpses were those of at least two chiefs, White Antelope and War Bonnet, who "had Ears and Privates cut off." Soule wondered about the massacre's implications for the project of civilizing the Plains: "You would think it impossible for white men to butcher and mutilate human beings as they did there, but every word I have told you is the truth, which they do not deny."[42]

Understood broadly, Soule's letter to Wynkoop raised questions about the interwoven projects of preserving the Union and settling the West. Sand Creek left Soule unsure about the prospects of a society founded on so loose a definition of civilization that such fell deeds could take place beneath its banner. When, for example, he related the tale of the mother who had killed first her children and then herself rather than allowing her family to be gunned down by the Colorado volunteers, or of the eviscerated pregnant woman, her unborn child ripped from her body and then scalped by white soldiers, he relied on moral suasion, steeping his Sand Creek stories in cultural currents that ran throughout the era's abolitionist literature. He also undercut Chivington's charge that all Indians were alike, little more than faceless savages. This fit with Soule's broader depiction of the Cheyennes and Arapahos as individuated: sometimes good and sometimes bad, sometimes peaceful and sometimes violent. But ultimately, he took care to extend his critique only so far. He separated himself from the massacre but never from the struggle first to reunite the nation and then to expand it onto the Great Plains. Had Chivington targeted hostile rather than friendly Indians, Soule made clear, he would have fought beside his commander. The Union remained sacrosanct; the West had to be settled.[43]

Accordingly, when apportioning blame for the massacre, Soule focused on Chivington. In this way, he exempted decent soldiers present at Sand Creek, including himself, from responsibility for the slaughter, while also shielding federal Indian policy from culpability. Soule charged that Chivington, driven by his ambitions, had planned and executed the attack not because he believed that Black Kettle's and Left Hand's people were hostile, but as a way of securing a promotion. Using the Civil War as an engine for mobility was common, Soule knew—in 1861, he had written to a friend that he would volunteer if he "could get a Lieutenant's commission"—so it stood to reason that Chivington hoped "to be made General" in the wake of the attack. Given that, Soule conjectured, the colonel had inflated both the threat from the Indians at Sand Creek and also the number of dead: "Chivington reports five or six hundred killed, but there were not more than two hundred." And of those, Soule continued, the vast majority were women and children. Worse still, though Chivington claimed that Sand Creek would make the Plains safer, Soule argued that more violence would actually result. "Our best Indians were killed," Soule mourned of the peace chiefs cut down by Chivington's men. Recriminations would flow from Sand Creek, he warned, suggesting that in its aftermath, "we will have a hell of a time with Indians this winter."[44]

Before Sand Creek, Soule held different views of Chivington and of the region's Native peoples. In the months leading to the massacre, Soule corresponded regularly with his family. His letters included updates about his prospects, the occasional complaint about money woes, and reassurances about his behavior. In midsummer, he sent a note to his sister, Annie, joking, "You and Mother write for me to be a

Christian and not be wild &c but the Army don't improve a fellow much in that respect." Still, he promised, there was hope, thanks to the efforts of his commanding officer, Colonel Chivington: "I think there is not much danger of my spoiling—our Col. is a Methodist Preacher and whenever he sees me drinking, gambling, stealing, or murdering he says, he will write to Mother or my sister Annie, so I have to go straight." But in August, Soule's tone changed. Writing again to his sister, he stated, "We have considerable trouble with the Indians—they would like to scalp us all." By October's end, though, he thought the danger had passed, at least temporarily. Of the same tribes, Soule said: "they are quite peaceable at present." Black Kettle had recently parleyed with Chivington and Evans in Denver. Following that meeting, the chief had waited with his people "within a mile of [Fort Lyon] . . . for the purpose of making peace." Reading the mood within the garrison, Soule noted ruefully, "I think Government will not make peace with them." "If that is the case," he guessed, "we shall have some fighting to do this winter." Chivington arrived at Fort Lyon less than a month later.[45]

Four days after sending his letter to Ned Wynkoop, Soule wrote to his mother. He recounted that two weeks earlier, he had been "present at a Massacre of three hundred Indians mostly women and Children." He explained that the Indians had been "friendly" and promised that he had "not let [his] Company fire." Sparing his mother few details of the carnage, Soule mourned the "little Children on their knees begging for their lives" who had "their brains beat out like dogs." He next wrote to his mother early in January 1865. He remained convinced that he had done right by refusing to burn powder at Sand Creek. He had since combed the "battle ground counting dead Indians." He noted, "There were not as many as reported, not more than one hundred and thirty killed." The putrefying remains of the Cheyenne and Arapaho people mocked Chivington's vainglorious claims of 500 or 600 dead. As for the idea that the camp had housed dangerous warriors, Soule again noted that the evidence he had since recovered suggested otherwise. The corpses were mostly those of "women and children and all of them scalped." He hoped that "authorities in Washington [would] investigate the killing of these Indians." If they did, Soule was certain that his actions would be vindicated.[46]

When Soule got his wish and federal investigators inquired into the attack in February 1865, he offered an official rendition of his story, refuting Chivington's history of Sand Creek. In early fall 1864, Soule reported, he and Ned Wynkoop had tried to recover several white captives from a group of Cheyennes and Arapahos camped near the Smoky Hill River. When "Major Wynkoop asked them to give up the white prisoners," Soule recalled, the Indians had said "they were desirous of making peace with the whites." Wynkoop replied that "he had not the power to make peace, but if they would give up the white prisoners he would take them to Denver before the governor [John Evans], and pledged himself to protect them from Denver and back." After Black Kettle handed over a woman and three children—captives taken earlier in the summer during raids on outlying white settlements—Wynkoop held up the first part of his end of the bargain: he brought several peace chiefs, including Black Kettle, to Denver. The controversial parley with Chivington and Governor Evans took place a few days later.[47]

Soule reported that the group had gathered in Denver at Camp Weld. "The Indians," he said, had "seemed very anxious to make peace." Governor Evans, though, insisted that he "could not make peace with them," that they must instead "look to military power for protection." Soule remembered Chivington telling "them that he left the matter with Major Wynkoop; if they wanted peace they must come into the post and subject themselves to military law." Soule continued, "Major Wynkoop told them to bring the Indians of their tribe who were anxious for peace to Fort Lyon, and camp near the post." Wynkoop then sent word to General Curtis "to see if peace could not be made." Meanwhile, "the Indians complied with Wynkoop's orders, and camped near the post." Even after Scott Anthony relieved Wynkoop as commander of Fort Lyon, the Native people still believed that "they were protected . . . until the messenger returned from General Curtis." Soule lamented that no instructions had arrived at the fort by late November. In sum, white officials repeatedly assured the chiefs that, pending further instructions from higher authorities, their bands would be safe; their fears allayed, the Cheyennes and Arapahos waited near Fort Lyon for word of their fate.[48]

On the evening of November 28, Soule stated, Chivington had arrived at Fort Lyon. The colonel asked if Native people were nearby.

Soule replied that, yes, "there were some Indians camped near the fort, but they were not dangerous." Instead, "they were considered as prisoners." Soule joined Chivington's command, marching overnight and arriving at Sand Creek just before sunrise. When asked by investigators for more details, Soule noted that "at the time of the attack" there were "white men in the Indian camp . . . by permission of Major Anthony to do some trading with the Indians." One of them, Soule related, had barely escaped the initial onslaught, running from a lodge with a white flag flying overhead. At the same time, many Cheyennes and Arapahos signaled their peaceful intentions by "holding their hands up." Chivington's men ignored their pleas, firing on women and children and later mutilating their bodies. Soule had not witnessed the fortifications that Chivington deemed evidence of the hostility of the Indian camp; he had seen "only holes under the banks in the sand" that he believed had been "dug the day of the fight."[49]

Following a brief recess of the inquiry, Chivington cross-examined Soule. As the accused faced off with his accuser, Chivington began by revisiting Ned Wynkoop's initial contact with Black Kettle's people, suggesting that some of them had been hostile. Soule agreed. Chivington then noted that after meeting with Wynkoop, those Indians had not delivered all of their white captives, as promised. Soule agreed again. Chivington, moving on to the weeks after the Camp Weld gathering, focused on the recalcitrance of the Dog Soldiers, the most militant Cheyennes, who had ignored Wynkoop's order to camp near Fort Lyon. Soule allowed that "none of the Dog Soldiers came in." Chivington next turned to the most controversial of Soule's earlier statements, regarding atrocities perpetrated by the men of the 3rd Regiment. He demanded to know if Soule had witnessed any barbaric acts being committed by soldiers. Soule replied, of the Indians at Sand Creek, "They were scalped I know; I saw holes in them, and some with their skulls knocked in." But, he admitted, he could not say for certain "how they were mutilated." He "saw soldiers with children's scalps during the day, but did not see them cut off." After seeking a few additional details, Chivington finished interrogating Soule.[50]

The next morning, the fifth day of Soule's testimony, investigators doubled back over the same terrain that Chivington had covered during the preceding sessions. Soule then replied to several more questions from Chivington, reiterating some of his earlier testimony and underscoring his sense that the Native people waiting in the Sand Creek camps had believed at the time of the assault that the troops at Fort Lyon would protect them: "I heard Wynkoop tell some of the chiefs, I think Black Kettle and Left-Hand, that—in case he got word from Curtis not to make peace with them, that he would let them know, so that they could remove out of the way and get to their tribe." With that, Soule finished. The federal investigators and Chivington left him to sift through his recollections of the bloodbath and where he fit into that grim history. Soule had no Sand Creek memorial where he could make a pilgrimage and seek expiation for his part in the massacre; he had only his unsettled thoughts.[51]

Nearly a century and a half later, Senator Ben Nighthorse Campbell knew the history of Silas Soule's struggles and considered him one of the heroes of Sand Creek. When Campbell strode to the dais at the historic site's opening ceremony, he wielded a potent combination of political and moral authority, rooted in an autobiography that read like a script treatment for a feature film. Born outside Sacramento, California, to a tubercular mother and an alcoholic father who denied his own Cheyenne heritage, Campbell sometimes lived in orphanages when his parents became overwhelmed by their responsibilities. After dropping out of high school, he entered the Air Force, served honorably in the Korean War, and earned a graduate equivalency degree. He then mustered out of the service and began studying at San José State University, where he found time to become a world-class judoka. In 1963, he won a gold medal in judo at the Pan-American Games before injuring his knee the following year while competing at the Tokyo Olympics, ending his athletic career. Campbell then got married and moved to his wife's home state, Colorado, where he began raising champion quarter horses. In the early 1970s, at the height of the Red Power Movement, he reconnected with his Cheyenne relatives and became renowned and wealthy designing jewelry inspired by Native American themes. He entered politics in 1982, winning a seat as a Democrat in the Colorado state legislature. He won again when he ran for U.S. Congress in 1986. And in 1992, Coloradans sent him to the U.S. Senate, still as a Democrat, before he switched parties in 1995. Campbell retired from politics in 2004, completing a run-of-the-mill Native-American-boy-transcends-hardscrabble-roots-to-become-Olympic athlete/horse breeder/jeweler/U.S. senator story.[52]

Campbell seemingly had more invested in the Sand Creek memorial than anyone else at the opening ceremony. And his goals for the site were both lofty and complex. He authored the legislation creating the memorial and shepherded the bill through the Senate. The site's opening realized a quarter-century's dream for him, capping a career in which he had used his political sway to champion Native American causes. At the ceremony, he served as a bridge, connecting the local, state, and federal officials who spoke before him with the Indian people who would follow him. This was a familiar role for Campbell, who inhabited two worlds throughout his adult life: Washington, where, as a senator, he was a member of what some people called the "world's most exclusive club"; and the Northern Cheyenne Reservation, a place he knew as "home," where he remained part of the Cheyenne Council of 44 Chiefs. On this day, his speech demonstrated that he saw the memorial as connecting the two.[53]

Wearing tribal regalia—a feathered headdress, its band adorned with elaborate beadwork; a vivid red and blue trade blanket draped over his shoulders; and an eagle staff in his left hand—Campbell played two roles at the opening ceremony: the authentic Indian and a senior statesman representing the U.S. government. Invoking a myth that dated back to the aftermath of Sand Creek, he claimed that the massacre had been perpetrated not by federal troops but by ragtag members of the Colorado militia, "raised, a good number of them, from the thugs and alcoholics and the ne'er-do-wells of Skid Row in Denver." Campbell then recalled Sand Creek's gruesome details, becoming the first speaker to do so, before returning to a refrain of healing, suggesting that the site offered forgiveness for those individuals willing to remember the dead. "Our tears," he said, "are tempered with the hope of a better future and a better relationship between people of all races." He concluded by absolving Sam Brownback and other gathered mendicants of their sins, seemingly closing the book on Sand Creek once and for all: "I think of the people here today that their hearts are good, they understand healing, and the circle is complete." Reconciliation had moved within reach because the memorial promoted cross-cultural interactions. And if Campbell's audience believed that the massacre had been the work of gun-toting drunks in the state militia, rather than a tragic result of federal policy carried out by the U.S. military—an idiosyncratic rather than a structural calamity, in other words—then healing would be easier to achieve for all concerned.[54]

By the same token, Campbell, like the other speakers at the ceremony, ignored the sinews that bound Sand Creek to the Civil War. He preferred that his audience recall that conflict as Silas Soule had hoped they would: a glorious struggle to preserve the Union, a moment when soldiers, white and African American alike, fought so that "a nation, conceived in liberty and dedicated to the proposition that all men are created equal" would not "perish from the earth." Remembered in that way, the Civil War occupied a sanctified place in the American imagination and served the interests of federal authorities. The conflict was a tragedy that consumed the lives of more than 600,000 men, but those deaths had not been in vain. Through shared sacrifice, the nation unshackled itself from the institution of slavery, redeeming itself in blood. Linking such transcendent recollections of a noble war fought in freedom's name to the murder and dispossession of indigenous people, to racial animosities rather than to soaring rhetoric of egalitarianism, to ill-trained cavalrymen committing atrocities rather than to volunteer soldiers lionized in American culture for fighting for their country, risked sullying popular conceptions of the Civil War. With U.S. troops dying overseas in Iraq and Afghanistan in 2008 and the nation already bitterly divided politically, Senator Campbell stepped carefully through the treacherous landscape of American memory.[55]

That Campbell segregated Sand Creek from the Civil War in his speech suggested that upholding patriotic orthodoxy sometimes demanded collective amnesia rather than remembrance. Monuments and memorials in the United States typically evoke neat visions of the nation's history (Maya Lin's stark Vietnam wall stands as an exception to this rule), rationalizing a chaotic and fractured past. But irredeemable episodes like Sand Creek remind Americans that as much as they might wish that their history proceeded in a regimented fashion, the past cannot so easily be trained to fall into line. Events like the massacre belie national narratives of steady progress and exceptional righteousness. They also call into question the legitimacy of the government's monopoly on violence. Had Senator Campbell acknowledged the massacre's connection to the Civil War, he would have underscored the consequences of imperialism on the borderlands. Had he examined the ways that U.S. history is shot through with ironies, he would have diminished the unifying power of collective memories surrounding the Civil War, a military endeavor viewed by most Americans as noble. Better then to forget Sand Creek's relationship to the Union war effort. Better to depict the massacre as the work of marginal characters, outliers led by a vicious madman.[56]

After three spokespeople read speeches for federal officials who could not attend the ceremony, reiterating the memorial's palliative qualities, the program turned to other tribal speakers, who revealed that competing narratives still swirled around the historic site, much as they had during the era of the massacre. Eugene Little Coyote, the Northern Cheyenne tribal president, spoke about how the Sand Creek story had scarred him as a child, leaving him distrustful of whites. After allowing that the memorial's creation held out some hope of healing for his tribe, he observed, "there are many important people here today, and in particular some of the highest-ranking state and federal officials." Turning to the senators, members of Congress, and governors arrayed behind him, Little Coyote asked "if the Cheyenne can trust the government to fulfill its . . . trust responsibilities, to insure that we have quality health care, quality education, and quality housing." As he intimated, his tribe faced huge problems: nearly four in ten Northern Cheyennes were unemployed; half lived in poverty; and because of disproportionate rates of chronic illness, diabetes, and heart disease especially, they died a full decade earlier than the national average for all Americans. Little Coyote reminded the assembled dignitaries that the Northern Cheyennes could not treat sickness with memorials, could not feed their children on apologies, and could not find shelter within multicultural bromides.[57]

As the ceremony took on an increasingly militant tone, William Walksalong shuffled to the microphone. A Northern Cheyenne spiritual leader and member of the tribe's Sand Creek Massacre Descendants Committee, he rejected the equation of reconciliation with healing, offering instead Native identity and self-determination as alternative medicine for what ailed his kin. "The majority of Indian people today," he observed, "do not want to become plain Americans. Our desire is to retain our own way of life." Walksalong suggested that if federal officials wished to promote healing, they should honor the treaty, signed after the massacre, promising reparations to the victims' families: "I humbly and respectfully request of American leaders . . . to help us fulfill the promises made to them at the Treaty of the Little Arkansas in 1865." Walksalong explained that he was not offering "a concession, but rather" viewed fulfillment of treaty obligations as "a measure of justice necessary for genuine forgiveness and reconciliation to occur." Kind words and earnest sentiments were nice, he noted, but restitution for the massacre had to precede real healing. In this way, Walksalong, like Little Coyote before him, echoed the views of George Bent.[58]

Looking back on the massacre at the beginning of the twentieth century, George Bent viewed Sand Creek as a hinge in Cheyenne history, an event that ended a relatively peaceful and prosperous era for the tribe and began a more violent and impoverished one: the Plains Indian Wars and the reservation era that followed. Bent, like Senator Campbell a hundred years later, often moved between worlds. His father, William Bent, was a trader and federal Indian agent, whose eponymous fort served as a hub for the bustling commercial networks on Colorado's Eastern Plains. His mother, Owl Woman, was matriarch to the Cheyennes' most prestigious kinship group and daughter of the Sacred Arrow Keeper, the tribe's revered spiritual leader. Although George Bent was schooled in Missouri among whites, he typically felt more at home with his Cheyenne relatives. Nevertheless, at the start of the Civil War, he volunteered to fight for the South, eventually joining the 1st Missouri Cavalry. He saw action in several battles, including Wilson's Creek and Pea Ridge, until Union troops captured him in summer 1862. After Bent swore a loyalty oath to the United States, he returned to his father's ranch. But with anti-Confederate sentiment running high in Colorado at the time, Bent decided that it would be safer for him to live with the Cheyennes. In November 1864, he camped with Black Kettle near Sand Creek.[59]

Bent was wounded in the massacre but lived. Still, federal officials inquiring into the violence apparently sought neither his testimony nor that of any other Native survivors of the ordeal. But even if he had been asked for his story, Bent likely would have declined in the aftermath of Sand Creek. He later recalled that following the massacre, he

and his kin had been "afraid of going into any fort" or federal installation. And yet, despite institutionalized pressure to forget—the Cheyennes struggled against coercive programs in the 1880s and 1890s, the
so-called era of assimilation, including violent reprisals for preserving
tribal histories or maintaining traditional practices like the Sun Dance—
Bent resolved to keep memories of Sand Creek alive. Americans at the
time worried about what historian Frederick Jackson Turner labeled
the closing of the frontier; pondered what conservationists warned
would be the imminent extinction of the bison, not to mention that of
the tribes dependent for their survival on those great beasts; and greed-
ily consumed piles of dime novels about cowboys and Indians. With
the West at the center of debates about the nation's future, Bent worried
that Native people were not speaking for themselves. So he began relating tribal lore to James Mooney, a renowned Smithsonian ethnographer; George Bird Grinnell, one of the fathers of professional anthropology; and George Hyde, a relatively obscure historian.[60]

Bent quickly soured on Mooney (he "always thought he was right in
every thing") and eventually on Grinnell too (he would not "give credit
to any body, only himself"). By contrast, for more than a decade Bent
collaborated with Hyde. In 1905 and 1906, they placed a series of six
articles in a monthly magazine, the *Frontier,* published out of Colorado
Springs. In those essays, Bent went public with his stories of Sand
Creek, calling it a massacre and fixing blame on John Chivington and
his men for the years of violence that followed: "The real causes of the
Indian War on the plains were the wanton attacks made by the Colorado volunteers on friendly Indians." Bent then turned Chivington's
history of the era on its head. He said of the Civil War backdrop that
although "some men in Colorado talked about 'Rebel Plots'" and
charged that he had worked as a "Rebel Emissary," he had only served
the Confederacy very briefly. Nevertheless, he admitted, "some Texas
officers [had] schemed to bring their men up the Arkansas [River] in
the spring of 1863, and, with the aid of Indians to attack and capture
Ft. Larned and Ft. Lyon." But, Bent noted, he had not participated in
that doomed plot, which had foundered because the targeted tribes,
"the Kiowas and Comanches, inveterate foes of Texas, refused to have
anything to do with the scheme." So too the Arapahos and Cheyennes,
who, Bent said, likewise carried no brief for the Confederacy.[61]

Bent extended his critique of Chivington in the *Frontier*, scoffing at
the claim that a pan-Indian alliance, united under the banner of various Sioux tribes, had represented an existential threat to whites prior
to Sand Creek. The sovereign identities of the Plains Indians made such
a thing impossible. "Some Sioux did come down that winter [1863–1864]
with a war-pipe," Bent allowed, but "the Cheyennes and Arapahos refused to smoke, thus showing that they intended to remain at peace."
The Kiowas and Comanches, pursuing their own political agenda, also
rejected the Sioux's entreaties. Bent then reiterated the real cause of the
violence that had spiraled out of control at Sand Creek: American attacks on friendly Native people. This aggression, he noted, was born in
the hothouse of the Civil War, as white racial anxiety ran rampant at
the time, fostering paranoia and misapprehensions about mono-
lithic Indian identity. At the same time, the Civil War grew out of
a long-standing fight between the North and the South for control of
the West. The same struggle gave rise to the Indian Wars, which involved different parties vying for dominance in the same region. Regardless, the Plains Tribes had not formed an alliance until after Sand
Creek, Bent said, when memories of the massacre had provided them
with a rallying cry, a common cause around which they ultimately
had united.[62]

Turning to the massacre's prehistory, Bent's perspective again differed sharply from Chivington's. Whereas Chivington viewed the escalating mayhem in 1864 as evidence that the entire Cheyenne and Arapaho tribes were waging war on white settlers, Bent recalled those episodes
as ones in which many of his people had actually demonstrated remarkable forbearance. Bent remembered Colorado troops, in May 1864,
murdering Chief Lean Bear in cold blood, even though a year earlier
the chief had visited Washington as part of a peace delegation "and
had papers to show that he was friendly." In the event, when Lean Bear
approached a group of soldiers, "intending to show his papers and
shake hands," their commander ordered them to fire. "Then the troops
shot Lean Bear to pieces, as he lay on his back on the ground." Other
similar episodes followed, Bent wrote, suggesting that cumulatively
these attacks "made the Cheyennes very angry." Belligerent tribal fac-
tions eventually "began fighting, and were soon joined by the Arapahos." Before too long, "the Kiowas and Comanches 'chipped in' and so

nearly all the Indians on the Plains were at war." But even then, Bent noted, many Native people did not fight.[63]

Bent reported in the *Frontier* that at the end of summer 1864, peace chiefs, hoping to rehabilitate relations with whites, had struggled to end the violence. In August, Black Kettle, for instance, sent emissaries to Fort Lyon proposing prisoner exchanges. Ned Wynkoop, Bent wrote in passages that fleshed out Silas Soule's recollection of these events, had agreed to meet with Black Kettle. At that gathering, Wynkoop recovered several white captives and convinced the peace chiefs to travel with him to Denver to parley with Governor Evans. In his letters to Hyde, Bent recounted that after the fruitless Camp Weld meeting, Wynkoop had "told Black Kettle and other chiefs that they could move to Fort Lyon and they would be protected" and that additional white officials had "told Black Kettle to move there and no harm would be done them." Bent remembered, "This was the reason the Cheyennes moved toward Fort Lyon that winter." Shortly after that, Bent returned to Black Kettle's village, "now on the Big Bend of Sandy Creek, about thirty-five miles northeast of Ft. Lyon." Approximately one hundred Cheyenne and ten Arapaho lodges waited there, where Chivington's men attacked them a month later.[64]

As for the massacre's particulars, Bent related that when the soldiers arrived at Sand Creek just before dawn, he had heard shouts warning of their approach. Startled, he dashed from his lodge and "saw that Black Kettle had a flag up on a long pole, to show the troops that the camp was friendly." Chivington's men ignored the signal and "opened fire from all sides." Bent then scrambled two miles upstream and discovered "the main body of Indians, who had dug pits under the high banks of the creek." These makeshift "holes" in the sand were the trenches that Chivington later insisted proved that the Cheyennes and Arapahos had prepared in advance for combat. At day's end, Chivington finally "drew off his men," having concluded "the largest slaughter of Indians ever on the Plains." But by Bent's reckoning Chivington's body count far outstripped the facts, which were tragic enough. "About one hundred and fifty" corpses littered the field, "(three-fourths of them [from] women and children)," as soldiers cast about for macabre trophies.[65]

For Bent, the ruthlessness of Chivington's men, evidenced by their mistreatment of women, children, and the dead, made a lasting impression, suggesting a lack of basic humanity among the Colorado volunteers. In his *Frontier* articles and letters he wrote to Hyde, Bent emphasized the desecration of Native bodies at Sand Creek, intimating that these atrocities—like the earlier killing of Lean Bear—had enduring repercussions in the region. For example, in the wake of the massacre, he recalled, a Cheyenne war party had attacked a group of soldiers that had fought under Chivington, finding in their baggage "2 scalps and lots of things that had been taken at Sand Creek." The Cheyennes recognized "the scalps of White Leaf and Little Wolf that were killed at Sand Creek." The outraged warriors revenged themselves upon their defeated foes, mutilating their corpses.[66]

Blessed with nearly half a century's hindsight, Bent's most powerful refutation of Chivington's Sand Creek stories pivoted on the massacre's consequences. Whereas to his dying day Chivington insisted that Sand Creek had pacified the Plains Tribes, clearing the way for civilization's spread throughout the region, and Soule only suggested that the opposite might prove true, Bent knew for certain that the bloodletting had touched off the brutal Indian Wars. As he recounted in the *Frontier,* the day after the massacre, he and a group of battered survivors had made their way northeast, rendezvousing with a Cheyenne camp on the Smoky Hill. Once there, they swapped stories of Chivington's perfidy, of Black Kettle's unrequited efforts to avoid violence, and of the Colorado volunteers' depravity. Although Bent wrote that some Cheyennes, including Black Kettle, had "still stood firmly for peace with the whites," he recalled that "most," upon hearing what had happened to their kin at Sand Creek, "were for war." The militants then joined Spotted Tail's and Pawnee Killer's bands of Brule Sioux, along with the Cheyenne Dog Soldiers and some Northern Arapaho warriors, in a winter camp. They plotted their reprisals, eventually taking the unusual step of dispatching raiding parties during the year's coldest months.[67]

In the remaining *Frontier* articles, Bent recounted the region awash in violence. Blood first spilled at Sand Creek could not easily be staunched. It overflowed the Plains' river basins—the Platte, the Arkansas, the Smoky Hill, the Republican, the Powder, the Tongue—running through eastern Colorado, into Kansas and Nebraska, north to Wyoming and Montana, before flowing back south again. Bent suggested of the Cheyennes and Arapahos that, haunted by memories of Sand

Creek, they refused to yield to federal troops. He recalled General Winfield Scott Hancock asking the Dog Soldiers to parley in 1867, but "Tall Bull, head chief of the Dog Soldiers, told Hancock that would not do." If the Cheyennes saw soldiers approaching, Tall Bull explained, "they would say another Sand Creek Massacre." After all, "it had been only three years since Chivington had attacked." Together, Native warriors disrupted the mail, menaced stage lines, and drove off workers building railroads. Chivington, Bent explained, had wrought with Sand Creek the very thing that the colonel claimed to have prevented: a conflict that threatened expansion in the West. U.S. troops commanded by Thomas Moonlight, William Fetterman, and, most famously, George Armstrong Custer all fell in the fighting. The *Frontier* series finished there, with Custer's Last Stand at the Little Bighorn. That episode completed a tragic and potentially transgressive narrative arc: from an episode of violence deemed a battle by most white Westerners but a massacre by Bent, to another deemed a massacre by most white readers early in the new century but a battle by Bent.[68]

Bent still had stories to tell. After experiencing the initial thrill of appearing in print, like many first-time authors he found himself craving more. His articles created a bit of a stir in Colorado, where some of Chivington's partisans resented Bent's revisionism, but he received little attention beyond that. He did not become rich or famous, and he blamed the *Frontier*. "I don't think the *Frontier* is much of a paper," he complained to Hyde. The *Frontier* then shut its doors, leaving Bent searching for another outlet for his prose. Hyde, for his part, assured Bent that the market craved a book about the Cheyennes and that he was the man to help produce such a volume. Bent agreed. And so, for another decade, he wrote to Hyde, the subjects of his letters ranging from the poetic (accounts of Cheyenne rituals) to the geographic (maps of important events from the tribe's past, including depictions of the massacre) to the prosaic (Bent's circuitous quest for an effective safety razor).[69]

Although Bent died long before the fruits of his labor with Hyde found their way into the public eye, their book, *Life of George Bent: Written from His Letters,* offers the Cheyenne historian's last word on Sand Creek. The chapter on the massacre begins with discussion of a map, which George Hyde regretted had been lost some time before the book's publication. Bent explains that he had produced the drawing with the help of tribal elders, "who were in the camps at the time of the massacre." Working together, they had sketched out details of the violence, including the location of the Cheyenne and Arapaho villages during the assault, the shape of the stream in November 1864, and the direction from which the Colorado volunteers had approached Sand Creek.[70]

As in his *Frontier* articles, Bent then recalls that Black Kettle had an "American flag tied to the end of a long lodgepole and was standing in front of his lodge . . . the flag fluttering in the grey light of the winter dawn." He adds, "When the soldiers first appeared," neither Black Kettle nor White Antelope, who a year earlier had traveled with Lean Bear to Washington on a peace mission, could "believe that an attack was about to be made on the camps." Waving his flag, Black Kettle kept signaling to the onrushing troops that his bands were friendly. White Antelope, for his part, "had been telling the Cheyennes for months that the whites were good people and that peace was going to be made." He had even "induced many people to come to this camp, telling them that the camp was under the protection of Fort Lyon and that no harm would come to them." Now, though, ashamed of his complicity in the unfolding slaughter, he "made up his mind not to live any longer." He "stood in front of his lodge with his arms folded across his breast, singing the death song: 'Nothing lives long, Only the earth and the mountains.'" The soldiers obliged White Antelope; they "shot him and he fell dead in front of his lodge."[71]

In this telling, Bent spills little ink recounting how troops mangled the corpses of fallen Native people—"this butchers' work"—focusing instead on the massacre's aftermath. "There we were," he recalls, "on that bleak, frozen plain, without any shelter whatever [Chivington's men had burned the remnants of the camp after the fight] and not a stick of wood to build a fire." Covering their exposed kin with grass, able-bodied Cheyennes and Arapahos shambled downstream, walking among "the naked and mutilated bodies of the dead" as they combed the field for "wives, husbands, children, or friends." Bent concludes, "That night will never be forgotten as long as any of us who went through it are alive." So it came to pass. Word spread that Chivington's troops were being feted "as heroes" in Denver, that some of them had taken "ghastly souvenirs" from Sand Creek—including "tobacco bags made of pieces of skin cut from the bodies of dead Cheyenne women"— while others were exhibiting Indian scalps at a Denver theater as "the audience cheered and the orchestra rendered patriotic airs." The ordeal's survivors, meanwhile, carried only bitter memories with them from the massacre. For two hundred more bloody pages, *Life of George Bent* catalogs how those recollections helped fuel the Indian Wars, the author remembering how violence begat violence, a final challenge to John Chivington's claim that Sand Creek had quieted the Plains.[72]

Because Bent viewed Sand Creek through the lens of Cheyenne history, he quickly moved beyond struggles over whether the violence should be recalled as a battle or a massacre—in part because for Native Americans that question had long since been answered, but also because focusing on the controversy over nomenclature threatened to diminish the event's significance. Yes, of course Sand Creek had been a massacre, Bent observed, but it had been more than that: it had been the moment when it became impossible for even the most idealistic chiefs to hope for peace with white settlers. Bent consequently placed Sand Creek in the deeper context of the federal government's long-standing dealings with Indian peoples. And when it came to the Cheyennes, he made certain to portray that relationship as reciprocal. His people, Bent always insisted, had not merely been buffeted by the political crosswinds whipping the Great Plains after the Civil War; they had fought to chart their own course during that stormy period.[73]

Whereas Chivington and Soule depicted the Plains Tribes as purely reactive, their fates shaped solely by decisions external to their communities, or as hardwired by racial destiny for eventual ruin, Bent stressed the political independence of the Cheyennes. Although he never employed the words "sovereignty" or "self-determination," his writings presaged these concepts, highlighting how his people had always relied on their own institutions—fractured and ineffectual though they sometimes were—for civil governance and military leadership. Still, for all his emphasis on tribal autonomy and the political give-and-take between Cheyenne and white authorities, Bent laid the blame for Sand Creek at the feet of federal officials. The U.S. government, he suggested, working blindly in service of an expansionist agenda, had used violence to uproot the Plains Tribes. The massacre, in this light, looked less like a one-time event, an exception rather than the rule, and more like a predictable outgrowth of public policy.[74]

In another way as well, Bent's Sand Creek stories differed from Chivington's and Soule's: Bent suggested that hypocrisy sometimes attenuated Civil War–era patriotism. He did this most often by leveraging allegorical meanings attached to the American flag. The Civil War began in April 1861 when Confederate general P. G. T. Beauregard ordered an artillery barrage on Fort Sumter, the federal garrison located in Charleston harbor. After holding out for more than a day, the fort's commander, Major Robert Anderson, surrendered the installation. Anderson later carried Fort Sumter's flag, a powerful image of the nation besieged, with him to the Union. American flags of all kinds then became resonant symbols throughout the war; by 1864, the flag served as a synecdoche for the United States. Bent often recounted that the Colorado volunteers had fired on Black Kettle even as the chief draped himself in the flag, displaying his peaceful intentions by running Old Glory up over his lodge or waving it from a pole in his hand. Chivington's Sand Creek stories charged Bent with treason, pointing to his service in the Confederate Army. Bent responded to such allegations with stories of his own, about the desecration of the flag, calling into question Chivington's love of country.[75]

In the end, Bent did not write to rebut Chivington's Sand Creek stories or to amend Soule's. He wrote so that his people's ongoing struggle for survival would be remembered accurately. By the time that Bent began working with James Mooney, George Bird Grinnell, and George Hyde, the Southern Cheyennes lived on a reservation surrounded by the state of Oklahoma, approximately one hundred miles west of Oklahoma City. The Northern Cheyennes, who skirmished with the U.S. government late into the nineteenth century, had won a reservation sited on the Tongue River, roughly ninety miles east of the Little Bighorn Battlefield in southeastern Montana. Despite dire predictions of their impending demise, the Cheyennes had not vanished. They had survived Chivington's onslaught and the Indian Wars. But what, Bent wondered, of another existential peril? What of modernity? Federal authorities continued trying to strip the Plains Tribes of their distinctive identity: sometimes shipping their children off to be acculturated at boarding schools; sometimes threatening traditional people, who struggled to preserve the tribes' history and ancient ways, with retribution; and sometimes, as part of the Dawes Act, allotting parcels of their communally held land to individual proprietors. At the same time, popular fiction and historical accounts bastardized the Cheyennes' past; in Bent's words, "whites never get it straight." As it became clear that sedentary farming, private property regimes, and coerced Christianity did not suit many Cheyennes and that mass culture threatened to sweep away their traditions, Bent worried that his tribe's heritage might die out after all. He responded by devoting the last decades of his life to his memory project, gathering scores of tribal histories for publication.[76]

But on the eve of his death, in 1918, Bent worried that the trio of scholars he had chosen as partners and publicists had failed him. At the time, all Bent had to show for his years of toil were his essays in the *Frontier,* which, in his view, had come up wanting, and Grinnell's *Fighting Cheyennes,* which, though successful, buried Bent's efforts in the footnotes and amid the contributions of other informants. Two years earlier, Hyde had completed the bulk of an early draft of Bent's memoir, but he had failed to secure a publishing deal. He kept searching until 1930, when, with the nation slipping into the Great Depression, he gave up and sold the manuscript to the Denver Public Library. There it languished for nearly forty more years until finally, in 1968, as the Red Power moment arrived, so did *Life of George Bent.* The book captivated tribal activists and students of history. Bent's people had survived still more hardships. His stories had survived, too, and they would serve modern Cheyennes as a primer on their past.[77]

Chivington's and Soule's stories, archived as part of the federal inquiries into Sand Creek, also survived the century after the violence. And when, in the 1990s, the NPS began thinking about how best to memorialize the massacre, dissonance between the competing accounts became deafening. Lasting repercussions of continental expansion; the power of racial ideologies in shaping the West; ongoing battles over the political and cultural sovereignty of Native peoples; the role of state-sponsored violence during the Civil War era; and the painful contradictions embedded in American nationalism: these were the core elements contested in Bent's, Soule's, and Chivington's Sand Creek stories.

It is no wonder, then, that as federal officials, tribal representatives, and local people living on Colorado's Eastern Plains reopened debates surrounding the legacy of Sand Creek, they found themselves engaged in bitter disputes over the meaning of history and memory. Looking back to Bent's, Soule's, and Chivington's massacre stories, they fought over many of the same issues and, because of the contingent nature of collective memory, others more in line with contemporary concerns.[78]

The process of commemorating Sand Creek proved that the massacre remained a "history front" in a simmering "culture war," as contested perceptions of the past revealed fault lines in the present. In many ways, participants in the Sand Creek memorialization project had incommensurable goals: national unity versus local autonomy versus tribal sovereignty. And so, while each new fight over American memory highlights the difficulty of agreeing on a single historical narrative within the confines of a pluralistic society, the case of Sand Creek proved unusually complicated. Time and again, the process nearly blew up because the United States is a nation of nations; because the Cheyenne and Arapaho tribes are sovereign political entities, distinct cultures with unique understandings of the past; and because residents of Kiowa County have their own perspectives on history, shaped by their own political interests and by features of their own community, which often diverge from the federal government's or from Native peoples'. Collective remembrance in this case, it became clear, was as likely to tear scabs from old wounds as to heal them. But the Sand Creek site did eventually open its doors, because at critical moments each of the interested parties understood that a commitment to remembering the past meant accepting the existence of multiple, sometimes even competing, recollections rather than a single, unified collective memory. The story of how a diverse group of people worked to bridge cultural divides in order to find and remember a misplaced massacre is the subject of this book. That story began with a mystery.[79]

2

LOOTERS

In late summer 1993, two amateur artifact collectors traveled to a southeastern Colorado ranch owned by a man named William Dawson. Variously described by people familiar with the effort to memorialize the massacre as "history buffs," "treasure hunters," or, with tongue in cheek, "looters," the men drew attention to themselves in Eads, a Ford pickup kind of town, by arriving in a luxury car. Passionate about Western history, they wanted to return home with a small part of the past, to own a piece of one of the region's greatest tragedies. They came looking for arrowheads, minié balls, regimental pins, or any other materials associated with the Sand Creek massacre. And they chose Dawson's land because conventional wisdom dictated that Black Kettle's and Left Hand's people had, on the night of November 28, 1864, camped in a large bend in the creek there. The next morning the massacre reputedly had begun at that spot, before continuing upstream, a running engagement, for several miles. Oddly, though, no matter how hard the two men scoured the ground, systematically working a series of grids with their metal detectors, they found none of the relics that should have been spread across a site where more than a thousand people had fought for their lives during a daylong slaughter. The absence of artifacts made no sense. Unless, that is, there was a simple explanation: the men were prospecting in the wrong place.[1]

Puzzled, the two collectors traveled to Denver, where they contacted David Halaas, the chief historian at the Colorado Historical Society.

They told Halaas, "the ground was completely sterile, there wasn't any evidence at all that a massacre happened there," and suggested that maybe the slaughter had taken place in another creek bend, eight miles to the north of the Dawson ranch. Halaas, a native Coloradan and one of the leading experts on the massacre's history, at the time was almost finished writing a book about George Bent. Although Halaas found the prospect that the site had been misplaced "potentially earthshaking," akin, in his words, to "suddenly losing track of the Gettysburg battlefield," he remained uncertain about the story's credibility. Neverthless, he approached his coauthor on the Bent book, Andy Masich, who, as vice president of the Historical Society, also served as Halaas's boss at the time. Together, they began the initial search for the Sand Creek massacre site.[2]

Their hunt ultimately would prove significant less for its results than for the interdisciplinary methodology it introduced, for bringing a disparate cast of characters together, and for touching off a series of nettlesome controversies—all of which would later shape the National Park Service's (NPS) effort to create the Sand Creek Massacre National Historic Site. Still, even if Halaas and Masich's search would end in anticlimax, it began dramatically. The two historians convinced the Colorado National Guard to take them up in Huey helicopters during a training exercise on September 1, 1993. Halaas, recalling the film *Apocalypse Now,* noted how much he regretted not having brought along a recording of Wagner's "Ride of the Valkyries" for background music. The gunships took off from Buckley Field, near Denver, and headed southeast before flying over Dawson's property and then further upstream to a second large bend in the creek. After spending a day in the air and poking around on land, Halaas, Masich, and the colleagues they brought along found no compelling evidence of the massacre at all. Still, they believed that Dawson's ranch might have hosted the bloodshed. "It looks right, feels right, and meets all contemporary descriptions," Masich wrote after their field trip. But he also cited "an archeological rule of thumb": "no battle-related artifacts, probably no battlefield." The two men decided that the search was "way too big of a project for a weekend kind of thing." So they turned for help to the Colorado State Historical Fund (SHF), one of the nation's most ambitious historic preservation initiatives.[3]

The SHF disbursed grants underwritten by taxes levied on legal gambling in the Colorado mountain towns of Cripple Creek, Central City, and Black Hawk. The grants, ranging from small sums to well into the six figures, supported preservation efforts that "demonstrate[d] public benefit and community support" throughout the state. In the case of Sand Creek, the SHF solicited an application from a professor named Dick Ellis, who directed the Center for Southwest Studies at Fort Lewis College, in Durango. Ellis was a typical Westerner. Which is to say, he was originally from somewhere else. Growing up on Long Island, he heard tantalizing stories about the wonders of Colorado from a family friend, who came back from vacations there with pictures of mountain vistas and aspen groves. After graduating from Colgate University in upstate New York, Ellis made his way to Colorado and entered the PhD program in the University of Colorado–Boulder's history department, where he met David Halaas. Ellis earned his doctorate in 1967 and then spent a year teaching at Murray State, in Kentucky (while there, he shared an office with the eminent historian of country music, Bill Malone), before landing a job at the University of New Mexico. Although he enjoyed his time in Albuquerque, he longed for Colorado, and in 1987 happily exchanged city life for Durango's small-town living. Six years later, Halaas, who recalled that his graduate school colleague had a great deal of experience working closely with Native Americans, came calling.[4]

When Halaas contacted Ellis in 1993, asking if he wanted to "put together an effort to find the site of the Sand Creek Massacre," Ellis replied, "When did you lose it?" But like nearly everyone else who heard about the mystery, Ellis found himself hooked. Sand Creek remained an unusually ugly plot point in the state's creation story. Chivington had attacked the peaceful Indians camped at Sand Creek, most historians agreed by the 1990s, not only because of his personal ambition to enter politics, but also as a way of vaulting Colorado beyond territorial status and toward statehood in the wake of the Civil War. Native Americans, from Chivington's perspective, stood in the way of progress's steady march westward. They had to be removed, or, in the case of Sand Creek, exterminated outright. That same story, tailored to fit particular circumstances, might describe much of nineteenth-century Anglo-Indian relations throughout the West. So if David Halaas exaggerated somewhat in likening the loss of the massacre site to misplacing the Gettys-burg battlefield, he did not inflate the case by much—at least not for most Western historians, who, as the twentieth century wound down, viewed the massacre as a critical flash point in the decades-long wars between the U.S. Army and Native peoples on the Great Plains, con-flicts that only ended with the infamous massacre at Wounded Knee in 1890. Eager to play a role in shaping how and where the critical event would be remembered, Ellis signed on to the search.[5]

Because of ongoing controversy surrounding the massacre in Colo-rado, and because Sand Creek occupies a central place in the histories of the Cheyenne and Arapaho peoples, the SHF offered an initial grant, allowing Ellis to consult with the tribes, prior to moving forward with a full-blown search for the site. Ellis and his team spent eighteen months working on "diplomacy," making multiple trips to the North-ern Cheyenne Reservation in Lame Deer, Montana, the Northern Arap-ahos' Wind River Reservation in Ethete, Wyoming, and the Southern Cheyenne and Southern Arapaho Reservation in Clinton, Oklahoma. Ellis recalled trying to "figure out who was who," learning, in other words, who needed to be involved in the project. As time passed, he dis-covered that each of the tribes had groups, some more formal than oth-ers, devoted to representing the massacre's descendants: for the North-ern Arapahos, the Ridgelys, Eugene Sr., a painter and tribal elder, and Gail and Eugene Jr., his sons, both educators; for the Cheyenne and Arapaho Tribes, Chief Laird Cometsevah and his wife, Colleen, a gene-alogist who had, for more than two decades, been tracing links back to Sand Creek; and for the Northern Cheyennes, the members of the Sand Creek Massacre Descendants Committee, led by Steve Brady, headman of the Crazy Dogs Society, and his younger brother, Otto Braided Hair, who oversaw the tribal descendants' Sand Creek office.[6]

For many of the descendants, stories of the massacre were dearly held, passed from one generation to the next, a family heirloom akin to a sacred text. Across nearly a century, from the start of the reservation era until relatively recently, Cheyenne and Arapaho people were dis-couraged, sometimes violently, from telling their Sand Creek stories. Boarding school administrators, Bureau of Indian Affairs officials, and other white authorities believed that keeping alive memories of the massacre preserved links to the past, to a traditional way of life, hindering acculturation. These stories, consequently, took on added significance because they were endangered and thus preserved away from prying eyes. Steve Brady, for instance, learned about Sand Creek when he was a little boy. He lived in a one-room log house with his paternal grandparents, who oversaw his cultural education. When night fell, Brady often crawled into bed with his grandfather, who told "creation stories, stories of the battles his parents had fought, stories of ordeals, of the massacre, of the good times and the hard times they endured." Laird Cometsevah heard the story of Sand Creek from his father, who recounted the family's history outside, usually on camping trips, away from nosy outsiders. And Norma Gorneau, another member of the Northern Cheyenne Sand Creek Massacre Descendants Committee, explained that she always cried when relating her family's massacre story, knowing that her memories of Sand Creek came down to her at great cost through the generations.[7]

The massacre remained a living memory for many descendants; it shaped their daily lives, helping to forge their individual and collective identity, as well as their relationship to family and tribal history. Many Sand Creek stories depicted the massacre as a watershed, suggesting, much as George Bent once had, that it was the moment when even Black Kettle's peace faction finally had to reckon with the apocalyptic consequences of onrushing white settlers' endless land hunger and the rapacious nature of the U.S. government. Steve Brady, well aware that he might have sounded melodramatic, nonetheless suggested that the betrayal at Sand Creek "taught the Cheyenne people that whites would never let us live in peace." Laird Cometsevah agreed with that stark assessment. "After Sand Creek," he said, "the Cheyennes understood that the white government would always take what it wanted, right or wrong." Brady, Cometsevah, and other descendants' Sand Creek stories underscored that Chivington had attacked bands that both wanted and believed they had already secured peace with whites. Memories of the massacre suggested, consequently, that Indian people should be wary of promises made by non-Indians. That many descendants were forced through the years to safeguard their Sand Creek stories from white censorship only amplified this painful lesson as time passed.[8]

Luckily for Dick Ellis, he did not represent the federal government. Luckier still, when he traveled to the Arapahos' and Cheyennes' reservations, he often brought along David Halaas, who became a close friend and confidant of Brady and Cometsevah, the most influential of the Cheyenne descendants. Steve Brady was an imposing man. He stood about six feet tall, was wide across the shoulders and thick around the middle, and usually wore his jet-black hair in a ponytail. He walked slowly, as though savoring his surroundings, and spoke in a rumbling baritone. But he rarely said much and often intimidated his audiences with long silences. When he did talk, the words usually came out deliberately. And he punctuated much of what he said with a deep belly laugh and a mischievous gleam in his eyes. Like many Cheyenne people, Brady used humor, rooted in good-natured teasing, to leaven even the most somber situations—except when he got angry, frightening storms that, if one managed to weather them, proved to be both exceedingly rare and usually deployed for effect. Laird Cometsevah, by contrast, carried himself with an air of almost preternatural calm. More than six feet tall, wiry as a long-distance runner, he wore his gray hair cropped short and loped through space with graceful strides. Cometsevah commanded any room, no matter how large or full, that he entered, even though he almost never raised his voice above a loud whisper and spoke in a raspy tenor marked by a mild Oklahoma accent. He possessed grace, charisma, gravitas; people were drawn to him. The two men, Cometsevah and Brady, often worked as a formidable duo. Over time they became useful allies for Ellis.[9]

That alliance went both ways, proving Ellis lucky thrice over, as the descendants' interests aligned with the site searchers' goals. The head of the Cheyenne and Arapaho Tribes' business committee pointed Ellis toward the Cometsevahs, who proved sympathetic, arranging a meeting with "thirty or forty descendants." Ellis then went to the Northern Arapahos, whose tribal government suggested working with the Ridgelys. Next came the Northern Cheyennes. Steve Brady, laughing, recalled Ellis, Halaas, and Andy Masich arriving in Lame Deer for the first time: "three white guys . . . thinking about pursuing the massacre site." Brady's Descendants Committee had tribal authorization to deal with all issues related to Sand Creek, and he indicated that its members would be willing to cooperate with the site search. Mildred Red Cherries, who also served on that committee, explained the choice: "We decided it was all right for them to get funding and try to find it

[the site] since we needed the location to try to go after Article 6." Red
Cherries meant that many of the Northern and Southern Cheyenne
descendants had already begun pursuing the reparations promised in
Article 6 of the Treaty of the Little Arkansas but never delivered by federal authorities. Both Brady and Laird Cometsevah believed that looking for the site would further that goal by publicizing the injustice of
Sand Creek.[10]

Having secured tribal support, Ellis received funding to start searching. Choosing not to rely on any single scholarly discipline for guidance, he devised a plan elegant for its methodological breadth but, in
the end, short on results. Gary Roberts, a historian whose dissertation
represented the gold standard among studies of Sand Creek, would
comb through archives, looking for hints of the site's location in the
documentary record. An aerial photographer would try to locate the
trails that Black Kettle's people had traveled on their way to camp prior
to the slaughter. A team armed with metal detectors would reconnoiter
possible sites for relevant artifacts. An expert in remote sensing would
search deeper beneath the earth's surface. And the tribal representatives
would offer guidance. As time passed, each of these efforts yielded nothing but frustration: Roberts learned that historical documents offered
little clear evidence about the site's placement; from above, the trails pe-
tered out when they crossed land that had been regularly cultivated for
more than a century; the remote sensors discovered little of consequence;
and the Cheyennes and Arapahos, who never really had any doubts about
the site's location, looked on bemused. The team of metal detectors,
meanwhile, waited for Doug Scott, a renowned battlefield archeologist,
to find time in his busy schedule to coordinate their efforts.[11]

Although the preliminary results disappointed Ellis, these early efforts to pinpoint the massacre's location proved more significant than
he realized at the time. Many of the relationships, some friendly, some
adversarial, forged during the search became critical when the NPS attempted to find and protect the Sand Creek site. David Halaas became
close with Steve Brady and Laird Cometsevah. Brady and Cometsevah,
in turn, grew comfortable working together on projects related to Sand
Creek. And William Dawson, who owned the land that most observers
believed had hosted the violence, changed a number of his deeply held
views because of his experiences during the search: he accepted that

Sand Creek had been a massacre, whereas he had long insisted that it had been a battle; he became close with several of the Cheyenne people, whom he had distrusted for decades; and, perhaps most important of all, he eventually decided that he wanted to sell his property and leave Kiowa County, the place where he and his wife had lived most of their lives.[12]

A rancher who had spent the better part of his life working outdoors, Bill Dawson carried himself with a sense of quiet power. Often taciturn, when he felt challenged or sank his teeth into a subject that held his interest, he became suddenly expansive. Declarative sentences then tumbled from his mouth in rapid-fire bursts. To hammer a point home, he would slow his cadence, weaving didactic tales filled with dramatic irony and sarcastic asides, revealing himself as a born storyteller. Dawson was also, at first glance, a bundle of contradictions. He was a deeply learned man, an autodidact and lightning-quick study, with an insatiable appetite for fine-grained information about military history and ordnance. But he mostly held intellectuals in contempt for their soft lives. He was a committed patriot, proud of his honorable service in the U.S. Navy. But he believed that the federal government was little more than a dangerous nuisance: intrusive, imperious, and prone to flights of fancy. He was unafraid to throw his weight around and could be a bully. But he went out of his way to charm people with courtly manners. He loathed "political correctness" and scorned contemporary trends toward identity politics. But he admired the Cheyennes, counting Laird Cometsevah, Steve Brady, and Otto Braided Hair among his friends. He was a complex man, in his own words "brutally honest" and "a bit ornery."[13]

For three decades prior to the beginning of Dick Ellis's site search, Dawson had owned the property that most people believed had hosted the bloodletting. That assumption rested on an earlier era's effort to commemorate Sand Creek. Although the word "massacre" represented an uncomfortable compromise for many local people when the national historic site opened in 2007, Kiowa County had a long history of deploying memories of Sand Creek, typically sanitized for mass consumption, to spur its economy. On August 6, 1950, for instance, the county unveiled two Sand Creek historic markers at an elaborate public ceremony. The first sat atop a small rise overlooking a lazy bend in

The Sand Creek Battle Ground marker, ca. 1950s, seen from the top of the monument overlook. The photographer was facing upstream, looking along the ridgeline (to the left) and down into the dry creek bed. The earth around the monument has subsequently filled in, so the base of the marker sits flush with the surrounding soil. *(Denver Public Library, Western History Collection; Opan Harper, photographer; X-32025.)*

the creek, located several miles north of State Highway 96. At a time before most Americans traveled via interstate highways, the chambers of commerce in Eads and Lamar, the area's two largest towns, paid for the historical marker, hoping to entice motor tourists to stop for a rest in their communities. The hilltop monument hewed closely to the Sand Creek story that had circulated in the region since John Chivington and his troops had returned to Denver after the massacre in December 1864. The ochre marble slab featured an image of a "lifelike Indian" wearing a "full war headdress" above the words "Sand Creek Battle Ground." Paul Steward, who produced gravestones in Lamar, had carved the monument. Boosting the event, the local press conferred legitimacy on the artist's rendering by describing Steward as a "lifetime student of Indian lore." And at the unveiling, Levi Rutledge, who owned the property at the time, promised that interested sightseers would always be welcome to visit his land.[14]

The hilltop marker did its work by pairing with the second monument, an obelisk sponsored by the Colorado Historical Society, fashioned of stone and located just outside the small town of Chivington, just off Highway 96. Bearing a bronze plaque headed by the mixed message "Sand Creek: 'Battle' or 'Massacre,'" the state's column suggested that by 1950, cultural politics had already begun complicating efforts to memorialize the violence. The monument recounted the barest facts of the massacre, relying on the passive voice to obscure responsibility for the bloodshed, and pulling its punches still further by avoiding any mention of atrocities or even the number of Indian people killed. By contrast, the marker placed Chivington's losses precisely at ten dead and thirty-eight wounded. The text concluded by calling Sand Creek "one of the regrettable tragedies of the conquest of the West"—all in all, an ambiguous set of messages, whispering of the need to placate wealthy Historical Society donors, the people of Kiowa County, and other Colorado taxpayers. After eating a celebratory dinner, roughly three hundred people, including Colonel Chivington's granddaughter and descendants of some of the Native Americans present at the massacre, drove to the highway marker. They wound their way from there in "a caravan of autos" to "the actual battle ground," where Paul Steward gave a tour of the "battle area." Leroy Hafen, Colorado's chief historian in 1950, oversaw both dedication ceremonies.[15]

Hafen apparently understood the enduring controversy surrounding collective remembrance of Sand Creek, particularly the knotty question of whether the bloodshed would be memorialized as a battle or a massacre. His private notes from the period indicate that for months he had wrestled with the implications of the wording for the Colorado Historical Society's roadside marker. And in a short essay on the slaughter published in the *Lamar Daily News* four days before the monuments' unveiling, Hafen tried to explain the inexplicable: how white Coloradans had perpetrated such a heinous crime. He described Sand Creek as "perhaps the most controversial subject in Colorado history," noting, "some have called it a 'battle' in which the Indians got what they deserved, while others have labeled it an 'unjustifiable massacre.'" In Hafen's telling, the "tragic engagement" grew out of "contact" between the "incompatible cultures of the red man and the white man." Sand Creek, in other words, had been an inevitable and unfortunate

A state-sponsored obelisk, which was erected near Chivington, Colorado, in 1950 to memorialize Sand Creek. Its plaque read, "North eight miles, east one mile, is the site of the Sand Creek 'Battle' or 'Massacre' of November 29, 1864[.] Colorado volunteers under the command of John Chivington attacked a village of Cheyennes and Arapahoes encamped on Sand Creek. Many Indians were killed; no prisoners were taken. The white losses were ten killed and thirty-eight wounded. One of the regrettable tragedies in the conquest of the West." *(Courtesy History Colorado, Scan 10025732.)*

outgrowth of American expansion onto the Great Plains. After placing the violence within that frame of reference, Hafen concluded his essay: "As is common in human relations, there are various points of view, and right is not all on one side." At the time, such insights represented a relatively nuanced treatment of Sand Creek. In retrospect, though, Hafen's essay reads like equivocation—particularly when placed side by side with the wording of the Colorado Historical Society monument on Highway 96.[16]

One thing Hafen did not mention, in either his speech or his newspaper article, was the relationship between Sand Creek and the Civil War. Divorcing the massacre from its historical context, as opposed to linking the violence to the Civil War as at the memorial on the capitol steps in Denver, made sense in these years. Between the run-up to World War I and the years after World War II, federal authorities sometimes drummed up support for involving the United States in overseas conflicts in part by encouraging Americans to look back to the Civil War as a virtuous and glorious fight, emblematic of the nation's commitment to defending freedom against tyranny. President Lincoln's standing as the great liberator, as well as the stock of citizen soldiers cast as the Union's saviors, soared in these years. Sand Creek, though, increasingly perceived in an ambiguous light even in Colorado—"'Battle' or 'Massacre'"—and throughout the West, did not fit into this popular vision of the Civil War as a good war. Disentangling the massacre from the Civil War, consequently, served both nationalist and internationalist aims at the time. The 1950-vintage memorials, both the one atop the overlook and the other near the state highway, reflected these priorities, as did Leroy Hafen's speech and newspaper essay, which painted Sand Creek against the bloody backdrop of the Indian Wars only.[17]

By 1997, the roadside obelisk had disappeared from the Kiowa County landscape. The hilltop marker, though, remained on Bill Dawson's property, still proclaiming the land below it the "Sand Creek Battle Ground." For more than half a century, out-of-town visitors had come there to contemplate the horror of the massacre and to pay their respects to its victims, leaving all manner of tributes: small bolts of cloth, tobacco, flowers, jewelry, and the occasional animal skull.[18]

The historical and spiritual significance of the site, and the pilgrims who arrived there through the years, had slowly broadened Bill Dawson's vision of Western history. He met people on his land that he otherwise would not have, and forged unlikely friendships, including with Laird Cometsevah, who regularly arrived there to perform sacred rituals and mourn his ancestors. As Dawson grew "curious why some folks would sit on the creek bluff on my north forty and gaze out across the countryside," he also became dissatisfied that all he knew about Sand Creek had come from his "eighth grade Colorado history" class. He began studying the subject. He had always defended the soldiers under Chivington's command, seeing them as kindred spirits: Coloradans who had volunteered to serve their country. He had insisted that Sand Creek had been a battle, ugly perhaps, but nevertheless righteous. By the mid-1990s, though, as he consumed more history books and developed close ties with Indian people, especially Cometsevah, who patiently explained the ceremonies he performed at the site, Dawson's view of Sand Creek slowly shifted. His sympathy for Chivington's troops slackened as his identification with the Cheyennes tightened. He eventually decided that Sand Creek had been a massacre.[19]

Throughout those years, Dawson remained a committed and capable steward of the land. He improved the property both for his mid-sized ranching operation—for his personal gain in other words—and also because he viewed his piece of prairie as somehow akin to a community trust, a historical treasure that required considerable protection. Despite his ironclad faith in untrammeled private property rights, Dawson even accepted that the land's association with the massacre conferred upon it something like quasi-public status. He typically allowed sightseers, curious about the massacre, and Indian people, who wanted to perform traditional rituals, onto his property. He asked only that these guests take their trash out with them and, beginning in the early 1980s, that they also leave a small donation in a collection box that he nailed to a fence post near the monument overlook. For more than twenty years this unlikely relationship between accommodating landowner and uninvited guests worked relatively smoothly.[20]

Eventually, though, yet another commemorative project began complicating Dawson's site management. In 1986, the Colorado Historical Society replaced the 1950-vintage obelisk located near State Highway 96 with an updated interpretive marker, still sited approximately a mile east of the town of Chivington. The new sign, embodying a turn in the state's official understanding of its own history, bore the heading "Sand Creek Massacre," dropped the word "battle" entirely, thus casting the event in an unequivocally tragic light. The marker also gave clear driving directions to the site without indicating that the land remained in private hands. That oversight, coupled with the word "Massacre," outraged Dawson, whose perspective on Sand Creek had not yet shifted entirely. He penned an angry letter to James Hartmann, the vice president of the Historical Society at the time, insisting that the "whole damn historical marker is hogwash," nothing more than politically correct pandering to "Native American groups." Dawson then vowed to close his property to visitors. Although Hartmann suggested that debates about whether Sand Creek had been a battle or a massacre were likely to "continue well into the future," he agreed to post a notice that the site was private property. Still, the number of visitors to Bill Dawson's ranch kept increasing.[21]

Around that same time, Dawson observed a change in the behavior, a perceived erosion of courtesy mirroring a decline he sensed in the broader culture's values, among the people who came to his property. Instead of relatively well-informed history buffs, tribal people, and the occasional harmless New Age seeker hoping to commune with a mythic version of the American West's past, more and more "idiots" showed up at Dawson's land. These guests increasingly searched not for immutable truths or spiritual sustenance but for a place to party. And while there, as they walked the consecrated earth they also trod on Dawson's property rights. Visitors, he recalled, arrived "for an amazing assortment of reasons. Some came to clean out their automobiles, display their large collection of beer bottles, condoms, whatever." Dawson eventually hit "a point where [he] was overwhelmed and just couldn't cope." The strain of overseeing such a controversial piece of real estate, a symbol of the costs of westward expansion and a sacred site for Indian peoples, exhausted him. As more time passed, his famously short temper frayed completely. He found himself mired in a series of bitter confrontations.[22]

By the late 1990s, even after Dawson successfully lobbied the Colorado Historical Society to remove its highway sign entirely, episodes of gate crashing signaled that the time had come for him to move. One such disturbance took place in spring 1997, as Dick Ellis's site search wound down. A woman named Pat Muckle and her brother, Mark Berge, sightseers from Boulder, arrived at Dawson's land on March 3. As daylight faded, they ignored a posted sign asking for a $2 per person donation and instead "walked around the area" near the hillside marker. Dawson by this time had lost patience with inconsiderate guests and had begun staging morality plays for unwitting tourists. On March 3, he removed the license plates from Muckle's car. When she and Berge returned from hiking around the site, Dawson, who had parked his truck behind their vehicle, demanded that they pay him $25 before he would return their tags. In a complaint Muckle later swore out against Dawson, she said that she had not realized that the site was privately held and that the proprietor's aggressive demeanor had convinced her that he had a gun. It would not have been the first time that Dawson threatened visitors to his ranch, including cases in which he menaced people he deemed "trespassers."[23]

The Muckle incident unleashed a flood of criminal charges, more than a dozen in all, against Dawson, including possession of an illegal firearm, false imprisonment, and extortion. Dawson eventually pled out the case. But first, he had to spend a night in jail and "waste," in his words, more than $20,000 on attorney's fees. Then the trouble lingered, depleting reserves of social capital that he had accrued over time. News of his legal woes "spread like wildfire" in Kiowa County. As one local resident put it, "If you don't know about this, you're living in a cave." Because Eads is a small town with an unusually stable population, judgments about longtime residents are based on hard-won reputations. The criminal proceedings diminished Dawson's stature in his community. He had previously served as a municipal judge in town, earning "$200 per month to hear everybody's dog disputes and various traffic things," but the Eads City Council stripped him of that job. Worse still, his relationship with his neighbors suffered, damage that not even good fences could put right. Although he and his wife had lived in Kiowa County for more than three decades, the Dawsons began considering a move away from Colorado's Eastern Plains.[24]

After leaving jail, Dawson returned home and locked his gates, barring strangers from his property. But keeping visitors away proved more difficult than he expected. Two weeks later, his phone rang. Dawson found himself on the line with Ward Churchill, a scholar of Native American studies at the University of Colorado–Boulder. Churchill, who since then has become notorious for intemperate comments he made about the 9/11 attacks, informed Dawson that he and a colleague wanted to visit Sand Creek. Dawson remembered replying: "I'm sorry, no, you won't be seeing the massacre site. It's closed." A shocked Churchill asked if Dawson would sell his property rather than keeping the public from it. Dawson pulled a figure from the air, "maybe $1.5 million," and Churchill responded that he would be back in touch soon. Six weeks later, Churchill rang Dawson again, asking if he would consider selling to cable television magnate and Western history enthusiast Ted Turner. Although Dawson, still smarting from his arrest, laughed at the idea, thinking, "nothing would give me more satisfaction than inflicting Turner and his wife [then the actress and antiwar activist Jane Fonda] on Kiowa County," he knew that such a thing "wasn't going to happen." Another six months passed, and Churchill called again, this time announcing, "I have a buyer for your place." Churchill was serious; he had contacted Ben Nighthorse Campbell, who wanted to acquire the land.[25]

By then, James Doyle, Senator Campbell's communications director in Colorado, had read about Dawson's legal woes in the local papers. So when Dawson asked for a moment of Campbell's time at a Republican Party fund-raiser held in southeastern Colorado in spring 1997, Doyle and Campbell knew that they might have an opportunity to move the site from the private to the public realm. After shaking the senator's hand, Dawson remembered saying, "I'm the son of a bitch who owns Sand Creek," before explaining that he might, for the right price, be ready to sell his land. Campbell had long been fascinated by the massacre. Some of his forebears had been killed there, and he had often visited the site through the years, "hearing, in the wind," he said, "the sound of people crying." At the time, Campbell held seats on the Senate Appropriations Committee, a position of power that allowed him to advance his legislative agenda, and on the Subcommittee on National Parks, part of the Committee on Energy and Natural Resources, a post that offered him a chance to shape NPS policy. In short, Doyle recalled, Campbell had "not just the will, but the ability to actually move on Sand Creek." He began investigating the best way to acquire and preserve the property, which, he decided, meant designating the Sand Creek killing field a national historic site and opening it as a unit of the National Park System.[26]

Senator Campbell immediately inquired about the NPS's interest in Sand Creek while, at the same time, trying to firm up Bill Dawson's commitment to selling. NPS officials, in response to a detailed questionnaire they received from Campbell's office, scrambled to reassure the senator that they had long considered the Sand Creek site "extremely worthy" of preservation. And Dawson promised Campbell that he wanted to leave Kiowa County—assuming that he could get the right price for his land. Attempting to maximize his profits from the coming transaction, Dawson coyly admitted to a Denver reporter that he did indeed hope to sell out. But he would not reveal more than that: "My granddad said, 'You never ask anybody how much land you got or how much cattle you got.' We consider it poor form." Reassured by the NPS that the commemoration process, if not necessarily the land acquisition process, would proceed smoothly, Campbell introduced a bill in the Senate on March 2, 1998 to purchase Dawson's ranch. Editorials in Denver-area newspapers hailed the idea: "If Sen. Ben Nighthorse Campbell has his way, history buffs won't have to contend with a gun-toting rancher to visit the site of the infamous Sand Creek Massacre on Colorado's southeastern plains." For the moment, it seemed that the Sand Creek property would quickly become a national historic site.[27]

There was just one hitch: nobody knew for certain where the massacre had taken place. Dick Ellis had not yet completed his site location study. But his preliminary research already indicated that a Sand Creek massacre national historic site located on the Dawson ranch might well be misplaced. And David Halaas, who then worked closely with Ellis on the search, suggested as much in an interview with the *Denver Post*. "What we have here is a significant historical site that's lost," Halaas explained. Again comparing the unsolved mystery to the disappearance of Gettysburg's hallowed ground, an analogy that he believed "conveyed the gravity of the situation," Halaas insisted, "we shouldn't be talking about acquiring it until we spend the money to find it." He concluded wryly: "It was a well-known place at the time. But I guess no one thought to write down the coordinates."[28]

Those coordinates would have spared Senator Campbell and the NPS a great deal of trouble. As it happened, though, the site's precise location was something that many Coloradans—like the prospectors who had, in 1993, come up empty while surveying Dawson's ranch—assumed that they knew well, but upon closer examination perhaps did not. Misconceptions about the site's placement had been documented since at least 1908, when four veterans of Chivington's 3rd Colorado Regiment—Morse Coffin, W. H. Dickens, David Harden, and P. M. Williams—took a nostalgic tour of the site of their past exploits with *Denver Post* reporter C. E. Van Loan. Their driver, a local cowboy, assured the men "that he knew the exact site of the 'battle ground,' as the old timers persisted in calling it." After setting out from Kit Carson, a hamlet located approximately twenty miles due north of Eads, the men bounced across the prairie, searching without luck for recognizable landmarks. A rancher they happened upon insisted that he could point them toward the proper site; he had found arrowheads and human remains there, he explained. But when they arrived at the location he described, "Mr. Coffin did not think so. The ground did not 'look right' to him." And the telltale signs of carnage, the remains still on the field, turned out to be bones from "beef critters." Before night fell, each of the men "had found a site which pleased him," but they could not agree on a single place in common.[29]

Their trip down memory lane continued early the next day, when the four men found still "more battlegrounds." Van Loan, the bewildered scribe along for the ride, quipped: "It was a good thing that four instead of forty of the old-timers turned up for the reunion, else there would have been forty battlegrounds and 400,000 arguments." The veterans, he related, had sown confusion wherever they had traveled in southeastern Colorado: "Before the visit of the survivors every man between Kit Carson and Chivington knew exactly where the fight took place. Now nobody is sure about it." Van Loan then traded in romantic rhetoric common at the time: Native Americans were a vanished race. Their disappearance, he suggested, had been inevitable, "a foregone conclusion." But in the reporter's telling, this familiar story carried more than a whiff of lament. When the Cheyennes and Arapahos had retreated before the floodtide of white civilization, washed out of Colorado by Chivington's men—"It wasn't nice work, but it had to be done," P. M. Williams recalled—those tribes had taken their indigenous knowledge of the local landscape with them. "The plains Indian was once intimately acquainted with [this place]," Van Loan wrote, "but the red man is now nothing more than a vivid memory—fading away like everything else connected with the aboriginal owners of the soil." Well into their dotage, and without Native guides to orient them, the quartet of veterans "left the site of the battlefield unmarked."[30]

It remained that way well into the future. In 1923, the *Rocky Mountain News* asked, "Where was the stage upon which the tragedy of Sand Creek was enacted?" and concluded, "The place is indefinite." Nearly twenty years later, the federal Works Progress Administration, an arm of Franklin Delano Roosevelt's New Deal, could do little better in its Colorado guidebook, directing parties interested in seeing the site to "inquire directions locally." That was not bad advice, given that some residents of Kiowa County—like the confident ranch hand who had driven the four veterans on their tour in 1908, or the local proprietor who had misdirected them to a pile of cow remains—still believed that they knew exactly where the violence had transpired. Disparate theories provided the fodder for what became a decades-long game of telephone: the massacre happened right here, no over there, blood had been shed just across that next rise, or perhaps nowhere nearby. The uncertainty lingered until 1950, when, with the ceremony dedicating the hilltop memorial bearing the words "Sand Creek Battle Ground," a mason distilled scattershot perspectives into something that looked an awful lot like historical precision. The massacre site was there for anyone to see, just beneath the monument overlook located on Bill Dawson's ranch.[31]

Unless it was actually somewhere else entirely. Roughly half a century later, as Senator Campbell contemplated buying Dawson's property, it seemed that the memorial served as an ironic reminder of the haziness of collective memory in southeastern Colorado rather than as a useful guide to the massacre site's actual whereabouts. When Campbell held hearings on March 24, 1998, to discuss the fate of his memorial legislation, NPS officials testified that nobody knew the massacre's exact location. Over the previous six months, NPS personnel, already aware of Campbell's interest in memorializing Sand Creek, had begun investigating the possibility of turning the Dawson property into a national historic site. Cathy Spude, one of the NPS staffers charged with vetting the project's viability, remembered that Jerry Rogers, her boss at the time, "had very strong views about the integrity of the sites incorporated into the Park System." Rogers shared Campbell's passion for memorializing Sand Creek, later arguing that the NPS needed to "fill the huge empty space of sites that deal with American Indian history and culture." But Rogers also worried about an ongoing public relations disaster surrounding the establishment of another national historic site, which was still embarrassing the NPS. His familiarity with that episode colored his perception of the Sand Creek project.[32]

A decade earlier, Congress had created the Charles Pinckney National Historic Site, honoring the "forgotten founder," a slaveholding patriot who fought in the Revolutionary War, helped draft and later signed the Constitution, and served as governor of South Carolina and then as a U.S. senator. Pinckney's estate, located near Charleston, provided visitors with a period tableau, including a building that the NPS believed was the original plantation house. George Washington once dined there, a claim to fame that recalled a bygone era when preservation decisions hinged on associating structures with famous individuals. The NPS at the time had no units owned by signers of the Constitution. And in the late 1980s, the Pinckney property faced threats from encroaching development. These factors convinced the NPS that the Pinckney estate merited protection. In 1988, the NPS supported its establishment as a historic site. Three years later, though, a survey suggested that the Pinckney mansion had not been constructed until approximately 1830, long after Charles Pinckney had sold his property to pay off debts. The NPS, humiliated that it apparently had created a national historic site in what seemed to be the wrong location, began searching for the original Pinckney house. That hunt, ultimately successful, was still under way when Senator Campbell began considering memorializing Sand Creek.[33]

With the Pinckney debacle serving as an ugly backdrop, Jerry Rogers, despite his desire to memorialize the massacre, initially handled Sand Creek with caution. An update about preliminary—and negative—results from Dick Ellis's site search only deepened his doubts about Campbell's plan. Rogers thought that the senator, because of his committee assignments and history of high regard for the NPS, had to be treated deferentially. But he also believed that the NPS could not support a bill "designating, without any further investigation, where the site would be." If it later turned out that Dawson's property was the "wrong site," that the "historic event hadn't taken place there," the NPS would be left holding a sprawling ranch in southeastern Colorado, equal parts white elephant and black eye. Alluding to the structure at the center of the Pinckney fiasco, Rogers wrote his subordinates: "No more Snee farms for this kid." More worrisome still, because of the politically charged nature of the event in question, Sand Creek might further poison federal-tribal relations. So when the NPS's witnesses appeared at Senator Campbell's hearing, they suggested that instead of buying Dawson's land and creating a memorial right away, putting the cart before the horse in their view, they should focus first on "finding the site."[34]

Dick Ellis, meanwhile, was trying to do just that. Six months earlier, Doug Scott, the archeologist Ellis had tapped to oversee the fieldwork for the Sand Creek site search, had finally surveyed Dawson's land. After decades of digging in far-flung and dangerous locales, Scott looked like artifacts would begin falling from his pant cuffs if you turned him upside down and gave him a shake. And they probably would have: fragments of shrapnel, shattered glass, and splintered bone. One of the pioneers in the emerging field of battlefield archeology, Scott could sometimes re-create the ebb and flow of scenes of mass violence by pulling bits and pieces from the ground, reading them like texts, and then assembling a chronology from what looked to the untrained eye like a random sample from the town dump. He was an affable, outgoing man, confident in his abilities; he enjoyed recounting stories of his successes, which spanned continents and decades. He first cemented his reputation at the Little Bighorn Battlefield, in Montana. He unearthed evidence suggesting that Cheyenne and Lakota warriors had outfought Custer's men, rather than tricking them, an insight that allowed the NPS, which oversaw the site, to reinterpret the bloodshed there. After that triumph, Scott's professional standing soared. He next excavated other sites from the Indian Wars and the Civil War. Immediately prior to coming to Kiowa County, he had worked in Bosnia and Rwanda, gathering evidence used in several war crimes prosecutions.[35]

Despite Scott's experience canvassing similar settings, the peculiar case of Sand Creek left him shaking his head. Before sending a large team of experienced metal detectors—members of the Pikes Peak Adventure League, accompanied by Steve Brady, the Ridgelys, Laird Cometsevah, and several other massacre descendants—out to sweep the Dawson ranch in late September and early October 1997, Scott drew up a detailed work plan. Despite his preparations, his team, after covering acres of prairie terrain, came up nearly empty: no spent cartridges from Chivington's troops and very little of the detritus that should have been cast off by the Arapaho and Cheyenne bands camped on the banks of Sand Creek. In short, the searchers found almost no hard evidence at all. Scott, though, still believed that they were looking in the right place. He kept repeating, "I don't know why we're not finding anything. It just ought to be here. All of the historical evidence points in this direction." Still, after a week of looking, he gave up and pulled his team from the site. When he later compiled a report on his fieldwork, he noted that the archeology had been "inconclusive at best."[36]

The Cheyenne descendants, by contrast, were undeterred. They remained resolute in their conviction that the massacre had taken place on Dawson's property. Steve Brady recalled, "you could just feel that we were in a very special place." Upon arriving for the archeological reconnaissance, he, Laird Cometsevah, and Joe Big Medicine, another Southern Cheyenne massacre descendant, "conducted a ceremony," and, in Brady's words, "without any question at all, we knew that we were in the right place at that time." He continued, "It was our cultural understanding that we were at the massacre site. It was just unequivocal." In part, the Cheyenne representatives to the project drew upon deeply held feelings, a sense of place they associated with the massacre of their ancestors, whose spirits, they believed, still roamed that land. They also knew that other observers from their tribes, including Senator Campbell, had heard voices, often those of crying children, near the monument overlook. And most important of all, two decades earlier, in 1978, Cometsevah and the Sacred Arrow Keeper, the Cheyenne spiritual leader, had consecrated the ground there. In Cometsevah's words, they had "reclaimed the land," making it "Cheyenne earth." Still, despite the descendants' consensus, Brady worried: "white people aren't going to believe that kind of thing without hard scientific evidence." He was right. Ellis remained unconvinced by the Cheyennes' certitude and later produced a report echoing Doug Scott's findings, suggesting that the entire search had been inconclusive.[37]

So when Senator Campbell held his Sand Creek hearings in Washington, DC, on March 24, Steve Brady and Laird Cometsevah, confident that they knew the site's true location, testified about the importance of buying Bill Dawson's property and creating a national historic site there. But Kate Stevenson, the NPS's key witness before Campbell's committee, demurred, warning that without "solid physical, archaeological, scientific, historically documented evidence," purchasing the Dawson ranch would be rash and perhaps could wind up embarrassing the NPS. Stevenson concluded by suggesting, "To commemorate the event on the wrong spot would dishonor the victims, distort the history, and deceive the visitor. Nothing about your consideration of this legislation could be more important than to make certain that we have the correct location." Frustrated that NPS officials were ignoring their cultural authority on the subject of Sand Creek, thereby undercutting the validity of the "traditional tribal methods" the descendants had used to locate the massacre site, Brady and Cometsevah nonetheless supported the NPS's call for another investigation into where the slaughter had taken place. Senator Campbell, by then certain that such a process would be the best way to "acquire and preserve with honor and dignity" the Sand Creek killing field, sponsored the site location legislation. Both houses of Congress passed identical versions of the bill in September 1998. On October 6 of that year, President Clinton signed the Sand Creek Massacre National Historic Site Study Act into law.[38]

Although he stood with the NPS during the Capitol Hill hearings, an irritated Steve Brady came away from the experience "reminde[d] of the way that white government always operates when dealing with Indian people: ask Indians for help, maybe get our help, and then thank us by hanging us out to dry. It's the same as it ever was." With the phrase "the same as it ever was," Brady linked the nascent effort to commemorate Sand Creek with the era of the massacre itself. Time and again during the memorialization process, President Lincoln's mystic chords of memory would begin to feel more like cords, cinching past to present, sometimes biting uncomfortably tight. For the descendants, especially, federal officials working in the NPS would appear guilty of recapitulating episodes from the road to and from Sand Creek.[39]

In this case, Brady alluded to a plea for cooperation issued by Governor John Evans in June 1864. In the aftermath of the gruesome Hungate murders, with the city of Denver slipping into panic, Evans responded in two ways. First, he redoubled his requests for help from federal authorities. Second, he tried to separate Native people in Colorado Territory into two clearly identifiable and mutually exclusive groups: "friendlies" and "hostiles." Working through "agents, interpreters, and traders," on June 27 Evans reached out to "the friendly Indians of the plains," asking for their help. He observed that some "members of their tribes ha[d] gone to war with white people." Because of that, he warned, "the Great Father is angry, and will certainly hunt them out and punish them." But, Evans continued, despite the escalating violence, white authorities still hoped to "protect and take care of" peaceful Indians "who remain[ed] friendly." The governor then asked those

Native people to go to "places of safety," including, for the Cheyennes and Arapahos, Fort Lyon. "The object of this" plan, Evans concluded, was to "prevent friendly Indians from being killed through mistake." As for Native people who had attacked whites, there could be no mis-construing their fate: "The war on hostile Indians will be continued until they are all effectually subdued."[40]

Through the end of June, Evans's maneuver seemed to be working, as relative calm settled on Colorado's Eastern Plains. In mid-July, though, soldiers fired without provocation on Chief Left Hand, a diehard propo-nent of peace with American settlers, and more Cheyennes and Arapa-hos began to wonder if Governor Evans could be trusted. Some bands joined raiding parties, lashing out at settlements along the Platte route, while others migrated toward places that they deemed safe—places that sometimes differed from the ones Evans had specified. Colonel Chiving-ton observed these movements and the intensified attacks some bands levied on stage stations and outlying ranches; he insisted that the tribes had joined with pro-Confederate guerrillas and belligerent Sioux bands. He also attended to politics, traveling the territory advo-cating for statehood and his own prospects. In early August, though, more bloodshed forced him to narrow his focus from civilian to military affairs. On August 7, Cheyenne, Arapaho, and Sioux warriors attacked several outposts, murdering some forty settlers and taking at least six women and children captive. Black Kettle, still hoping for peace with white authorities, attempted to demonstrate his good faith in late Au-gust by handing some of those hostages over to Ned Wynkoop. But it was too late by then. Governor Evans had convinced himself that the Plains Tribes posed an existential threat to Colorado Territory. Settlers, he believed, needed to do everything in their power to safeguard white civilization from what he saw as unchecked Indian savagery.[41]

Governor Evans begged General Curtis and Secretary of War Stan-ton to send troops to Colorado or, failing that, to authorize him to raise a regiment of Indian fighters from the local population. While he waited for a reply, on August 11 Evans issued a second proclamation, this time urging "all citizens of Colorado, either individually or in such parties as they may organize, to go in pursuit of all hostile Indi-ans on the plains." He asked members of the state-sanctioned mobs that he was creating to "scrupulously avoid" peaceful Indians who had responded to his earlier call. But the governor offered no clues as to how whites should differentiate between hostile and friendly Native people. Instead, he provided incentives for "citizens, or parties of citizens" who chose to "kill and destroy . . . all such hostile Indians": the right to "take captive, and hold to their own private use and benefit all the property" of their victims. "The conflict is upon us," he concluded, "and all good citizens are called upon to do their duty for the defense of their homes and families." The next day, he received authorization from the War Department to raise a regiment for a hundred days—the 3rd Colorado—a force recruited, in Evans's words, to "pursue, kill, and destroy all hostile Indians that infest the plains, for thus only can we secure a permanent and lasting peace." Just a month and a half earlier, he had asked Colorado's Native peoples for help, promising them safety in exchange for their assistance. More than a century later, Steve Brady recalled episodes like that one as he wrestled with whether or not to keep assisting the NPS to memorialize Sand Creek.[42]

By 1998, Brady, along with Laird Cometsevah and several of the other descendants, had spent decades struggling against what they perceived as overweening federal authority, their efforts one part of a national movement to secure cultural sovereignty and self-determination for Native Americans. One of the fronts on which that fight had played out was the quest to reacquire parcels of land taken throughout the nation's history from tribal peoples. In light of those pitched battles, as well as the lessons drawn from betrayals during the massacre era, having the NPS ignore their traditional practices—the implications of the Sacred Arrow Keeper's ceremony conducted on Bill Dawson's land twenty years earlier, the contact some tribal people had with their ancestors' spirits at that spot, and the stories of Sand Creek passed from generation to generation—left the descendants more committed than ever to ensuring that they would have a meaningful say in the memorialization process. They would protect the Sand Creek site, reclaiming a parcel of their ancestral homeland. Then they would narrate their tribes' history on that ground. They would preserve the past by embedding their stories in a sacred place.[43]

Although their treatment at the Senate hearings still rankled, the Cheyenne descendants nonetheless celebrated the passage of Senator Campbell's legislation, because it served their interests. To begin with, there apparently would be no more linguistic debates surrounding Sand Creek memorials; the act defined the events of November 29, 1864, as a "massacre," plain and simple, seemingly rendering the "Battle" of Sand Creek a relic from self-serving histories white Westerners had crafted in the nineteenth century and promulgated in the twentieth. At the same time, Campbell's act acknowledged an unpaid debt, embedded in Article 6 of the Treaty of the Little Arkansas, owed by federal authorities to some Cheyennes and Arapahos. The legislation also noted, "the site is of great significance" to the descendants. Because of this, the tribes would have "the right of open access to visit the site and rights of cultural and historical observance." The act then laid out the task at hand: the federal government, represented by the NPS, would collaborate with officials from the State of Colorado and the four affected tribes—the Northern and Southern branches of the Cheyenne and Arapaho—to "identify the location and extent of the massacre area and the suitability and feasibility of designating the site as a unit of the National Park Service." Their detective work would have to be completed in just eighteen months, an ambitious timetable for an agency notorious for lengthy deliberation. And by placing the tribes on equal footing with the NPS, the act ensured that Cheyenne and Arapaho people would have voices in the memorialization process.[44]

The legislation included a final provision that touched off a number of unintended consequences for the way that Sand Creek would be remembered: land for the memorial could be acquired by the NPS from "willing sellers" only. The NPS would not be able to take property for the site through the legal mechanisms of condemnation or eminent domain. Upon hearing the news, some residents in Kiowa County, Bill Dawson especially, issued a sigh of relief. From the start of Dick Ellis's site search, rumors had flown around the plains of southeastern Colorado, suggesting that private property would be seized if government authorities deemed it historically significant. That this scuttlebutt had amounted to little more than nonsense had not allayed many people's fears. Then, Senator Campbell rested his act upon one of the bedrock principles of the Republican Party's Western caucus at the time: the federal government, which already owned more than 35 percent of the land in Colorado, should not take property from private hands and place it in the public realm. Campbell made this decision not only due to immutable political doctrine but also because he desperately wanted community support for the Sand Creek project. What he did not realize was how much power he had unwittingly vested in the hands of local landowners.[45]

Bill Dawson, by contrast, recognized two likely outgrowths of the Sand Creek Act's willing-seller-only stipulation: that he had instantly become a power broker in the process of commemorating the massacre, and that his land likely had gained considerable value overnight. So long as the descendants remained certain that the massacre had taken place on his property, Dawson controlled the fate of Senator Campbell's "pet project." If he refused to allow the NPS on his land to conduct further studies, or if he chose not to sell his ranch when the moment came to create the national historic site, there would be no Sand Creek memorial. At the same time, the real estate market holds heritage dear. Association with a significant historical event, coupled with the laws of supply and demand, can inflate a property's price tag. Dawson knew this. He understood that his ranch's value would fluctuate depending on its centrality to the massacre story, and that the tribal representatives, because of their role in the memorialization process, would help determine the importance of his land. The politically savvy Dawson thus played his cards carefully, nurturing his relationship with the Cheyennes and consolidating his position whenever he could.[46]

Even before the site search legislation passed Congress, Dawson demonstrated his mastery of the memorialization process's shifting political landscape. Homer Flute, president of a pan-tribal organization known as the Sand Creek Massacre Descendants Trust, a splinter from Laird Cometsevah's Cheyenne-only group, wrote Dawson in spring 1998, informing him of the group's upcoming visit to the site for ceremonial purposes. Dawson by then had grown quite close with Laird and Colleen Cometsevah. Because of that friendship and also because of Dawson's understanding of the ramifications of prescriptions on property acquisition likely to be lodged in the Sand Creek Act, he guarded his ties to the Cheyenne descendants' groups jealously. He knew, too, that the Cometsevahs disparaged Flute as an interloper and a potential rival for a future reparations claim based on Article 6 of the Little Arkansas treaty. Dawson, accordingly, wrote back to Flute that his group would be neither welcome nor allowed to enter the property. Flute, apparently certain that his cultural authority would trump Dawson's property rights, replied that the rancher could not ban Indian people from performing their traditional rituals at the massacre site. Dawson dashed off a rejoinder, saying that, as the sole proprietor at the site, he could and would prevent the group from entering his land. When Flute and his descendants' organization nevertheless arrived at Sand Creek, Dawson proved his point. Sheriff's deputies met approximately three dozen Native people at the county road. Dawson had secured a restraining order, barring them from his land.[47]

The deputies escorted Flute and his party to a spot nearby, where they mourned the dead and performed a pipe ceremony, separated from the monument overlook by barbed wire. At the close of the ritual, the trust's attorney, Larry Derryberry, announced to the crowd, "the next step is to ask assistance from those in Washington, to take this issue to Congress and to the President." Claiming a place for the massacre descendants near the pinnacle of a well-established hierarchy of victimization, Derryberry explained that his organization would seek "reparations comparable to those given Holocaust survivors, Japanese-American internees, Haitians, Ugandans, Rwandans, etc." One of the descendants, Dorothy Wood, looked on with tears streaming down her face. She diagrammed the massacre in the sandy soil at her feet, noting where the lodges of Black Kettle and her ancestor, White Antelope, had been positioned during the slaughter. Wood then joined a somber parade of cars making the long drive back east to Oklahoma. The local press, revealing southeastern Colorado's ongoing ambivalence about how to categorize Sand Creek, reported on the gathering in two adjacent articles, one describing the violence as a "massacre," the other calling it a "battle."[48]

At around the same time that Dawson faced off with Homer Flute, the NPS began gearing up to find the site—still months before Campbell's bill became law. Aware that there would be little time to complete the search after the legislation passed both houses of Congress, NPS officials crafted a plan of action and tried to secure cooperation from all of the concerned parties. Cathy Spude, who at the time led the NPS's Sand Creek search initiative, began pondering the composition of her team, using Dick Ellis's experience as a guide. The site search, true to its origins under Ellis, would remain an interdisciplinary effort.

Historians would scrutinize documentary sources. Anthropologists would collect ethnographies from descendants. Aerial photographers would search from above for historic trails. Geomorphologists would determine if Sand Creek had shifted its course since the time of the massacre, or if deposition or erosion had altered the earth's shape significantly enough to render landmarks gleaned from the historical record useless. And finally, depending on the results of the above studies, battlefield archeologists would search all of the possible sites for artifacts. Before any of that could happen, though, Spude needed to gain the descendants' trust while keeping Bill Dawson happy.[49]

Neither proved to be an easy task. Lingering resentments, born of the descendants' treatment at the Senate's site hearings, exacerbated their long-standing skepticism regarding the federal government and its proxies in the NPS. To bridge the divide, Spude turned to Colorado's chief historian, David Halaas. "Because of the connections he had already made with the descendants," she hoped that Halaas would act as a "liaison" between the NPS and the tribal represenatives. He rejected that role. Halaas's relationship with the Cheyenne descendants, forged during the first site search, coupled with the research he was completing for his biography of George Bent, defined his identity far more than did his job at the Colorado Historical Society. Spude, who had begun her work with such high hopes for Halaas's contribution, found herself "disappointed" by him, "unsure of where his loyalties lay at any point." For his part, Halaas looked back without regret on the choices he made at that time. He recalled deciding to "throw his hat in with the Cheyennes when forced to pick sides." As a result, his vision for the site search often clashed with that of the NPS. And when the NPS would lock horns with the Cheyennes, Halaas always backed the descendants.[50]

Because of Halaas's relationship with the Cheyenne representatives, Spude was correct that he did not embrace the NPS's site search as his top priority in summer 1998. While she focused on Kiowa County and Bill Dawson's ranch, Halaas's gaze lingered closer at hand, drawn by a Sand Creek memory fight heating up just a few hundred feet from his office door. In 1909, the Colorado Pioneers Association placed a Civil War monument on the state capitol steps in Denver. The Pioneers' memorial—a Union cavalryman cast in bronze, on foot and carrying his rifle, peering westward into the middle distance where the foothills of the Rocky Mountains rise just outside Denver—featured a plaque affixed to its base, cataloging all of the "battles" in which Coloradans had fought throughout the Civil War. Sand Creek was listed among them. This perspective gathered significance because of the memorial's placement. Located just outside the capitol's front door and looming high above Civic Center Park, Denver's most important municipal public space, the monument offered a de facto city- and state-sponsored memory of the bloodshed at Sand Creek.[51]

In 1909, the Colorado Civil War memorial represented a local manifestation of a generational commemorative impulse sweeping the United States. Around the turn of the twentieth century, most members of the 1st and 3rd Colorado Regiments had died or were nearing the end of their lives. The same was true for Civil War veterans nationwide. The result was a huge campaign around the country to archive documents, publish regimental histories, and build monuments. All of this activity comprised part of an organized but diffuse effort to shape, for posterity, the way future generations would remember the war and the people who fought it. This upsurge in memorialization was akin to what students of collective memory call "the invention of tradition," the way that societies create historical narratives or rituals to suit contemporary political or cultural conditions. Invented traditions are often crafted to maintain power relations and uphold the status quo. In the case of turn-of-the-century Civil War commemorative activity, communities were dealing with anxieties over massive changes facing the United States: industrialization, urbanization, and, among others, immigration. Nostalgia reigned, consequently, as Americans idealized the Civil War generation for its virtues and sacrifices. The monuments that cropped up were designed to inspire onlookers to venerate a shared iteration of the past and to embrace a reconciliationist narrative of the war.[52]

For members of the Pioneers Association, as well as other stewards of the Civil War's collective memory in Colorado, including the local chapter of the Grand Army of the Republic, Sand Creek presented something of a problem. Beginning during the era of Reconstruction and continuing through the early part of the twentieth century, a heroic narrative of the war predominated, in which both the Union and the Confederacy had fought hard, fought well, and fought for just causes. Unresolved issues, like the war's deeper causes—including slavery, other ongoing racial inequities, and the lingering consequences of westward expansion—could be forgotten in service of an amicable reunion and the goal of getting back to the business of doing business. No room for events like a Sand Creek "massacre" existed in this story of the war and its aftermath, no room for atrocities, and, given the still-simmering conflict with indigenous people on the Plains, no room for Native Americans at all. If Sand Creek were to be part of this emerging national Civil War narrative, as Coloradans hoped in 1909, it would have to be cast as a "battle," for there had been few "massacres" in that noble war.[53]

On July 24 of that year, the Pioneers Association unveiled its memorial, designed by John Howland, who had served in the 1st Colorado Regiment during the Civil War. With Colorado's governor, John Shafroth, waylaid by a rockslide in the mountains, the state supreme court's chief justice, Robert Steele, oversaw the ceremony before a parade of elderly veterans and a crowd of admirers numbering in the thousands. The press reported that "a hush of patriotic awe" fell over the throng as the American flag shrouding the monument slipped away. A twenty-one-gun salute pierced the thin air, a band played "Marching through Georgia," balanced next by "Dixie," and Senator Thomas "T. M." Patterson then remarked, in the spirit of reconciliation: "We are all Americans today, and we all glory in one flag and in one country." Ignoring Sand Creek's impact on the Arapahos and Cheyennes, General Irving Hale, who spoke later, suggested that the "Civil War ... made freedom universal." The Pioneers Association had, it seemed, sanded down the massacre's rough edges and carved John Chivington's narrative of the slaughter into stone by including Sand Creek among the twenty-two Civil War "battles" in which Coloradans had participated.[54]

Eighty-nine years later, though, amid a storm of publicity generated by Senator Campbell's plans for memorializing the massacre, Sand Creek seemed misplaced yet again, this time among the list of engagements arrayed on the Pioneers Association monument. On May 5, 1998, the Colorado legislature, whose members sometimes walked by the Civil War memorial on their way to work in the capitol building, decided to correct an "insult to the memory" of the "Native Americans who were killed at Sand Creek" and also to the "Colorado Civil war veterans who fought and died in the *actual* Civil War battles that are listed on the memorial." The state legislature passed a joint resolution

The Colorado Civil War Memorial, Denver. Originally unveiled in 1909, the memorial sits on the west side of the state capitol, facing Civic Center Park and the foothills of the Rocky Mountains beyond. *(Courtesy History Colorado, C-Denver-Buildings, Govt-State-Capitol-Exterior, Scan 10037235.)*

noting, "Sand Creek was not, in fact, the site of a battle, but of a massacre" and therefore would "be removed from the memorial." Put another way, the words Sand Creek" would literally be erased from the list at the foot of the statue. A local sculptor would detach the plaque on which the twenty-two "battles" appeared, grind away the offending text, sandblast the remaining twenty-one, apply a patina to match the original color, and then reinstall the bronze plate at the foot of the statue. It seemed in that moment that generations of public remembrance could be scraped away and recast, the sins of the past wiped clean, all for the bargain price of $1,000.[55]

But then David Halaas heard about the resolution. He was still collaborating with Dick Ellis on the first site search at the time and was also just becoming involved with the NPS's early efforts to memorialize Sand Creek. He had already established close ties with the Cheyenne descendants, especially with Laird Cometsevah and Steve Brady, who by then viewed Halaas as a friend and occasional advisor. Halaas also headed the Colorado Historical Society's Roadside Interpretation Project, an initiative that placed displays throughout the state, offering surprisingly nuanced drive-through analyses of key episodes from the recent and distant past. This combination of duties arguably made Halaas the state's most influential public historian, the person with the greatest understanding of and impact on how Coloradans experienced their heritage. As a result, Halaas had a keen interest in both shaping and protecting Colorado's collective memories. At around the same time that Cathy Spude began doubting his loyalties, Halaas believed that he had found an important task—the struggle over the fate of the Civil War memorial—in which he could represent his employer, the State of Colorado, and his friends, the Sand Creek descendants, without any conflict of interest.[56]

Halaas feared that the legislature's benign revisionism might inadvertently undermine the impact of Senator Campbell's memorialization efforts. After learning that State Senator Bob Martinez, the monument resolution's sponsor, had not consulted "the tribally recognized and official Sand Creek Descendants organizations in Oklahoma and Montana," Halaas contacted Cometsevah and Brady, soliciting their views of the proposed changes to the plaque. Chief Cometsevah appreciated the "sentiment that Sand Creek should be considered a massacre and not a battle worthy of celebration" but worried nevertheless that the massacre had already been forgotten often enough in "history books and the public mind." He also "pointed out the absurdity of Senator Campbell supporting a national bill to commemorate and remember Sand Creek while at the same time the Colorado Legislature supports

A plaque affixed to the base of the Colorado Civil War Memorial. The list includes every Civil War "battle" in which Coloradans fought. Sand Creek is included on the bottom right. (*Photo by author.*)

a state resolution erasing Sand Creek." Cometsevah and Halaas then suggested a compromise: instead of "removing Sand Creek from the statue, we should inform the public about the massacre through historical markers." They would, in other words, apply the principles of the Roadside Interpretation Project to the Civil War memorial on the state capitol steps.[57]

When Cathy Spude asked Halaas to woo the Sand Creek descendants on the NPS's behalf, he instead busied himself with lobbying Colorado's legislature to reconsider its Civil War memorial resolution. At the same time, Halaas secured Spude's unwitting support for his efforts, suggesting that the NPS sponsor a preliminary site location meeting with the descendants, a gathering that would be timed to coincide with the state legislature's hearings on the Civil War memorial. Halaas also encouraged a diverse coalition to pressure the lawmakers. Activists within Denver's Native American communities had long viewed the memorial's text as an "assault on Colorado's Indian history," but they supported the idea of reinterpreting the monument rather than "erasing Sand Creek." Tom Noel, a history professor at the University of Colorado–Denver and a local public intellectual, penned an op-ed in the *Denver Post*, advising the legislature to "keep the words 'Sand Creek'" on the Civil War memorial on the capitol steps. Noel then pitched the importance of historical contingency to his readers, observing, "if each generation censors the monuments ... of predecessor generations, history becomes hopelessly shortsighted. The story of Sand Creek, with all its various interpretations, needs to be left open for public discussions and reflection." Finally, Halaas asked Brady and Cometsevah to appeal directly to the Colorado legislature—a request they honored with an impassioned letter imploring the state's well-meaning lawmakers to foster remembrance rather than institutionalize forgetting of Sand Creek.[58]

Defenders of the status quo, meanwhile, mobilized to keep the statue intact. Duane Smith, a colleague of Dick Ellis's at Fort Lewis College in Durango, bristled about meddlesome do-gooders, insisting, "it's absolutely stupid to take [Sand Creek] off." He admitted, "I know I sound like a bigot, [but] two American Armies were fighting for their homeland. That is not unusual in world history. We're making it into something it's not." Of the statue's original sponsors, Smith noted, "[they] weren't devils incarnate." The memorializers had understood what they were doing, he continued, believing that "for the future of Colorado, Sand Creek was a tremendously important Civil War battle." Mike Koury, a local author, editor, and active member of a national heritage organization known as the Order of the Indian Wars, agreed with Smith and also parroted John Chivington: "I firmly believe that there were hostiles in that camp." Political correctness run amok, he warned, would "dishonor people who fought in the Civil War." Anyway, it did not matter, Koury continued, "whether [Sand Creek] was a massacre or not." The men who fought there "were soldiers" who deserved to be hailed for their patriotism. After all, "they went where they were ordered to go and did what they were ordered to do." Finally, Koury echoed Tom Noel: "Taking [Sand Creek] off a statue is not going to make it disappear. You gain nothing by hiding it under a blanket." The only reasonable course, and certainly the only patriotic course, was to celebrate Colorado's history, including Sand Creek.[59]

When the legislature's Capitol Advisory Committee met on July 31 to discuss the controversy, Halaas and Cometsevah testified that Sand Creek should remain part of the memorial—accompanied by a new plaque providing historical context. Halaas stated that the massacre had, in fact, been part of the Civil War. The previous day, he had made this point to the Colorado Historical Society's president, Georgianna Contiguglia: that the best source for historians of the war, *The War of the Rebellion: A Compilation of the Official Records of the Union and Confederate Armies* (also known as the *Official Records of the War of the Rebellion*), included details of Sand Creek; that the soldiers "involved in Sand Creek were Civil War troops"; that Governor John Evans "believed the Cheyennes and other plains tribes were allied with the Confederate government"; and that Chivington was a "Civil War officer." Halaas's perspective broadened the war narrative and de-emphasized reconciliation, allowing for the inclusion of injustices like Sand Creek. Cometsevah, in turn, read aloud his and Brady's letter to the legislature, "respectfully request[ing] that the words 'Sand Creek' presently engraved on the Civil War memorial be retained" and that new "signage be placed around the Civil War statue that would inform and educate the public about the holocaust of Sand Creek." After hearing other witnesses, the committee recommended reconsidering the resolution. Within months, the legislature would adopt all of Halaas's suggestions.[60]

Cathy Spude, meanwhile, managed to work around the skirmishes taking place on the capitol steps. She convened a preliminary meeting with the descendants on July 25, hoping to secure their cooperation for the upcoming site search. The gathering proved disastrous, deepening the descendants' frustration with the NPS. After Spude explained that the NPS would be dealing with the tribes on a government-to-government basis, Steve Brady exploded. Spude's proposed structure, he argued, ignored intratribal divisions and the authority vested in the descendants on matters relating to Sand Creek. Laird Cometsevah then wondered why there had to be another site location study at all: "It is not the Cheyennes . . . but white people who question the location of the Sand Creek Massacre." The descendants, he reiterated, knew where the bloodshed had taken place. Cometsevah and Brady then tag-teamed Spude, "explaining that this [memorializing the massacre] was not a tribal but a descendants' matter." Recalling their frustration at the way their cultural authority had been ignored by the NPS during Senator Campbell's Sand Creek hearings, Brady and Cometsevah next insisted that tribal "oral histories would be part of any site study." Finally, they demanded assurances that a prospective memorial would "not void Article 6 of the 1865 [Little Arkansas] treaty . . . which granted as yet unpaid reparations to the victims of the massacre or their descendants."[61]

Looking back on that fractious episode with a hint of a smile creeping across his face, Brady admitted that he and Cometsevah, along with worrying about the particular issues they raised, also were sending the NPS a message: the descendants would not be ignored by the federal government this time; their voices would be heard throughout the memorialization process. Regardless, a chastened Spude reassured the frustrated descendants that she would do everything in her power to comply with their demands. She then managed to steer the agenda at the meeting to a discussion of geomorphological investigations, explaining that "ground-disturbing" work would have to be done at the site. The descendants, having cooperated with Doug Scott in similar endeavors already, had no objections to that or the prospect of additional archeological surveys. The meeting adjourned on relatively good terms.[62]

But controversy lingered. Spude, it turned out, had blundered by excluding Bill Dawson from the gathering with the descendants. She and

Dawson had met twice already. Spude had traveled to his ranch first on July 7 and then again on July 23, just two days before convening her meeting in Denver with the Sand Creek descendants. At her first discussion with Dawson, the rancher acknowledged that he wanted to sell his property; he even showed her a copy of the letter, including his $1.5 million asking price, that he had written to Ward Churchill more than a year earlier. Reading the note reassured the jittery Spude, who knew that, because of Senator Campbell's willing-seller-only provision, the site search likely could not proceed without Dawson's cooperation. At the same time, the rancher's attitude worried her. Dawson insisted that although he wanted "to actively participate in efforts to confirm the location of the massacre," he would do so *only* as an active participant." Spude suspected this meant that Dawson wanted what she called "editorial control" over the process. Their next meeting deepened her concerns. Dawson became visibly upset when he learned that there would be no "press embargo" surrounding the search; he demanded a lump sum payment to secure his participation; and when he heard that Spude had not invited him to the upcoming meeting with the descendants, he seethed.[63]

Spude's reasons for excluding Dawson seemed sound at the time. Not knowing how deep the rancher's ties ran with some of the descendants, Spude assumed that the tribal representatives would not want to meet with outsiders present. She believed that Dawson's presence might prove disruptive. From Spude's perspective, Dawson "wanted to be calling the shots all the way from the beginning." Dawson, in turn, viewed Spude "as a government bureaucrat"—as nasty a slur as he had in his repertoire—"a Park Service person who says that we're going to do it my way and you're going to like it or else." Spude also did not realize that Dawson would use the perceived slight as an opportunity to consolidate his power in the search by asserting what amounted to veto power over the process. He did so first by attacking Spude for being secretive, demanding a "verbatim copy" of notes from the meeting. Spude responded icily, suggesting that the rancher file a Freedom of Information Act request if he wanted the documents so badly. Dawson then labeled her move a "breach of trust," prompting Spude to reply that the descendants "did not wish for [him] to receive a copy of the meeting notes." Dawson next wrote to John Cook, head of the NPS regional office in Denver, telling him, "problems with Ms. Catherine Spude have caused me to withdraw support for this project." On another occasion, Dawson warned Cook: "If you want cooperation from the landowner of the focus piece of property, you'd better lose Cathy Spude, because I am not going to have anything more to do with her." Dawson was not bluffing; the project would not move forward until he got his way.[64]

Aware of the threat, on September 15, 1998, Cook met with Dawson, promising him that Cathy Spude would no longer direct the Sand Creek project. Spude, for her part, only learned about that decision at the end of a contentious NPS planning meeting for the site search team—a gathering at which she found herself, in her words, "treated as an adversary, rather than a collaborator." The difficult news, and the way she received it without any advance warning, "devastated" her. Spude had been certain that the job was hers. She had devoted months of her life to the Sand Creek project. And she hated the idea that Bill Dawson had pulled the strings that had unseated her. For the moment, though, she remained on the memorialization team, coordinating the archeological investigations. Then Dawson gainsaid even that. Eventually, after he and Spude clashed yet again, she realized that her participation "wasn't going to help the Park Service any." She informed her replacement, Rick Frost, then the Sand Creek site search manager, "I can't work on the project anymore because Dawson is going to use me as an excuse to make trouble for you." Frost accepted her resignation from the team, and Dawson, who chuckled when recalling his successful power play, said of Spude: "I'll be real frank. She wasn't involved in the project because of me." NPS officials, having given in to Dawson's demands on personnel matters once, would learn later, when grappling with him again, that they had emboldened rather than placating the rancher.[65]

With Dawson at least temporarily mollified, Rick Frost put together the Sand Creek team. A native of Colorado who grew up in the foothills outside Denver, Frost looked like the poster boy for an NPS employee, a backcountry ranger even. He was tall, square-jawed, and handsome. In 1998, when John Cook tapped him to manage the site search, Frost had, only the previous year, joined the NPS as regional communications director. Still, with a wealth of experience in the fed-

eral bureaucracy, Frost was not exactly Bill Dawson's kind of guy. He
came to the NPS having worked a series of jobs in Washington, DC,
both on and off Capitol Hill: as a staffer for Congressman Robert Tori-
celli; as legislative director for Congresswoman Rosa DeLauro; and
then, just prior to joining the NPS, as communications director at the
Consumer Products Safety Administration. Frost understood and ex-
celled at politics and diplomacy, one reason that Cook selected him to
head a high-profile project that was already stirring controversy. NPS
shorthand suggested that, as a newcomer to the organization, Frost
might not yet "bleed green," but while working on the Sand Creek project, he would prove his loyalty time and again to his new employer.[66]

A number of talented researchers worked on the team under Frost.
Doug Scott, who led the archeological investigations during Dick
Ellis's site search, returned for round two. His friend, Jerry Greene,
joined him as one of the historians working on the Sand Creek project.
If Scott was rough-hewn, Greene appeared bookish, a walking stereo-
type of the scholar he was. Tall and slender, he spoke in soft tones
lightly inflected with the flatness of the upper Midwest, where he went
to school, rather than the rounder vowels of the West, which later became his home and the focus of his life's work. Well known for his
slender monograph *Evidence and the Custer Enigma,* Greene was a stick-
ler for archival research and a demon for detail. His masterpiece was
one of the most influential accounts ever written about the Battle of
the Little Bighorn. With its publication, Greene proved himself every
bit the sleuth Scott was—the two had worked closely together on projects through the years—by treating the infamous fight as a kind of
crime scene, sifting through evidence and debunking myths about
how Custer and his troops had perished. One of the nation's foremost
experts on the Plains Indian Wars, Greene had been with the NPS for
twenty-five years when he joined the Sand Creek team.[67]

Working with him were Gary Roberts, a history professor and author of "Sand Creek: Tragedy and Symbol," an unpublished dissertation that remained the finest available study of the massacre, and two
other NPS historians, Lysa Wegman-French and the team captain,
Christine Whitacre. At the time, Wegman-French referred to herself
and Whitacre as "Tweedledee and Tweedledum" because they shared so
much in common. Unlike Greene or Roberts, who both specialized in

the history of the American West and the Indian wars, Whitacre and Wegman-French were generalists, asked to master new topics and produce work for the NPS in short order. Both were successful public historians, not academics. They were especially concerned with the intersection of history and place, including the impact of historic preservation on built landscapes. In that capacity, they compiled special resource studies, detailed assessments of whether a proposed site merited selection as a unit of the National Park System. The two women were also committed to the NPS, convinced that they had the "best job[s] in the world," and proud of the work they did. Finally, both were outgoing and generous with their time, admired by colleagues and superiors alike. Together, Whitacre and Wegman-French would handle the archival research within driving distance of the Denver regional office, while Roberts and Greene would travel to document collections further afield. In addition, Whitacre, a graceful and enthusiastic writer, would compile her team's findings for publication as part of the NPS's site search.[68]

The last two members of the NPS lineup, Alexa Roberts and Barbara Sutteer, would be assigned the most politically fraught and culturally precarious jobs in the search: working closely with the tribal descendants. Sutteer, the Indian liaison for the NPS, had spent her career in similar situations. She had worked for the Bureau of Indian Affairs before joining the NPS in 1989. At that time, she became just the second Native American (Northern Ute/Cherokee) superintendent in the NPS. Her superiors charged her with overseeing the public relations powder keg at the Little Bighorn Battlefield in Montana, a site that has long occupied a pivotal position on the front lines of the fight over how the NPS interprets the West's indigenous history. She lasted four years at the job. And though she could look back on many triumphs, including shepherding through the decision to open an Indian memorial at the site, she described that time as "rough." The experience, like her tenure working on the NPS's failed effort to memorialize the Wounded Knee massacre, thickened her skin. But the Sand Creek search would still prove alienating. Because of her heritage, Sutteer recalled finding herself in a series of "awkward positions." She had an "inherent knowledge and understanding of Indian people that the Park Service does not," but, at the same time, she said, "the tribes looked at me as a government person which made me not part of their circle." She would find herself caught between worlds throughout the project, with her professional identity inside the NPS and her tribal heritage constantly in question.[69]

Alexa Roberts, responsible for collecting oral histories from massacre descendants during the site search, also had a complicated relationship with her status as an NPS employee. At a bit over five feet tall, Roberts kept her brown hair shoulder length and looked young for her age. A quick laugh and unstinting optimism countered her sad eyes. For a woman working across cultural lines, often in patriarchal settings, these traits could be disarming. But Roberts's charm and sunny disposition led people to underestimate her. Although she preferred compromise to confrontation, she was unafraid to stand her ground. And she had a utopian streak that left her committed to her core values: the importance of multiculturalism and public service. Roberts grew up in Albuquerque and stayed there for her undergraduate and graduate education, at the University of New Mexico, where she earned a PhD in anthropology. She studied the relationship between archeological evidence and tribal oral histories on the Navajo reservation in Window Rock, Arizona. After taking a contract position with the NPS in 1984, Roberts went to work full-time for the Navajo Nation, helping the tribe increase its involvement with federal historic preservation projects. Much of her work involved "inserting tribal perspectives into what had formerly been an Anglo-dominated preservation movement." She had often found herself, she recalled, at odds with the NPS. But in 1991, she went to work there, hoping to change the agency from within. The Sand Creek project, Roberts believed, offered a rare opportunity to begin reconciling tribal and federal interests in representing the past.[70]

Roberts's dream would not be realized so easily. Even though the NPS search team members all viewed the Sand Creek project as exciting and important and threw themselves into their work with something like evangelical zeal, it remained for them just that: work. Memorializing the massacre never meant for the NPS what it did for the descendants. Again, this was not because the NPS personnel did not act in good faith; they almost always did. Rather, the politics of memory separated them from the tribal represenatives. The members of the NPS team saw a potential Sand Creek National Historic Site as many things, including a symbol of the NPS's commitment to

pluralism and incorporating Native voices into the national narrative
the agency constructs; a template for future cooperation between federal authorities and Indian peoples; and a way to satisfy a select group
of influential politicians who wanted the massacre memorialized. The
descendants were not necessarily opposed to any of those goals. But
they also had their own: honoring the massacre's victims to promote
healing within their tribes; leveraging collective remembrance of Sand
Creek in service of reparations claims; and maintaining cultural and
political sovereignty throughout the painful memorialization process.
As time passed, these disparate aspirations would broaden the divide
separating the NPS from the descendants, no matter how much they
shared in common.[71]

3

THE SMOKING GUN

Historical research and writing are neither streamlined nor aesthetically pleasing tasks. Instead, they are often painfully similar to the process of accretion—and sometimes seem to play out across similar sweeps of geological time. Historians frame questions about the past and then read, watch, or listen to huge numbers of "texts," the current term of art for their sources. Sifting through these materials, they take notes, retaining tiny fragments of relevant information for later use. After doing this for months, years, even decades in some instances, they assemble the evidence they have collected, fashioning strata of ideas from an aggregate of facts, before arraying these layers, one atop the next, usually in the form of analytical narratives structured by a central argument. In this way, scholars transform fine-grained information into knowledge about the past. This is the historian's method, tortuous and somewhat arcane by design, an outgrowth of turn-of-the-twentieth-century efforts to approximate the practices of then-ascendant earth and life sciences. And this methodology, albeit sometimes far more fluid than depicted here, sits at the core of most historians' disciplinary identity, their sense of themselves as professionals both bound and elevated by shared scholarly practices.[1]

This work may be difficult, lonely, even tedious. But it is rarely boring, especially not when research hinges on historical sleuthing, carrying with it the thrill of the chase. For instance, urgency animated the historians' team early in the site search. Lysa Wegman-French and

Christine Whitacre, focused on the chance to help solve an enduring mystery, relished the prospect of finding Sand Creek. They felt like cold-case detectives. As an added bonus, they believed their work would serve not just the National Park Service (NPS) but also the affected tribes. Wegman-French recalled that when news of the site study began filtering through the halls of the NPS offices, located in the foothills west of Denver, she said to herself, "This will be fantastic." In summer 1998, with Whitacre temporarily detailed to Yellowstone National Park, Wegman-French began familiarizing herself with the published literature on the massacre as well as conducting preliminary research in local archives. The following fall and winter, after Whitacre returned to her regular post, the two women continued searching through document collections in Denver, Colorado Springs, Pueblo, and a variety of other regional repositories.[2]

The NPS historians benefited from having a narrow research agenda, defined by a small set of questions, guiding their inquiries. They asked only what the historical record could contribute to the search with regard to the location and shape of Sand Creek in November 1864; the distance and route the Colorado volunteers had marched toward the Cheyenne and Arapaho camps; where Chivington and his troops had bivouacked after the massacre; and if period maps could shed light on any element of the slaughter's location. They hoped to learn, based on documentary evidence, where, exactly, the violence had unfolded. The broader context surrounding the massacre lay outside the scope of their task. This was true for Wegman-French and Whitacre, and also for Gary Roberts and Jerry Greene, both of whom culled documents from collections located nationwide, including the Library of Congress and the National Archives.[3]

As the team's work progressed, its members weighted firsthand accounts more heavily than other perspectives. This represented an easy choice, because historians typically value primary more than secondary sources. By utilizing these materials, scholars believe they are able to get closer to the subject of their inquiries, just a step removed from events and actors otherwise shrouded by the mists of time. For Jerry Greene, especially, decades of ordering the chaos of cross-cultural warfare had taught him to distrust hearsay and place his faith instead in "participant testimony"; time and again, such sources had helped him unravel historical mysteries. Given Greene's stellar reputation—Wegman-French called him "the Park Service's recognized expert on the Indian Wars"—his opinion carried added significance during the search. In fact, he had been offered the team captaincy before Christine Whitacre accepted the job. Greene only turned down the position because he worried at the time about offending new colleagues at the Harpers Ferry National Historical Park, where he had just accepted a post when the NPS began assembling personnel for its site study. As Greene sifted through evidence, trying to locate the massacre site, he kept looking for accounts from "people who were there." This preference meant that the team often relied, by default if not design, on narratives produced by the men under Chivington's command.[4]

By studying the 1st and 3rd Colorado Regiments' Sand Creek stories, collected in written sources ranging from sworn testimony to memoirs, the NPS historians gleaned a great deal of useful information. The soldiers who mentioned the massacre's proximity to Fort Lyon, for example, placed the distance between the two at twenty-five to forty-five miles, with most recalling that they had marched forty miles the night before the slaughter. Luckily for the NPS, Fort Lyon's location, unlike Sand Creek's, remained well known: about thirty-five miles south of Bill Dawson's ranch. Several men also recalled walking a well-worn "Indian trail" on their way to the Cheyenne and Arapaho camps. As for the carnage itself, many soldiers suggested that blood had been spilled near the "Big Bend" or the "South Bend of Sandy Creek"; almost all of them sited the killing on the stream's north side; of those who remembered the sand pits, the fortifications Chivington pointed to as proof that the Indians at Sand Creek had been hostile, most thought they had been between a quarter mile and a mile from Black Kettle's village; and they overwhelmingly suggested that the engagement had sprawled across an area more than five miles long and well over a mile wide. Finally, in the aftermath of the chaos, Chivington, his subordinates reported, had bivouacked within a mile of the killing field.[5]

What the NPS team could not find when searching through archives was much Native American testimony about the massacre—though not for lack of interest or effort. The NPS historians hoped that their study would feature indigenous voices. Lysa Wegman-French, for her part, had trained at the University of Colorado–Boulder (CU) with Patricia

Nelson Limerick, a leading scholar among the so-called New Western historians, a group whose work placed the experiences of Native Americans on par with those of Euro-American settlers. Limerick's masterpiece, *Legacy of Conquest: The Unbroken Past of the American West,* argues that Westerners today live with the consequences of their bloody history, including events like Sand Creek—even if she never mentions the massacre specifically in her book. Arguing against Frederick Jackson Turner's so-called Frontier Thesis, Limerick suggests that there was no discernible moment when a line of Euro-American settlement overcame the region's roughhewn identity, replacing it with something all new and relatively refined. Instead, she writes, reverberations from the past thunder through the West's present. For the NPS historians studying Sand Creek, an event whose implications still shaped the experiences of whites and Indians throughout the region, Limerick's work had special resonance.[6]

During the site search, Wegman-French sometimes thought about her time at CU, where she had experienced the massacre's lingering power. A fight over Sand Creek's legacy had engulfed the Boulder campus in spring and fall 1987, when OYATE, a Native American student organization, "resurrected a 20-year-old campaign to strip" Nichols Hall, a university building, of its name. Captain David Nichols, the hall's namesake, had served in the 3rd Colorado Regiment and commanded troops at the Sand Creek massacre. Local legend also held that he later had made a midnight ride from Denver to Boulder, a trip that formed a cornerstone of CU's founding myth. Because of his centrality in the university community's collective memory of the school's origins, in 1961 CU renamed a dormitory in Nichols's honor. Native American students, pointing to the atrocities committed at Sand Creek, had intermittently protested that decision in the years since. But the conflict intensified in 1987. Children of the Red Power Movement, steeped in a campus culture that increasingly viewed Western history through a postcolonial lens, began demanding that the university suture an "open wound that keeps the bigotry from healing."[7]

CU's chancellor at the time, James Corbridge, dealt with the controversy by asking Patty Limerick to study whether Nichols's name should be erased from the dorm (a question similar to the one later asked by the Colorado legislature about the Civil War memorial on the capitol steps). Limerick spent months investigating a series of issues surrounding Sand Creek and Captain Nichols: Had the bloodshed been a battle or a massacre? How had Nichols understood his role at Sand Creek, as well as the event's place in the sweep of Colorado's settlement? Was there any truth to the midnight ride story? And how did grim episodes from the West's history relate to the controversy over the naming of buildings at CU? Limerick later produced a document, "What's in a Name?," a 138-page study, long on nuance and documentation, of what she labeled an "ideal topic to raise the crucial questions of Colorado's complex history."[8]

Throughout her report, Limerick struggled to reconcile history and memory by balancing competing perspectives from different eras: 1864, when Chivington and his men perpetrated the massacre; 1961, when CU dedicated Nichols Hall; and 1987, the contemporary context in which the naming controversy erupted. Of Nichols's worldview, Limerick suggested, "the founding of universities and the killing of Indians represented service in the same cause. The project was to 'bring civilization' to Colorado." More broadly, 1864-vintage Coloradans "saw Indian resistance as something comparable to the Confederate rebellion: an illegitimate revolt against a legitimate authority." By contrast, Limerick noted, that same resistance appeared to modern eyes like "a logical, even predictable response to invasion, a defense of homeland." As for the decision to name the building for Captain Nichols: "In 1961, in the minds of those who proposed his name for a building . . . war activities did not detract from his achievements; on the contrary, they added to them." And on the validity of revisiting that decision, Limerick argued, "When a name that most people take for granted brings distress to a significant number of people within the University, then the University has an obligation to look into the problem."[9]

Turning to the superheated question of whether Sand Creek had been a massacre or a battle, Limerick maintained her cool. She allowed that "to members of the Third Colorado, the engagement felt like a battle, and not like a massacre, because they were, at various times, scared to death." But then, after detailing the promises made by Ned Wynkoop to Black Kettle in the months leading to the slaughter, and also noting that the Arapahos and Cheyennes had camped at Sand Creek only because white authorities had guaranteed them safe harbor there, Limerick surveyed other renowned historians of the West and the Indian Wars. These scholars all agreed that Sand Creek had been a massacre. Robert Utley, for example, explained, "where noncombatants were killed deliberately and indiscriminately, I regard massacre [as] an appropriate term." And yet he still recommended retaining the name of Nichols Hall. Arguing both as a historic preservationist and a professional historian, he suggested: "To readjust the nomenclature in order to appease the sensibilities of the present, however valid, is to do violence to the past, to the opinions and actions of previous generations." He concluded that "Nichols Hall should remain Nichols Hall, not as a monument to Sand Creek, but as a reminder of how a previous generation felt about fellow Coloradan David Nichols."[10]

Limerick disagreed. She discounted Utley's concerns about preservation, as the dormitory had carried Nichols's name for less than three decades. She also found that the heroic narrative of Nichols's midnight ride, the story that connected him to CU, likely was apocryphal. And finally, while she had initially hoped that the naming controversy could serve as a teaching tool, a chance to educate the university community about moral ambiguities woven throughout Colorado's history, that goal, no matter how worthy, did not outweigh the anguish expressed by Native American students over the veneration, on the Boulder campus, of a man who had participated in depraved acts at Sand Creek. As a result, Limerick concluded: "The University [should] change the name of Nichols Hall, and carefully choose a replacement." What had been an isolated conflict on the CU campus then escalated into a regional memory fight.[11]

Word of Limerick's report leaked out at the start of the fall semester in 1987. By that time, Richard Nixon's backlash had long since devolved into Ronald Reagan's culture wars. Historians around the United States found themselves on the front lines of skirmishes over how the past should be remembered. Upon hearing of Limerick's findings, CU regents Roy Shore and Hugh Fowler mounted an offensive, characterizing "What's in a Name?" as "revisionism," little more than liberal propaganda. Shore claimed that Limerick was "biased," that she "denigrate[d] people," and suggested that rather than changing Nichols Hall's name, it would be better to "let the dead bury the dead." Armed with talking points seemingly plucked from a Vietnam-era time capsule, he insisted that "minority students were totally unaware of who Capt. Nichols was until the agitators brought up his name." Both he and Fowler then accused Limerick of a historian's sin: presentism, using contemporary standards to judge past events. Fowler also suggested, "if we decide to pull down all the statues of bad guys, we would not have any statues left." Limerick, in this view, had abdicated her professional obligations in service of a radical multicultural agenda.[12]

For months the controversy dragged on, capturing attention throughout the state. Claims of political correctness prompted counterclaims of insensitivity or full-blown racism. Captain Nichols's descendants eventually weighed in, defending their family's honor and insisting that the protestors were "trying to fight a war that's been over for 100 years." With the board of regents bitterly divided, Chancellor Corbridge backed Limerick, saying that he wanted the name changed. Finally, on November 19, 1987, the university regents voted, 5–3, to remove Nichols's name, prompting a spokesperson from OYATE to proclaim it "a great day." Still the conflict lingered. It took the regents another eighteen months to rename the dormitory Cheyenne-Arapaho Hall. Only then did the controversy finally abate. Years later, as she began looking for clues leading to the massacre site, Lysa Wegman-French remembered how Sand Creek could inflame people's passions by bringing Colorado's past and present into close proximity.[13]

Neither Jerry Greene nor Gary Roberts had experienced anything as dramatic as the fight over Nichols Hall. But both men had long been familiar with Sand Creek, and they both hoped that Native American sources might help them find the site. Greene, throughout his career, had included Indian voices in his military histories of the West. And though Roberts had completed his dissertation more than a decade before the NPS started its site search, his work still represented a model of interdisciplinary inquiry, incorporating Cheyenne oral histories with more traditional manuscript sources. But in 1998, even as the NPS team made "every attempt . . . to locate and consider Cheyenne and Arapaho *participant accounts* of the Sand Creek massacre," the thousands of pages of primary documents produced by Chivington and his men far out-stripped both the number and impact of the indigenous sources the historians consulted.[14]

That was the case not only because written records of nineteenth-century Cheyenne and Arapaho history are relatively rare, but also because none of the federal inquiries into Sand Creek featured deposi-tions from Native American witnesses. Few Indians were U.S. citizens at the time of the massacre. Their second-class status would linger, with some exceptions, until the Indian Citizenship Act of 1924. Native people, consequently, rarely testified in federal proceedings. At the same time, as George Bent explains in his writings, the Cheyennes and Arap-ahos who lived through the massacre distrusted whites for the rest of their lives. As Laird Cometsevah suggested, these "folks had complied with the white government's wishes and then were betrayed anyway." They camped on Sand Creek at John Chivington's and Major Scott An-thony's behest; Black Kettle flew the American flag on the day of the massacre, signaling that his was a peace camp; and they were slaugh-tered for their trouble. Most of the survivors of the ordeal then fled Colo-rado for the Republican River country, joining the bulk of the Cheyenne and Arapaho tribes, as well as many Lakotas, camped there. Cometsevah scoffed at the idea that they then would have come in to testify. "They weren't fools," he said. All of this meant that Jerry Greene, because of his reliance on written documents, would have almost no Native American sources available to him as he did his research.[15]

There was one notable exception: George Bent's letters and writings. Around the turn of the twentieth century, Bent's work with George Hyde constituted an intellectual threat to the Civil War memories propagated by veterans of the 1st and 3rd Colorado Regiments. Follow-ing John Chivington's death in 1894, many of these men tried to embed their colonel's Sand Creek stories in the glorious Civil War narrative being constructed by heritage groups around the United States—work that culminated in Colorado with the unveiling of the memorial on the state capitol steps in 1909. These efforts upset Bent, who responded by writing his own narrative of the slaughter for the public. He based his account on his own and other Cheyenne stories, recasting what Chivington had called a battle as a massacre in articles for the *Frontier* in 1905 and 1906. Bent's essays outraged Chivington's surviving loyal-

ists. In the *Denver Times,* Major Jacob Downing deployed racial stereotypes in this memory war, calling Bent's father, the renowned William,
a "squaw man" for having married Owl Woman. He then trained his
sights on George, denigrating him as a "cutthroat, and a thief, a liar
and a scoundrel, but worst of all, a halfbreed." Having littered the field
with reputations, Downing finally assured readers that Sand Creek
merited celebration as a noble part of civilizing Colorado and winning
the Civil War in the West.[16]

Nearly a century later, due to shifting cultural values, Bent's heritage
made it more rather than less likely that his Sand Creek story would be
taken seriously and that his massacre narrative would shape future
collective memories. Bent's private correspondence and published writings offered the NPS historians rare insight into Cheyenne perspectives on the massacre. And two maps that he produced with George
Hyde between 1905 and 1914 seemed even more useful than his prose.
In the preface of *Life of George Bent,* Hyde bemoans those maps' disappearance. But thirty years later, as the NPS began looking for the site,
the charts had long since turned up again. Though both appear at first
glance like mere line drawings, each contains a wealth of information.
The first, held by the Western History Collection at the University of
Colorado, depicts a large, gentle curve in Sand Creek; the whole of the
massacre site is enveloped within that bend. Several chiefs' camps are
noted, along with "Chivington's trail," the placement of the Colorado
volunteers, the site of the sand pits, and other details, including spots
where women and children were killed. The second map, housed at the
Oklahoma Historical Society, also encompasses the slaughter within a
large bend (somewhat sharper in this case) in the creek. Elements of
the massacre, including artillery positions, are marked with numbers,
interpreted by an annotated key at the bottom of the page. Beyond
that, most of the particulars are similar to those of the first sketch.
Bent apparently worked with other massacre descendants to produce
these drawings, in effect mapping Cheyenne memories of Sand Creek
onto the page, seemingly a boon for the NPS historians' team.[17]

But Jerry Greene had doubts. Although he recognized the politics
surrounding Bent's recollections of Sand Creek, understanding that a
Cheyenne survivor of the ordeal wielded extraordinary cultural authority that might impinge on the NPS's interpretation of sources,

George Bent's maps of Sand Creek, produced between 1905 and 1914. His maps feature a variety of details, including where various bands of Cheyennes and Arapahos camped on the eve of the violence, the shape of the stream at the time of the attack, the location of artillery there, and the so-called sand or rifle pits during the massacre. *(University of Colorado at Boulder, University Archives, Bent-Hyde Collection, Box 1, Folder 1, Sand Creek Map, 1 image; Oklahoma Historical Society.)*

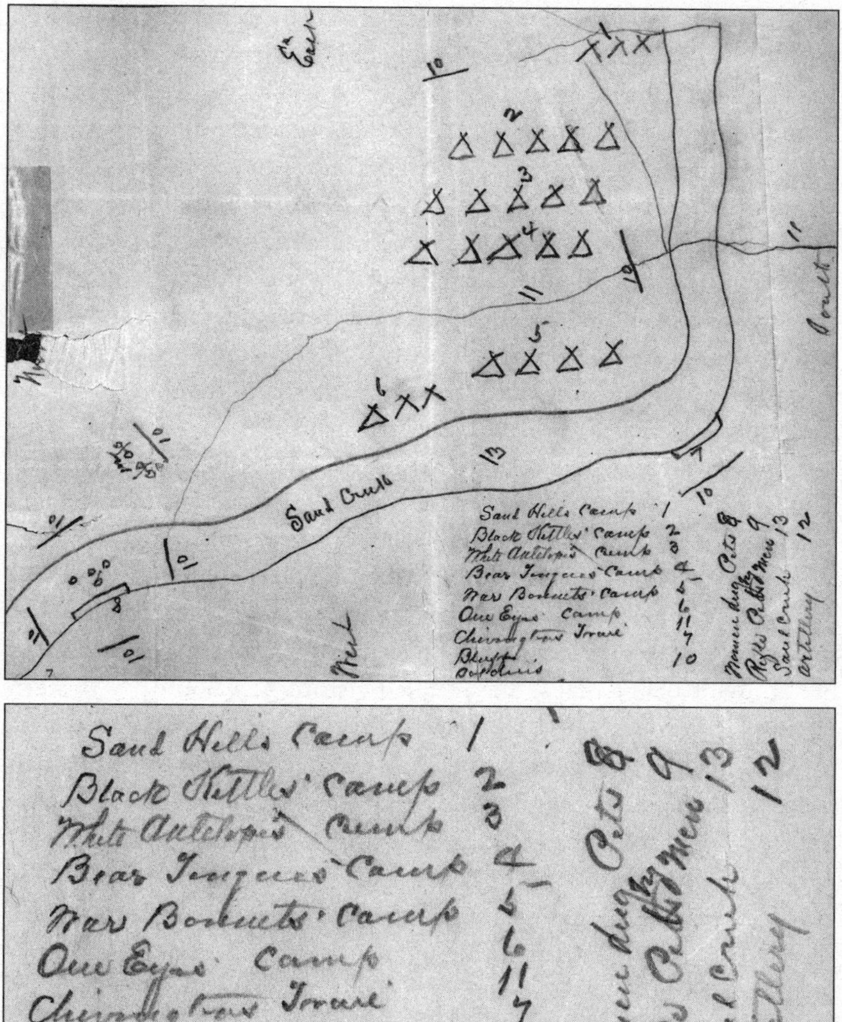

Sand Creek

Sand Hills Camp   1
Black Kettle's Camp   2
White Antelope's Camp   3
Bear Tongue's Camp   4
War Bonnet's Camp   5
One Eye's Camp   6   11
Chevington Troure   7
Bluff   10
Soldiers

Mouncie Dug Outs   8
Ryes Cattle or Men   9
Sand Creek   13
Artillery   12

Greene remained skeptical about the maps' accuracy. He worried especially because Bent had produced his drawings so long after the fact—
"more than forty years later"—an interval that threatened to cloud even
the most vivid memories. Worse still, Bent had not worked on the maps
alone, leaving Greene unsure whether the drawings represented unme-
diated first-person perspectives, his preference for primary sources, or
consisted instead of composite sketches of recollections. Greene fretted
about whether the maps' details might have been derived from an unknown group of people who had not been present at the massacre. And
if memory is malleable under the best of circumstances, he knew, its
transmission from one person to the next, across space and time, only
makes it more so. So Greene, who valued Bent's drawings for their indigenous provenance and their graphic depiction of Sand Creek, could
not resolve his mixed feelings about their utility.[18]

In late summer 1998, two revelations pushed Greene beyond ambivalence toward outright skepticism. George Bent, in addition to having
twice drawn the massacre site, had produced two other maps depicting
the region in which the slaughter had taken place. For Lysa Wegman-
French, the corpus of Bent's cartography seemingly held the "key" to
unlocking the site mystery. With infectious enthusiasm, she recounted
her study of Bent's maps. She recalled visiting CU Boulder's Western
History Collection, where she viewed a sketch, brittle with age, on the
brink of disintegration, and experienced a "historian's moment," a pal-
pable thrill at possessing the source that she thought would lead to her
quarry. Wegman-French remembered thinking: "George Bent held this
paper in his hands; this is his handwriting." But after returning home
and scrutinizing the paleography on copies of Bent's regional maps,
she realized that the script on them appeared not to have been a prod-
uct of his hand. It seemed that Bent had not drawn those maps himself. Instead, George Hyde had likely rendered the maps' broad strokes
before sending them on to Bent, who then had added particulars about
the massacre's location based on his memories and research.[19]

There was more. While poring over copies of the Bent-Hyde regional
maps, Wegman-French observed that the sketches seemed to mirror an
1890 U.S. Geological Survey (USGS) map of southeastern Colorado sitting nearby. The two documents, upon further inspection, were nearly
identical. When Wegman-French slid the Bent-Hyde diagram on top of

the USGS map, she concluded that Hyde must have traced the map
before forwarding it to Bent. Because of the excellent reputation enjoyed by USGS maps, Wegman-French initially believed that her discovery heralded great things for the search team. "The base map is as
accurate as the USGS map," she wrote to other members of the site
search. In that case, the Bent-Hyde maps, in Wegman-French's view,
represented a "real place," not just a landscape found only in Cheyenne
memories; with the sketches guiding the NPS team, it would just be a
matter of time before they discovered exactly where the massacre had
taken place. But then Wegman-French learned that 1890 had been a
horrible vintage for the USGS's regional maps. Hyde, in other words,
had apparently copied a flawed original, leaving "poor George Bent
looking at this inaccurate map." That the massacre site had been misplaced on Bent's map suddenly made a great deal more sense. How to
find it, though, remained a mystery.[20]

Jerry Greene and David Halaas happened upon a possible answer
around that same time. At the start of the NPS site search, the two
friends met regularly to exchange news of their progress. After having
lunch together one day early in August, they returned to Halaas's office, where he rummaged through files, looking for materials to share
with Greene. In the midst of his excavation, Halaas pulled out a copy
of a map, passed it to Greene without comment, and returned to his
search. Second Lieutenant Samuel Bonsall had prepared the document
in 1868, while escorting Lieutenant General William Tecumseh Sherman, then in charge of all of the U.S. Army's forces in the West, on a
tour of "frontier" military sites—including Sand Creek. Bonsall's map
was "discovered" in 1992 by an archivist named Scott Forsythe, who, because it had been miscataloged in the Chicago branch of the National
Archives, labeled it "something of an oddity." Forsythe then forwarded
a copy to Halaas, who at the time worked on Dick Ellis's site search.
Halaas apparently had not thought much about it since then. But
Greene remembered stopping short as he scanned the sketch, thinking to himself: "I can't believe what I'm seeing. Nobody's interpreted this
thing at all." He believed that the map could become the NPS historians' "Rosetta Stone."[21]

Bonsall followed army rules while preparing his "strip map and
journal," a document featuring an unadorned line drawing, running

from bottom to top along its left side, depicting his multiday journey from Fort Lyon to Cheyenne Wells with General Sherman, and lengthy annotations along its right side. Army regulations stated that "commanding officers of troops marching through a little known country" should keep such a precise record, "whose object . . . is to furnish data for maps and information which may serve future operations." Consequently, "every point of practical importance should therefore be noted." Bonsall did his duty; he followed these instructions to the letter. He recorded minute details about his expedition, including times and distances between "remarkable features of the country." One of those landmarks, located near but not within one of Sand Creek's large bends, he labeled in the style of the day: "Chivington's Massacre." That Bonsall would have used this language reflected two facets of contemporary perceptions of the violence: first, because of the army inquiry's findings in 1866, some military personnel, even those serving in Colorado, referred at the time to Sand Creek as a massacre; and second, linking the bloodbath to Chivington alone, rather than to a place name, individualized culpability, evading questions of context. It was Chivington's massacre, not the army's, and not the federal government's.[22]

Beyond that, Bonsall indicated that his detachment had left Fort Lyon near daybreak on June 16, at 5:30 in the morning. After traveling approximately thirty miles that day, Bonsall and company arrived at the site of "Chivington's Massacre" late in the afternoon. Once on the scene, Sherman, who wanted to bring artifacts from notable Western battlegrounds back with him to Washington, DC, had his men scour the field for "relics." The troops found human remains (skulls, some apparently from children, and several scalps), arrows, knives, "and many other things too numerous to mention." They "collected nearly a wagonload" before camping overnight. Bonsall then noted that his group had moved on the next morning. He highlighted a spot on his map, roughly seven miles north of their campsite from the previous evening, where the road split into the so-called Three Forks. After opting for the center of the trio of paths, the group delivered General Sherman to a stagecoach that would take him to a rail junction. Sherman would begin his long trip back east from there. Bonsall and his men, for their part, returned to Fort Lyon several days later, their route again taking them past the massacre site.[23]

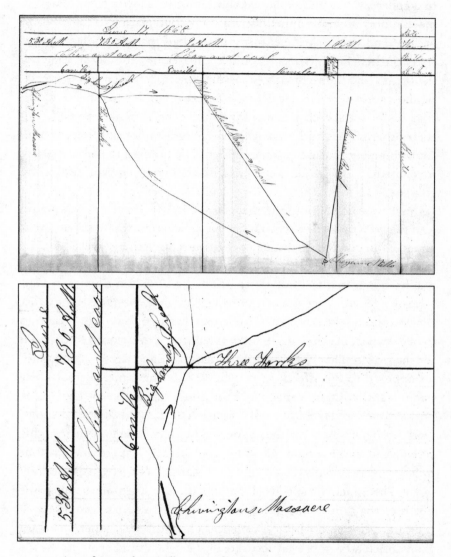

A section of Samuel Bonsall's map of military sites along the Western frontier, 1868. It includes a site marked "Chivington's Massacre" and, just to its north, one labeled "Three Forks." *(National Archives.)*

With Bonsall's map in hand, Greene dashed off an enthusiastic note to a colleague. Greene explained that Bonsall's drawing "is to me the most important and compelling thing I've seen relating to the location of the Sand Creek site." Because Bonsall had included mileage notations on his sketch, Greene could compare the landmarks that the lieutenant had highlighted to a modern map. The Three Forks in particular captivated him. He believed that it might be possible to locate that historic trail. Greene suggested that the searchers should stop their other efforts and focus exclusively on the Bonsall map, saying, "our immediate future endeavors should be tailored to corroborating its content. . . . [It] could well comprise the 'smoking gun' to finding this site."[24]

Intensive study of Bonsall's map, coupled with two other sources, did lead the NPS historians to what Greene called a "Eureka moment" that appeared to confirm the value of their interdisciplinary methods. The NPS team first located the paths of the Three Forks on aerial photographs taken in the 1930s by the Soil Conservation Service, a New Deal–era federal agency created to ensure that the disastrous Dust Bowl would not be repeated. Greene then married that information to data drawn from a geomorphological report commissioned by the NPS for the search. That document indicated that Sand Creek's flood plain (as opposed to the stream itself, which might have meandered) likely had not shifted significantly since the mid-nineteenth century. Greene next extrapolated from Bonsall's notation of the Three Forks' distance from his detachment's campsite on the night of June 16, 1868 (roughly six miles), and the spot of "Chivington's Massacre" (approximately four miles). Greene, finally, could place the Sand Creek site relatively precisely. The attack, he surmised, had begun just seven-tenths of a mile north of the hilltop memorial found on Bill Dawson's land, the area typically associated with the violence. The location further upstream than anticipated, if proven accurate in the field, would explain why the massacre had been misplaced for so long.[25]

The NPS historians delighted in their "discovery" and celebrated the source upon which it rested. But because of Jerry Greene's exacting standards for evidence, they also dug deeper into Bonsall's experiences at the Sand Creek site, contrasting his knowledge with George Bent's. Aware that Bent's drawings enjoyed more cultural clout than did Bonsall's, the historians' team highlighted the former's shortcomings as a source. Bonsall had sketched his map just four years after the slaughter, they noted. And he had visited the site multiple times: first with General Sherman, and then when he returned, two years later, to collect more crania for the Army Medical Museum. He sent those skulls to Washington, where researchers studied the effects of gunshots on human anatomy, a grisly scientific outgrowth of the Indian Wars. For Greene, though, the precise nature of Bonsall's connection to Sand Creek mattered little, so long as the historical record confirmed that the mapmaker had known the place well enough to produce a reliable source. Satisfied of that, Greene extolled Bonsall's map as "the most directly compelling contemporary information . . . about the location of the Sand Creek Massacre." It became the cornerstone of the historians' efforts, far and away the most influential document they consulted.[26]

Late in 1998, Greene found an opportunity to field test his theory. Based on his reading of the Bonsall map, Greene believed that the massacre had taken place less than a mile north of the monument overlook, traditionally accepted as the location of the bloodshed. On December 13 and 14, the NPS, hoping to drum up support from the community surrounding the presumptive site, held a consultation meeting, this time at the Cow Palace hotel in Lamar, thirty-five miles south of Eads. Following that gathering, Greene accepted an invitation from Chuck and Sheri Bowen to visit their home. Chuck Bowen's father, Charles Bowen Sr., owned a sprawling ranch just upstream from Bill Dawson's. Because of that, Chuck and Sheri Bowen, though they had asked Greene over for a visit, remained wary of cooperating with the NPS. Like many of their neighbors, the Bowens worried that if the NPS determined that their property had hosted the massacre, the government would evict them without recompense—no matter Senator Campbell's strategic decision to include the willing-seller-only provision in his legislation. As Chuck Bowen remembered it, "people's land had been condemned over this kind of thing. So yeah, we were concerned." Still, the Bowens had a story to tell; they believed that their family ranch was the proper Sand Creek site. They wanted the world to know.[27]

Chuck and Sheri Bowen seemed like mild-mannered people. They owned a small business in Lamar, a photography shop located on a tree-lined street, removed from the commercial bustle of the city's main drag. They typically shied away from political discussions, avoided conflict when they could, and found refuge in their church and marriage. Their bond dated to a childhood friendship forged while growing up in Eads. Like most residents of Kiowa County, they had known about the massacre for as long as they could remember; familiarity and proximity had woven Sand Creek's threads into their family histories. A scrapbook documented that warp and weft: a fading picture captured a frozen scene of Sheri's aunts and mother reenacting the event as youngsters; a yellowed newspaper clipping revealed her mom playing the accordion at the ceremony opening the highway marker in 1950; another photo depicted a Cub Scout trip Chuck took to what he then knew as "the Sand Creek battleground"; and a map produced for a tour the Bowens led of the "traditional site"—the South Bend on Dawson's ranch—reminded them that even in high school they had shared a keen interest in local history.[28]

In 1993, their relationship to Sand Creek changed. With the news that the site had been "lost," the Bowens started their own search. What had been an intermittent and satisfying hobby became, Sheri Bowen remembered, an "obsession." She combed through thousands of pages of documents while her husband haunted his family's ranch, crisscrossing the land with a metal detector, probing the earth for relics. Of her husband's passion for the hunt, she recalled: "He got up and thought about Sand Creek, then he thought about Sand Creek during the day, and he went to bed thinking about Sand Creek." Across the years, stacks of notes and boxes of antiquities piled up: bullets, arrowheads, regimental pins, utensils, and mysterious items awaiting identification by expert eyes. By the time the NPS began its site study, picking up in 1998 where Dick Ellis had left off, the Bowens had concluded that a significant portion of the massacre had taken place on their family's property.[29]

When Jerry Greene arrived at their home in 1999, the Bowens, who at great personal expense had fashioned themselves into lay historical archeologists—they had even produced a documentary film, a sort of vernacular dissertation chronicling their efforts—relished the prospect of an NPS official finally lauding their achievements. Chuck Bowen remembered, "We had made a significant discovery, which we should have been credited with." The Bowens detailed their theories for Greene and then displayed "three or four boxes of artifacts and a bucket of stuff we thought was junk." Greene contemplated the treasures arrayed before him. He picked up a seemingly innocuous hunk of metal, which he quickly recognized as "very significant." Although he remained cagey—he was unconvinced by the Bowens' conclusions but wanted to avoid offending them—Greene knew that he was holding a remnant of shot from a mountain howitzer, a piece of artillery that had been fired by Chivington's men at the Sand Creek massacre. Here was seemingly irrefutable forensic evidence linking the Bowen property to the slaughter and, barring a hoax, final vindication of the accuracy of Samuel Bonsall's map.[30]

Greene understood that the Bowens remained "suspicious" of him and the NPS, but he nevertheless asked to see exactly where Chuck Bowen had found the shrapnel. The Bowens agreed to show him the location. Early in the new year, Greene toured their ranch. Since the start of the NPS's site search, he had struggled to assemble a detailed chronology of the massacre. The effort had forced him to wrestle with competing eyewitness testimony while determining the relative accuracy of conflicting sources. It was not until he walked the area where the Bowens had found the telltale fragment of howitzer shot that Greene finally put the pieces together. As he gazed southward from a small rise, he saw, perhaps a mile and a half away, the hilltop monument on Bill Dawson's property. Greene recalled that, in that moment, "it all came together in a flash. I couldn't believe it. These were the sand pits, where we were standing. And then everything that I'd been studying for the last several months just made sense." Greene swallowed his excitement and walked off to gather his thoughts. On a map that he brought with him, he marked the precise spot where he believed the archeologists should dig.[31]

Using "evidence gleaned from the Bonsall map, the two Bent maps, and a host of participant testimony and other documents," by early spring 1999, the NPS historians had arrived at a series of hypotheses, including the following: Black Kettle's village had stood on the north side of Sand Creek; the sand pits, the trenches where the Colorado volunteers had concentrated their artillery barrage, had been located less than a mile upstream from that point; the Arapahos had placed their lodges downstream from the Cheyennes'; Chivington and his men had

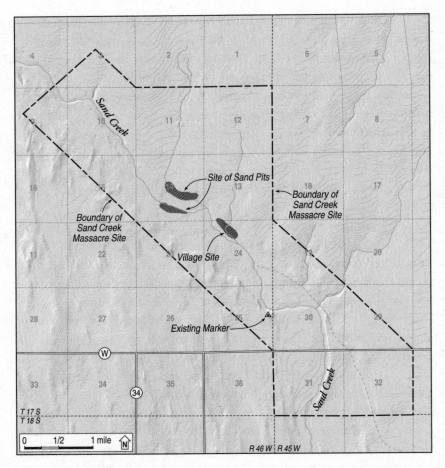

Site of the Sand Creek Massacre, based on archival projections. *(Adapted from the Sand Creek Massacre Special Resource Study, U.S. Dept. of the Interior, National Park Service.)*

approached the camp from the southwest; the troops had divided before the violence had begun; and following the carnage, the soldiers had bivouacked adjacent to the bloody field. Finally, the historians concluded: "The archival record leaves little doubt that the Sand Creek Massacre took place in the area of the South Bend of Sand Creek," though "not precisely at the bend." Here they aligned themselves with Jerry Greene's interpretation, departing from George Bent's efforts at mapping Cheyenne history. Instead, the event had unfolded upstream from the traditional site, apparently about three-quarters of a mile from the spot depicted by Bent. Archeological fieldwork, the NPS team hoped, would confirm this theory.[32]

Working on a track parallel to the historians, Alexa Roberts worried less about her sources' credibility and more about her own. Charged with collecting ethnographies from the massacre descendants, she had to overcome their anxieties about federal authority and convince them to share their oral histories. This proved difficult because the descendants had generations of practice guarding their Sand Creek stories, especially from white outsiders. Compounding the challenge, Roberts had to work on an abbreviated timetable: the eighteen months laid out in Senator Campbell's site search legislation. Cathy Spude worried that the tight calendar jeopardized the whole process. Because the oral histories represented the NPS's best chance to forge relationships with the descendants, Spude thought, "the time frame was just not suitable to the task. We should have had at least three years to gain the tribes' confidence." But Roberts did not have the luxury of time. She got right to work, using a consultation meeting to begin discussing her plans with the leaders of the various descendants' groups.[33]

That gathering, unfortunately, threatened to further poison relations further between the tribal representatives and the NPS. Held on November 14 and 15, 1998, two weeks before the massacre's 134th anniversary, the meeting took place in an antiseptic conference room in a Denver chain hotel. The descendants, who had traveled from as far away as Montana, Wyoming, and Oklahoma, streamed in bleary eyed, bone tired, and, in some cases, late. The issue of timing would crop up throughout the search. The Arapahos and Cheyennes seemingly arrived when they pleased, oblivious to schedules, calibrating their movements to so-called Indian time. Mildred Red Cherries explained, "Indian people don't walk away from someone until we're done talking. We don't leave a relative or a friend just to be on time." Norma Gorneau laughed, adding, "Well, there's Indian time, then there's *Cheyenne* time." Otto Braided Hair noted that the phenomenon stemmed from his tribe's long view of historical processes: "We've been waiting for more than a century for a memorial. And people like Laird and Colleen [Cometsevah] have been fighting for this for decades. We're in no rush." Context, though, did not matter to the NPS officials who anticipated the descendants' arrival on the morning of November 14. Tardiness in that moment seemed less a marker of cultural difference than of disrespect.[34]

In part, the NPS representatives' irritation emerged from anxiety. If the descendants were wary of working with federal officials, the NPS team was skittish about the politically fraught task before them. Trying to alleviate these concerns, Mike Snyder, deputy director of the NPS, kicked off the meeting by welcoming the participants. Snyder kept circling back to one theme in his remarks: persistence. Finding the site, he acknowledged, would be difficult; the gulf dividing federal employees and the tribal delegates yawned wide. But because of their shared commitment to a common goal, they would, Snyder insisted, work together. They would persevere. Then, at the meeting's first break, he left. The descendants wondered why an NPS official had just lectured them about constancy and then "bolted without so much as a goodbye." Laird Cometsevah contemplated an appropriate way to respond to Snyder's insulting behavior. Steve Brady smoldered, insisting, "We cannot trust the Park Service now."[35]

Rick Frost, the coolly efficient and politically savvy regional communications director tapped to replace Cathy Spude as head of the NPS search, then took over the meeting. This would be his first chance to place his stamp on the process with the descendants present. Frost recognized the challenge. Five government entities would collaborate on the project: the Northern Cheyenne, the Northern Arapaho, the Cheyenne and Arapaho Tribes, the State of Colorado, and the United States. Aware that keeping their representatives together, despite histories of antagonism, would be difficult, Frost cast himself as a court of last resort for the grievances that he believed inevitably would arise. As he recalled it, Mike Snyder had spoken in the morning and then strategically left the meeting, because "people would only deal with me if I was the person they *had* to deal with." So he laid down ground rules: everybody would "have a voice." But he "had to be seen as the person in charge." Frost then announced that the search would be "an American project, not an Indian project." This did not sit well with the descendants. Already reminded by Snyder's performance of injustices that had punctuated centuries of Native-white relations, the Cheyennes saw in Frost federal arrogance embodied. Steve Brady and Laird Cometsevah decided to derail the meeting, simultaneously establishing the tribal representatives' cultural authority and political autonomy.[36]

The two men asked David Halaas if he would serve as the Cheyennes' proxy, explaining to the NPS officials the massacre's impact on the tribes. Halaas agreed. The next morning, after the meeting reconvened, Cometsevah interrupted Rick Frost and introduced Halaas. Halaas then played a role once familiar to George Bent, the man whose life story Halaas was writing: cultural intermediary and Cheyenne advocate. A gripping narrator, Halaas spoke with swinging rhythms, built characters like a novelist, and wove telling detail into his stories. On that day, he became emotional recounting the run-up to the slaughter, the desecration of bodies at the massacre, and the lingering effect on Cheyenne politics and culture. "There isn't any other incident like Sand Creek," he explained, "that resonates through the years like it has, whose importance is so central to understanding the relationship between Indians and whites thereafter." Halaas's story carried a message: the massacre was a watershed event in U.S. history, to be sure, but it was also too central a part of the Cheyennes' past and future to entrust its narration to federal authorities; pursuing the site would not be business as usual for the NPS; the tribes' cultural and political autonomy would not be sacrificed in service of other goals, even memorializing Sand Creek, because tribal sovereignty and persistence, as it had been for George Bent a century earlier, was their principal goal.[37]

Rick Frost, to his credit, realized what had happened and why. He recalled: "What I learned from that initial meeting was the tremendous emotional resonance of this event for the tribes, the deep impact it had had on an entire people, a civilization, a culture." And also, as David Halaas explained, that Sand Creek "was, for them, not a historical event, but an emotionally and psychologically present event." These insights led Frost to abandon his one-size-fits-all strategy, a top-down approach that Steve Brady scorned as the "Park Service's sacred playbook." Frost instead adopted a pluralistic vision for the search process. He had never worked with Native people before, and only after Halaas hijacked the consultation meeting did Frost decide, "We were talking about two really different worldviews"—different enough that he realized, "if I was going to approach this thing insisting that everybody adopt my worldview, it was going to fail, that there had to be a deep and abiding recognition that there were two, at least two, clearly distinct ways of looking at things, and that they both had to be considered." At the time, Frost explained contritely: "I've come to realize that this project belongs to Indian people." For the descendants' purposes, that revelation represented a significant triumph.[38]

Steve Brady next took over the meeting, cementing the impression that the Cheyennes had imposed their will on the process and would not allow themselves to occupy a position subordinate to the NPS. After that, the tension did not evaporate, but it abated somewhat, in part because Rick Frost drew on his experience in politics, equating stoicism with professionalism: "The National Park Service, the Intermountain Region, had goals and objectives and criteria that I needed to meet." Frost, therefore, imposed a gag order on himself: "Never respond to an attack on me or the federal government or on what my intentions were or the federal government's intentions were, because you could be trapped in that argument forever." From that point on, he would not allow any slight, no matter how damning—including being labeled a "Chivingtonite" at that meeting—to wound him. This was wise, because the barbs were usually tactical rather than personal. As Brady noted: "Sometimes I had to say some pretty harsh stuff about the Park Service folks. Because history teaches me that the federal government lies. Then, after I'd kick them around a bit in the meetings, I'd still shake their hands later." It was not quite the level of trust the NPS hoped to establish, but it was the beginning of a working relationship.[39]

Alexa Roberts, drawing on her experiences with Indian peoples, struggled to build atop the shaky foundation constructed at the consultation meeting. The descendants worried about the ethnographic element of the search, especially questions of "confidentiality and the chance that the government would somehow capitalize on their oral histories." Here, again, George Bent's specter loomed over the site search. David Halaas, Steve Brady, and Laird Cometsevah all believed that James Mooney and George Bird Grinnell had exploited Bent. Even George Hyde had broken some of his promises to Bent. From the descendants' perspective, whites had used Bent's stories for their own purposes. And in the view of Conrad Fisher, head of the Northern Cheyenne Cultural

Center, not much had changed since. Fisher observed, "White scholars and Park Service employees come onto the reservation and take what they need." Steve Brady made the same point with a joke: "You know the makeup of a traditional Cheyenne family, right?" He answered his own question: "A mother, a father, a few kids, maybe a granny, and an anthropologist with graduate students in tow." The descendants did not want their stories to be objects of study, to be manipulated by outsiders; they wanted to assert control over own their heritage.[40]

As well as worrying about intellectual property and exploitation, the descendants viewed oral histories as crucial to their cultural sovereignty. For Laird Cometsevah, oral traditions were the best way of transmitting Cheyenne history. Pointing to a link between language and identity, Cometsevah noted, "Some of us my age are real fortunate. We grew up at a time when Cheyenne was real fluent in our daily living. Our folks talked Cheyenne, and English was second." Tribal history moved through "family stories," from person to person, related in the Cheyenne language. Cometsevah recalled: "As young people we grew up with parents, grandparents, great-grandparents that experienced some of these [events], and that's how we passed our information to our young people." In his telling, poverty, ironically, helped the tribe's culture persist, as the "Cheyennes never did have a book, pencil, typewriter; they kept [history] in their memories, and it was handed down that way." "Today we do a lot of research, and I've met a lot of authors, professors, and anthropologists," Cometsevah explained. "They're afraid to go out of the boundary of the book to accept the truth of what happened to the Cheyennes." Steve Brady concurred; the spoken word was "*the* traditional method of passing Cheyenne history" across generations. For Cometsevah and Brady, oral history was tribal history, not something to be dismissed as less legitimate or reliable than written accounts.[41]

Because of their ongoing struggle to perpetuate traditional cultural practices, for Brady and Cometsevah the oral history project loomed larger than the site search's other parts. Although neither man disparaged Jerry Greene's forays into the archives for manuscript sources (Brady and Cometsevah were avid readers of tribal histories), and while both eagerly anticipated the site study's archeological component (assuming that the sacred ground and any artifacts pulled from it would be handled with respect), the descendants would collect their ethnographies using "traditional approaches." They would gather indigenous knowledge using indigenous methods. And because some of the Sand Creek stories would come from tribal elders nearing the end of their lives, the last generation of Cheyennes to have spoken directly with the massacre's survivors, the descendants hoped that the collected memories would connect past and present, promising healing on tribal terms, rather than the false restoration through assimilation that the Cheyennes believed the federal government was offering them.[42]

After the Cheyenne representatives to the site study met with David Halaas and Steve Chestnut, their attorney, they drafted an "agreement that laid out principles that were good for the tribes." They insisted on leading the search's ethnographic component; they would rely on Alexa Roberts as a consultant only. Roberts, while working for the Navajo Nation, had often clashed with the NPS over questions of cultural sovereignty. Over time, she had "quit thinking of [her]self as an archeologist . . . because digging sites or documenting sites is not what the Navajo people do or how they perceive their past." Having embraced ethnography instead, she sympathized with the descendants' skepticism of outsiders, especially federal officials attempting to document the past with approaches suspect to some Native people. And she saw the Sand Creek stories, gathered using "traditional methods," as a "sacred matter," the principal way that the descendants "would know their history." Roberts agreed that the ethnography project could succeed only if the tribal representatives designed and implemented their own protocols for collecting histories. She would help when asked; otherwise she would do her best to "stay in the shadows."[43]

Roberts understood the cultural politics underlying her part of the search. When the descendants prepared to gather their oral histories, she shared her expertise and provided direct funding so that the Arapaho and Cheyenne delegates could administer their projects as they wished. Working in early 1999 with the NPS historians and Doug Scott, captain of the archeologists' team, she compiled a list of questions intended to elicit information about the site's location. Even then, Roberts took care not to appear prescriptive, explaining that the "questions were intended to be used as an interviewing guide . . . rather than as a formal questionnaire, and also were intended to be modified as considered appropriate by each tribe." Finally, between November 1998 and June 1999, she traveled to the reservation towns of Concho, Ethete, Riverton, and Lame Deer, convening fora where she discussed the oral history project with various tribal constituencies.[44]

From spring 1999 through winter 2000, the descendants collected their oral histories, with the Northern Arapahos first out of the gate. On April 6, 1999, Roberts drove from Denver to the Wind River Reservation, a four-hundred-mile trip graced by breathtaking views of the Rocky Mountains rising from the plains. Wind River sat less than two hours from the mountain playground of Jackson, Wyoming, one of the centers of the ersatz West, where trophy homes boasted prices that skied into the millions and visitors were greeted at the edge of town by a multistory arch fashioned from elk antlers. Grand Teton National Park, whose jutting peaks and Snake River were emblazoned in the American imagination by Ansel Adams, spread out an hour beyond Jackson. Yet Wind River, which the Northern Arapahos shared with their historical enemies, the Eastern Shoshones, could not have felt further away from such iconic landscapes for Roberts. It, too, was beautiful, ringed by the relatively modest peaks of the Wind River Range: rounded, densely forested, often shrouded in mist. The reservation itself, though, was crushed by poverty—roughly 50 percent of its residents were jobless—and attendant problems: drug abuse, violence, and chronic illness. But if economic woes and social pathologies were what most outsiders saw, Roberts knew that they were no more Wind River's whole story than arcing antlers were Jackson's.[45]

After arriving on the reservation, Alexa Roberts met with the Ridgelys: Eugene Sr., an artist, and two of his sons, Eugene Jr. and Gail, both educators. Together, they would oversee the Northern Arapahos' oral history project. At Eugene Sr.'s house, Roberts viewed his painting, *The Sand Creek Massacre*, Northern Arapaho history depicted in oils on an elk hide canvas. The group then toured Wind River, as Gail Ridgely described his family's ties to the massacre—his great-great-grandfather, Lame Man, had survived the ordeal—and their interest in the Sand Creek project. "Creating a national historic site," he explained, "will allow our people to remember their ancestors and help put their suffering to rest." Roberts and Tom Meier, a historian and advisor to the Ridgelys, cooperated with the Northern Arapaho team on their oral history project. With Roberts's help, the following day they collected

stories from two tribal elders at a community school in Ethete, one of
the largest towns on the reservation. The Arapahos interviewed two
more descendants on the reservation in July 1999 and then another two
in February 2000, bringing their total to six.[46]

Less than two months after visiting the Northern Arapahos in April
1999, Roberts got back in her car and headed for the Cheyenne and
Arapaho Tribes' reservation. Unlike the journey to Wind River, this
time she left the mountains in her rearview mirror and traversed the
open expanse of the Great Plains. As she sped east on I-40, the soil gradually turned from Colorado's brown clay to the red earth of Oklahoma.
After six hours of driving, she arrived in Clinton, a small town of 8,000
people that puffed itself up as the "Hub City of Western Oklahoma"—a
decidedly humble claim to fame. Hub or not, Clinton looked very much
like other communities scattered across the country's midsection: the
highway defined it geographically; the usual array of fast-food restau-
rants, inexpensive chain hotels, gas stations, and twenty-four-hour con-
venience stores littered its compact business district; and a golf course,
flanking the Washita River, along with a few attractions ("Oklahoma's
Official Route 66 Museum!"), promised diversions for visitors who had
spare time on their hands. Given Clinton's proximity to the Cheyenne
and Arapaho Tribes' homeland, the impact of the Native American
communities was less obvious than one might have anticipated. But a
huge casino run by the tribes and a Cheyenne cultural center reminded
tourists that they were indeed in "Indian Country."[47]

When she arrived in Clinton, Alexa Roberts met Laird and Colleen
Cometsevah, who, along with their daughter, Carolyn Sandlin, and David Halaas, would direct the Southern Cheyennes' ethnography project.
The Cometsevahs approached the collection of oral histories more in-
formally than had the Northern Arapahos. They advertised locally
that there would be an open house at the Cheyenne and Arapaho Elderly Nutrition Center in Clinton. Descendants could go there and
share Sand Creek stories if they chose to. In part, the Cometsevahs'
relatively casual approach emerged from work they had already done:
years of genealogical research on Sand Creek descendants, support
material for an eventual reparations claim they planned. But Laird
Cometsevah's social position also guided their efforts; Cometsevah, a
chief, took responsibility not just for protecting his tribe's traditional

practices but also, at times, for dictating what they would be. His Sand Creek story carried additional weight, a kind of representative history for the Southern Cheyennes. Regardless, the Cometsevahs' team gathered eight ethnographies on June 1–4, 1999, at the Elderly Nutrition Center and a ninth from a descendent living in a nearby nursing home. The Southern Cheyennes organized a second session in August 1999, interviewing three more people, bringing their total to twelve.[48]

Because of tribal protocols and politics, the Northern Cheyennes only began collecting oral histories late in 1999. But they wasted no time while they waited. They focused on other ways of memorializing Sand Creek. In early fall, Otto Braided Hair opened the Northern Cheyenne Sand Creek Office, an administrative arm supporting the tribal descendants' committee chaired by his older brother, Steve Brady. Braided Hair then coordinated a Sand Creek Massacre Spiritual Healing Run. On November 25–29, approximately five hundred participants, mostly young people, ran a relay between the two most significant sites commemorating the massacre in Colorado. The runners began their journey with a prayer and a blessing, snaking out in a long line from the creek bed beneath the monument overlook on Bill Dawson's property. They continued their journey across nearly two hundred miles of Colorado's back roads, until they reached the Civil War memorial on the capitol steps in Denver. The Cheyenne runners and their families gathered there, listening to speeches and drum groups, symbolically reclaiming land that once had belonged to their forbears. As Braided Hair explained, the run promoted healing by using "traditional ceremonial practices" and offering some Cheyenne families their first chance to "return to their ancestral home" since the massacre's aftermath. The Healing Run would become an annual event, reminding the descendants and the people of Colorado to consider Sand Creek's ongoing significance on the massacre's anniversary.[49]

Six weeks after the run, Alexa Roberts hit the road again, this time bound for Lame Deer on the Northern Cheyenne Reservation. The first part of the drive replicated her earlier trip to Wind River. But instead of veering off I-25 and heading west amid the low-slung sprawl of Cheyenne, Wyoming, Roberts continued north. She next passed the city of Casper, at the foot of the Laramie range, before entering the verdant Powder River country, where year-round streams connected small pine stands shadowed by miniature mountains. In the years following Sand Creek, some Cheyenne and Lakota people fought a war to protect this land from federal troops. Historical markers scattered along the highway's edge narrated part of that grim story: Fort Fetterman, the Connor Battlefield, Fort Phil Kearny. At those spots and others, tribal warriors engaged with U.S. cavalry as part of a doomed effort to keep white settlers from overrunning territory where, in the postbellum years, some of the last remaining bison herds in the American West roamed free. In the midst of this area, Roberts drove by the cities of Buffalo and Sheridan and then hit a steep climb leading up into the Bighorn Mountains and the Montana border beyond. Another hour and she turned east at the Little Bighorn Battlefield, where Cheyennes and Lakotas bested Custer and his men on June 25–26, 1876. Roberts made a right there, at the town of Crow Agency. After one more hour, she reached her destination.[50]

Luke Brady, younger brother of Otto Braided Hair and Steve Brady, hosted Roberts during her ten-day stay on the reservation, starting January 17, 2000. Intense and sometimes bellicose, but also famously good-hearted and funny, Luke Brady was an iconoclast, a champion of the oppressed, and a fierce defender of tribal traditions. To introduce Roberts to the Northern Cheyennes' culture, and particularly to the lasting impact of Sand Creek on the tribe, Brady took her on a tour of his community. The Northern Cheyenne reservation, Roberts learned, occupied 440,000 acres of fiercely glaciated and widely varied terrain. Brady brought Roberts from its eastern boundary, Ashland, where the St. Labre Indian School sat; to the piney mountains in its center; through Lame Deer's tiny strip of a downtown, where tribal government buildings, Dull Knife College, and a few beleaguered stores held fast; then to the small district of Busby; and finally on to the reservation's western edge at the border of the Crow Reservation. He tried to impress upon Roberts the problems, in his view traceable to the massacre, plaguing his people: crude living conditions, rampant joblessness, widespread addiction to drugs, and high rates of heart disease and diabetes, as well as many other public health concerns. Having worked with the Navajos, Roberts understood the difficulties of reservation life. She found the Northern Cheyennes' struggles poignant and the place where they lived somehow "familiar, like home."[51]

Following the tour, Roberts and Luke Brady, with support from Steve Brady, Otto Braided Hair, and Arbutus Red Woman, began interviewing massacre descendants. From the first, the process was more fraught with tension than it had been for the Northern Arapahos and Southern Cheyennes. Luke Brady struggled to convey to Roberts the gravity of the task before them, but he remained frustrated with the NPS's tight schedule. Time constraints, he believed, threatened to undercut the sanctity of their endeavor. Otto Braided Hair agreed. He recalled that the descendants' committee, because of the NPS's looming deadline, could not prepare adequately for the interviews, and as a result had not "earned" the right to ask tribal elders for their sacred stories. Had "time allowed . . . a respected, knowledgeable, older tribal member would have visited in advance and at length with each person from whom" the NPS sought an oral history. The descendants would also have received "a gift commensurate with the storyteller's intellectual property." And they would been allowed "as much time as they needed to think about whether or not [they] wished to give a story normally reserved only for family members." Instead, Roberts's and Brady's youth, coupled with "a lack of time and access to funding," undermined "traditional protocols." From Brady's perspective, these constraints "adversely affected the ability to gather stories." In the face of these considerable difficulties, the Northern Cheyennes nonetheless collected more than thirty oral histories.[52]

Even still, Luke Brady remained angry about the timeline and also concerned that the ethnographies might be misused or misinterpreted by NPS employees. On this point, he spoke for many of the descendants, who feared that the NPS would translate the oral histories inaccurately, robbing them of meaning and perhaps even rendering them false. For those "Cheyenne speakers . . . with important social positions, such as Chiefs or Society Men," this worry was particularly acute. "Unwritten rules about truthfulness in storytelling" bound these people, who, because of venerable protocols, had to repeat their oral histories "exactly as they had heard" them. To do otherwise, even unintentionally, would dishonor the individual who had originally shared the massacre story and, in the process, undercut the memory keeper's status. Accuracy also hinged on linguistic nuance available only to storytellers working in the original Cheyenne. Alexa Roberts recalled: "Some

elderly Cheyenne speakers expressed concern that, as has often happened in the past, the rich meanings of the Cheyenne words would be
lost with too casual an approach to translation." Absent the subtleties
conveyed by the storytellers when speaking their own language, stories
of Sand Creek might become worse than useless: tribal history blighted
by the federal government's disrespect for indigenous culture.[53]

Here again, the past impinged on the search process. Throughout
much of the nineteenth century, federal officials often twisted the words
of Cheyenne and Arapaho leaders, achieving outcomes favorable to
U.S. interests by employing incompetent or corrupt translators during
negotiations. In one case, only a small faction of Cheyenne and Arapaho peace chiefs, including Black Kettle, White Antelope, and Little
Raven, signed the Treaty of Fort Wise in 1861. In doing so, they agreed
to cede to the U.S. government much of the land previously guaranteed their people by federal authorities in the Treaty of Fort Laramie,
ratified a decade earlier. But federal representatives later insisted that
the wording of the Fort Wise treaty bound all of the tribes' bands to a
small reservation in southeastern Colorado. Many Cheyennes, particularly the Dog Soldiers, viewed this perversion of the facts with open
contempt. Their antipathy deepened when Governor Evans used violations of the Fort Wise treaty as a pretext for his infamous orders allowing white Coloradans to hunt and kill "hostile" Indians in August
1864. Linguistic distortions, the descendants remembered in 2000,
had pushed Colorado Territory toward Sand Creek. They often "talked
about how the Cheyenne people ha[d] been misrepresented in treaties
and other legal processes." Luke Brady felt bound by honor to ensure
that nothing like that would happen again. One thirty-minute interview, consequently, took more than thirteen hours to translate.[54]

For most of the people involved in gathering and proffering the ethnographies, the oral history project prompted contradictory emotions. The stories included gut-wrenching accounts of brutality and
misery—at the individual and tribal level—the sorrow made more tragic
because, as Luke Brady kept insisting while guiding Alexa Roberts
around the reservation, the violence had left deep scars on his people.
Roberts agreed, writing that the oral histories provided "a direct link to
the events of November 29, 1864." She elaborated, "They represent a body
of the descendants' connection to the massacre that is still ongoing . . .

the multigenerational effects of the federal government's effort to con-
quer a people." Recounting and hearing the stories meant experiencing
painful ties between past and present. Still, Roberts also noted that
collectively the stories formed a narrative of both "ethnic cleansing"
and "cultural persistence." That these memories were preserved at all,
shared behind locked doors, after nightfall, or whispered from grand-
parent to grandchild, no matter the risks, underscored the durability
of traditional practices. For the descendants, recounting and documenting the massacre, tasks uplifting and unsettling, represented acts
of courage, self-sacrifice, and tribal patriotism.[55]

Ultimately, the oral histories, because of their content, proved more
useful to the tribes—particularly the traditionalists involved in the site
search—than to the NPS. Many storytellers indicted federal authorities
by focusing on the persecution descendants had since endured for preserving their memories. Another group echoed sentiments that George
Bent had shared in his memoir, suggesting that Chivington's decision
to fire on Black Kettle, who, in these stories, waited at the massacre
beneath an American flag, demonstrated that the U.S. government
would desecrate even "its own symbol of peace in the name of genocide, a practice that has characterized federal/tribal relations throughout history." Other storytellers insisted that socioeconomic problems
on the reservation could be traced directly back to the massacre, and
that only reviving traditional cultural practices would heal the lasting
wounds of Sand Creek, ensuring the Cheyennes' and Arapahos' future.
The tales collected during the site search documented too much anger,
and were both too substantively disparate and too culturally specific,
to be an integral part of a federally sponsored memorial, that, at root,
remained an assimilationist project in which even incommensurable
narratives of state-sponsored violence and dispossession would have to
be reconciled as part of a single story of the American past.[56]

In another way as well, the NPS struggled with the oral histories.
Read together, they suggested that no unified tribal memory of the massacre existed. And they offered little insight into the site's placement.
Instead, the descendants provided distinctive ethnographies, expressed
as individual and group memories, asserting the storytellers' place "in
the history of the family, which in turn is integral to the history of the
tribe as a whole." Each oral history contained singular details. A few

mentioned landscape features: bluffs, a fresh spring, water in the creek, hollowed-out tree trunks in which women and children had hid during the attack. Others did not. Some placed the number of people at the massacre in the thousands. Others tallied far fewer than that. One story even recalled that the violence had taken place far distant from Kiowa County, in Estes Park, Colorado. The ethnographies were literally all over the map. Alexa Roberts observed these disparities and the lack of precise information about the massacre location and realized that the descendants had passed along only "the most important aspects of these stories." Other "story elements," she noted, were "not salient enough to survive more than five generations." Rather than preserve memories shared by the tribe, the descendants, for the most part, had focused on their unique genealogies.[57]

Some members of the NPS team, unable to pluck either a unified narrative or useful details about the site location from the oral histories, chose to focus on what they ostensibly represented—an uptick in the descendants' trust in federal authorities, a step on the road to reconciliation—rather than their contents. James Doyle, who at the time still served on Senator Campbell's staff, remembered the ethnographies as the high-water mark for federal-tribal relations during the search. The oral histories, he noted, were "one of the first times an Indian perspective on Sand Creek has been recorded. . . . We were able to convince people who have an inherent distrust of the federal government to speak to representatives of the federal government about the massacre." In that moment, it "became clear that no matter how divided the various parties were, and as diverse as everybody's views were, everybody wanted the same thing"—to set aside differences in service of memorializing the massacre.[58]

It was not that simple. The descendants shared their oral histories not with government representatives but with other descendants; the ethnographies rested on intratribal, not tribal-federal, cooperation. Barbara Sutteer, the NPS's Indian liaison, dismissed the idea that the Arapahos and Cheyennes had begun trusting federal officials because of the site search. Instead, Sutteer suggested that the tribal delegates worked with the NPS out of necessity and only so long as the project suited their purposes—preserving family histories, invigorating traditional cultural practices, laying the groundwork for a reparations claim—and proceeded on their terms. Sutteer remembered "hearing one of the Park Service people say, 'Well, the tribal people trust me.'" She replied, "You really don't get it. Because the last thing feds will ever get from a tribal person is trust." Alexa Roberts agreed, suggesting that the descendants might have trusted individuals in the NPS but never their employer. It might be more accurate to say that Roberts trusted the descendants, allowing the ethnographic research to proceed. In the end, as Laird Cometsevah said, "We have no reason to trust the U.S. government or the Park Service. They don't respect our culture or Indian ways." The final component of the site study seemed to prove Cometsevah's point.[59]

On April 19–20, 1999, the NPS held another consultation meeting at the Cow Palace, the by-then-familiar convention hotel located on Lamar's main street. Rick Frost planned to take stock of the site search's progress and also to ensure that the "stakeholders"—the NPS, the State of Colorado, various tribal delegations, and local officials and landowners—"remained at the negotiating table despite their differences." But as so often happened at these events, the gathering exacerbated frustrations and fears rather than allaying them. The descendants remained concerned with the fate of their ethnographies. The Northern Arapahos had collected their oral histories two weeks earlier. The Southern Cheyennes would follow suit in early June, approximately six weeks after the meeting in Lamar. The Northern Cheyennes would wait until the new year before starting to collect their Sand Creek stories from tribal elders. At the Lamar meeting, the assembled site searchers touched on that controversial element of the project and then discussed the historical research before turning their attention to the upcoming geomorphological and archeological fieldwork, which would take place just a few weeks later.[60]

Rick Frost understood that both the geomorphology and the archeology would churn earth sacred to the tribes, raising the difficult question of what would happen if the search teams uncovered human remains or other artifacts during their digging. As Joe Big Medicine, a Southern Cheyenne Sand Creek and NAGPRA (Native American Graves Protection and Repatriation Act) representative remembered, "We didn't like the idea of disturbing our ancestors who were murdered there. They hadn't rested since Sand Creek." Laird Cometsevah then raised the issue of ownership, given that the dig would take place on private property. "I personally feel that human remains have priority for return (to Native people)," he explained. Other "artifacts can be dealt with somewhere down the line." Doug Scott, who would direct the archeological fieldwork, had a great deal of experience working with tribes around NAGPRA issues. He and Frost assured the descendants that the NPS would follow established protocols. Excitement then crowded out anxiety for most of the people at the meeting. The NPS team members and the tribal representatives were curious to see what the archeology would turn up, to learn if they were closing in on the proper massacre site.[61]

Some local landowners, by contrast, remained wary, concerned that their property rights might be trampled amid the hubbub. Without their cooperation, the search process would grind to a halt. Rick Frost thus tried to calm the proprietors, those at the Cow Palace meeting and those who stayed away. Residents of Kiowa County said of August "Pete" Kern, whose land holdings sat to the north of Bill Dawson's, that "he buys land; he doesn't sell it." So it was in this case. Aware of the search legislation's willing-seller-only provision, Kern politely insisted that the NPS would not buy any of his property. But he would not obstruct the search, because he was not threatened by it. Bill Dawson, though, hoped that the project would conclude with him selling out. Still, he had other concerns. It had been a very damp spring, and Sand Creek, often bone dry, ran relatively high at the time. Dawson relied on his ranch for economic survival, and he knew that his land would be even more fragile than usual. Until the NPS assumed liability for any damage its efforts caused, he worried that the searchers would tear up the fertile creek bottom. Once he was sure that he had no financial exposure, though, Dawson agreed to open his gates.[62]

Chuck and Sheri Bowen would not be placated so easily. By spring 1999, their long-standing wariness of the NPS had hardened into outright distrust. Aware that his upcoming dig required their consent, Doug Scott had visited the Bowens in mid-March, laying the groundwork for the upcoming site location meeting in Lamar. Like his friend Jerry Greene, Scott spent hours listening as the Bowens explained their elaborate theories of how the massacre had played out on their property. Scott was more interested in the artifacts they had unearthed, especially a fragment of mountain howitzer, "a very important item" in his view. He left the Bowens, having asked them to consider forgoing their ad hoc reconnaissance in favor of professional efforts. He also reassured them that he would take them seriously, though he believed that the archeological record, as evidenced by their vast collection, did not support their perspective.[63]

In spite of Doug Scott's visit, the Bowens stewed. They worried that their land might "be condemned" if the NPS determined that it had historical significance. And even if the NPS paid for their family ranch, the sum would be inadequate, they believed. The NPS could only offer "fair market value" for land. Such an assessment, the Bowens knew, would not account for "future lost earnings" or "the history associated with the place." The price would be calculated based on the cost of "dry land, grassland, Kiowa County ranchland." It would not be enough, the Bowens concluded, to compensate for the sentiment attached to their family's property. They also believed that NPS officials had been high-handed during the search. They were especially annoyed with Jerry Greene. The Bowens recalled "liking Greene personally," but they believed that he had discounted their expertise and was hostile to the idea that the massacre had taken place on their land. They were half right. Greene suspected that the massacre had spilled onto the Bowens' property. It seemed likely to him that the sand pits had been located on their ranch. Still, he deprecated the Bowens' research methods. They had "pulled artifacts from the ground without thinking," he later complained, thus complicating future investigations. For Greene, a meticulous scholar, the Bowens' recklessness was nearly inexplicable and entirely unacceptable.[64]

The Bowens' fears about dispossession also colored their perceptions of the tribal representatives. They insisted that they were "not anti-Indian in any way, shape, or form." But like most everyone in Kiowa County, they had little experience with Native people. They had read about Cheyennes and Arapahos in old-fashioned histories filled with cartoonish portraits of Indians: savages either bloodthirsty or noble, but rarely in between. The descendants, by contrast, were human beings, not archetypes. And after the Cow Palace meeting, having been confronted with the tribal representatives' rough edges, the Bowens assumed that they wanted their ancestral land back, including the massacre site, and that the NPS, bowing to "political correctness," could not be trusted to protect the interests of local proprietors. Worse still, the Bowens believed that the NPS and the tribes had colluded with Bill Dawson, stacking the deck so the search would conclude that the slaughter had taken place on his land. This made sense, the Bowens reasoned, because Dawson wanted to sell and they did not. Finally, Rick Frost's decision to allow the meetings to start late grated on the Bowens. As the Cheyennes and Arapahos slowly filed into the hall, the punctual Bowens read the Indians' tardiness as contempt.[65]

Concerned that they were being cast to the margins of the search, Chuck and Sheri Bowen replied by insisting that they had ironclad proof that the massacre had taken place on their ranch. The descendants responded coolly. Laird Cometsevah resented the Bowens' challenge to his authority. Then a rumor began swirling around the Cow Palace that the Bowens had offered to sell their land for $18 million. Six weeks earlier, a man named Robert Perry, claiming to represent the Bowens, had written to Laird Cometsevah, noting that the "true site" could be had for that price. For the NPS, statutorily bound to pay only fair market value for property, such a sum was completely out of reach and did not merit a second thought. But for the Arapaho and Cheyenne delegates to the search, the figure was an affront. It seemed that the Bowens were holding tribal history hostage in hopes of extracting a huge ransom. Joe Big Medicine summed up the descendants' views by describing the Bowens as "greedy people." The meeting ended with the Bowens upset at the NPS and the tribes. Yet the couple nonetheless agreed to allow the site searchers on their property. They wanted recognition for their hard work and feared that they would be cut out of the process otherwise. To be ignored in that moment, the Bowens reckoned, was worse than being mistreated.[66]

The day after that contentious meeting, the geomorphological investigation proceeded. On April 21, a team began a two-day survey of the Bowen and Dawson properties, boring three-inch-diameter holes several meters into the earth at forty spots along Sand Creek. The samples they retrieved revealed little buildup of soils over time, suggesting that only small changes had taken place in the land since the era of the massacre. Laird Cometsevah greeted the news with awe. He realized that when he "visited the massacre site" he "walked on the same earth

[his] ancestors walked," underscoring the collision of past and present at Sand Creek. Doug Scott was also thrilled with the results. He planned to use metal detectors to search for artifacts during the upcoming archeological phase of the study. Because there had been "little ag-gradation" (buildup of soil) since 1864, Scott felt confident that metal detectors would be "well within their range," a "nearly ideal inventory tool." It was just a question of whether the searchers would look in the right place.[67]

If historians drift comfortably between the humanities and the so-cial sciences, and anthropologists typically identify with the latter cat-egory, archeologists are social scientists who flirt with harder sciences. And for a young subdiscipline like battlefield archeology, questions of scholarly taxonomy or methodological orientation became all the more important. So it was that Doug Scott designed his research protocols with rigid scientific standards—and perhaps police procedural dramas, popular on television at the time—in mind. Scott said, "I love using crime scene analogies. Historians equal detectives. In the archives, they interview witnesses and possible suspects. Victims, too, if they're still alive." From those materials, they "get a story down on paper." But historians are often left with "conflicting stories." That is when the "fo-rensic scientist, the archeologist" steps in, "gathering hard evidence." Only by mating the two disciplines is it possible to "complete a more ac-curate picture of the past." Scott, consequently, hoped that his data would be unimpeachable, answering, without any doubt at all, the ques-tion of where the Sand Creek massacre had happened, and perhaps hint-ing at how the bloodletting had unfolded—though the latter issue was beyond the scope of the site search.[68]

For eleven days, May 17–27, members of the search team spread out in a broad phalanx, usually four to six people across, standing approxi-mately thirty feet apart. Advancing in unison across the landscape, the group surveyed targeted sections of property, their arms sweeping back and forth like windshield wipers, as though washing the sandy soil with the metal detectors they held. With each new "beep" the team stopped and marked the spot with a pin flag, signaling the presence of a piece of metal buried in the earth. The line of searchers then moved on. A recovery crew armed with spades and trowels followed immedi-ately in their wake, excavating the material found by the detectors. The

artifacts then rested next to their telltale pin flags, awaiting a final recording crew, which assigned each specimen a number, jotted down its
provenance, collected the object, and then refilled the hole from whence
it had come. Finally, Doug Scott entered each of the artifacts the
searchers found into a portable data collector and then uploaded the
plotted coordinates onto a computerized map, creating a comprehensive inventory of every object the team pulled from the earth.[69]

The archeological survey began on May 19–20, on Bill Dawson's land.
The searchers started by covering terrain enveloped in the South Bend
of the creek. Across the two days, the team gradually worked its way
from the shadow of the monument overlook to the east side of Dawson's property. They turned up a great deal of metal as they advanced:
baling wire, tin cans, even some bullets. But they found nothing dating
from the nineteenth century. It was frustrating, particularly for the
Cheyenne descendants, most of whom remained convinced that the
massacre had played out in that crook of Sand Creek. Laird Cometsevah's confidence rested in part on George Bent's work. Guided by Bent's
text and maps, Cometsevah had visited the Dawson South Bend for
years, performing sacred rituals there. In that time, he "heard the voices
of children, of mothers, crying for help." As a result, he recalled, he
"knew that's where Black Kettle's people were killed." The absence of
physical evidence from that spot did not deter Cometsevah. He remained convinced that he was right.[70]

The archeological investigations continued the next day, with the survey moving gradually north on Dawson's ranch. Approximately three-
fifths of a mile from the monument overlook, the metal detectors began
steadily shrilling. The recovery team carefully dug artifacts from the
ground and then waited impatiently for the recording crew to confirm
their suspicions: the materials they had found dated to the massacre
era. The searchers eventually unearthed an oblong band, three hundred
feet wide by twelve hundred feet long, peppered with period pieces: bullets, an arrowhead, telltale fragments from a mountain howitzer shell.
For Doug Scott, "this concentration of artifacts was an exciting find."
Noting that "archaeological investigations are based on the use of the
scientific method as expounded in the field of the physical sciences,"
Scott later surmised that the artifacts had lodged there when Chivington's troops had fired on Cheyennes and Arapahos fleeing the massacre.

In that case, Scott believed, there should have been relevant materials to the north and west as well. But the search team found no evidence in either of those directions. Scott, sticking to his methodology, then generated a second theory: the artifacts had lodged in the earth when Chivington's men had overshot their targets, which suggested that more materials would be found to the east.[71]

Scott deployed the searchers in that direction to test his new conjecture. "Within minutes" their metal detectors began bleating like a flock of sheep. Red pin flags, a field of artificial poppies, sprouted in the soil of Bill Dawson's ranch. The searchers turned up more than three hundred artifacts in a swath stretching approximately a quarter of a mile long and a tenth of a mile wide. Team members pulled a vast array of equipment from the ground: ordnance, including bullets, arrowheads, and cannonball fragments, to outfit a small army; domestic materials, including skillets, kettles, knives, forks, spoons, cups, plates, bowls, and a coffee grinder, to prepare a grand feast; and hardware, including nails, barrel hoops, horseshoes, awls, and several crude scrapers, to stock a general store. It was an amazing and suggestive haul. Rick Frost, focusing on one artifact in particular, remarked, "shrapnel from the 12-pound howitzers is pretty sound evidence," because "the only recorded use of howitzers in the area was along Sand Creek." The search team, it seemed, had unearthed the massacre site.[72]

Doug Scott celebrated finding the artifact concentration. Once again in his storied career, Scott had proven the utility of battlefield archeology in historical investigations. But he realized that he had not achieved his goal without the help of others. To illustrate the point, he spun a lovely (and hyperbolic) yarn. Referring to the moments after the team found the artifacts, he recalled, "I had to get on the cell phone to call Jerry Greene and tell him that he was wrong: the site wasn't where he had predicted it would be; he was off by about ten feet." In fact, Scott later acknowledged, Greene's projections had missed the mark by several hundred feet. Still, Scott's story fashioned a usable past from the fragments of his memories of the search, creating a tale that legitimated not only months of hard work but also the disciplines involved in the hunt. In this telling, the scientific methods held dear by Scott and Greene could help solve even the most complex historical mysteries.[73]

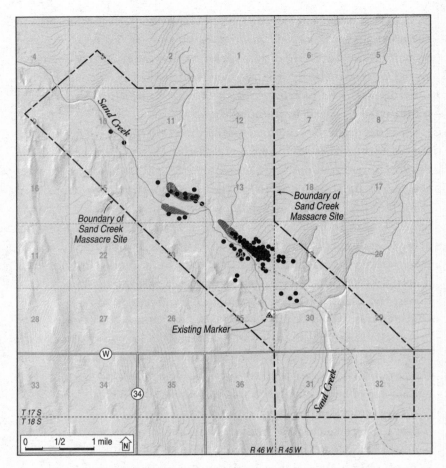

Archeological findings at the Sand Creek Massacre site; dots show artifact sites. *(Adapted from the Sand Creek Massacre Special Resource Study, U.S. Dept. of the Interior, National Park Service.)*

Members of the NPS team also recalled the scene at Dawson's ranch as a cross-cultural triumph, a moment when the tribal representatives and federal government set aside differences to achieve a common goal. Doug Scott said, "It was fascinating to watch the excitement build among the Arapahos and Cheyennes . . . to the point that they would grab a shovel from one of the volunteers and literally go out and dig up some of their own heritage." Rick Frost trailed behind the metal detectors, working on the recovery team next to Mildred Red Cherries, a Northern Cheyenne descendant. "I must have dug up, I don't know, two,

three dozen pin flags that day," Frost recalled, "and I was right next to
Mildred. And nothing I ever dug was more than a piece of barbed wire,
an old tin can, or something like that." But "every time Mildred dug
something up, it was an actual artifact: a piece of howitzer, a minié ball,
an arrowhead." He said, "It was stunning, something that made you feel
the hand of fate in the mix, something that said, this is her place, her
history, she's going to be the one that makes the significant finds."
Then, as the sun fell, Luke Brady and Laird Cometsevah conducted a
pipe ceremony to honor the massacre's victims. Frost remembered being overcome by the moment and thinking, "it was hard to get past the
feeling that we were in a consecrated place."[74]

Many descendants, by contrast, recalled that day not as a success but
as another instance of federal insensitivity to tribal traditions, cultural sovereignty, and basic propriety. Laird Cometsevah worried that
the artifacts' location, more than half a mile from the monument overlook, would be construed as challenging his grasp on Cheyenne history. Shaking his head, Cometsevah recounted his frustration: "the
Park Service never admitted that we knew that place. Our ancestors
were scattered across that land. The site should have been treated like a
cemetery. There was no call for all the whooping and hollering they
were doing." The celebration smacked of disrespect to Steve Brady and
Mildred Red Cherries as well. Brady noted, "Archeologists were jumping up and down, doing cartwheels and back flips when they found
something. But the Cheyennes, they just walked off. You know, two
different worlds." Red Cherries echoed this sentiment: "It was emotional for us to find things like bullets or cannonballs. We wondered if
they killed one of our ancestors. Meanwhile, the white people out there
were laughing and feeling good. It was hard." Of the pipe ceremony,
which had so impressed Frost and other NPS observers, Barbara Sutteer suggested, "the tribes felt like the Park Service didn't understand
how to behave, how to watch quietly from a polite distance." In the
end, what had seemed to the NPS like a day of reconciliation and healing had in fact reopened old wounds for the tribal representatives.[75]

Relations only deteriorated from there. After spending a day on Pete
Kern's land and then another day at a ranch several miles to the south,
the searchers prepared to visit the Bowens' property. But there was a
catch. Still suspicious that the federal government would employ dirty

tricks to seize their land, the Bowens asked all of the searchers to sign a release, absolving the ranchers of liability in the event of an accident. The request outraged the descendants, especially Mildred Red Cherries, who refused to sign away her rights. The Bowens responded that the document "wasn't anything," just protection so that nobody could "sue if [they] tripped or got bit by a snake or something." Red Cherries would not relent. She turned away and began the long walk back toward Lamar. Other descendants rallied around her. Rick Frost worried that the search might splinter. A member of the NPS team eventually drove Red Cherries back to her hotel while the archeological investigation proceeded on the Bowens' ranch.[76]

As often happened during the search, the participants' views on contemporary developments could in part be traced back to the era of the massacre. For the NPS staff, though immersed in the project and committed to their partnership with the descendants, Sand Creek was a subject of study and the site search a job that needed doing. For the tribal representatives, though, the massacre shaped their daily lives. As the ethnographies demonstrated, for the descendants, "the Sand Creek Massacre is not an event relegated to the past, but is a very real part of the Cheyenne people's contemporary identity." That was never more obvious than in Mildred Red Cherries's reaction to the Bowens' demand that she sign a legal release before entering their ranch. Red Cherries recalled worrying that the Bowens were asking her, in her official capacity as a representative to the search team, to sign "for the tribe." She insisted that she did not have the authority to do that and would rather walk away from the search entirely than risk committing her tribe to a document that she did not entirely understand handed to her by people that she did not trust.[77]

In that moment, painful lessons drawn from the contested history of the Treaty of Fort Wise guided Red Cherries. In the wake of an 1859 gold strike in Colorado, tens of thousands of white migrants flowed into the Front Range, and territorial officials began pressuring the federal government to remove local tribes from the plains east of Denver. The Indians there stood in the way of progress, whites argued, threatening instant towns that were cropping up to mine the miners working claims in the mountains. In summer 1860, panic-stricken Denverites worried that the Cheyennes and the Arapahos, in cahoots with other

Indian peoples from the region, would descend on the city, slaughtering its inhabitants. William Byers, editor of the *Rocky Mountain News*, responded to this ostensible menace by releasing a stream of inflammatory broadsides. Respectable whites would take matters into their own hands if the army did not pacify the tribes, he warned: "forbearance will cease to be virtue, public sympathy will be aroused by some overt act, or terrible outrage committed by the Indians, and a horrible and indiscriminate war will ensue." Byers received satisfaction in July, when Congress appropriated funds to treat with the tribes.[78]

In September of that year, Arapaho and Cheyenne peace chiefs, including Little Raven, Left Hand, and, somewhat later, Black Kettle and White Antelope, arrived at a ranch owned by William Bent, George Bent's father, a trader who also held a commission as the federal Indian agent for the region. At Bent's property, tribal leaders planned to meet with Commissioner of Indian Affairs A. B. Greenwood. Late in the month, negotiations began, culminating in an agreement that limited the tribes to a triangular reservation located between Sand Creek and the Arkansas River in southeastern Colorado. By design, the site would bring the Native people into contact with the supposedly civilizing influence of white settlers, a move that reflected federal Indian policy at the time. Greenwood also believed that the land offered the Cheyennes and Arapahos the best chance of abandoning their bison-based economy and embracing sedentary agriculture instead. The tribes, though, continued hunting buffalo. And the reservation's proximity to whites, coupled with food scarcities caused by the ongoing colonization of Colorado, ushered in escalating depredations in spring and summer 1864. Those depredations then led to reprisals from white settlers, to Governor Evans's decision to raise the 3rd Colorado Regiment, and finally to the massacre.[79]

Searching for the site nearly a century and a half later, Mildred Red Cherries knew that history. She knew, too, that Black Kettle and White Antelope had insisted, when striking their deal with Greenwood, that they "would enter into such an agreement, and settle down, *and allow the remaining portion of their tribe to locate where they saw proper.*" In other words, the peace chiefs had clarified that they spoke only for those bands that followed them. The rest of the Cheyennes, including the more militant soldier societies, whose leaders at the time scorned peace, could go their own way. In the ensuing years, however, territorial and federal authorities, including John Evans and John Chivington, ignored this element of the Fort Wise treaty. Evans and Chivington relied on divide-and-conquer tactics, insisting that the accord bound the entire tribe to the reservation that Black Kettle and White Antelope had accepted only for a small fraction of their people. Now, Red Cherries, serving in her capacity as a tribal Sand Creek representative, drew on that history when she confronted the Bowens. She reacted by insisting that that she did not have the authority to sign for the Cheyenne people. No matter how many times the Bowens claimed that they simply wanted her as an individual to release them from liability, they could not persuade her to believe them.[80]

The controversy at the Bowen ranch did not scuttle the site search. But it did further erode what little trust the Cheyenne descendants had in the NPS and local landowners (other than Bill Dawson, who remained in their good graces). The day following the debacle at the Bowens' ranch, rain confined the searchers to their hotel. The tribal representatives met privately, discussing their grievances. Even after they spent the next day surveying the rest of the Bowens' land, the Cheyenne descendants remained angry about how Mildred Red Cherries had been treated and anxious about the implications of the artifact concentration's location. Rick Frost and Doug Scott, meanwhile, still believed that the archeological fieldwork represented a moment of reconciliation in federal-tribal relations—even as the cross-cultural partnership actually was sinking beneath waves of ill feeling.[81]

Scott's and Frost's misapprehensions stemmed from positive interactions they had at the time, including evening visits with the Cheyenne descendants. Laird Cometsevah, Joe Big Medicine, and Mildred Red Cherries often knocked on Scott's hotel room door, asking to see the artifacts they had pulled from the ground earlier in the day. On the last night of the survey, after the second day spent at the Bowens' ranch, Steve Brady joined the group. As Scott unboxed materials for the descendants, Cometsevah asked about the next step in the process. Seeking common ground with the chief, Scott explained, "Well, it may sound funny coming from me, an archeologist and white guy, but I'm going to listen to these artifacts." He allowed that "They're not going to speak to me spiritually the way they speak to you. But they'll still tell me how old they are; they'll tell me at least part of what they were doing there; and with that information, I'll be able to tell a story about them." He promised, "The story I tell will be fitted with your memories of the place, and the spiritual meaning of it, and also what the history says." Considering all that transpired after that, Scott later grimaced, saying, "It was a wonderful conversation. It was exciting. When we separated that evening it was very jovial, very congenial. We believed we had discovered the Sand Creek site."[82]

Again, though, the Cheyenne descendants recalled that interaction differently than Scott did. Steve Brady recognized the artifact concentration's significance, viewing it as "absolutely unequivocal" proof, if not of the exact site of Black Kettle's village, at least of the massacre's general location. But for him and Cometsevah, the accession numbers that Scott attached to the artifacts brought to mind the way the massacre's victims had been treated in the wake of Sand Creek. Brady thought of the museums that still housed human remains lifted from the killing field and pondered the "ballistics research that had been conducted on some of the Cheyennes slaughtered at Sand Creek." Of Scott's exacting research methods, Brady said, "Not everything has to fit into a box. And some things really shouldn't, even if they can." Cometsevah voiced similar concerns. "Numbers," he began, "why do white people feel like they have to put numbers on everything, no matter how sacred?" To Cometsevah, Scott "seemed like he never considered that those bullets might have killed one of our ancestors. He was too busy slapping numbers on them and getting ready to study them in his laboratory." Barbara Sutteer, the NPS Indian liaison, viewed that moment as a turning point in the process. Had the NPS treated the artifacts with more respect, Sutteer contended, much trouble might have been averted later. "But the Park Service way was to deal with tribal materials as objects ready for museum cases," she lamented.[83]

Doug Scott, meanwhile, had no idea that problems were afoot. He returned to his home, in Lincoln, Nebraska, elated about the discoveries the search team had made at the dig and eager to interpret the antique materials they had found; these varied objects would, as he had promised Cometsevah, speak to him. And because the searchers had found the artifact concentration so near where Jerry Greene had suggested they would, Scott quickly settled on a working hypothesis that he and Greene had batted around for some time. This was their ideal outcome: the searchers had discovered "Black Kettle's village," the precise spot where John Chivington's men had descended upon the unsuspecting Cheyennes on the morning of November 29, 1864. Scott could not yet be sure, of course. He still had more work to do, applying scientific methods to test his theory. But he was confident that additional research would prove him correct.[84]

Alexa Roberts greeted this theory with dread. At the time, she had not yet reached the midpoint of the ethnographic component of the site search, and already some of the stories the Arapaho and Cheyenne elders had shared suggested that Scott's certitude about the precise location of Black Kettle's village was badly misplaced. Roberts recalled riding from the archeological dig with Scott around that time and "distinctly hearing the words 'village site' being used a lot." Speaking of "*the* village site, just one, especially right there"—distant from the monument overlook, the spot mapped by George Bent—did not square with what the descendants were telling her. Roberts later asked her colleagues if any other nomenclature might possibly be attached to the find. "Could it *not* be called the village site?" she wondered. "Maybe we could just call it *part* of the village site? The artifact concentration? Evidence of domestic artifacts? You know, *a portion* of the village site? Potential north end of the village site?" Growing more desperate as her pleas fell on deaf ears, she implored, "Is there anything else it can be called other than *the* village site?" No. "Zealousness and understandable enthusiasm took over," Roberts remembered, "and it became *the* village site." Her instincts were impeccable; more trouble was on the horizon for the search.[85]

4

ACCURATE BUT NOT PRECISE

The coffee was watery, the cigarette smoke stale, the re-criminations bitter. On October 5, 1999, the site searchers met in Denver at yet another chain hotel, a concrete, steel, and glass tower plopped just off a busy artery in the city. The participants in the Sand Creek project had not gathered as a group since Doug Scott had completed the archeological fieldwork half a year earlier. The day began with updates from the National Park Service (NPS) teams. The drone of business as usual filled the room, interrupted only by the descendants "caucusing" or pulling Alexa Roberts and Barbara Sutteer aside for conversations about their ongoing oral history projects. It seemed that things might proceed without a hitch, deepening the NPS representatives' impression that "everyone had reached consensus at the dig that we had found Sand Creek." Then Rick Frost unfurled "a map of the length and extent of the massacre site." On it, the NPS had marked the location of Black Kettle's village, roughly a mile north of the hilltop memorial on Bill Dawson's ranch. Frost, cringing, recalled that the NPS had labeled the map "DRAFT." But even that precaution could not defuse "an explosion of emotion . . . on the part of the tribal folks." The descendants were outraged; they believed they had been "betrayed."[1]

Although he remembered being livid—"not surprised, mind you, because I never figured I could trust the federal government . . . but still hopping mad"—Laird Cometsevah unfolded his long legs from beneath the table where he sat next to his wife, Colleen, and strode deliberately to the front of the conference room. In those moments, with Cometsevah on the march, Rick Frost could feel his grip on the project slipping. He realized that the NPS "had made a huge mistake, that once something appeared on paper, the message to people was, this is a fact, this is it, this is done." After staring for a moment at the NPS's map, pondering the implications of the graphic representation of the massacre site, Cometsevah, using a red magic marker, "corrected the diagram." He redrafted the NPS's draft map, nestling Black Kettle's village in the crook of Sand Creek, exactly where George Bent had located it at the start of the twentieth century and below where the monument still rested on Bill Dawson's ranch. The room detonated into sharp discussions, testy back-and-forth sniping in which NPS personnel wondered if the Cheyenne representatives were acting in bad faith, while the descendants countered that the NPS was engaging in bureaucratic imperialism or "cultural genocide." Cometsevah slowly walked back to his seat, having irrevocably altered the dynamics of the search.[2]

Cometsevah's gambit stunned the NPS officials. Based on misapprehensions during the final days of the archeological reconnaissance, the NPS team had been confident that all of the searchers, including the descendants, were on the same page: they had "found the site." And yet, roughly a year into the eighteen-month window that Senator Campbell had opened to look for Sand Creek, Cometsevah had defenestrated the NPS. "Not so fast," he warned. "The federal government shouldn't be so certain it knows what Indian people are thinking about their own history." Cometsevah, in other words, demanded that the descendants be allowed to interpret their own past, without "meddling" from federal officials. Doug Scott remembered feeling "floored, caught flat-footed," and deeply hurt by the suggestion that his findings ran roughshod over tribal history and traditional cultural practices. Only later, after regaining perspective, did he comfort himself by depersonalizing the experience: "There was such mistrust of the government's representatives. So while Laird . . . may like us [members of the NPS team] as individuals, we still represent an entity he distrusts." Christine Whitacre, meanwhile, looked on as Cometsevah redrew the NPS map. Aghast that the site study appeared to be crashing before her eyes, she thought to herself, "maybe this isn't going to work."[3]

Cometsevah's reaction blindsided Whitacre and her colleagues in part because the NPS's conclusions, depicted on the draft map, rested on ostensibly irrefutable evidence. During the archeological fieldwork, the search team had unearthed a vast concentration of artifacts, stretching nearly 1,500 feet long and approximately 500 feet wide. Doug Scott, after investigating those materials, had dated many of them to the era of the massacre. The NPS representatives then tried to prove that the fruits of their digging had once been part of a Cheyenne village. The NPS historians compared the artifacts with lists of goods that the federal government had provided as part of mid-nineteenth-century annuity programs to the Cheyennes, Kiowas, and Comanches. Next, because Chivington's men had not maintained an account of the objects they had taken from Sand Creek, the NPS looked to complete catalogs of materials seized by federal troops following other violent encounters with Indians around that time: a Cheyenne and Lakota village, destroyed near Fort Larned, Kansas, in 1867; Black Kettle's camp, razed by George Armstrong Custer's troops at the Washita in 1868; and a gathering of Dog Soldiers, killed by U.S. cavalry at Summit Springs, Colorado, in 1869. In each case, as with the federal annuity lists, the NPS found significant overlap, suggesting that the "Sand Creek assemblage" likely represented part of "an 1864-era Cheyenne camp."[4]

But questions lingered: was the artifact concentration all that remained of Black Kettle's village, destroyed at the massacre? Or might the searchers have found detritus from another Cheyenne camp? Again, the evidence seemed both ironclad and, NPS personnel believed, likely to engender the descendants' support and gratitude. Munitions unearthed during the search's archeological dig matched lists of weapons wielded by the 1st and 3rd Colorado Regiments in fall 1864. Most telling, fragments from a mountain howitzer shell (as noted earlier, a cannon fired at the massacre) offered "mute testimony," "nearly unequivocal" proof that the search had indeed located the correct site. Most of the artifacts also had been battered—bowls cracked, cutlery flattened, tools ruined—suggesting that Chivington's men, after they had butchered some of the Indian people at Sand Creek, had destroyed the remnants of their camp. This kind of violence was typical of engagements during the U.S. government's conflict with the Plains Tribes, as federal soldiers fought a total war against Native people they deemed savages.

At Sand Creek, the Colorado volunteers tried to obliterate the posses-
sions they found littering the field. The troops rendered useless what
little remained of the Indian encampment for any Cheyenne and Arapaho survivors who might return to scour the field, trying to piece together some of what they had lost there.[5]

A final element of the archeology had even broader implications for
students of Sand Creek, including the descendants. The archeological
reconnaissance turned up hardly any artifacts from weapons the
Arapahos and Cheyennes "might have fired at the Colorado attacking
force." Considering that the bloodshed had involved hundreds of Native people desperately struggling to survive, a lack of weapons traceable to the tribes seemed revealing. For Doug Scott and Jerry Greene,
"the absence of definitive artifacts of resistance [was] consistent with
Indian oral tradition that the attack came as a complete surprise." As
many of the oral histories collected during the search suggested, the
Indians at Sand Creek had not been passive or weak. They had not accepted their fate without resisting. But they had been too surprised and
unprepared to mount a vigorous defense. The bloodshed had been a
massacre: a shocking and devastating attack followed by indiscriminate killing of individuals who for the most part had not fought back.[6]

Leading to the October consultation meeting, Scott and Greene had
thought the tribal representatives would be thrilled by their analysis,
which seemed to ratify with science the descendants' massacre stories.
From the fact that the village had been unguarded, to the enduring
image of American and white flags flying over Black Kettle's lodge, to
the tragic case of White Antelope singing his death song as bullets cut
him down, the Cheyennes and Arapahos recalled their massacred ancestors as peaceful individuals double-crossed by violent whites. Even
if the documentary record remained divided—with Colonel Chivington and his partisans insisting that the attack had been a battle, war-
ranted because Black Kettle's village had been filled with hostile warriors, and Silas Soule, George Bent, and others countering that Sand
Creek had been an outrageous act of moral cowardice, a massacre—
Scott and Greene believed that the archeological evidence had settled
the matter once and for all. Black Kettle's people had been victimized
by Chivington and his troops, just as the descendants contended.[7]

As for the fact that the NPS's blend of documentary and archeological sources undercut many of the descendants' perceptions of where the massacre had taken place, Scott and Greene had an answer for that as well. Relying on terms of art more typically used by scholars describing the collection of quantitative data, the men insisted, of both the Bent maps and oral histories, that they were "accurate but not precise." Greene noted, "Bent's account *was* very useful not in terms of where, exactly, the village was located, but more in a schematic sense of placing the massacre in the general vicinity of the South Bend on Dawson's property." He added, "So when you think of Bent's drawing, it's complementary to where we finally found the site." Scott made a similar argument about his findings' relationship to the oral histories: "I don't see it as a problem. I see it as the difference between accuracy and precision. Their stories are accurate. The massacre occurred in a bend of Sand Creek. But if you want to talk about precision, that's where the physical evidence and the historical record puts it a little further north." Because, in their view, the archival and archeological research remained compatible with Bent's maps and the tribal oral histories, Scott and Greene were "taken aback, really kind of shocked that the descendants didn't want to accept the scientific data."[8]

NPS officials explained away the controversy as a by-product of antithetical epistemologies. The NPS looked to empirical methods: archival research and archeological fieldwork. The massacre descendants, by contrast, relied on indigenous cultural practices: oral traditions, ancestor veneration, and guidance from the spiritual realm. "There's this schism," Frost suggested. "We're very much a culture that likes to put everything on paper, get everything written down, and have notebooks and binders and Xeroxes." He concluded, "It was a mistake to be dealing with people who have an oral culture by presenting them constantly with written stuff." Christine Whitacre went a step further, suggesting that the divide could not be reduced to comfort with oral versus written sources. She believed something deeper separated the searchers. "Archeological evidence and historical documentation carried little weight with many of the tribal representatives," she remembered. Laird Cometsevah, for one, "heard voices on the site." Because of that, Whitacre said, "I don't think it was oral history so much as traditional tribal knowledge he valued." The search, in this view, had become a clash between a people of history, the NPS, and a people of memory, the descendants.[9]

The conflict was never quite that stark. In part, the tribal representatives were, as the NPS officials suggested, upset at the Denver meeting because the NPS map undercut the oral histories and traditional methods that allowed some descendants to "feel where Sand Creek happened." Steve Brady and Laird Cometsevah had long believed that they knew exactly where the massacre had taken place: right where George Bent had mapped it at the beginning of the twentieth century. When Brady and Cometsevah visited Bill Dawson's ranch through the years, their ancestors spoke to them, marking the field with the sounds of women screaming or children crying. Guided by those experiences, an exasperated Cometsevah fumed before the archeological dig: "The Cheyennes feel the Dawson site is the original site. It's not the Indians that's looking for it." He continued, "But according to the National Park Service they have to document or pinpoint the Sand Creek area." And in the wake of the fieldwork, he reiterated, "The Cheyenne have always known where it is. It has always stayed in the Cheyenne mind." Brady, for his part, accepted the archeology's importance. But he inverted Doug Scott's and Jerry Greene's claims about methodological precision: "the digging proved we found part of the site, sure. But our elders told us what happened there. And the Cheyennes already knew exactly where Black Kettle's people camped." In choosing to ignore this evidence, Brady believed, the NPS evinced "typically high-handed behavior, another effort on the government's part to dictate to us important chapters from our own history."[10]

Cheyenne traditionalists, especially Laird Cometsevah, had another reason for locating the site in the shadow of the monument overlook on the Dawson ranch. Two decades earlier, Cometsevah had accompanied the Sacred Arrow Keeper, the tribe's most important spiritual leader, to Sand Creek. The Arrow Keeper consecrated the soil in the South Bend, making "Cheyenne earth" there. For Cometsevah, memories of that ritual loomed over the search: "Spiritually and religiously, [we] claimed that spot for the Cheyennes. I'm going to do everything I can to fulfill that ceremony. The Arrow Keeper wasn't wrong." Cometsevah's usually quiet voice rang as he insisted: "*I* wasn't wrong. That's exactly where the massacre happened. That's right where Chivington killed our people." In sum, Cometsevah had an enormous, albeit intangible, investment in his contention that Dawson's property had hosted the massacre. If it turned out that the Arrow Keeper had been wrong, that Cometsevah had been wrong, he might lose standing in the search process, credibility in future reparations claims, and perhaps even some of his cultural authority as a chief. He had to be right.[11]

As for oral histories, the Northern Cheyennes had not yet started collecting theirs. Luke and Steve Brady, along with their brother, Otto Braided Hair, still struggled to comply with traditional protocols before asking tribal elders to share their memories of the massacre. The NPS's compressed timeline threatened their efforts, but the Bradys refused to hurry. Recalling the chronology and that her tribe's elders still "hadn't shared their stories of Sand Creek," Mildred Red Cherries felt like she had been "stabbed in the back" when the NPS revealed its map. And because the NPS had ignored pertinent details from the Southern Cheyennes' oral histories, which had already been recorded, as well as traditional methods and the Arrow Keeper's claim to part of the Dawson ranch, Laird Cometsevah snapped, "They're calling our ancestors liars. They're discounting our whole history." He raged, "The Park Service folks gave their word they'd listen to us. We've got stacks of paper proving it. But they don't care about Cheyenne earth or whether our ancestors died or the stories our elders passed down from Sand Creek. And they don't care about their word when it comes to Indians."[12]

Cometsevah's accusation highlighted an issue that NPS personnel overlooked in the wake of the Denver meeting. The descendants, and the tribes they represented, were not exclusively a people of memory, steeped only in an oral culture. They also studied written history; they were well versed in the archival record. Cometsevah and Steve Brady, especially, had an encyclopedic knowledge of many of the documents relating to the massacre. Both men could recite passages from Governor Evans's fateful proclamations during summer 1864, from George Bent's memoir, and from the key treaties signposting the road to and from Sand Creek: Fort Laramie, Fort Wise, and the Little Arkansas. Both men also believed that across the nineteenth and twentieth centuries white authorities had repeatedly broken written promises to the Cheyennes. And both men were determined that the NPS would not be allowed to repeat that history during the Sand Creek search or after the memorial opened to the public. Accordingly, Brady and Cometsevah struggled to bind the NPS, using a series of written rather than oral agreements, to weigh tribal evidence prior to reaching any conclusions during the site study.[13]

Before writing the Sand Creek legislation, Senator Campbell had spoken with Brady and Cometsevah, the tribal leaders he deemed most influential on issues related to the massacre. Campbell learned that the Cheyenne descendants would cooperate with the NPS only if the agency incorporated tribal perspectives into its search. NPS officials then reassured Campbell that they were eager to collaborate with the tribes. Still wary because of historical precedent, elements of Campbell's legislation—along with parts of Executive Order No. 13804 and the National Historic Preservation Act—tied the NPS to the descendants and shaped the tribal representatives' sense of their own power during the process. Campbell's bill mandated, for instance, that the NPS "work in consultation with the" Cheyennes and Arapahos. Executive Order No. 13804 required that federal agencies, when dealing with indigenous people, partner with tribes on a government-to-government basis. And the preservation act stipulated that any time the NPS undertook a project that might affect "American Indian lands or properties of historic value to the tribes," the NPS had to consult with the relevant Native groups.[14]

Using these documents—rather than traditional practices or oral histories—as a foundation, the descendants later built more safeguards into their relationship with the NPS. When asked by the NPS to sign so-called cooperative agreements or memoranda of understanding for the search, tribal representatives balked. After consulting with their attorney, they insisted on inserting passages of restrictive language, clarifying the search process's intent and the relative power that participants would wield during the study. The NPS finally offered the descendants several written guarantees: it would weigh evidence gleaned from "methods of the tribes' choosing to help determine the site location"; it would "work to help achieve the goals of the Cheyenne and Arapaho with respect to the management and use of the site"; the "Cheyenne and Arapaho [people would] be a full partner in the project"; and it would make its "best efforts . . . to obtain the concurrence and signa-

ture of each Tribal Government on the location of the Massacre Site."
At the same time, the NPS hedged, noting, "the project is intended to
also be of benefit to all American people." Regardless, the descendants
believed that they had protected their interests, that their voices would
be heard. The NPS's draft map, though, seemed to signal that the federal government, as it had so often throughout the nation's history,
was once again reneging on written agreements forged with Native
people.[15]

That the NPS had concluded, no matter how tentatively, anything
about the site's location without consent from the tribal representatives
seemed to the Cheyennes to echo ugly episodes from the past. And that
NPS officials, faced with the descendants' ire, insisted that the disagreement was a misunderstanding rooted in Native traditionalism
compounded the Cheyenne delegates' outrage. Rick Frost believed that
the Cheyennes "had their oral traditions and their Arrow Keeper, who
came and consecrated the earth in the bend. And for them that was all
the evidence they needed about where the site was." But, Steve Brady
countered, the descendants also had written history, rather than just
memory and traditional cultural practices, on their side. Brady pointed
out that the Cheyennes relied on archival sources, including the Bent
maps, in addition to ethnographies and indigenous methods of gathering knowledge, to support their contention that the massacre had
taken place inside the Dawson South Bend. "Even then, they still don't
believe us," Brady said. "They don't believe Bent's map. Bent was there.
He was wounded. He had a white man's education. But still they don't
believe his map." In the end, this was the most infuriating thing for the
Cheyennes: the conflict had not emerged out of a clash of methodologies or incompatible epistemologies; the NPS had not chosen written
over oral sources, or Western science over Native traditions; the NPS
had instead chosen one map over a second map as its guide in producing a third map.[16]

The history of those first two maps and their makers, Samuel Bonsall and George Bent, exacerbated a tense situation following the site
location meeting. Bent was part of the Cheyenne tribe and a proud
member of the Crooked Lances, a military society. Working with James
Mooney, George Bird Grinnell, and George Hyde, he became one of
the most effective stewards of his tribe's cultural resources. Since its

publication, Bent and Hyde's *Life of George Bent* had served as a reference; for traditionalists, it remained an essential source of history and lore. Its sections on Sand Creek were especially influential for the descendants. Bent, after all, bucked conventional wisdom in Colorado and throughout the West, arguing that the bloodshed had been a massacre rather than a battle. He could credibly make that claim because he had been shot in the hip at Sand Creek and had barely escaped with his life. Through the years, his drawings also provided descendants with a guide to one of their most sacred sites. Bent mapped the tribe's history. And as time passed, and other links to the massacre disappeared, many Cheyennes mapped their identities onto Bent's drawings.[17]

No ethnographer or anthropologist ever interviewed Samuel Bonsall; no historian ever collaborated with him on a book about his life. His father was not a borderlands power broker, a renowned trade tycoon and liaison between federal authorities and tribal peoples; his mother was not an important cultural figure in her community, the daughter of a revered spiritual leader. Bonsall, unlike George Bent, lived most of his life in history's shadows. What scholars know of him are bits and pieces gleaned from his service record. He hailed from Indiana. Just four months after the start of the Civil War, when he was only twenty-two years old, he enlisted in the Union Army. He fought bravely in several battles before mustering out in spring 1866. He promptly rejoined the army, serving another six years in the West, until his commanding officer finally recommended that he resign his commission because of a drinking problem. As noted earlier, Bonsall mapped the massacre's location when he helped escort General William Tecumseh Sherman on a tour of western battlegrounds in June 1868. Bonsall then returned to Sand Creek, likely two years later, again combing the hallowed ground for human remains, including skulls that he shipped back east to the Army Medical Museum in Washington, DC.[18]

The NPS's reliance on Bonsall rather than Bent frustrated the Cheyennes, who focused on differences in the men's biographies, their relationships to Sand Creek, and their behavior in the years after the massacre. Bent was Cheyenne, Bonsall white. Bent was wounded by federal troops at Sand Creek but lived. He was both a victim and a survivor of the massacre. Even if Bonsall had served in the Civil War's eastern theater, more than a thousand miles away from Colorado when Chivington attacked Black Kettle's village, the descendants nevertheless believed that he had been in league with the perpetrators. Most of all, Bent produced his maps as a means of preserving tribal history and culture. Bonsall, by contrast, penned his diagram only after desecrating Cheyenne corpses that he found scattered on the killing field at Sand Creek. And he later returned, in the descendants' view recapitulating war crimes committed by some of Chivington's men at the massacre, when he plundered the human remains at Sand Creek for a second time, in 1870. Given that, Steve Brady waved aside Jerry Greene's insistence that Bonsall was the better source of the two mapmakers: "He [Greene] claims that he wants eyewitness testimony. Well, Bent was there. He had the scars to prove it. Bonsall only showed up years after the fact to pick at our ancestors' bodies, like a vulture."[19]

Laird Cometsevah, too, found it "insulting" that the person hailed for producing the NPS's "Rosetta Stone," the key to decoding the site mystery, had on more than one occasion defiled Cheyenne corpses. Cometsevah was especially stunned to learn that the NPS viewed such "depraved acts" as evidence of the mapmaker's credibility—one NPS report suggested that "the most compelling argument giving weight to Bonsall [was] the FACT that he collected skeletal remains on the site." Cometsevah could not forget that Colorado authorities had repeatedly used the mistreatment of white bodies as a pretext for ginning up a war against the Cheyennes in summer 1864. The mutilation of corpses symbolized the horror of the massacre. Bonsall—"a grave robber," in Cometsevah's words—had taken part in these "crimes against humanity." Here again, the ghosts of Sand Creek haunted the site search.[20]

Confronted with the NPS's defense of Bonsall, the descendants rejoined by recalling a series of atrocities committed in spring, summer, and fall 1864. At that time, Governor John Evans became increasingly unhinged about the threat Native people posed to white Coloradans. In part, Evans's fears emerged from the fact that federal troops were deployed elsewhere fighting the Civil War, leaving frontier settlers especially vulnerable to Indian attacks. Two years earlier, the Dakota Sioux, frustrated by years of treaty violations, had rebelled in Minnesota, killing hundreds of whites before the army crushed their uprising. With the Civil War ongoing, and the majority of Union soldiers fighting back east, the Dakota War cast a pall over Colorado in 1863-1864. Evans grew

especially alarmed after receiving intelligence stating that Sioux emissaries had approached several local tribes about forging an alliance in
fall 1863. He responded to these rumors by asking military authorities
to keep more troops in the vicinity. When that request did not work, he
sent desperate pleas to Secretary of War Edwin Stanton, warning that
a confederation "of several thousand warriors" waited nearby, "wild
savages" who might "sweep off our settlers." Evans intimated that the
blood of white Coloradans would be on Stanton's hands if the secretary failed to dispatch help.[21]

After writing to Stanton, Evans left for New York, where he lobbied
colleagues on the Union Pacific Railroad's board of directors to run track
through Colorado. But he worried that the territory's Native peoples
might complicate his development schemes. Indians represented an
impediment to progress in Evans's view. This perspective, shared widely
throughout the region, offered another reason to pacify or remove the
tribes. At the same time, President Lincoln hoped to bring Colorado
into the Union as a Republican state in 1864. More Republican votes
would improve the chances of legislation pending in Congress, as well
as Lincoln's own uncertain reelection prospects the following November. Evans, for his part, delighted in the idea of statehood; he longed to
serve as Colorado's first U.S. senator. But when officials paved the way
for statehood by calling for a constitutional convention in July 1864,
racial violence on the plains threatened the plan. In sum, economic as
well as political concerns impelled Evans toward Sand Creek.[22]

For the moment, though, most of Colorado's tribal peoples waited
on their reservations, struggling to survive the winter of 1863–1864 despite chronic food shortages and frequent disease outbreaks. Evans's
paranoia about Indians abated. But with spring's arrival his anxiety
returned, and Evans renewed his campaign for federal protection. He
soon discovered to his dismay that Samuel Curtis, the region's newly
minted military commander, rightly believed that the ongoing up-
heaval in Kansas represented a greater threat to the Union than did
bands of starving Indians conducting occasional attacks on outlying
white settlements. Evans raised the specter of the Dakota War, warning Curtis that Sioux bands were on the warpath. Curtis coolly replied
that he appreciated the information but needed to focus his attention,
and troop strength, elsewhere. Curtis maintained that posture until

rumors of livestock theft began spreading in April, signaling that renewed trouble might be imminent as the Cheyennes and Arapahos
launched spring raids.[23]

With troops fanning out to keep the peace, hostilities became more
rather than less likely. Skirmishes, including a brutal fight on April 12,
1864, at Fremont's Orchard, soon followed. Governor Evans responded by
peppering General Curtis with missives about the hazards of inaction.
And though the plains remained quieter than they had the previous
spring, fear gripped Colorado, among both settlers and Cheyennes,
who, an officer in the field reported, were "very much alarmed and appeared to be very anxious to remain on good terms with whites." It was
not to be. On May 3, soldiers under Major Jacob Downing attacked a
Cheyenne camp near Cedar Bluffs. Downing crowed to John Chivington: "I believe now it is but the commencement of war with this tribe,
which must result in their extermination." When Curtis received news
of the fight, he wrote to Evans, imploring him to contain further hostilities, as "the fate of the nation depends much on the campaigns of this
season against the Great Rebellion." But just two weeks after that, Lieutenant George Eayre's men killed Lean Bear and Star, two peace chiefs,
who rode out to parley with the federal troops. Many of the surviving
Cheyenne witnesses vowed revenge. Governor Evans had lost control of
the situation.[24]

On June 11, with chaos stalking Colorado, a ranch foreman named
Nathan Ward Hungate worked with another hired hand (recorded only
by his surname, Miller) in the pastures of Van Wormer's property. The
ranch stood approximately thirty miles southeast of Denver, near the
banks of Box Elder Creek. The landscape rolls gently in that part of
Colorado, and the plains usually remain bright green early in the summer. As Hungate and Miller tended the stock they supervised, a column
of smoke billowed above one of the ranch buildings, catching their eye.
Hungate dropped his work and sprinted toward the fire, thinking of his
family back at the ranch house. Miller dashed off in another direction,
looking for help. When neighbors arrived on the scene, they found
Hungate, his wife, and their two daughters, one four years old, the other
an infant, dead. Some accounts suggested that Hungate's wife had been
raped. Because the corpses had been scalped and mutilated, the onlookers assumed that Native people were responsible for the murders.

The crowd then carried the broken bodies to Denver, where they lay "in a box side by side, the two children between their parents."[25]

Equal parts public memorial and cautionary tale, this gruesome display stood on one of the city's main streets, inciting violence by playing off the fears of captivated spectators. An incredulous newcomer to Colorado, a chemistry professor just arrived from Brown University in Providence, Rhode Island, wrote to his wife, "all the people of the town with a few honorable exceptions went to see them [the bodies]." As news of the murders circulated throughout the area, terrified settlers, fearing an all-out assault from a confederation of belligerent tribes, poured into Denver from the plains to the east. The Hungates' ruined corpses became the centerpiece of a community gripped by collective panic. When rumors of additional Indian attacks spread, they tipped the city over the edge. On June 15, 1864, reports surfaced that a force of Indians, "three thousand strong," stood poised to strike Denver. "Every bell in the city sounded," and "men, women, and children pushed through the streets . . . literally crazed with fear." With armed gangs on patrol, Denverites hunkered down for a long night spent waiting for an attack that never arrived. The next day, it turned out that the army of hostile Indians had actually been drovers, their cattle kicking up dust on the way to market.[26]

Governor Evans, overmatched in the wake of the Hungate murders, redoubled his efforts to convince General Curtis to send a "regiment" to protect the city, implying that the conspiracy Evans had anticipated for months had finally claimed its first victims. As evidence, he pointed to the "murdered and scalped bodies brought in today." There would be more corpses if help did not arrive soon, the governor warned. Absent credible evidence, he blamed the Cheyennes. In fact, a small party of Northern Arapahos, seeking revenge against Van Wormer for a perceived injustice from the previous year, had likely committed the murders. Regardless, Evans's paranoia and politics combined, as he assembled unrelated violent episodes into a jigsaw puzzle depicting a coordinated threat. Only federal troops could save the day, he argued. Evans then imposed a curfew, organized the militia, and wrote to William Dole, commissioner of Indian affairs, suggesting that Colorado's friendly tribes should be concentrated in places of safety. Finally, he asked for permission to raise a regiment of hundred-day volunteers devoted to fighting Indians. Evans would not abandon any of these schemes, or his paranoia, until after the massacre.[27]

In the event, John Chivington rallied his men on November 29, 1864, by recalling the fate of the Hungates and whites taken captive on the plains the previous summer. The Colorado troops exacted vengeance by committing atrocities against the Cheyennes and Arapahos. In the wake of the bloodletting, when Chivington's men returned to Denver, they paraded through town with grisly mementos from Sand Creek. "Cheyenne scalps," the *Rocky Mountain News* reported, "are getting as thick here now as toads in Egypt. Every body has got one, and is anxious to get another to send east." Two area theaters mounted productions in which "trophies of the big fight at Sand Creek" served as props. One of the plays, *The Battle of Sand Creek,* was the first reenactment of the carnage in Colorado. As for the bodies left unburied on the bloody ground, they froze in winter's cold. Years later, Lieutenant Samuel Bonsall despoiled those remains.[28]

More than a century after the massacre, the descendants remembered how their ancestors' bodies had been treated. Several of the tribal delegates to the site search also served as Native American Graves Protection and Repatriation Act (NAGPRA) representatives. NAGPRA became federal law in 1990, capping a long struggle by Native activists who wanted human remains, along with other sacred materials, returned to their tribes. Repositories, ranging from archeology departments on university campuses to the Smithsonian Institution, had until then often stored or displayed such items around the nation. These artifacts were ugly reminders of the years around the turn of the twentieth century, when white observers had considered Indians a "vanishing race." Anthropologists who hoped to preserve evidence of these endangered people began collecting indigenous antiquities at that time. NAGPRA would allow the affected tribes to reclaim their cultural patrimony. Some of the descendants had already spent years struggling to repatriate the remains of several victims slaughtered at the massacre. They hoped that eventually there would be a cemetery at the Sand Creek site, a place where their "ancestors could finally rest, easing their spirits."[29]

After the Denver meeting, body parts scattered across the United States became another painful link between the massacre and the site search. When General Sherman visited Sand Creek in 1868, he asked his subordinates, Samuel Bonsall among them, to "hunt all over the battleground" for trophies, including human remains. And when Bonsall later returned to the site, he retrieved at least two more skulls, which he then shipped back east. Experts at the Army Medical Museum studied those remains in an effort to understand the impact of munitions on Native bodies. The crania next made their way to the Smithsonian. There they waited, in the bowels of the National Anthropological Archives, stripped of humanity, known only by accession numbers. The skulls that Bonsall removed from the massacre site were used not just to improve the army's ability to kill more Native Americans, but also by anthropologists, practicing "racial science", who claimed that Indians were of inferior stock. This history did not make Jerry Greene's claims about Bonsall's reliability, or Doug Scott's boasts about the unassailable nature of archeological evidence, more compelling for the descendants.[30]

As the dispute over competing cartographies intensified, most of the NPS team members maintained that they had done nothing wrong. Quite the contrary, they insisted, they had succeeded where others had failed: the NPS, using an interdisciplinary toolkit and working within a circumscribed schedule, had pinpointed the massacre site. Nobody involved with the project would have disputed that broad contention. But because of the ongoing conflict surrounding the NPS's map, a narrower question still threatened the project: Where had Black Kettle's people camped on the morning of November 29, 1864? Inside or outside what the site searchers knew as the Dawson South Bend? That query, and the history and politics attached to it, left Rick Frost worried that the Cheyennes might scuttle the entire initiative. Frost and his colleagues struggled throughout winter 1999–2000 to craft a compromise that would keep the disaffected descendants in the fold.[31]

It would not be easy, because the Cheyennes preferred no memorial at all to one built upon the ruins of their cultural and political sovereignty. From the first, the tribal representatives had explained that they would not participate in the search if their voices were not going to be heard. And the "village controversy," as people began calling it, suggested that the NPS would not, in the end, let the descendants' Sand Creek stories guide the process. Instead, the NPS wanted to narrate key parts of the massacre from the perspective of Bonsall, an officer in the U.S. Army and a man who had taken part in what some of the Cheyennes labeled "the imperialist projects of westward expansion and forced Indian removal." For all of the talk of healing that surrounded the memorialization process, this seemed to the descendants more like the NPS rubbing salt into old wounds. Consequently, the disagreement over Black Kettle's village devolved into personal attacks, with some of Cheyenne representatives to the search accusing NPS personnel, most often Doug Scott and Jerry Greene, of recapitulating elements of the massacre itself, albeit "with documents rather than bullets" this time. It was, Frost remembered, the most difficult moment in the memorialization process.[32]

The NPS responded with a plan to placate the Cheyenne descendants and maintain the search's integrity: its *Site Location Study*, the publication associated with the project, would suggest creating a memorial large enough to encompass all of the competing theories about the location of Black Kettle's village. The boundaries of the proposed historic site would stretch for miles across the Kiowa County countryside, including the Dawson South Bend, the location of the artifact finds, and chunks of the Bowens' property. With just six months left before the NPS's deadline to share its findings with Congress, Christine Whitacre started writing. She would have to weave together methodological loose threads—the archival investigations, the oral histories, the tribes' traditional cultural practices, and the archeology—as well as provide a brief history of the search process, an environmental impact assessment of the historic site proposal, and an abstract of the public's response to the NPS's inchoate plan. Under the best of circumstances, it would have been a daunting task. But in this case, Whitacre also had to try to reassure the Cheyenne descendants that the NPS had taken their views seriously. Her effort would be further complicated by the fact that the Northern Cheyennes had not yet started collecting their ethnographies, suggesting that their elders' Sand Creek stories would have little bearing on Whitacre's work.[33]

The blowback Whitacre encountered as she assembled the *Site Location Study* demonstrated how the village controversy had splintered the

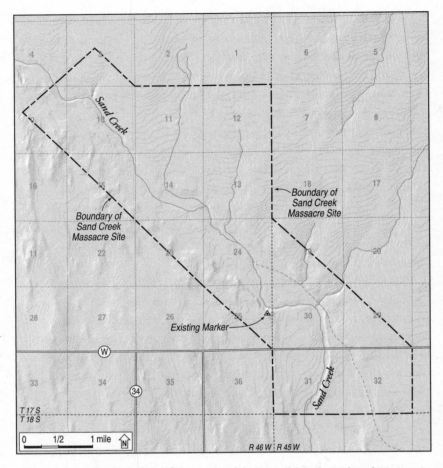

Boundary of the Sand Creek Massacre site. *(Adapted from the Sand Creek Massacre Special Resource Study, U.S. Dept. of the Interior, National Park Service.)*

fragile search. Problems reached beyond federal-tribal friction and into the NPS's relations with the State of Colorado, which to that point had typically been "cordial." By challenging George Bent's Sand Creek story, the NPS reinforced David Halaas's already strong ties with the descendants while forcing Susan Collins, the state's other representative to the memorialization project, to choose sides. Collins would have to back the federal government or the descendants.[34]

Susan Collins received a PhD in anthropology from the University of Colorado–Boulder before becoming Colorado's state archeologist.

In that capacity, she helped administer the State Historical Fund, the agency that had granted Dick Ellis the money needed to conduct the first site search. When the NPS later began looking for Sand Creek, Collins saw Doug Scott as a friend and colleague. But she could not escape the sense that the NPS seemed more confident about its conclusions than the data merited. In a long, diplomatic letter to Christine Whitacre, Collins and David Halaas outlined their concerns. They supported the NPS's proposed site boundaries while suggesting that the report they had seen demonstrated a "level of specific knowledge that is not fully supported by" the available evidence. Especially when it came to the location of Black Kettle's village, Collins and Halaas believed, it made sense to project doubt rather than certitude. They also wondered why the NPS had rushed to judgment. On the one hand, the search had to be finished on deadline. On the other hand, they noted, "Greene and Scott wrote their reports without reference to the Cheyenne and Arapaho oral histories."[35]

The NPS team members knew by then that their interactions with the Cheyennes had strained to the breaking point. And they suspected that David Halaas's loyalties lay with the descendants and George Bent, the subject of his book, rather than his colleagues at the NPS or the Colorado Historical Society. Looking back, Halaas concurred: "If you're caught in between them like I was, you have to decide: what do you think? And I was with the Cheyennes." Of the NPS's overconfidence during the village controversy, he suggested, "you can disagree with Laird Cometsevah about any number of things. But when you start saying your theory is ironclad, that you've got science and history on your side, well, what are you doing?" He concluded, "And not to understand the implication of that kind of claim, and not be more sensitive about making it just shocked me." At the time, Halaas still worked with the descendants on the memory fight unfolding on the capitol steps in Denver. At his, Laird Cometsevah's, and Steve Brady's urging, the state legislature had agreed to rescind its resolution removing Sand Creek from the list of battles on the Civil War memorial. Colorado would reinterpret rather than erase the statue's text. But even though the NPS understood Halaas's identification with the Cheyennes, the letter from him and Susan Collins suggested that the federal agency had alienated some of its most important allies.[36]

Rick Frost replied to Collins and Halaas with a point-by-point rebuttal stretching across seven pages. He defended the NPS's methods and conclusions. On the most controversial point, the placement of Black Kettle's village, Frost did not give an inch. Collins and Halaas wrote back, pointing out that there was no reason to dig in about a "relatively minor disagreement." After all, following the archeological survey Doug Scott had allowed that there was still more work to be done at the site. Given that, Collins and Halaas suggested, the NPS had a clear path out of the village controversy: allow for the possibility that Black Kettle's encampment had been larger than the draft map indicated. If the village had actually stretched from the location of the artifact concentration into the Dawson South Bend, where Bent had mapped it, all the searchers might be satisfied. Collins and Halaas concluded by dangling the possibility of consensus in front of Frost: "In short, we agree with the Massacre Monument boundaries proposed, congratulate you on the 1999 discoveries, respectfully suggest that the village extent may be considerably greater than that shown on current NPS maps, and encourage continuing research to develop an interpretive plan." Still the NPS team members were not ready to concede the key points in the controversy, and so they continued preparing to publish their *Site Location Study*.[37]

In the meantime, the NPS received backing from an unexpected source: the Northern Arapahos. About a month after the NPS unveiled its map, Ben Ridgely, cochair of the tribe's governing council, wrote to Rick Frost: "The Northern Arapaho Business Council supports the documents of Dr. Doug Scott and Jerry Greene, and findings of the National Park Service in regard to the Site Location." The Ridgelys later explained that they had made their choice after "looking at the data objectively." Because both Ben and Gail Ridgely were educators who "respected science," they noted, they had concluded that the NPS had the facts on its side. As far as Frost and Christine Whitacre were concerned, the Ridgelys' reasoning mattered less than did their endorsement. The NPS finally had a tribal backer. But James Doyle, Senator Campbell's staffer, realized that the Northern Arapahos' letter also reaffirmed that no single collective memory of Sand Creek bound all of the descendants. "You would think that because all four tribes had people descended from the massacre that they would have had the most commonality in the whole search process," Doyle observed, "but really they didn't." Dividing the tribal representatives within the turmoil of the village controversy, he fretted, might have disastrous consequences moving forward. As it turned out, events would bear out Doyle's concerns.[38]

If the Northern Arapahos' support of the NPS highlighted the varied nature of tribal memories of Sand Creek, Ben Ridgely's letter also suggested that the descendants' recollections of the massacre were captive to politics. By fall 1999, the Ridgelys had wearied of what they labeled the Cometsevahs' "sensationalism" and "hostility." Several times during the search, the Cometsevahs insisted that there had been no Arapahos at the massacre. "The Northern Arapahos had nothing whatsoever to do with Sand Creek," they stated flatly. Colleen Cometsevah also claimed that the Ridgelys had "no real oral histories because their people weren't even there." The Cometsevahs even suggested that the Arapahos had no historical identity distinct from the Cheyennes. The former had always orbited around the latter, the Cometsevahs said. The Arapahos were "pests," Laird and Colleen Cometsevah charged. These claims infuriated the Ridgelys. And when Laird Cometsevah thundered that the Northern Arapahos had "betrayed their heritage by siding with the government," the slight deepened the Ridgelys' conviction that their interests more closely aligned with the NPS than with the Southern Cheyennes.[39]

The Ridgelys did not allow what they saw as unprovoked attacks on their tribe's historical and cultural legitimacy to stand. Rather than pointing to their recently collected Sand Creek ethnographies, though, they worked with Tom Meier, a historian and friend, to produce a seventeen-page annotated bibliography documenting the Arapahos' presence at the massacre. Some of their sources originated with Cheyennes. For example, several times in his correspondence with George Hyde, George Bent mentioned Arapahos who had been at Sand Creek. That convinced David Halaas. "I believe the Arapahos were there," he said. "I have to, because my guy [Bent] says they were." Halaas even tried to persuade the Cometsevahs, pointing to "document after document," but to no avail. Steve Brady also accepted that the Arapahos had suffered at Sand Creek. Once again forswearing oral histories in favor of the documentary record, Brady cited the Treaty of the Little Arkansas, which mentions the Arapaho and Cheyenne tribes. Even

Article 6, Brady conceded, applied to "certain bands" of the two tribes. Because of that, he said, "we have to be inclusive with all of the tribes. We have to work together." Still the Cometsevahs would not budge— because, as ever, they too looked back to details of Article 6.[40]

On October 12, 1865, emissaries of the U.S. government, including William Bent and Kit Carson, met on the banks of the Little Arkansas River in south-central Kansas with Black Kettle's Cheyennes and Little Raven's Arapahos. In prepared remarks, Little Raven revealed what he had learned from Governor Evans's misuse of the Treaty of Fort Wise: the chief insisted that future agreements between his people and white authorities would bind only the signatories. Black Kettle then looked back to Sand Creek, admitting that he had been guilty of hubris for thinking that he could forge a lasting peace with white settlers. "[My] shame is as big as the earth," he mourned. Two days later, the parties signed a treaty guaranteeing "perpetual peace" between them. Written at a time when the federal government acknowledged its culpability in the massacre, Article 6 of the document "repudiate[d] the gross and wanton outrages perpetrated against certain bands of Cheyenne and Arapaho Indians" at Sand Creek. Those "Indians were at peace with the United States, and under its flag," and so Washington wanted "to make some suitable reparation for the injuries then done." Restitution would include both land and other material compensation for survivors who had lost loved ones or property during the slaughter. But the treaty lasted only two years (even by the U.S. government's standards, that span represented a loose definition of "perpetual") and federal officials made good on few of the promises contained therein, including Article 6.[41]

For nearly a century after that, the reparations promised in Article 6 taunted the Sand Creek descendants, another broken vow punctuating the story of federal-tribal relations following the massacre. Then, in the early 1960s, the U.S. government began negotiating with both branches of the Arapaho and Cheyenne tribes to extinguish outstanding land claims from the treaties of Fort Laramie, Fort Wise, the Little Arkansas, and Medicine Lodge. With the case proceeding before the Indian Claims Commission toward a settlement—resulting in payments of roughly $3 million to the Northern Arapahos, $4 million to the Northern Cheyennes, and $15 million to the Cheyenne and Arapaho Tribes—federal officials realized what many Sand Creek descendants had long known: that Article 6 of the Little Arkansas treaty promised compensation not to the tribes, but to specific individuals, those Cheyenne and Arapaho people who had lost loved ones or property at the massacre. Several Southern Cheyennes, all descendants of Chief White Antelope, began pursuing the reparations that their forebears had been guaranteed in 1865.[42]

The group actually had its origins in another struggle over Sand Creek memory. In 1938, curators at the Laboratory of Anthropology (currently known as the School of Advanced Research) in Santa Fe, New Mexico, put up an exhibit featuring an 1850s-vintage Navajo textile, renowned for its extraordinarily fine craftsmanship and vivid colors, known as the Chief White Antelope blanket. A soldier in the 3rd Colorado Regiment had taken the weaving from the body of the dead chief at Sand Creek. After wending its way through multiple owners, the blanket finally arrived in Santa Fe, where the Laboratory of Anthropology displayed it, earning critical acclaim. At that time, Kish Hawkins, a descendent of White Antelope, began doing research at the Oklahoma Historical Society, before deciding to try to recover his family's property. Officials at the Laboratory of Anthropology, though, maintained that they had acquired the artifact legitimately. They refused to return it to Hawkins. Hawkins then joined forces with Sam Dicke, another of White Antelope's living descendants. The two of them, with help from an Oklahoma City attorney named Bliss Kelly, worked together on the issue until Hawkins died sometime in the mid-1950s.[43]

While looking into the provenance of the White Antelope blanket, Hawkins and Dicke familiarized themselves with the Treaty of the Little Arkansas. And as they sparred across years with the Laboratory of Anthropology, the two men opened a second front in their memory fight. In 1949, they convinced their congressman, Toby Morris, to sponsor legislation clarifying the jurisdiction in which an Article 6 reparations claim would be heard. The bill languished in committee and, after Morris tried to reinvigorate it in 1953 and 1957, it died without ever having come to a vote. The Cheyenne descendants renewed their efforts in the early 1960s, part of their tribe's huge settlement with the federal government. After chartering an organization known as the Sand Creek Descendants Association, the group began lobbying John Jarman, their new congressional representative, to introduce legislation to fulfill the government's obligations under Article 6. But Jarman's bill, like Morris's, never made it to a vote in the House of Representatives. The claim remained open.[44]

In the early 1970s, Laird Cometsevah picked up the quest. Cometsevah recalled worrying that "young people were losing touch with the Cheyenne way of life," so he banded together with a group of other traditionalists to preserve their tribe's culture. A few years later, Chief Cometsevah turned his attention to Article 6 reparations. He continued working with other traditional people, while his wife, Colleen Cometsevah, began assembling a vast genealogical archive: boxes and boxes of files establishing the lineal descendancy of contemporary Cheyennes to Sand Creek's victims. By the time the NPS search started in the late 1990s, the Cometsevahs had spent more than two decades pursuing an Article 6 claim. They saw a Sand Creek national historic site as the thin edge of a wedge: memorializing the massacre, they hoped, would lay the groundwork for forcing the government to acknowledge their open treaty claim.[45]

The Cheyenne descendants saw reparations and memorialization as intertwined, part of a broader project of revitalizing their tribes' sovereignty and traditional culture. Colleen Cometsevah suggested, "Every time the Cheyennes signed a treaty we wound up with the short end of the stick. The reservation got smaller and smaller, and white people tried to destroy our way of life." The antidote for that poisonous history could be found in Article 6 and the massacre site: "Now all we ask is that the government make good on its promises after Sand Creek. Protecting Sand Creek is part of it. Reparations are the other part." Steve Brady agreed. Recalling his tribe's decision to extinguish land claims with the United States in the mid-1960s, Brady's jaw set: "Our people didn't understand the long-term implications of the settlement. And we still suffer as a result today. We signed away our treaty claims— with the exception of Sand Creek. That is the remaining flicker we have, a flame of hope." In the early 1990s, when the Northern Cheyennes tapped Brady to preside over their descendants' committee, he hoped to pile fuel atop that fire. Along with repatriating their ancestors' remains and preserving the Sand Creek site, the Northern Cheyennes, like their southern kin, would seek Article 6 reparations.[46]

So when they faced off with the Ridgelys, the Cometsevahs were not merely playing a high-stakes game of misery poker. They were policing the historical record and protecting their cultural authority in advance of a planned reparations suit. Because such a suit would hinge on the plaintiffs' ability to demonstrate lineal descendancy to victims of the massacre, it seemed to the Cometsevahs that they had to protect their own credibility as a way of safeguarding their prospective claim. Once they announced publicly that no Arapahos had been at Sand Creek, they could not turn back, even if their assertions split the tribal representatives, leaving them vulnerable to what Steve Brady called the NPS's "divide-and-conquer" tactics. "The U.S. government has always played that game," Brady said with a grimace, "playing Indians off against each other."[47]

But as it happened, divisions between the descendants ended up undercutting the NPS's interests. The Northern Arapaho representatives typically did not focus on reparations; they saw memorialization as their principal goal. "We wanted a historic site to honor our ancestors," Gail Ridgely recalled, hinting that invocations of Article 6 endangered the search. The Ridgelys also increasingly resented being called traitors by the Cometsevahs. By January 2000, they were so angry that they walked out of meetings if they believed the Cometsevahs had insulted them. Coincidentally, Rick Frost decided at that time to update Senator Campbell about the NPS's preliminary conclusions. Frost's letter focused on the prospective historic site's expansive boundaries, skirting the village controversy by noting that the search team had "not yet fully concurred on the precise locations" of some of the massacre's "core features." Frost then suggested that as the study wound down, "we intend to sort out and resolve by agreement any differences which may arise regarding such precise locations." The Ridgelys, surprisingly, refused to sign the letter. They did not want their names on a document suggesting unity within the search team. Only after Frost implored them to reconsider did the Ridgelys comply with his request.[48]

The Cheyennes' emphasis on reparations placed Senator Campbell in an awkward position. He believed that the descendants deserved restitution for the abuses at Sand Creek. Recalling broken promises in the Treaty of the Little Arkansas, he suggested, "I'm supportive of giving reparations." Nonetheless, he wondered how Congress would determine who should receive payment more than a century after the fact. Pointing to the approximately $1.6 billion that the federal government had recently meted out to families of Japanese Americans interned during World War II, the senator explained that eligibility in that instance had been clear-cut. But even then, there had been controversy, as the internees' case reopened long-simmering debates about reparations for the descendants of African American slaves. "Where do you draw the line?" Campbell asked. Considering the political realities, he answered his own question: "When it comes time to get Sand Creek reparations passed in the Senate," it would be "a nonstarter." He then instructed James Doyle, his liaison to the search team, to disentangle the process of memorialization from an Article 6 claim. "Reparations is a separate issue," Campbell insisted, warning that confusing that goal with memorialization would complicate the prospects of any legislation creating a national historic site.[49]

On the morning of February 9, 2000, Rick Frost, hoping finally to move beyond the village controversy, waited for another consultation meeting to start. But the question of reparations threatened to derail the process yet again. Representatives from the NPS, the State of Colorado, and the tribes arrived in Billings, Montana, approximately a hundred miles west of the Northern Cheyenne Reservation, where Luke Brady and Alexa Roberts were compiling the tribe's recently collected oral histories. The consultation meeting's agenda included a preliminary discussion of how the Sand Creek site would be managed—assuming Congress authorized its establishment as a unit of the National Park System. With that contentious issue already on the docket, the tension mounted further because of lingering bad feelings surrounding the NPS's draft map of the village site and the widening rift between the Southern Cheyenne and Northern Arapaho descendants. Then, as the search team members began trailing into the hotel conference room, both Laird Cometsevah and Steve Brady noticed that a newcomer, Homer Flute, apparently intended to join the meeting.[50]

In the early 1990s, Flute and Cometsevah worked together on the issue of reparations. As time passed, though, Cometsevah decided that Flute was a "fraud" whose bad judgment concerning who qualified as a descendent—in other words, who would be eligible for compensation under the Little Arkansas treaty's provisions—would doom any Article 6 claim. Flute, for his part, considered Cometsevah "arrogant" and believed he defined descendancy too narrowly. Cometsevah, Flute argued, focused excessively on cultural politics and blood purity when considering eligibility for reparations. From Flute's perspective, Cometsevah's insistence that only full-blooded Cheyennes should receive funds from an Article 6 payout meant that he was not representing "all of the descendants," including some Northern and Southern Arapahos. Such a contention rankled Cometsevah, whose research and public pronouncements, as noted earlier, suggested that no Arapahos had been at the massacre. At the same time, Flute believed that Cometsevah worried only about "Cheyenne traditional [people]" at the expense of other deserving descendants. Years before the site search started, the two men had parted ways, forming competing organizations to pursue an Article 6 settlement.[51]

Laird Cometsevah and Steve Brady treated Homer Flute's unexpected arrival in Billings as an opportunity to kill two birds with one stone. First, they would seize the moment to reassert their centrality in the search, reminding Rick Frost that without the Cheyenne descendants' cooperation, the process could not move forward. Second, Homer Flute would learn again that he stood on the outside looking in when it came to preserving the Sand Creek site (Bill Dawson, remember, had turned Flute away from his ranch nearly two years earlier). Cometsevah and Brady explained to Frost that Flute should not be allowed to enter the meeting room. Flustered by Flute's claims of cultural authority—he was a massacre descendant, after all—Frost replied that the gathering was a matter of public record and open to all comers. Cometsevah and Brady then pointed to Senator Campbell's legislation, noting that they were the official Cheyenne representatives to the search, and that the NPS had an obligation to work with them and them only. Either Flute had to leave or they would. Still uncertain, Frost announced that he would call an NPS lawyer. Brady, chortling, remembered: "So he talked to his lawyer, or maybe he talked to himself in a broom closet—I don't know. But he came back ten or fifteen minutes later and patted me on the back. 'You know what?' he said. 'My lawyer agrees with you. Homer Flute can't be here.'" With that, Flute left and the meeting proceeded.[52]

The Cheyennes' attorney, Steve Chestnut, believed that his clients had made a crucial stand. "It was big," Chestnut noted with a smile.

Moving ahead, he recalled, as the NPS team members decided important issues, including finalizing the historic site's capacious boundaries, they "seemed like they just didn't want to tangle with the Cheyennes." Joe Big Medicine, a Southern Cheyenne Sand Creek representative, agreed: "We showed Rick Frost and them that we wouldn't let them push us around. We'd push back if we had to." So in early 2000, the memorialization process remained in tatters: the Southern Cheyenne and Northern Arapaho descendants were not speaking because of the latter's ostensible apostasy during the village controversy and the former's insistence that no Arapahos had been present at the massacre; all of the Native people involved in the process, except the Ridgelys, believed the NPS had betrayed them; the NPS team thought the Cheyenne descendants were acting in bad faith; the State of Colorado's representatives believed that the NPS had misread some of the evidence turned up during the archeological investigations; and local proprietors in Kiowa County, Bill Dawson and Chuck and Sheri Bowen especially, were preparing to flex their muscles.[53]

In the months after that, as the descendants continued preparing progress reports on their oral history projects, the NPS oversaw several additional consultation meetings in Oklahoma, Montana, Wyoming, and Colorado. These gatherings offered the tribal representatives a final opportunity to provide the NPS with feedback and the public its first chance to comment on the search results. On March 22, 2000, the NPS convened with both the Northern and Southern Cheyenne and the Southern Arapaho descendants—the Northern Arapahos, still wary of the Cometsevahs, had chosen to meet with the NPS the previous week. The gathering unfolded much as others had over the previous year and a half; by that time, it seemed everyone involved in the search knew their roles by rote. The Cheyennes railed about Black Kettle's misplaced village. The NPS defended itself by pointing to the boundary compromise. Then everyone went their separate ways. A bit more than a month after that, Laird Cometsevah fired off yet another broadside aimed at the NPS. In a letter to Rick Frost, Cometsevah reiterated that he wanted "to go on record as in total disagreement on said location of the campsite, which is located one and a half miles north of Dawson's South Bend." Pointing back to George Bent's maps, Cometsevah insisted, "the correct location of the campsite and sandpits [should be] within Dawson's South Bend." The NPS then turned its attention to its obligation to solicit feedback from the public before adding new units to the National Park System.[54]

The NPS's outreach efforts—press releases, a direct-mail campaign, a website, and a series of open houses—yielded responses from thirty-two states and the District of Columbia, with nearly half of those replies coming from within Colorado. The stacks of comments heralded future triumphs and a number of challenges still facing the effort to commemorate the massacre. Nearly two-thirds of respondents believed that the federal government should create a Sand Creek Massacre National Historic Site, as opposed to less than one-tenth of commenters who called for no further action at all. Nearly 75 percent of those who favored a historic site hoped that the affected tribes would own the property with the NPS managing it. Many of these responses pointed to open questions of recompense, suggesting that Indian peoples had been displaced from the land in question and thus should be allowed to return to it: "It is only right that the tribes should own the property since it is stained with the innocent blood of their people." Several other commenters acknowledged that while the federal government had the resources and expertise necessary to operate a historic site, only tribal ownership could guarantee that the hallowed ground would be treated with proper respect.[55]

As for the memorial, replies looked forward and backward, focusing on honoring victims of the violence, healing wounds between white and Native peoples, and ensuring that something like the massacre would never happen again. "Sand Creek is a holy place," one comment suggested, "a link to another time, to the spirits of their ancestors, and honoring that site as a National Historic Site not only shows reverence for the role played in our history by native people and remorse for a great wrong but also affirms a commitment to see that such tragedies not play out again." Others noted that whites had a responsibility to confront the most horrific episodes from the nation's history before true healing could begin: "The United States must face its past and recognize it, no matter how tragic." Put another way: "the story needs to be told." Or, more poetically: "Because ignorance thrives in darkness, shine a light on past wrongs and there is more hope for the future." At the same time, many of the responses focused on the meaning of Sand Creek not for the dominant culture, but for indigenous people: "This project is for tribal people and ancestors lost." Because of that, the descendants, several people suggested, should have special access to the site for ceremonial purposes.[56]

Although the vast majority of respondents supported creating a national historic site, a small minority raised red flags. Screeds about the perils of left-leaning revisionism cropped up next to warnings about Kiowa County's deep-seated hostility to federal authority. Several comments suggested that it might be appropriate to commemorate the massacre, but not if such an undertaking meant diverting property away from agricultural use: "a smaller memorial would be adequate"; "it is way too much land"; "using the larger acreage for this historic site is quite out of reason." Other skeptics worried that federally funded political correctness would run amok at the historic site. "Enough is enough," one offended observer insisted. "There was plenty of injustice to go around. But asking the taxpayers to pay for an expensive memorial because it is presently popular is not where we need to spend our money." As ever in southeastern Colorado, for many people government was the problem. "You must understand," wrote one aspiring John Galt, "that the words 'Federal Government' are not some of the most endearing and confidence inspiring in Kiowa County." Another advocate of property rights railed, "I think the United States Government needs to leave the private lands alone. . . . These lands belong to the people and it is about time we say 'NO MORE!' Washington, D.C. GET OUT of Colorado and STAY OUT!" With local whites as well as the tribal representatives deeply distrustful of the federal government, the NPS had its work cut out for it.[57]

Having just finished an eighteen-month sprint, Rick Frost and his colleagues were exhausted. But they had no time to rest. The deadline for their report to Congress loomed only months ahead. With the search team still bitterly divided, Christine Whitacre faced pressure to produce a document that would satisfy all comers—or at least avoid stoking additional conflict. What to do in such a moment? Throw a party, of course. On June 8, 2000, the searchers gathered in Denver for a final consultation meeting. They reviewed the public comments and hammered out some unresolved details for the site study. In a gesture of goodwill, the NPS then served everyone dinner. The NPS team would break bread with the Cheyennes, who would sit side by side with the Northern Arapahos, who would put aside their bruised feelings for the evening. The NPS intended the meal as a celebration of the search's central achievement: finding the Sand Creek site. At the appointed hour, the team members gathered at a huge U-shaped table. Trays arrived. Then a pall settled over the room. Everyone gulped down food before going their separate ways. The NPS had planned a gala but instead had hosted something like a wake. When it was over, it was time to get back to the work of documenting the results of the memorialization effort to that point.[58]

Stretching across nearly 550 pages, the two lavishly illustrated volumes of the NPS's published report on the search are themselves monuments to the politics of memory surrounding Sand Creek. Christine Whitacre, who either compiled or wrote most of the document, found herself facing competing mandates: reconciling sometimes incompatible theories born of a grab bag of methodologies; mollifying the Cheyenne descendants, who, in the wake of the village controversy, fumed that the U.S. government once again had run roughshod over their political and cultural sovereignty; reiterating that Arapaho people had indeed been present at the massacre; tiptoeing through the minefield of unresolved Article 6 reparations; reassuring proprietors in Kiowa County, ranchers often hostile to federal authority, that the NPS would not seize their land; demonstrating to Congress that, because of its historical significance, the Sand Creek site merited inclusion in the National Park System; and finally, satisfying those same lawmakers that the NPS had found the killing field. The document, therefore, is built atop a bedrock of certainty, but its greatest virtue is its flexibility, expressed through a willingness to tolerate doubt. Whitacre acknowledged that when narrating a story as complex as the massacre's, clashing interpretations are not only unavoidable but also useful reminders of deeper conflicts embedded in the nation's history.[59]

In the *Site Location Study*, volume 1 of the *Sand Creek Massacre Project*, Whitacre balanced the relative weight of the evidence gathered during the search. Laughing, she recalled the challenge: "We were going to go where the evidence took us." And "based on the preponderance of evidence, we'd figure out where the site was." But as she began writing, she found herself thinking, "That just doesn't work. Because 'preponderance of evidence'?

Whose evidence? That was really what it came down to in the site study." Whitacre chose to explain the project's interdisciplinary research design, outline the five possible locations the searchers had considered, and then allow each of the teams—historians, archeologists, and ethnographers (who included the tribes' traditional methods)—to present their findings. Readers first encounter Jerry Greene's extravagant praise for the Bonsall map and his explanations of the Bent drawings' deficiencies, then view images of spent ordnance and graphic plots of the artifact concentration, and finally contemplate the sustained horror and anguish preserved in the oral histories. By the book's last chapter, the contradictions have piled up like cordwood.[60]

In her conclusion, Whitacre continues to walk a fine line between bold assertions and couched qualifiers. First: "Through a multidisciplinary approach that included historical research, tribal oral histories and traditional methods, and archeological investigations, the National Park Service Sand Creek Massacre Site Location Study resulted in a *definitive identification of the massacre site*." But then: "As with any historical event, however, our understanding of the Sand Creek Massacre is still limited and obscured through time, in this case 135 years. Thus, although the length and extent of the Sand Creek Massacre have been conclusively identified, there are—as the preceding chapters indicate—differing views regarding some of the specifics of the massacre within that boundary." Those specifics included the location of Black Kettle's village. So even as the study ends with cross-cultural comity—"The task has been completed, and the location and extent of the Sand Creek Massacre has been conclusively identified to the satisfaction of the National Park Service, the Cheyenne and Arapaho Tribes of Oklahoma, the Northern Cheyenne, the Northern Arapaho, and the Colorado Historical Society."—a cartographic coda bespeaks lingering controversy. One map depicts Doug Scott's and Jerry Greene's interpretation of Sand Creek, the other, the Cheyennes' and Southern Arapahos' vision of the violence. Together they draw the curtain on the site search, suggesting that the massacre might still be misplaced.[61]

The second volume of the *Sand Creek Massacre Project* considers the best plan for creating a national historic site. But first, in a telling section, Whitacre grapples with the descendants' frustrations with the NPS. "Throughout this project," she allows, "the tribes, particularly the Cheyenne, also have expressed dissatisfaction with the consultation process." More specifically, "they believe . . . that the National Park Service does not listen to the tribes." And "there also are tribal feelings that the oral histories are not being given the same weight as the scientific studies." Again, though, as during the village controversy, Whitacre suggests that the problem is both overstated and rooted in misunderstandings. "Consultation associated with this and other projects," she notes, "has revealed differing opinions of what consultation means. Some tribal governments view consultation as a seat at the decision-making table. The National Park Service views consultation as gathering of information that will influence policy and decision-making." After reading that passage, Laird Cometsevah snorted and said: "I honestly can't say what that means. All I know is that the Park Service folks promised they would pay attention to our oral histories. They promised our traditional methods would matter. They promised they would listen. They didn't. They broke those promises."[62]

After that, the report covers somewhat less controversial material: the likely environmental and socioeconomic impacts of the proposed memorial; the various site management alternatives considered by the NPS; and, perhaps most important of all, the historic significance of the massacre, the reason it should be the focus of one of the federal government's first attempts at memorializing an event in which American citizens were neither heroes nor victims, but perpetrators.[63]

Jerry Greene wrote that section, and in it he tried to mend fences with the descendants. He first had to steer clear of intertribal divisions. Greene begins, "In the lives lost at Sand Creek, both the Cheyennes and Arapahos experienced familial and societal disruptions that have since spanned the generations of their societies." Likely with an eye on the Cheyennes, he adds: "While the event thus impacted both tribes, it most directly carried devastating physical, social, political, and material consequences among the relatively small (ca. 3,000) Cheyenne population, and indisputably changed the course of tribal history." Because the Cheyennes lost so many chiefs—among them One Eye, White Antelope, and Yellow Wolf—as well as the headmen of several soldier

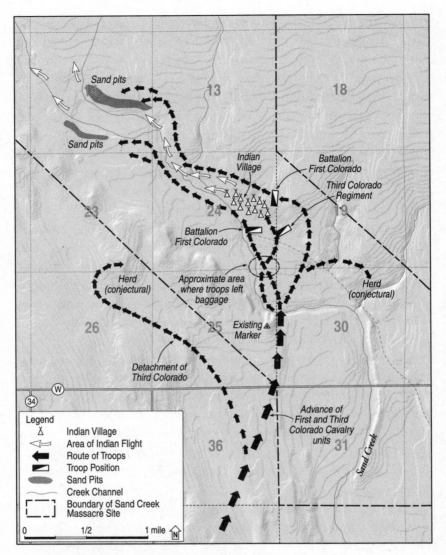

National Park Service map of the Sand Creek Massacre site, based on reports by Jerome Greene and Douglas Scott. (*Adapted from the Sand Creek Massacre Special Resource Study, U.S. Dept. of the Interior, National Park Service.*)

societies at such a critical moment, with the tribe already fractured by the fallout from the Treaty of Fort Wise, Sand Creek's impact reverberated across generations. Then, apparently nodding at the issue of Article 6 reparations, Greene notes that the tribes suffered enormous material losses as well. He continues by explaining that the massacre's impact

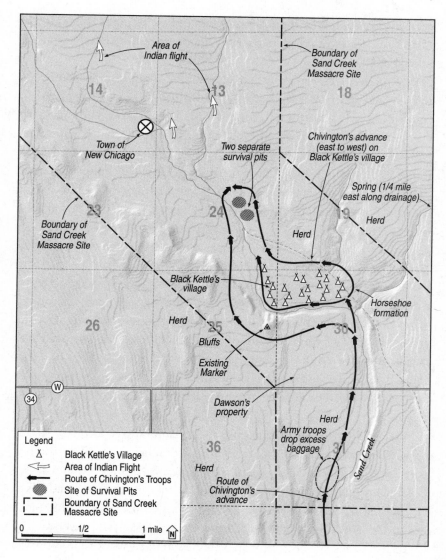

Southern Cheyenne, Southern Arapaho, and Northern Cheyenne map of the Sand Creek Massacre site, based on traditional tribal methods, oral histories, and maps by George Bent. (*Adapted from the* Sand Creek Massacre Special Resource Study, *U.S. Dept. of the Interior, National Park Service.*)

spread beyond the tribes, shaping Native-white relations "over ensuing decades." Next, in a section headed "An Atmosphere of Pervasive and Nervous Distrust," Greene details how Sand Creek not only poisoned interactions between the U.S. government and Native peoples, but also set the stage for reforming federal Indian policy. To make that case, the historian directs his readers back to the period immediately after the massacre.[64]

Having overseen the slaughter of his most likely partners in peace, John Evans snared himself in a self-fulfilling prophecy in early 1865: the Indian war that he had long dreaded. Following the massacre, enraged Cheyennes prepared for a winter offensive against whites, allying themselves with bands of Lakotas and Northern Arapahos. The tribes gathered in a huge camp, composed of more than a thousand lodges, located in the Republican River country of northwestern Kansas. From that base, warriors attacked before moving beyond the reach of retaliating whites. As early as January 6, the hostilities began when a multitribal force struck the road near Julesburg, Colorado. The violence spread until, by month's end, Native people controlled the most important routes in the region. The U.S. Army's efforts at beating back this offensive, including setting thousands of acres of the plains ablaze, failed. The violence only subsided after the tribes withdrew from the field, joining their kin in the Powder River country to the north. By that time, more than fifty settlers had lost their lives and hundreds of thousands of dollars in property had been destroyed. The city of Denver again stood perched on the brink of panic.[65]

Most of the federal troops stationed in Colorado had mustered out early in the new year, leaving territorial officials in a familiar and uncomfortable position: begging distant generals for protection. Ulysses Grant had just reassigned Samuel Curtis, who in the past had often turned a deaf ear to Governor Evans's pleas, and tapped in his place Major General John Pope. Dick Ellis, the professor who oversaw the first Sand Creek site search, argues in his scholarly work that Pope was the army's foremost expert on Indian policy. An advocate of reform, he believed that the treaty system had "worked injustice and wrong to the Indian" and "entailed heavy and useless expense on the government." In Pope's view, tribal peoples accommodated to reservation life should be removed to distant lands, beyond the reach of white settlement, where they could thrive. As for "wild" tribes, including the Arapahos, Cheyennes, and Sioux peoples, he thought they could live as they wished—so long as they remained at peace with whites. But at the first sign of violence, federal troops would "attack them, march through their country, establish military posts in it, and, as natural consequence, their game will be driven off or killed." For the moment, though, Pope's grand vision had to wait. He had a more immediate problem to solve.[66]

With hostile Indians apparently still menacing the plains to the east and north of Denver, Pope's subordinate, Major General Grenville Dodge, pondered the best way to pacify the allied Cheyenne, Arapaho, and Sioux bands. Early in the Civil War, Dodge, then still a colonel, had headed a brigade at the Battle of Pea Ridge. Later, as a brigadier general, he had commanded a corps during William Sherman's assault on Atlanta. Dodge, then, had experience on the frontier and had demonstrated that he would not shy from a fight. He also did not lack manpower in February 1865. Reopening trade on the Plains had become one of the military's priorities, and General Pope allowed Dodge to pull troops from Kansas and Nebraska to assist in that effort. Still, Dodge had a problem: he lacked an enemy to engage. The main concentration of Native warriors had moved to the Powder River country, one of the few remaining spots in the region entirely controlled by Indian peoples. Dodge's men, left behind, chased their own shadows. Upon hearing word of the warriors to the north, General Pope planned a spring attack. But that offensive and others like it foundered in the mud or were hamstrung by poor planning.[67]

Similar problems plagued military operations on the Southern Plains. By the end of May, Senator James Doolittle, head of a delegation hoping to negotiate a peace with the tribes in the area, had arrived at Fort Larned, Kansas. Doolittle believed that further reprisals would only incite more violence. In a passionate letter to his former colleague in the Senate, newly minted Secretary of the Interior James Harlan, Doolittle explained: "As yet no great amount of bloodshed has taken place, except for the treacherous, brutal, and cowardly butchery of the Cheyennes on Sand Creek, an affair in which the blame is on our side." Displaying empathy for Indians rarely seen among federal officials, he suggested, echoing Silas Soule's and presaging George Bent's Sand Creek stories, "It is that affair [the massacre] which has combined all the tribes against us. And why not? They were invited to place themselves under our protection. The sacred honor of our flag was violated, and unsuspecting women and children butchered, and their bodies horribly mutilated, and scenes enacted that a fiend should blush to record." Only victims of the massacre, he insisted, still wanted war. And thus, Doolittle suggested, "As a matter of policy, even, as well as duty, I would propose terms to the Cheyennes for their losses at Sand Creek. It is just." Perhaps so, but the gulf standing between justice and federal Indian policy still yawned wide.[68]

Although Secretary Harlan proved sympathetic to Doolittle's entreaties, he had little patience for hostile Indians. He believed that Commissioner Dole—whom Harlan soon forced out—had abdicated his responsibilities, allowing the army to seize unfettered control of Indian affairs. With Dole gone, Harlan would try to reclaim that policy portfolio for the civilian branch of the government by enacting a series of new initiatives. In a letter to Major General Pope, Harlan later proposed relocating Native people to small reservations far from whites, an idea very similar to one recommended by Pope to Secretary of War Stanton more than a year earlier. Harlan argued that peaceful tribes, facing scarcities of game and helped along by white authorities, would eventually abandon their traditional ways. In the meantime, he warned, violence on the path to assimilation would be met with overwhelming force. Harlan also informed Dennis Cooley, the new commissioner of Indian affairs, that the army should handle belligerent Native peoples. In effect, Harlan hoped to establish a partnership between the Departments of the Interior and War: the former would work with peaceful tribes; the latter would squash resistance.[69]

After Sand Creek, a tribal alliance sought revenge, attacking white settlers across the Plains. The U.S. Army repeatedly failed to engage these warriors, in the process losing its dominion over Indian affairs. As federal authorities later examined the causes and consequences of the tribal insurrection, they decided that peace made more sense than war. Although many settlers in Colorado still longed for a policy of extermination, the tide had turned in Washington. Observers pointed to Sand Creek as the reason why, noting: "The history of the Chivington massacre is too fresh in the public mind, and will be forever too atrocious in history for the preaching of any further doctrines of that sort." In a letter to Senator Charles Sumner, Samuel Tappan, an advocate of

Indian rights who had served under Chivington, offered a more pene-
trating analysis. Blaming his former commander for Sand Creek obscured more than it revealed, Tappan suggested. The root rather than
proximate cause of the slaughter "rest[ed] with those highest in authority, for not having fixed and well understood policy that would have
frustrated the possibility of a Sand Creek massacre." In that context,
federal emissaries negotiated the Treaty of the Little Arkansas, including within it Article 6's promise of reparations. The Arapahos and Cheyennes had earned themselves a reprieve, even if it would not last.[70]

Christine Whitacre took account of that history in the second volume of the *Sand Creek Massacre Project,* buttressing the claim that the
Sand Creek site merited inclusion within the National Park System.
"In its immediate, direct, and long-range impacts upon the Cheyenne
and Arapaho societies and the plains Indian community," Whitacre
writes, "as well as in its immediate and subsequent bearing on the pro-
gression of federal Indian and military policy respecting the plains
tribes, the Sand Creek Massacre comprised an event of outstanding
significance as reflected within the broad national patterns of United
States history." Here was the argument the NPS would make when tes-
tifying before Congress: the massacre had shaped both Native and national history.[71]

In spring 2000, the effort to memorialize the massacre took another
sharp turn. Rick Frost sent a draft of the site study to Senator Campbell. From the beginning, Campbell had received updates on the process
from his trusted Colorado press secretary, James Doyle, and also from
his friends Steve Brady and Laird Cometsevah. The senator knew that
the village controversy—"a little bit of a disagreement," he understated—
still divided the search. But though he did not want "to offend the
tribes," the NPS's boundary compromise alleviated his concerns. Of the
contested terrain he suggested, "let's take the whole thing," reasoning,
"if you got the whole area, we can split hairs later whether the campfire
was here or there." That might not have been good history, but it
seemed like excellent politics. And since Campbell typically understood history as an extension of politics, he scheduled Senate hearings
for mid-September, planning to discuss a new unit of the National Park
System: a Sand Creek massacre historic site.[72]

Two weeks before the Senate took up the question of memorializing Sand Creek, a woman named Linda Rebeck arrived at the Colorado Historical Society. Rebeck brought with her a stack of letters that had belonged to her grandfather, Marl Blunt. She had stumbled upon the correspondence in her mother's keepsake trunk, stored away in the attic of her home. Blunt, it appeared, had settled in Colorado in 1859, and some of the papers that he later passed on to his heirs related to the massacre. Among them were documents previously unavailable to historians and other researchers, including gruesome dispatches from Silas Soule and Lieutenant Joseph Cramer, detailing their experiences at Sand Creek. Officials at the historical society immediately recognized the importance of Rebeck's find and sent the materials along to Senator Campbell in Washington. Campbell made the documents the centerpiece of his hearings.[73]

David Halaas and Gary Roberts suggested that the Soule-Cramer letters were so important because they "validate[d] much of the testimony taken during the congressional and Army hearings" that looked into Sand Creek. In notes to Ned Wynkoop, their former commander, Soule and Cramer justified their decisions not to commit to the fight. They corroborated that surrender flags had flown in Black Kettle's camp. They verified that members of the 1st and 3rd Colorado Regiments had mutilated Native bodies, including taking men's and women's genitalia as trophies. They substantiated charges that the Colorado volunteers had murdered an infant and eviscerated a pregnant woman. They confirmed that Chivington had stationed pickets around Fort Lyon, so officers horrified by his plan to "massacre the friendly Indians camped on Sand Creek" could not leave without first receiving permission. And they bore out scattered claims that several chiefs at Sand Creek, confident that they had consummated an agreement with white authorities at the Camp Weld conference months earlier, initially had greeted the onrushing troops as friends.[74]

Because they ratified elements of the Arapahos' and Cheyennes' oral histories, Soule's and Cramer's words captured the descendants' attention. Steve Brady believed that the letters were critical because they originated with white soldiers rather than Native Americans: "It's one thing when these stories come from Indians. When white people hear us bitching and complaining about the massacre, they say to themselves, 'There they go, whining again.' But when these reports come from the cavalry that was there assaulting the village, well, that's something else again. That's something that will force whites to sit up and take notice." Almost immediately, the Northern Cheyennes began honoring Soule and Cramer in much the same way that Holocaust survivors venerate so-called righteous gentiles, non-Jews who saved Jewish people during the Shoah: as individuals whose basic humanity transcended ethnic or racial differences in a critical moment of history. Otto Braided Hair began inviting Soule's and Cramer's descendants to attend Sand Creek ceremonies, including the healing runs, where the soldiers' letters would be read aloud on the steps of the capitol in Denver, or at graveside ceremonies held at the city cemetery where Soule was buried.[75]

Silas Soule, especially, impressed the descendants as one of only a few white martyrs of Sand Creek. Not only did he stand down during the massacre, but he also was among the first people to spread the word about what had happened there. Soule wrote his note to Ned Wynkoop a bit more than two weeks after Sand Creek. He hinted that Wynkoop might pass along the information to a well-connected friend, Samuel Tappan, who had long feuded with Chivington. Tappan, in turn, would presumably reach out to his friend, General John P. Slough, who formerly had commanded the 1st Colorado but who by then was stationed outside Washington, DC. At the end of 1864, Wynkoop followed the script to the letter: he contacted Tappan, who wrote to Slough. Wynkoop next received orders to return to his old command at Fort Lyon, where he looked into the massacre. His damning report on Sand Creek led directly to congressional and military investigations. When the latter convened in February 1865, Soule rose as the first witness, with Joseph Cramer following soon after. Their testimony undercut the claim, popular in Colorado at the time, that Sand Creek had been a glorious battle. The military commission recessed on April 20, 1865, allowing Chivington time to organize his defense. Three days after that, two men changed the course of the inquiry and recast public memories of Sand Creek.[76]

On the night of April 23, Silas Soule was with Hersa Soule, his bride of just three weeks, out visiting friends in Denver. As Soule and his wife headed home around 10 p.m., he heard the sound of gunfire. When he investigated the source of the shots, Charles Squires and William

Morrow, both soldiers in the 2nd Colorado Cavalry, reportedly am-
bushed him. Soule squeezed off a round from his revolver, winging
Squires, before dying of a gunshot wound to the face. Denverites knew
that Soule had just testified against Colonel Chivington. The murder
transfixed the city. A bit more than a week earlier, on April 14, President Lincoln had been assassinated. The manhunt for John Wilkes
Booth continued as Denverites wrestled with their own apparently political murder. Samuel Tappan, taking a rest from investigating the
massacre, wrote in his diary, "The barbarism of slavery culminated in
the assassination of Mr. Lincoln, the barbarism of Sand Creek has culminated in the assassination of Capt. Soule." Tappan was not the only
observer to make that connection, as Soule died at a moment when
Americans were more willing even than usual to embrace conspiracy
theories and make heroes of the dead. Soule's funeral, consequently,
turned into a municipal occasion, with many of Denver's elites paying
their respects. John Chivington, though, remained at his home, likely
preparing testimony for the ongoing Sand Creek investigations.[77]

After killing Soule, Charles Squires and William Morrow fled Colorado. Morrow seemingly disappeared without a trace. On June 13, however, the *Rocky Mountain News* reported that Squires had been appre-
hended in New Mexico by Lieutenant James Cannon. A month later, on
July 11, Cannon brought Squires back with him to justice in Denver.
Two nights after that, Cannon died in his hotel room, apparently poisoned. Some observers believed that Chivington's supporters had killed
again on their colonel's behalf, though no evidence came to light to substantiate that contention. Squires, meanwhile, waited in jail for his
trial. But just after his court martial finally began in October, somebody picked the lock on Squires's cell. He escaped and was never
caught. It turned out that Squires had powerful allies—his brother
edited a prominent newspaper, and the Squires family counted among
its friends General Daniel Sickles and General John Pope, as well as
many others—some of whom apparently helped him avoid capture.
Soule's martyrdom, and the mysterious circumstances surrounding
his death, became important again when the U.S. Senate took up the
matter of a Sand Creek memorial.[78]

On September 14, 2000, Senator Craig Thomas gaveled to order hearings of the Senate Subcommittee on National Parks, Historic Preserva-

tion, and Recreation. Senate Bill 2950, the Sand Creek Massacre National Historic Site Establishment Act of 2000, was on the docket. The bill's sponsor, Senator Campbell, rose first to speak on behalf of his legislation. Rather than offering his own testimony, Campbell read the Soule and Cramer letters aloud and then introduced them into the Senate record. Before ceding the floor, Campbell noted, "I do not know of any worse atrocity, frankly, in American history." John Warner, one of the most respected voices in the Senate at the time and a renowned champion of the nation's armed forces, rose after Campbell. Steve Brady, on hand to speak in support of the bill, wondered if Warner would defend the troops under Chivington. Instead, a visibly shaken Warner revealed that Campbell's testimony had been "the most moving and compassionate reading of a tragic chapter of American history" that he had ever heard.[79]

After a representative from the NPS suggested that the federal government had remained silent about the massacre for too long, Steve Brady spoke. First, he took care of business, stating that the search had accomplished its goals. "It is unquestionably clear, absolutely clear," he said, brushing aside the village controversy, "that there is no more room for ambiguity. The location and extent of the massacre site and area has been identified." Brady next grappled with more complicated issues, including the open question of treaty claims: "Although Congress admitted responsibility [for] the atrocities, the acts of genocide, committed at Sand Creek, and promised reparations to the Cheyenne and Arapaho through Article 6 of Treaty of Little Arkansas of 1865, this remains an empty promise." Finally, he spoke about NAGPRA, wagging his finger at museums that "presently hold within their collections those that were killed, mutilated and taken as trophies and/or specimens at Sand Creek." David Halaas then reiterated the importance of the Soule-Cramer letters, before Senator Campbell entered affidavits of support from the Kiowa County commissioners into the Senate's record. With that, Senator Thomas adjourned the hearing, and the waiting began.[80]

Senator Campbell's hearings generated publicity in Colorado, where the use of the Soule-Cramer letters as evidence ignited yet another memory fight surrounding Sand Creek. The brouhaha began when the *Denver Post* quoted Patty Limerick, the University of Colorado historian who had studied the question of renaming Nichols Hall in 1987, saying that the documents contained little fresh information. Noting that the various Sand Creek investigations had turned up plenty of brutal testimony about the massacre, Limerick suggested that rather than providing new insights, the letters offered "more of a confirmation of what's already on the record." An outraged David Halaas responded, explaining that beyond the extraordinary good fortune of finding the papers on the eve of the Sand Creek hearings, Soule's and Cramer's correspondence had, more than a century earlier, thrown back the curtain on the massacre. "Everything that came later flowed from these letters," he explained. Limerick backtracked, insisting that she had been selectively quoted in the original story and that, after reading the letters, she found their contents "dazzling." By then, other local scholars had piled on, questioning the legitimacy of the accounts in some cases and attesting to their importance in others. Congress, meanwhile, deliberated about Senator Campbell's memorial bill.[81]

As Coloradans bickered over the Soule-Cramer letters, the Senate passed the Sand Creek Act on October 5; the House followed suit on October 23. Three weeks shy of the massacre's 136th anniversary, on November 7, 2000, with Americans casting ballots in a general election that would be among the most contentious in the nation's history, President Clinton signed the Sand Creek legislation. The act embedded in federal law elements of George Bent's and Silas Soule's interpretation of the violence: Chivington's troops had attacked "a peaceful village of Cheyenne and Arapaho Indians"; more than 150 of those Native Americans, "most of whom were women, children, or the elderly," had died in the slaughter that ensued; and "during the massacre and the following day, the soldiers committed atrocities on the dead before withdrawing from the field." The act also justified memorializing the violence by noting that the massacre was both "of great significance to descendants of the victims" and "a reminder of the tragic extremes sometimes reached in the 500 years of conflict between Native Americans and people of European [descent]." The NPS, after obtaining "sufficient land," would establish and manage the Sand Creek Massacre National Historic Site.[82]

Observers who read the legislation closely might have predicted that the politics of memory would continue to shape the effort to commemorate Sand Creek. For example, the memorial would be huge, embodying the boundary compromise, the NPS's solution to the village controversy. The historic site would span more than 12,000 acres of southeastern Colorado prairie. The act also reflected the affected tribal representatives' concerns. A portion of the memorial would be dedicated to a cemetery, where the repatriated remains of the massacre's victims would be interred. The descendants would have special access to the site for traditional cultural practices. They would also continue to have a say about the future of the memorial: "any reasonable need of a descendent shall be considered in park planning and operation." As for local proprietors, Senator Campbell safeguarded their interests as well. The NPS would be allowed to acquire land through a variety of methods: donation, exchange, or purchase, but "only from a willing seller." The NPS would also "give priority to the acquisition of land containing the marker in existence on the date of enactment of this Act, which states 'Sand Creek Battleground, November 29 and 30, 1864'"—the so-called Dawson South Bend. In other words, as with the earlier Sand Creek legislation, the NPS would not be able to seize private property via condemnation or eminent domain, a sop to Kiowa County landowners, especially William Dawson. But it turned out that satisfying Dawson and the descendants would prove more complicated even than Senator Campbell anticipated at that time.[83]

5

INDELIBLE INFAMY

On a chilly night in mid-November 2000, the Northern Cheyennes marked the passage of the Sand Creek Massacre National Historic Site Establishment Act with a powwow held in the reservation town of Lame Deer. Women at the celebration wore brightly colored dresses. Men arrived clad in traditional regalia: feathered headdresses, patterned tunics and breeches, and intricately beaded moccasins. Deep into the night the descendants reveled in their recent success, honoring the memories of their forebears. They stepped, swayed, spun, and shuffled as members of a small drum group pounded out steady beats and sang in the Cheyenne language. Otto Braided Hair remembered feeling "like we had accomplished something for our tribe, especially for our ancestors killed at Sand Creek." Quieter events took place on the Northern Arapahos' Wind River Reservation and within the Cheyenne and Arapaho Nation. After the bill passed, Gail Ridgely recalled thinking, "the spirits can finally rest." Laird and Colleen Cometsevah, for their part, took comfort knowing that "generations will die out, but now Sand Creek will always be protected. Our great-grandchildren will be able to go there, to learn what happened there, and understand our people's history."[1]

As the descendants exulted, people throughout the West congratulated themselves for having opened a door to cross-cultural reconciliation. Some Coloradans, including Georgianna Contiguglia, head of the Colorado Historical Society, viewed the Sand Creek legislation as heralding a new era of open-mindedness in the region's perception of its past. "We now have enough homes of the rich and famous designated as historic sites in Colorado," Contiguglia suggested. "We need more places and sites that relate to ordinary and more diverse people." Senator Ben Nighthorse Campbell, speaking to a reporter from the *Denver Post*, extolled the nation's resilience and explained of the memorial that it would salve old wounds: "After years of denial and dishonor, America has found the courage to face the flaws of our past and honor those killed at Sand Creek." Allowing that "creating a national historic site where so much innocent blood was shed cannot undo the past," Campbell nevertheless suggested, "it can serve as a living symbol of healing." Editors at the *Omaha World-Herald* amplified this message: "America's increasing maturity as a society is demonstrated by an act of Congress in the closing days of this year's session." Still, the article sounded a cautionary note: "monuments can be healing or they can be divisive," before suggesting to readers, "the 21st century is approaching; the time is long past for Americans, no matter what ethnicity or personal family history, to be divided over things that happened in the 19th." The Sand Creek site, in this view, would serve not only as a memorial to the Native people killed at the massacre but also as a prompt for individuals eager to forgive and forget historical tragedies.[2]

Bill Dawson, too, initially delighted in the act's passage. Senator Campbell's legislation directed the National Park Service (NPS) to prioritize Dawson's property when acquiring land for the historic site. Dawson, consequently, believed that he would soon realize his goal of cashing out his ranch and leaving Kiowa County for greener pastures. He had worked hard over the preceding years, playing his cards carefully and well. He had cultivated friendships with Laird Cometsevah, Steve Brady, and several other descendants. He had influenced the NPS personnel process during the site study. And even when he had not been invited to consultation meetings, he had outmaneuvered his opponents, maintaining a central place for himself in the search process.[3]

The village controversy remained the greatest obstacle to Dawson's long-simmering plan to extricate himself from his ranch. Confronted with Doug Scott's and Jerry Greene's findings about the massacre site's location, Dawson produced a competing thesis. Although carefully sourced, his theory ultimately rested on a claim of authority as a proprietor. Having worked the land for decades, Dawson explained, he knew its contours, its capacities, even its secrets. He respected Scott and Greene. "I thought those guys were top-flight," he recalled. Familiar with their work on the Little Bighorn battlefield, Dawson had "fought tooth and nail" to have the two experts attached to the Sand Creek project. As time passed, though, he lamented that Scott and Greene lacked the local knowledge necessary to temper what he saw as their intellectual arrogance. He viewed the village controversy as a threat to his pocketbook and his politics. If federal officials thought that academic expertise could trump hard-won experience, as Dawson believed happened often in the West, he would prove them wrong.[4]

Even when the site searchers unearthed relatively few relics from his ranch's soil, Dawson had an explanation rooted in his knowledge of local history: through the years, treasure hunters had picked the land clean. "It was a big thing back in the early days of settlement of this county," Dawson explained, "[for] homesteaders to pack a picnic basket and attach a team of horses to the wagon. They'd go to the Sand Creek site and have lunch, and the men would hunt artifacts." Dawson's grandfather, for example, had weathered lean years on the ranch, times so bad that when the wind howled the soil disappeared, exposing hardpan beneath. In those moments, "you'd walk out there and see stuff laying out everywhere. And people used to come with buckets and pick it up, literally take buckets full of artifacts away." The NPS's *Site Location Study* corroborated these stories, though some Kiowa County residents recalled searching for arrowheads and Civil War–era ordnance to the north of the marker on Dawson's property. Regardless, collectors had exhausted the South Bend's bounty, Dawson concluded. That there were so few remnants of the massacre still to be found in that spot—the "traditional site," he typically said, echoing Laird Cometsevah—made perfect sense.[5]

Making common cause with the Cheyenne descendants, whose moral authority, Dawson understood, buttressed the weight of his local knowledge and property rights, he kept insisting that the NPS had not, in fact, unearthed Black Kettle's village. Instead, he argued, the searchers had discovered the location where Chivington and his troops had camped following the massacre, when the Colorado volunteers had destroyed lingering remnants of the Indian village. Both Doug Scott and Jerry Greene were skeptical about this version of events, as well as about other facets of Dawson's theory. His views "did not accord with the historical record in any way, shape, or form," remembered Scott, who wondered if "pride of ownership" and a "desire to sell his land" had clouded the rancher's objectivity. Despite doubts within the NPS's ranks, though, Dawson emerged from the village controversy with his ranch still the centerpiece of the proposed historic site, thanks in part to backing from Laird Cometsevah and Steve Brady. Then, in October and November 2000, Dawson's erstwhile enemies became his allies: the federal government that he so reviled increased the value of his property. He would finally have his payday.[6]

But how much would Dawson be paid? And by whom? Those were two of the unresolved questions plaguing the memorialization effort throughout 2001 and into 2002. The longer it took for answers to emerge, the more frustrated Dawson became. The delay stemmed partly from the conditions that he had imposed on prospective buyers, including federal negotiators. He could not imagine running a ranch with "tourists wandering around the fence lines, trampling the grass and scaring the cows." The liability issues alone made such an arrangement unwieldy. He decided that he would not sell only a portion of his land; any deal would have to be all or nothing. And he would dictate the price. From as far back as his first interactions with Ward Churchill in 1997, Dawson had factored the property's historic significance into his asking price. He had set the number at $1.5 million then. His demands had remained consistent through the years. With passage of the Sand Creek legislation, that figure, approximately five times what his land would have fetched at market were it not associated with the massacre, seemed more reasonable than ever to Dawson. And after September 28, 2001, when the site joined the National Register of Historic Places, $1.5 million seemed like an outright bargain. A lucky bidder could own a piece of Western history.[7]

But the NPS, despite being the most likely buyer, could only pay fair market value for property. Federal regulators, safeguarding the public coffers, had long since tied the hands of NPS personnel in land negotiations. At a series of gatherings held in Colorado, Montana, and Oklahoma in 2001 and 2002, the NPS tried to educate the descendants and local proprietors about constraints governing the acquisition of land for units of the National Park System. Agricultural property in Kiowa County typically sold for between $120 and $264 per acre, depending on improvements and access to water. By contrast, Bill Dawson wanted approximately $1,000 per acre for his land. The Cheyennes supported him, insisting that he should receive his asking price because of the unique meaning of the site. Christine Whitacre, though, explained at a contentious meeting held in Colorado early in 2002 that as far as the NPS was concerned there was "no such thing as a higher price for historic value." Even though the NPS wanted to buy Dawson's ranch, it could not up its offer based on the property's cultural significance. An increasingly impatient Dawson found this "inflexibility infuriating" and wondered if it was a "negotiating ploy."[8]

Early in 2002, Dawson's frustration erupted into outrage. On February 14, the Conservation Fund, a national organization "dedicated to advancing America's land and water legacy," sent the NPS a valentine: it purchased 240 acres of property within the boundaries of the historic site from the Goodrich family and conveyed title to the NPS. Earl Goodrich had homesteaded the land in 1909, and his grandson, Marc, served as family spokesman when he announced to the press: "We are pleased that the NPS is moving ahead with the project." The Goodrich deal reflected fair market value, which worried Dawson. He grew more concerned, though, when the Internal Revenue Service investigated and then fined him around that time, citing him for not declaring consultation fees that the NPS had paid him during the site search. Dawson, incredulous about the timing of the audit, believed that someone at the NPS, either hoping to intimidate him into dropping the asking price for his land, or perhaps retaliating against him for past transgressions, had tipped off the IRS. This was typical behavior for thuggish bureaucrats, Dawson believed, an example of federal authority run amok. Hoping to put a stop to the perceived harassment, Dawson contacted Senator Campbell, who inquired with the NPS's regional director. Nothing more came of the charge, but the event became a trigger. In March 2002, a livid Dawson decided not to wait any longer. He put his ranch up for sale to the highest bidder.[9]

Bill Dawson was not the only Kiowa County resident angry with the NPS after the Sand Creek Act became law. The release of the NPS's two-volume report, coupled with details of Senator Campbell's legislation, deepened Chuck and Sheri Bowen's bad feelings toward the federal government. In its *Site Location Study,* the NPS downplayed the couple's claims about the massacre having taken place on their property. The report allowed that Chuck Bowen had "collected, literally, hundreds of artifacts," but then dismissed most of those finds because the materials dated to long after 1864. The Bowen property, Jerry Greene and Doug Scott believed, likely had hosted only the sand pits, the makeshift fortifications that the Arapahos and Cheyennes had dug at Sand Creek to escape the slaughter. As for the land that would form the bulk of the historic site, the Bowens insisted they were thrilled for their neighbor, Bill Dawson, that Senator Campbell had anointed his ranch. "We've never had an issue with Bill getting his money," Sheri Bowen explained. "In fact, like I said many times, we hoped everything would work out." But, Chuck Bowen added, Campbell's relentless focus on the Dawson South Bend suggested that the fix had been in from the first. In his view, the outcome looked like a foregone conclusion, part of a petty conspiracy. Dawson had wanted to sell; his family had not. Dawson had then become close to the Cheyennes. The NPS team, consequently, had played politics with its findings, knowing that the South Bend could be had for the right price and that its acquisition would placate many of the descendants.[10]

The Bowens expressed their opposition to elements of the memorialization process with the local press, using their property rights as a cudgel. The NPS plan, Chuck Bowen explained to a reporter after the Sand Creek Act passed, would "compromise" his family's ranching operation. Although the federal government, because of Senator Campbell's willing-seller-only provision, might not take their land outright, creating a unit of the National Park System next door would likely affect the same outcome: driving them out of business. But then, fueled by a sense of their righteousness and a quest they had not yet completed—Chuck Bowen recalled, "It [finding the site] was just driving us crazy. I kept thinking we've got to put this aside. But we just couldn't."—the Bowens remained engaged with the process. Based on more than 1,500 hours of detailed study of written sources and prospecting in the field, they had developed their "wood and water" theory of the site's location: "ya gotta have wood, ya gotta have water." In other words, their ranch, which boasted stands of trees and a freshwater spring, had the environmental features necessary to host a large Native American camp, whereas their neighbors' land did not. They also returned to the table with the NPS, hoping they would have a better negotiating partner, someone who might more seriously consider the merits of their perspective on the massacre than in previous years.[11]

With the ink from President Clinton's signature not yet dry on the Sand Creek legislation, Alexa Roberts and Rick Frost met in Denver to discuss the memorialization process. Although the NPS typically assigned a superintendent to a new unit of the Park System closer to the moment when the site opened, Frost explained to Roberts that Sand Creek would be different. Because the subject of the massacre remained politically fraught, and because the NPS saw the memorialization effort as an opportunity to burnish its multicultural credentials, the NPS would choose someone to helm the site immediately—a leader designated to steer it through the land acquisition process necessary before opening. Roberts, invested in the project and aware that Frost wanted to distance himself from the struggles surrounding Sand Creek, wondered who would be asked to take on that task. Frost, she recalled, perked up and asked, "Would you be interested?" Roberts laughed off the question, thinking that the position would be a political minefield. But Frost was serious. The following summer, based on her strong relationship with the descendants, the NPS tapped Roberts for the job.[12]

The Bowens, who had long since lost faith in Rick Frost, extended a clean slate to Alexa Roberts. In late summer 2002, hopeful that the NPS would reconsider its skepticism about the provenance of their artifacts, they asked Roberts and Doug Scott to review their collection again. On September 17, the NPS employees traveled to the Bowens' home in Lamar, Colorado. Viewing an enormous array of relics laid out on a table in the couple's basement, Scott found himself more impressed than he had been in 1999. He was particularly taken with a nearly complete cannonball from a mountain howitzer that Chuck Bowen had assembled. Bowen asked, "What do you think?" Scott answered, "I think you definitely have Sand Creek–related materials." He added, "You've got village materials, and you've got a lot of personal stuff," before speculating that the Bowens likely had the remnants of the sand pits on their property, as well, perhaps, as the spot where the Arapahos had camped in the days leading to the massacre. In other

words, it still was not Black Kettle's village, but Scott nevertheless reassured the Bowens, "There is no question you have part of the Sand Creek
site on your land. There never has been a question of it. But you've found
more." Then he promised the couple: "I will say it in print that you
found this, that you found a very important part of the site." This offer
pleased the Bowens, though they demurred when Scott asked if he
could return some time in the coming months with other archeologists, who would professionally catalog the collection.[13]

Scott and Roberts left the meeting confident that they had opened
up the possibility of improved relations with the Bowens. But Chuck
Bowen was not so sure. He sensed that Scott's parting query betrayed
the archeologist's lingering doubts about the authenticity of his collection. He was right in part. Scott understood that the Bowens were not
scholars and thus had not followed standard protocols when retrieving
objects from the earth. Nevertheless, he wondered, why hadn't they
even taken photographs of themselves collecting? Regardless, following the meeting, Bowen approached Jeff Broome, a Denver-area historian of the Indian Wars and a collector of artifacts from the period,
hoping Broome would examine his relics and help authenticate them.
Broome agreed. After visiting the Bowens' home, he called Doug Scott
to share his enthusiasm for what he had seen. Scott, in turn, wrote to
Chuck Bowen, asking again about cataloging his materials and also
raising the possibility of conducting further archeological reconnaissance on his land. Bowen, in a note to Alexa Roberts, then dropped any
pretense of cooperation, wondering: "In what ways would this benefit
me and be good for me to do? How could it possibly go against me or my
land? And also, with more archeology, how would I benefit?" Scott tried
and failed to reassure Bowen, noting, "Our work in 1999 was never intended to be the last word in the archeology of the site." But by then
the Bowens had turned their attention to coping with a family illness.
Only after a long convalescence would they reengage the NPS.[14]

Most Kiowa County residents had relatively tenuous connections to
Sand Creek compared to Bill Dawson or the Bowens. Janet Frederick,
director of the Kiowa County Economic Development Corporation,
suggested, "People know about it. It's part of our history. But it's not
who we are." Nevertheless, the news that the site would become a unit
of the National Park System generated mixed feelings in Eads. On the

one hand, the region was in grim shape. Between a drought parching the ranching industry and a general malaise gripping small towns nationwide, the prospect of tourists arriving with money to spend seemed hopeful—at least compared to no hope at all. On the other hand, local people loved their county's tranquility and stability. Hosting the historic site would mean newcomers, uncertainty, and maybe unfettered change. Then there was the name. Most area residents had deep roots in Kiowa County. For generations their families had known the prairie landscape near the monument overlook on the Dawson ranch as the Sand Creek *Battle*ground. Scout troops had visited the site, prospectors had hunted arrowheads there, and during high water some people had baptized their children in the creek. Now, with what seemed like little input from the local population, that familiar place would be renamed the Sand Creek *Massacre* National Historic Site. As Frederick said, "Folks just didn't know if they should feel ashamed, mad, or glad."[15]

Even some county officials were ambivalent about the historic site. Opening a unit of the National Park System in their backyard meant compromises, they realized. But they hoped to avoid what they saw as the ultimate devil's bargain: pulling up their agricultural roots and becoming another interchangeable part of the nation's exploding service economy. The county commissioners, including Rod Brown, had worked closely with Senator Campbell during the search process to protect their way of life. "We had all traded enough horses through the years," Brown recalled, "to know that there's always going to be a little give and take." And while they had been willing to give a little on nomenclature—despite occasional misgivings among their constituents, the word "massacre" had not been a deal breaker—they had held fast on property rights. After the legislation passed, members of the Kiowa County Economic Development Corporation pondered how to refashion Eads into a "gateway community," an attractive front door greeting visitors en route to a tourist destination. Janet Frederick and Rod Johnson understood that they had to walk a fine line, using a site of tragedy sacred to Native people to drive economic growth. The key, Johnson believed, would be avoiding "rubber tomahawk syndrome," lining Eads's streets with faux teepees filled with vendors selling kitsch. Johnson hoped his neighbors would do better than that because, despite their demographic homogeneity, they had "a lot in common with many of the Sand Creek descendants."[16]

Comparing his hometown of Eads to Lame Deer, on the Northern Cheyenne Reservation, Rod Johnson depicted small towns filled with people who focused on spirituality and their families. He also saw patriots, whites and Indians proud to fly the American flag and serve in the nation's armed forces. Considering his experiences with residents of Kiowa County and the descendants, he concluded, "we've got far more similarities than differences." At the time, Rod Brown agreed in part. The taciturn Brown offered the Ridgelys the highest praise he knew, calling them "ranching-type people." Beyond that, Johnson and Brown overlooked another point uniting these populations: both the residents of Kiowa County and the descendants saw the massacre site as a way to preserve their traditional way of life. Both groups were anxious about the future. Both felt threatened by external cultural pressures and economic hard times. Both worried that young people in their communities would be lured away from home and would abandon their values. Both believed that the site might help stave off those threats and protect their heritage. And for both, the memorialization effort necessitated uncomfortable partnerships. Neither the people of Kiowa County nor the descendants relished working closely with the federal government. At the same time, members of each group had misgivings about collaborating with the other. Still, they chose to set aside those concerns in service of a shared goal: cultural persistence. Rod Johnson believed that as long as they focused on what bound them together, they could work as a team, perhaps not always easily, but fruitfully.[17]

Then the events of September 11, 2001, changed everything–or so the cliché indicated. Terrorists struck the United States less than a year after Congress voted through Senator Campbell's legislation. A month and a week after that tragedy, with much of the nation still mourning, Alexa Roberts pondered the potential impact of the attacks on the effort to memorialize the massacre. Speaking on the campus of Fort Lewis College in Durango, Colorado, Roberts observed, "The nation and the world are just beginning to realize the consequences of a single morning on the freedoms we take for granted, on our global alliances, and on our trust in other people." She considered a historical parallel: "After 137 years, the Cheyenne and Arapaho people are still overcoming the consequences of a similar morning, in which near genocide changed forever the freedoms they had taken for granted, their alliances with the United States, and their trust in other people." She suggested, "the establishment of a national historic site to commemorate the Sand Creek Massacre is perhaps more relevant now than ever [because] it can remind us, as national monuments are intended to do, that our past shapes the present and the future." The site would prod visitors to consider "that only a fine line separates the history of our own culturally motivated treatment of other Americans from the kind of intolerance and aggression we will not accept from terrorist enemies today." Memorializing Sand Creek could foster empathy among all Americans, regardless of race or ethnicity, she hoped.[18]

As it happened, cross-cultural compassion seemed to be in short supply after 9/11. With smoke still shrouding the ruins of the World Trade Center, President George W. Bush and his advisors started ginning up support for two wars: in Afghanistan and later Iraq. Those conflicts, and the climate of hyperpatriotism that helped spawn them, had a huge effect on the effort to memorialize Sand Creek. First, after the September 11 attacks, with American troops fighting and dying overseas, people nationwide became fascinated by the mechanisms and content of collective remembrance. Second, the ostensibly omnipresent threat of terrorism prompted far-reaching discussions of state-sponsored violence, of the line dividing perpetrators from victims, and of the impact of American militarism. And third, as some members of the Bush administration began dividing the world into enemies and allies, with that sorting often hinging on race, region, and religion—white Westerners, steeped in Judeo-Christian values, versus nonwhite Easterners, typically Muslims—some residents of Kiowa County bristled at the prospect of a historic site in their community labeling the actions of U.S. soldiers a massacre.[19]

With federal authorities encouraging Americans to view the world through a black-and-white lens—us versus them—an event like Sand Creek, which raised questions about the consequences of American imperialism and the actions of the U.S. Army, prompted renewed controversy. And some people in Kiowa County knew where they stood in the ensuing conflict: not with Alexa Roberts or Rod Johnson and their calls for tolerance and pluralism, but with the troops. It did not matter that Native people served at greatly disproportionate rates in the American military. With racial anxiety on the rise, Janet Frederick lamented that for a few of her neighbors, it proved easier to "identify with Chivington and his men" than with Indians "who we mostly don't know and who can seem so different from folks around here." Ruthanna Jacobs, who ran the Kiowa County Museum, a combined historical society and repository of local curiosities, was Chivington's loudest defender in Eads. "The colonel was just doing his duty," she insisted. "Now, some of the volunteers may have gotten a little bit out of hand. But that kind of thing happens in war." Exhibiting empathy for the perpetrators rather than the victims, Jacobs added, "Chivington's men were frightened for their lives." Then she suggested that only Coloradans could judge the events at Sand Creek. "You have to understand that all the white people living here at that time were terrified. The Indians were on the warpath. They had raped and killed." Summing up a neo-Chivingtonite perspective, she concluded: "Massacre? That's just politically correct nonsense. I mean, how did white soldiers die if there were no warriors there? It surely was a battle."[20]

Jacobs's defense of the 3rd Colorado Regiment and its discredited commander sounded like faint echoes of the belligerent reactions in Denver after federal officials handed down the results of their inquiries in 1865. The investigations were politically motivated, Coloradans suggested at the time, the inquiries' flawed conclusions the work of eastern swells who could not possibly comprehend the hard realities of settling the West. Chivington, in this view, was an agent of civilization who catalyzed the region's development and hastened the inevitable decline of a doomed race. He covered himself in glory by saving the lives of countless innocent whites. And his detractors, the argument went, were fools or perhaps worse: outside agitators, intriguing at the expense of settlers who faced peril on the frontier. Above all, Sand Creek had been a battle. Labeling it a massacre insulted not just Chivington and his men but all of the people of the West. Such slights would not go unanswered.[21]

Word that the bloodshed would be subject to federal inquiry appeared in the *Rocky Mountain News* just before New Year's Day 1865. Referring to correspondence likely touched off by Silas Soule, the *News* reported, "Letters received from high officials in Colorado say that the Indians were killed after surrendering and that a large portion of them were women and children." The result would be a "Congressional investigation." Still, despite persistent rumors swirling around Denver that Chivington's men had indeed committed atrocities, some members of the local press corps continued to hail the attack and its perpetrators. Editors at the *Black Hawk Mining Journal* admitted of the violence that "perhaps it was wrong in the sight of heaven," but then suggested that it was not for them to judge, because they could "only see with eyes on earth. And looking with earthly, practical eyes, we see nothing to condemn but everything to approve in the action of the troops." Other articles established that the carnage had been a battle by insisting that the Indians at Sand Creek had been hostile. The *News,* for example, noted, "it is unquestioned and undenied that the site of the Sand Creek battle was the rendezvous of the thieving and marauding bands of savages who roamed this country last summer and fall," including the "confessed murderers of the Hungate family." Given that, critics had to be motivated by "political ambition" or greed, hoping to "put money in their pockets."[22]

Congress, meanwhile, set its investigatory apparatus in motion early in 1865. The army also looked into Sand Creek. On January 11, Samuel Curtis ordered Colonel Thomas Moonlight, then commanding the Military District of Colorado, to take charge of the matter. The next day, Ned Wynkoop arrived at Fort Lyon, where he began interviewing witnesses. And just three days after that, on January 16, Wynkoop wrote up his findings, denouncing the violence and blaming it almost entirely on John Chivington. "Numerous eye witnesses," Wynkoop reported, "have described scenes to me, coming under the eye of Colonel Chivington, of the most disgusting and horrible character. The dead bodies of females profaned in such a manner that the record is sickening." Less than a week later, Major Scott Anthony, previously one of Chivington's most stalwart advocates in Colorado Territory, resigned from his position as commander of Fort Lyon. Anthony explained that he had stepped down "on account of [his] connexion with the 'Sand Creek affair' which really disgraced every officer connected with it, unless he was compelled to go under orders." With even Chivington's staunchest allies turning against him, the various investigations into Sand Creek gathered momentum.[23]

On February 1, Thomas Moonlight, though far more concerned about Indians making war on nearby white settlements, nevertheless established a military commission to investigate allegations that Sand Creek had been a massacre. Moonlight selected Samuel Tappan to lead the inquiry. Tappan's preconceptions about Sand Creek, coupled with his long-standing animus toward Chivington, were well known in Colorado, fueling later claims that the investigation had been trumped up, part of a politically motivated vendetta against the heroic Fighting Parson. Tappan, for his part, rejected suggestions of bias: "As to my alleged prejudice and alleged personal enmity, even if true, I should not consider them at all influencing me in performing the duties assigned me in this commission, especially after taking the oath as a member." Those duties, Colonel Moonlight informed Tappan, included ascertaining whether the Indians at Sand Creek had fallen under the protection of the government; if so, by whose orders; whether Chivington had understood that to be the case at the time of the attack; whether the bands he had attacked were peaceful or, if not, whether they had engaged in depredations against whites; and whether Chivington had allowed atrocities to occur on his watch.[24]

On February 15, the commission began collecting testimony, calling Silas Soule to the stand. The proceedings continued, in Denver and at Fort Lyon, for three months after that, interrupted only by recesses and a break to honor Soule after his murder. Chivington's critics agreed on many points, including that the Cheyennes and Arapahos at Sand Creek had been peaceful and convinced that they were being protected by white authorities. Chivington knew this, witnesses asserted, but had still ordered the attack. Many of these people also claimed that Chivington had overseen the slaughter of women, children, and the elderly, and had allowed his troops to mutilate the dead. Chivington had then puffed up the number of warriors in the camp, as well as those killed, trying to transform an act of cowardice into one of courage. The colonel's defenders, by contrast, flipped the script, insisting that the troops at Sand Creek had found white scalps in the camp; that they had been outnumbered by hostile Indians, some entrenched in pits prepared before the fight; and that they had faced off with savages guilty of perpetrating vile acts against whites during the previous spring. In this view, Sand Creek had been a battle.[25]

Around that time, two other Sand Creek investigations began: one run by Joseph Holt, the army's judge advocate general, the other by Congress's Joint Committee on the Conduct of the War (JCCW). Although Holt later excoriated Chivington, calling Sand Creek a "coldblooded slaughter" and suggesting that the crime committed there would "cover its perpetrators with indelible infamy," his report generated relatively little controversy in the West. The muted reaction likely stemmed from Holt's limited power; he could not charge Chivington, who had already mustered out of the army, with a crime. But the JCCW, because of its high national profile, captured the attention of Coloradans. The JCCW began its investigation in March 1865, calling witnesses, including Governor John Evans, and entering reams of exhibits into the record. The committee worked until early May. Chivington provided a lengthy written affidavit on his own behalf. In that document, he maintained that he had not known that the Native people at Sand Creek had camped there because white authorities had asked them to. He also claimed that the Indians had not been peaceful. Quite the contrary, he insisted, his troops had discovered nineteen scalps in the camp, one of them still fresh with gore, on the day of the attack.[26]

When the JCCW issued its findings in early May 1865, the report represented the harshest assessment of Sand Creek to that time and perhaps since. The JCCW recommended that John Evans be fired as territorial governor and that John Chivington be cashiered prior to being tried before a military court—even though, again, he was already out of reach of the army, having resigned his commission months earlier. Appraising the host of outrages committed on Chivington's watch, the committee stated: "It is difficult to believe that beings in the form of men and disgracing the uniform of the United States, soldiers and officers, could commit or countenance such acts of cruelty and barbarity." As for Chivington, the report concluded that he had "deliberately planned and executed a foul and dastardly massacre which would have disgraced the veriest savages among those who were the victims of his cruelty." In sum, Colonel Chivington had perpetrated a horrifying massacre; he had committed what amounted to premeditated "murder";

and he had, in the process, rendered himself less civilized even than the Indians that his men had killed. While most of the federal officials investigating Sand Creek could agree that the Native people slaughtered there had been savages, this shared understanding still did not excuse whites who had violated the norms of civilized society during the violence.[27]

The national press seized on the investigations' lurid details, describing Chivington as a fiend and Sand Creek as an embarrassment. The *Washington Chronicle* called the attack a "bloody offense." The *Chicago Tribune,* which apparently purchased purple ink by the gallon, went one better, suggesting that the massacre had been "an act of hideous cruelty garnished with all the accessories of fraud, lying, treachery, bestiality." But many Western papers, evincing a combination of racism, regional pride, and willful disregard for the facts, disagreed. As the various commissions ground slowly toward their verdicts, borderlands journalists mounted spirited defenses of Chivington. Editors at the *Nebraska City News,* for instance, suggested that even if Chivington had attacked a peaceful village, they hoped other brave men would follow his lead, enlisting as soldiers in service of the West's Manifest Destiny. The same paper later reiterated its stance: "At present we are in favor of the Rev. Col. Chivington and a religious extermination of the Indians generally." And after the JCCW damned Chivington in its report, the *Rocky Mountain News* heaped scorn on the document, insisting that it was the work "of a few scoundrels who were blind to all else save the gratification of a petty personal malice." In Colorado, and for many white settlers throughout the West, Sand Creek would remain a battle for years to come.[28]

Whether as a battle or a massacre, the NPS could not memorialize Sand Creek without first acquiring the relevant property at the beginning of the twenty-first century. By spring 2002, though, Bill Dawson, never noted for his patience with federal officials, had moved beyond frustration with the NPS to unalloyed anger. Dawson preferred to see his ranch preserved for the use of the Sand Creek descendants and the public. But he needed leverage to negotiate with the NPS. In early March, having put his land up for sale on the open market, Dawson complained to a Denver reporter that the NPS's offer to that point had been "so low I could sell it to either of my two neighbors for more." He added, "the government has failed to negotiate in good faith." Dawson warned that he would not "sell out, move away and work as a Wal-Mart greeter in [his] 'golden years,'" noting with a hint of malice that if all else failed, he could repurpose his ranch as a private hunt club, catering to wealthy sportsmen. After hearing tidings of Dawson's discontent, Senator Campbell agreed, "it is historic land and should have some premium price," but went on to admit, "I'm not sure how much." Campbell then described himself as disgusted by the idea of the site hosting "more killing, even if it isn't people" and hoped that the government would find a way to match any offer Dawson might receive from another bidder.[29]

It never became necessary for members of Congress to hold bake sales or search for loose change between the couch cushions in their Washington offices. Instead, Laird Cometsevah, along with other traditional chiefs in the Cheyenne and Arapaho Tribes, began lobbying their business committee, the equivalent of the tribal council, to do what the U.S. government could not: buy Dawson's property. For Cometsevah, such a move would resonate symbolically; his tribe could reclaim a sacred place that had once belonged to it. But the issue remained money. The Cheyenne and Arapaho Tribes did not have the cash to make the deal. And Dawson was claiming that time was running out. Another buyer, whom he refused to identify, had begun negotiating with him. People hinted at the time that Dawson had fabricated the outside interest, hoping to pressure the NPS or descendants to act. Dawson, for his part, maintained that the other buyer was real. Regardless, the logjam broke. By early April, the Cheyenne and Arapaho Business Committee, though still lacking the funds necessary to complete the transaction, turned for help to a gaming corporation that managed the tribes' casino. Southwest Entertainment, run by a man named Jim Druck, would put up money to buy Dawson's ranch and then turn the property over to the tribes. In exchange, the tribes would renegotiate the terms of Southwest Entertainment's management agreement.[30]

The details of the deal were dramatic. Bill Dawson remembered that negotiations with his anonymous buyer—a man whom rumors later hinted operated a second gaming corporation—were almost complete when Laird Cometsevah stepped in at the eleventh hour. "They [the other buyer] had offered me well over a million dollars," Dawson claimed. "And I had to give them an answer by five o'clock that same afternoon." He recalled, "Sometime around four o'clock that day I got a telephone call from Laird, who said, 'Don't do anything. I've got the place sold for you.'" Dawson asked, "What do you mean?" Cometsevah elaborated: "We've got a guy that wants to buy your place at your price." Dawson, facing an inflexible deadline from his other buyer, explained to his friend, "You've got to be right about this, Laird." Cometsevah replied, "Trust me." Dawson did and waited to hear from Jim Druck. When Druck assured him that at the end of the three-party exchange he proposed, the South Bend, the massacre site marked on George Bent's maps, would belong to the Cheyenne and Arapaho Tribes, Dawson decided that he had found the right buyer.[31]

Jim Druck did not look the part of the stereotypical casino owner. He did not wear sharkskin suits, crocodile shoes, or silk shirts open to the navel. He did not drive around in stretch limousines, bark orders at lackeys, or surround himself with hired muscle. Instead, the squat, bright-eyed Druck favored jeans and T-shirts, motorcycles, and even tones when he spoke. His thoughts on hiring goons remained unknown. Most of the time, he looked like what he was: a Jewish lawyer transplanted from the Midwest to the mountains of Colorado, where he made what he described as "a good living in the gaming industry." Druck became involved with Sand Creek when, while in Oklahoma on business, he got wind that the Dawson property was for sale. As he worked to extend his management contract with the Cheyennes and Arapahos, one of his subordinates brought him a newspaper report on the Sand Creek stalemate. Years earlier, Druck had purchased a parcel of land for the tribes, which had then lengthened his contract in return. He hoped to do the same thing with the Dawson property. Druck broached the idea with the tribes' business committee, whose members he recalled were "panicking" because Dawson had a deal brewing with another buyer. "We weren't going to play poker with that," Druck remembered. He drew up a letter of intent with the committee, clarifying the deal: Bill Dawson would receive $1.5 million; the Cheyenne and Arapaho Tribes would extend their casino management agreement with Southwest Entertainment; and they would receive the Dawson ranch in return. Druck scheduled a signing ceremony for April 27 at his Cripple Creek, Colorado, casino to celebrate the deal.[32]

The sale initially looked like a "win-win" for all parties involved, a case of profit motive and private enterprise walking in lockstep with the politics of public memory. The Denver press, turning the page on one of the most gruesome chapters of the region's past, ran headlines like "Sand Creek Healing Can Begin" over sunny articles suggesting, "thanks to Southwest Entertainment's philanthropy, modern Colorado finally may get on the right side of history." Other stories featured the descendants, including Joe Big Medicine, who said that he finally had done something for his great-grandfather, one of Chivington's victims. Steve Brady justified the cost of the Dawson ranch by comparing the Sand Creek site to other hallowed national ruins: "If Ground Zero or the Murrah Building [the federal office building in Oklahoma City leveled in 1995 by domestic terrorists] were put on the auction block, people would pay any price." Robert Tabor, chairman of the Cheyenne and Arapaho Business Committee, suggested that acquiring the Sand Creek site would allow the tribes to maintain their traditional culture while carving out space for themselves within the national narrative. "The Cheyenne and Arapaho are doing this to preserve our history," he noted, "and to remind the government that this should never happen again. We do this to teach our children that this was not a battlefield as some would like to claim, it was a massacre site where our elders, women and children were killed." Tabor concluded, "Our people did not fight a battle, they were murdered and it should be remembered as such."[33]

Bill Dawson, for his part, had achieved the outcome he had long sought. He had sold his land for his price. He had also managed a neat trick: looking benevolent while cashing out. He appeared to have done both well and good. A decade earlier, such a turn of events would have been unthinkable. At the time, a belligerent Dawson still claimed that Sand Creek was a battle, insisting that any other interpretation amounted to politically correct pandering. Then, even after his views on the subject evolved, dealing with the public on his ranch embittered him. After menacing passersby and sightseers on his land, allegedly brandishing weapons in defense of his property rights, Dawson languished for a night in the Kiowa County jail, his reputation in tatters, his relationship with his hometown forever sundered. Finally, a U.S. senator and a venerated Cheyenne chief were lauding him as a "dedicated steward of a sacred site" and "a friend of the Cheyenne people." Dawson planned to leave Eads for his new home, Colorado Springs, where he and his wife would live comfortably, close enough to the Sand Creek site to visit for major events but far enough away to sleep well at night.[34]

Jim Druck also got the deal he wanted. And as he tallied his future earnings, he played the role of the philanthropist. Druck readily admitted that swapping the Dawson property for considerations in his negotiations with the Cheyenne and Arapaho Tribes had been a savvy financial transaction. But he also suggested that, because of his religion and family history, he could empathize with the Cheyenne and Arapaho peoples' historical suffering. He appealed to observers fascinated by the so-called Greatest Generation, revealing that his father's service in World War II had recently prompted him to make a pilgrimage to Dachau, one of the Nazis' most notorious death camps. Druck noted links between failed efforts to exterminate Europe's Jews and North America's indigenous peoples. Recalling a visit to the massacre site that he had made with several of the descendants, he explained: "At Sand Creek, I could see that they were feeling the same things that I felt at Dachau. . . . I could see in their eyes, I could see in their body language, what they were feeling. It's crushing. You can't talk. You can't say anything." Purchasing Bill Dawson's ranch, in this telling, had been much more than just a calculated business decision.[35]

By contrast, NPS personnel were skeptical about potential fallout from Druck's acquisition of Dawson's land. Alexa Roberts cheered the news that the property had changed hands. It seemed that the historic site might open sooner than she had previously hoped it would. But she worried that the extraordinary price tag would generate unrealistic expectations among other local proprietors, making it harder for the NPS to purchase more land. "We knew we'd just have to live with the consequences of the deal," she said. Initially, the NPS had calculated that acquiring property for the site would cost approximately $2 million. The NPS admitted in the wake of the Druck deal that "the sufficiency of that estimate is now questionable, considering the sale of the Dawson property for an amount far in excess of the appraisal approved by the Service." Surveying the changed real estate landscape in Kiowa County, Senator Campbell's aide, James Doyle, cringed: "When Jim Druck appeared on the scene, everybody understood that would be great for Bill Dawson, but we also understood that it was really going to complicate any future negotiations with landowners down there." Likely referring to Chuck and Sheri Bowen, Doyle noted, "Now we have people saying, 'If Dawson's property is worth X, my property, which has more artifacts on it, has to be worth Y.'" In short, "Mr. Druck kind of upset the apple cart in a way nobody anticipated." Nobody, that is, except Bill Dawson.[36]

As for Kiowa County residents, the specter of a casino in their backyard loomed over the sale of the Dawson ranch. Among stereotypes of the modern Indian—at one with nature, a pugnacious drunk, a stoic font of wisdom—the sharp dealer figures prominently in the American imagination. With a small number of tribes raking in huge sums from gaming ventures, there were people in Eads who wondered if their town would soon be illuminated by neon lights. Rod Brown recalled, "The first thing that came up around here when Mr. Druck bought the Dawson property was, 'Well, now we're going to have casinos.'" James Doyle scoffed at such concerns, saying, "There are more cattle than people in Kiowa County." He wondered if "the cows are going to gamble." But then Doyle admitted that although it was not "a viable option economically," he supposed that "a casino could be a legal option." Some people in Eads were not reassured. In addition to coping with tens of thousands of newcomers tramping through town annually and sacrificing some control over their local history and landscape, they might have to confront big-city vice as well.[37]

Or perhaps they would not have to do any of those things. The Druck deal generated so much controversy in the Cheyenne and Arapaho Tribes that its completion began to seem uncertain. Jim Druck had planned to own the Dawson ranch for "less than five minutes," just long enough to sign documents extending his management contract before handing the deed over to Robert Tabor. But when it came time to convey the land to the tribes, Tabor balked. It turned out that he did not have the votes necessary to complete the deal. Druck was stunned. Although he had worried that things were moving quickly—he had asked members of the business committee, "Are we going too fast?"— Tabor had reassured him that there would be no problems at the back end of the transaction. Now the casino magnate owned the Sand Creek site outright. He was not happy about it. "I didn't want to be responsible for that," he remembered. "It's far too valuable a historic asset for me. And that's not what I signed on to do." Bill Dawson shrugged as he recalled Druck's discomfort at the time: "Mr. Druck paid me a million and a half dollars. And he ended up with something he didn't quite know what to do with. He had a ranch in eastern Colorado and didn't own a cow. And he couldn't swap the damn thing to the Indians either. They were doing the whole deal on Indian time."[38]

The holdup actually stemmed from more prosaic issues than allegedly indigenous conceptions of time: tribal politics. Reports suggested that Robert Tabor had circumvented recalcitrant members of the business committee. Vera Franklin, one such committee member, responded to Tabor's tactics in an open letter. "You have exceeded your authority by acting outside the parameters of your position as chairman," she wrote, "and this constitutes misconduct." Franklin suggested that the issue should be brought before the entire tribe. Tabor replied that the business committee had the authority to handle the matter and insisted that Jim Druck had "donated the land to the tribes without conditions." Druck himself made no such assertions. Instead, he began lobbying members of the business committee directly, demanding that they make good on their part of the deal he had struck with them. As spring 2002 turned into summer and then fall, the descendants, the people of Kiowa County, Jim Druck, and key personnel within the NPS could only wait and hope for a quick resolution.[39]

In the meantime, other efforts to shift collective memory of the massacre finally came to fruition. On November 29, 2002, a crowd of Sand Creek descendants mingled with local dignitaries on the Colorado capitol steps in Denver. The crowd waited for the start of a ceremony rededicating the state's Civil War memorial. The statue, erected in 1909, included on its base a plaque listing all of the "battles" in which Coloradans had fought during the war. Sand Creek stood among them, a reminder that Colorado officially recalled the tragedy as a triumph. In 1998, a state senator named Robert Martinez sponsored a bill to remove Sand Creek from the bronzed catalog of battles. But in fall 1999, due to the efforts of David Halaas and the descendants, the legislature reconsidered. Senator Martinez wrote a second bill, reiterating, "Sand Creek was not the site of a battle, but rather was the site of a massacre." And yet, "instead of removing the words [Sand Creek] from the Civil War monument, an interpretative exhibit [would] be designed and placed near" it. A new marker would be cast, explaining the "historic significance of the Sand Creek massacre to Colorado and the United States." The state would reinterpret the offending passage of the text rather than erase it.[40]

It would not be easy. Crafting a pithy explanation of the massacre's importance, for state and nation, that would satisfy both observers at the Colorado capitol and also the descendants would require a deft touch. Further complicating matters, the work had to be done as a joint project of the state legislature and the Colorado Historical Society. Plus, David Halaas had taken a new job, leaving his replacement at the Historical Society, Modupe Lobode, in charge of the Civil War memorial. Starting early in 2002, Lobode began working on text. By late June of that year, she had a preliminary draft ready to share at a meeting of the legislature's Capitol Building Advisory Committee. That body agreed to consider the matter before meeting again in August. After receiving more input, Lobode produced a penultimate draft, approved on October 2, 2002. "An interpretive bronze plaque" would be "permanently installed at the base of the Civil War monument to clarify that Sand Creek is considered the site of a massacre and not a Civil War battle." The new marker would be unveiled less than two months later, on the massacre's anniversary.[41]

Unfortunately, without David Halaas overseeing the reinterpretation of the memorial and acting as liaison to the tribes, the descendants had not been invited to participate in the project. In late October, Otto Braided Hair, director of the Northern Cheyenne Sand Creek office, explained in a letter to the Capitol Building Advisory Committee "that he was very disappointed his people were not consulted regarding the content of the plaque text." He offered suggestions for substantive changes before noting that Joe Big Medicine—who, along with Laird Cometsevah, served as a Sand Creek representative for the Southern Cheyenne tribe—would need to do the same. Steve Tammeus, the legislative staffer overseeing the project, assured Braided Hair that he "would consider" the descendants' input. Tammeus told Modupe Lobode to "call the foundry and ask them to hold the plaque for final revisions" and to stay in contact with Braided Hair and Big Medicine in the weeks leading to the ceremony.[42]

On November 29, having just completed a healing run from the massacre site to the capitol steps in Denver, Otto Braided Hair led the Northern Cheyenne Singers in a version of White Antelope's death song. Gazing west toward the foothills of the Rockies, dusted with early snow, Robert Tabor remarked: "I look at the mountains today and I wonder what the Cheyenne and Arapaho were thinking 138 years ago." Considering all that had happened since, he issued a challenge: "Our people are still here." As drumbeats reverberated across Civic Center Park, Steve Johnson, chair of the Capitol Building Advisory Committee, explained the decision to update the memorial, noting, "History is not a static thing." Other local officials followed Johnson before several descendants shared their massacre stories. Laird Cometsevah detailed the atrocities committed by Chivington's men. Eugene Black Bear Jr. made a plea for empathy, suggesting that for Cheyenne and Arapaho people, the massacre "was akin to the Sept. 11 terrorist attacks." The crowd then turned to Bob Martinez, who stood by the memorial. The descendants had shrouded the new plaque with braided sweet grass. Members of the Southern and Northern Cheyenne tribes sang an honor song after Martinez unveiled the stele. Onlookers clustered around, contemplating the State of Colorado's new official memory of Sand Creek.[43]

The text, for the most part, focused attention on questions of memorialization rather than on the massacre itself. "The controversy surrounding the Civil War Monument," Modupe Lobode begins, "has become a symbol of Coloradans' struggle to understand and take responsibility for our past." The discussion of Sand Creek remained somewhat ambiguous, reflecting ongoing uncertainties in the historical and archeological record. The number of Chivington's victims, for example, stood at *"about* 160." The violence had played out *"about* 180 miles southeast of here." By contrast, on the key point, how the bloodshed should be remembered, Lobode took a clear position: Sand Creek had been a massacre. "Colorado's First and Third Cavalry," she writes, "commanded by Colonel John Chivington, attacked a *peaceful* camp of Cheyennes and Arapahos on the banks of Sand Creek," adding, "Though some civilian and military personnel immediately denounced the attack as a massacre, others claimed the village was a legitimate target." And despite the fact that "this Civil War Monument . . . was erected on

The controversy surrounding this Civil War Monument has become a symbol of Coloradans' struggle to understand and take responsibility for our past. On November 29, 1864, Colorado's First and Third Cavalry, commanded by Colonel John Chivington, attacked Chief Black Kettle's peaceful camp of Cheyenne and Arapaho Indians on the banks of Sand Creek, about 180 miles southeast of here. In the surprise attack, soldiers killed more than 150 of the village's 500 inhabitants. Most of the victims were elderly men, women, and children.

Though some civilians and military personnel immediately denounced the attack as a massacre, others claimed the village was a legitimate target. This Civil War Monument, paid for by funds from the Pioneers' Association and the State, was erected on July 24, 1909, to honor all Colorado soldiers who had fought in battles of the Civil War in Colorado and elsewhere. By designating Sand Creek a battle, the monument's designers mischaracterized the actual events. Protests led by some Sand Creek descendants and others throughout the twentieth century have since led to the widespread recognition of the tragedy as the Sand Creek Massacre.

This plaque was authorized by Senate Joint Resolution 99-017.

A revised plaque placed in 2002 at the Colorado Civil War Memorial, Denver. This plaque reinterprets the memorial by suggesting that "the controversy surrounding this Civil War monument has become a symbol of Coloradans' struggle to understand and take responsibility for our past." *(Photo by author.)*

July 24, 1909, to honor all Colorado soldiers who had fought in battles of the Civil War in Colorado and elsewhere by designating Sand Creek a battle, the monument's designers mischaracterized the actual events. Protests led by Native Americans and others throughout the twentieth century have since led to the widespread recognition of the tragedy as the Sand Creek Massacre."[44]

Laird Cometsevah, though pleased that the Civil War memorial had been reinterpreted, remained frustrated because of the turmoil complicating his tribe's efforts to protect the Sand Creek site. He worried also that the ceremony at the Colorado capitol would allow "white people to think they've paid their debts to the Cheyennes" and that the new plaque would not substantively shift collective memory of Sand Creek. The *Denver Post*'s coverage of the rededication ceremony suggested that Cometsevah had reason to be concerned. The *Post* perpetuated myths about the massacre and suggested that white Coloradans had secured for themselves expiation on the cheap. An editorial in the paper began with wishful thinking ("Colorado and the country finally are coming to terms with the saddest episode in state history"), then suggested that Sand Creek could be blamed on a small number of convenient scapegoats ("a mob of 700 half-drunk militia volunteers, armed with field artillery and commanded by Col. John Chivington"), before concluding with a misreading of current events ("the effort [to preserve the massacre site] was saved by businessman Jim Druck.... Three cheers for Jim Druck"). Cometsevah, meanwhile, insisted, "the soldiers *were* guilty, but the federal government was responsible for the genocide committed at Sand Creek. And the federal government still owes my people." Notwithstanding Jim Druck's help, the effort to memorialize the site had stalled because Cometsevah's "people were still dealing with what happened at Sand Creek."[45]

The *Post* article, and Cometsevah's reaction to it, recapitulated one of the enduring controversies surrounding the memory of Sand Creek: the question of ultimate responsibility for the bloodshed. In the wake of the violence, even those Coloradans, including Silas Soule, who allowed that Sand Creek had been a massacre pinned the blame on John Chivington or his ostensibly ragtag troops. Chivington, these people suggested, was an opportunistic coward, a politically motivated climber, a bloodthirsty madman, or some toxic combination of all of the above. His troops, another line of argument suggested, were the dregs of society: drunks, mental defectives, common criminals, or worse. From this perspective, the massacre could be dismissed as a one-off event, the work of a depraved element, marginal characters in no way representative of Colorado society. More than a century later, that view still proved alluring for some Denver-area journalists (just as it would for Senator Campbell at the site's opening ceremony). Blaming the massacre on fringe characters, or their debased commander, allowed editors at the *Post* to ignore the structural issues lurking beneath Sand Creek: how a murderous federal Indian policy, carried out by the army, abetted the settlement of the West. The bloodiest chapter of the region's history, then, could be redeemed through acts as simple as the casting and unveiling of a culturally sensitive plaque.[46]

Laird Cometsevah found such views maddening. His tribe remained mired in contentious politics that he viewed as one lingering by-product of the massacre. "The chiefs killed were important," he said, before turning to an analogy popular at the time among the descendants: "Imagine what it would have been like if the terrorists had flown planes into the Capitol and the White House. Chaos. Then how long would it have taken for the government to recover? My people still suffer from the losses at Sand Creek. Our government still hasn't recovered completely." Back in Oklahoma, where he spent his time performing a chief's duties—caring for elders at the tribes' senior center, safeguarding Cheyenne cultural practices, and preparing an Article 6 claim—Cometsevah waited. With his vision of preserving the massacre site as a step toward securing reparations for the descendants stalled, he believed that his tribe needed, more than ever, to embrace its traditions. Sitting with his wife, Colleen, Cometsevah suggested, "Our system of government just does not work." Colleen Cometsevah added: "Those of us who still respect our Indian ways are the only thing holding our tribe together now." The longer the impasse over the Druck deal persisted, the more frustrated the Cometsevahs became with the waiting.[47]

In the year after the ceremony at the Colorado capitol, what had once seemed like a placid union of casino gambling and the politics of memory threatened to end in an ugly divorce. Jim Druck, still "uneasy" about owning the massacre site, sought compromise with the Cheyenne and Arapaho Business Committee. But that body, made up of eight representatives drawn from throughout the tribes, remained evenly split. In the last week of April 2003, Druck traveled to Oklahoma to plead his case to the full tribal electorate. At a series of public meetings, he explained that his company collected approximately $1 million in profits for the tribes each month. He debunked rumors that he planned to build a casino on the Sand Creek site. And he produced a copy of the agreement that he had signed with the business committee a year earlier. Then Druck tried to leverage Laird Cometsevah's cultural authority within the community, recruiting the chief to lobby on behalf of the deal. The performance did not go well. Someone apparently manipulated the sound system when Cometsevah rose to speak. The audience heard only static. Cometsevah stalked out. Druck followed him at the microphone, but protestors shouted down the businessmen.[48]

The impasse only broke because, even if Sand Creek's commemoration mattered a great deal for the tribes, mammon sometimes trumped memory. In July 2003, Jim Druck accepted a shorter extension on the management agreement than he had originally negotiated with the tribes a year earlier, and the business committee voted through the deal. A relieved Druck informed Alexa Roberts that he would convey the Sand Creek property to the tribes early the following winter. Roberts had for months been trying to ease fears among her neighbors in Kiowa County: some still worried about the arrival of casino gambling in their community; others were more concerned that the national historic site might not open at all, another body blow for an economy already staggered by protracted drought. Roberts "was very happy to have some good news to share when [she] went to the grocery store" in Eads. The deed transfer, she said, would take place at the Cheyenne and Arapaho Tribes' casino sometime around the anniversary of the massacre.[49]

In the interim, the memorialization effort attracted more controversy, including renewed struggles over the designation of Sand Creek as a massacre and the proper placement of the historic site. On September 4, 2003, a crowd, mostly made up of middle-aged and older men, gathered in the ballroom of a Colorado Springs hotel. They arrived clad in raiment familiar to Western history buffs: pressed pants, cowboy shirts and boots, and bolo ties. Beneath chandeliers casting dim light and surrounded by oak paneling, they wandered around a book exhibit and gossiped with old friends about their hobby: "Did you see that article about the Earps in *Wild West?*" "Yeah, I did. It was pretty good, right? It kind of me reminded me of that talk we heard in Tucson a few years back." Participants had traveled from around the United States for the Twenty-Fourth Annual Assembly of the Order of the Indian Wars (OIW).[50]

Jerry Russell, a political consultant and advertising man from Little Rock, Arkansas, best known for jingles he wrote to help sell his candidates to voters in local and statewide elections, began the OIW in 1979. A longtime advocate of preserving Civil War battlefields, whether threatened by development or neglect, Russell had for years arranged popular "roundtables," traveling seminars accompanied by tours of key sites, focused on the "war between the states." He eventually decided, "It'd be neat to do Indian Wars stuff because that's what I'm interested in too." The Colorado gathering, highlighting Sand Creek and the Civil War in the West, united Russell's two historical passions. The meeting also allowed him to continue fighting against what he saw as a pernicious trend: the NPS's effort to include multicultural perspectives in its interpretation of historic sites.[51]

A bear of a man, possessed of a rich baritone and a jocular manner suited to his work in public relations, Russell groused: "It's tedious how politically correct we've become. We can't leave the past alone. We're constantly reinterpreting history guided by our own values." Years earlier, in an opinion piece he penned for his local newspaper, Russell laid out his philosophy of preserving Civil War sites. Condemning the NPS's shift in focus from military history emphasizing battlefield tactics and grand strategy to deeper questions surrounding the war's causes, context, and consequences, Russell suggested that multiculturalism had besieged the nation's history. He singled out Congressman Jesse Jackson Jr. for insisting that the NPS should "interpret slavery as 'the cause' of the Civil War." Russell contended, "Battlefields are not about 'causality' . . . battlefields are not about 'blame' or any political agendas or any socio-cultural agendas." Instead, he finished, "battlefields are about honor." In 2003, Russell announced that he had come to Colorado to redeem John Chivington's besmirched honor by touring "the Sand Creek Battlefield." He explained that as far as he was concerned, "[the NPS's] decision to use the word 'massacre' tells you all you need to know. Visitors won't have a chance to make up their own minds about what happened there. The government has already decided for them: it was a massacre." Russell wondered, "When did we decide that it's always white people bad, Indians good? When did we decide that Sand Creek was a massacre?"[52]

Russell might have addressed his questions to Dee Brown, an author he knew back in Arkansas. Born in a timber camp south of Shreveport in 1908, Brown lived in Louisiana until he was five years old, when his father died. His family then moved to southeastern Arkansas, where Brown grew up listening to his grandmother's tales of her father's exploits with Davy Crockett. Brown loved books and movies as a boy, devouring Mark Twain and Robert Louis Stevenson and going to Westerns when he had the chance. After graduating from high school, he attended Arkansas State Teachers College, where he studied history and prepared for a career as a librarian. For much of his adult life,

Brown worked at the University of Illinois library. In his off hours, he
wrote, relentlessly and with flair, eventually producing twenty-nine
works of adult fiction and nonfiction. In 1970, shortly before retiring
and returning to Arkansas, Brown published one of the most influential accounts of Native American history ever written: *Bury My Heart at
Wounded Knee.*[53]

As Brown's subtitle suggests, he wrote *Bury My Heart at Wounded Knee*
as an "Indian history of the American West." In the two years that he
banged out the book on a manual typewriter, he tried to examine the
region's conquest and settlement through the eyes of its dispossessed
tribal peoples. "I'm a very old Indian," he said of his authorial voice,
"and I'm remembering the past." The memories were bleak. Beginning
with the policy of removal under President Andrew Jackson, when the
U.S. government created a "permanent Indian frontier" beyond the
ninety-fifth meridian, and moving through the era of the Gold Rush,
Brown indicts federal Indian policy. The book then hits its stride when
he turns to the Indian Wars. He paints those conflicts as a series of
slaughters, suggesting that "the culture and civilization of the American Indian was destroyed." That process culminated with the murder of
the Lakota Ghost Dancers, in 1890, at Wounded Knee, South Dakota.
Underscoring the depravity of whites, ranging from elected officials to
U.S. cavalrymen, who participated in the bloody encounters he catalogs,
Brown ends his book in the wake of the carnage at Wounded Knee with
a macabre passage riddled with the era's painful ironies: "It was the
fourth day after Christmas in the Year of our Lord 1890. When the first
torn and bleeding bodies were carried into the candlelit church, those
who were conscious could see Christmas greenery hanging from the
open rafters. Across the chancel front above the pulpit was strung a
crudely lettered banner: PEACE ON EARTH, GOOD WILL TO MEN."[54]

The Cheyenne people figure prominently throughout *Bury My Heart
at Wounded Knee,* with Sand Creek occupying one of the book's longest
and bloodiest chapters. Relying on accounts produced by eyewitnesses
sympathetic to Black Kettle's bands, Brown adopts a narrative arc and
interpretive frame similar to those of George Bent and Silas Soule,
highlighting many of the same grim details: the spring skirmishes that
set the wheels of injustice in motion; Governor Evans's two summer-
time proclamations; the Camp Weld conference, where Chivington

offered the Arapahos and Cheyennes protection if they came in to Fort Lyon; the night before the bloodshed, when Chivington reportedly anticipated "wading in gore"; Silas Soule and Joseph Cramer replying, noting that targeting the Native people camped on Sand Creek would be "murder in every sense of the word"; the attack itself, when Black Kettle flew both white and American flags over his lodge, when White Antelope fell in a hail of bullets, calmly singing his death song, and when Chivington's men ran roughshod, slicing genitalia from their victims, including, in one observer's words, a "squaw cut open with an unborn child . . . lying by her side." For Brown, Sand Creek was a massacre, another grisly chapter among many in the West's history.[55]

Scholars greeted *Bury My Heart at Wounded Knee* with skepticism bordering on contempt. Most professional historians damned Brown's work with the faint praise reserved for well-told tales that do not rise to the level of the academy's analytical standards: he had produced a gripping narrative. From there, critics of *Bury My Heart at Wounded Knee* covered a lot of ground, but most agreed that the book failed as scholarship on several levels: Brown had eschewed balance, instead writing a "polemic"; he had not interrogated his Native sources, apparently "believing that Indians only spoke or wrote the truth"; and he had "committed errors" of fact and "distorted the evidence." Writing in the discipline's flagship journal, the *American Historical Review,* Francis Paul Prucha, the nation's foremost historian of federal Indian policy, leveled by far the harshest charges. Prucha treated *Bury My Heart at Wounded Knee* like a blanket infected with smallpox, suggesting that it was not merely flawed but dangerous. Brushing aside "praise given . . . by uncritical and unknowledgeable reviewers," he warned colleagues, "the unwary reader may falsely assume that the book is a scholarly historical work." He instead described Brown's work as "subtly dishonest" and filled with "a great many errors," adding up to "considerable misinformation." Prucha concluded, "It is to be regretted that this sort of 'Indian history of the American west' gains such popular acceptance."[56]

There was the irony. For no matter how much professional historians derided Dee Brown's work, his book captured the public's attention. As Prucha feared, reviewers outside the academy raved about *Bury My Heart at Wounded Knee.* Thomas Lask, writing in the *New York Times,* described it as "original, remarkable, and finally heartbreaking," concluding, "It is a book both impossible to read and impossible to put down." Phyllis Pearson, one of few Native Americans who evaluated the book in print, hailed it as "the first accurate and comprehensive account of how the western United States was taken from the American Indian." Congratulating Brown for his humanity and originality, she suggested, "This is a book every Indian should read" and also that "White people . . . should read this book, too." They did—in unbelievable numbers. *Bury My Heart at Wounded Knee* spent more than a year on the *New York Times* Best Seller List, sold in excess of 5 million copies in the time between its publication and Brown's death, and appeared in nearly two dozen foreign-language translations. The book became a phenomenon, one of the most popular histories of the American West ever written.[57]

Whatever *Bury My Heart at Wounded Knee*'s merits may have been, onlookers agreed that good timing helped account for its immediate success and its lasting impact. Brown published his book as Native people redoubled their struggle for civil rights, as public opinion about the nation's involvement in the Vietnam War reached a tipping point, and as many Americans searched for alternative spirituality during the so-called New Age. In 1968, a group of tribal activists formed the American Indian Movement. Just a year later, some of the organization's members helped take over Alcatraz Island, signaling the arrival of Red Power on the national stage. Meanwhile, eight days before the start of the occupation of Alcatraz, a then-obscure investigative journalist named Seymour Hersh broke the story of atrocities committed by American soldiers serving under Lieutenant William Calley in Vietnam. Calley's men, Hersh reported, stood accused by the U.S. Army of killing more than one hundred villagers in the hamlet of My Lai. By the time *Bury My Heart at Wounded Knee* appeared in bookstores, a majority of Americans disapproved of the Vietnam War and grappled with the capacity of U.S. soldiers to slaughter innocent civilians; the modern civil rights movement had captured the nation's attention, maintaining a steady focus on issues of equality and racism; and many white observers were fascinated by the traditional culture of Native people. As one reviewer understated, "Brown is clearly one of a few authors who manage to write the right book at the right time."[58]

Whether books or movies spur or mirror social change is always difficult to know for certain. But when *Bury My Heart at Wounded Knee*, along with films like *Soldier Blue* and *Little Big Man,* all released in 1970, captivated audiences eager to embrace critiques of American militarism, they helped galvanize sympathy for the plight of Native peoples. If Paul Hutton, a celebrated Western historian, exaggerated when he claimed of *Bury My Heart at Wounded Knee* that "we all went to bed thinking one way about the Indian Wars and the Indian people and we woke up the next morning after that book was published and we never thought the same way again," even Brown's critics agreed that his work had a significant impact on readers. Richard White, for example, another renowned historian of the American West, bemoaned Dee Brown's tendency to portray Native people as noble, passive victims, denying them an active role in their own history—"it's as if it didn't matter what Indians did, only what whites did to them"—but still allowed that, despite its flaws, *Bury My Heart at Wounded Knee* had inspired him. And Donald Fixico, among the leading lights in the field of Native American Studies, saw the book's publication as a taproot for his discipline. Sandy MacNabb, who worked in the Bureau of Indian Affairs during the Nixon administration, went further, suggesting that Brown's work, much like other important books of the era, including Rachel Carson's *Silent Spring* and Betty Friedan's *The Feminine Mystique,* helped shift federal policy by packaging complicated ideas for popular consumption: "you can't affect public opinion unless the public knows what you're talking about."[59]

By the time that Jerry Russell arrived in Colorado, wondering who to blame for the popular perception that Sand Creek had been a massacre, he could no longer put the question to Dee Brown, who had died less than a year earlier, at the age of ninety-four. Russell nevertheless acknowledged *Bury My Heart at Wounded Knee*'s importance in shaping the collective memory of Sand Creek, and the Indian Wars more broadly, for generations of readers. The book, after all, had been published during an early flash point, the struggle over the Vietnam War, in what became known as the culture wars in the United States, a conflict whose rearguard actions Russell and his troops in the OIW were still fighting. But Russell nevertheless argued, "we can't just blame Dee Brown for how politically correct this country has become in recent years." When asked to elaborate, he explained, "Some folks, bleeding hearts from back east, have been calling Sand Creek a massacre for a long time."

Russell concluded, "Maybe we ought to let Dee Brown off the hook and blame old Helen Hunt Jackson instead."[60]

Throughout most of her life, Helen Hunt Jackson ignored the plight of Native Americans, the vast majority of whom had long since been exterminated or removed from her childhood home in the mountains of western Massachusetts. Born in Amherst, in 1830, Helen Fiske grew up in a bookish home. Her father, a Congregational minister, taught Latin and Greek at Amherst College and authored a guide to classical literature. Her mother, who wrote children's books and graceful letters to friends and family, died when Fiske was fourteen years old; her father died three years later, but not before having arranged for his daughter to study at elite boarding schools, where she met influential friends, including a young woman named Emily Dickinson. In 1851, Fiske married Edward Hunt, then a lieutenant with a bright future in the U.S. Army Corps of Engineers. Two years after that, she gave birth to a son, who died before reaching his first birthday. She had a second son two years later, but personal tragedy remained her constant companion. In 1863, her husband died in an accident. And her second child died in 1865. Helen Hunt had spent most of her adult life mourning lost family. She decided to cope with her sorrow by following her deceased parents' example: she took up the pen.[61]

Ready to begin a new chapter in her life, Hunt placed a few short pieces in the *New York Evening Post* in 1865. The following winter, she looked for a setting more conducive to writing. She moved to Newport, Rhode Island, settling in a boardinghouse where Thomas Wentworth Higginson lived. Already established as a Civil War hero, a social reformer, an author, and an arbiter of good taste in New England literary circles, Higginson became Hunt's mentor. Over the next few years, her career blossomed. Her stories and poems appeared in the most prestigious journals of the day. But then, suffering from a respiratory ailment in fall 1873, Hunt decamped from the damp eastern seaboard. She moved to Colorado Springs, where she breathed crisp mountain air and began courting with William Sharpless Jackson, a banker and railroad speculator. They married two years later. Jackson, putting down roots in western soil, explored her adopted state, learned its history, and passed that knowledge on to readers in vivid travel essays. Although these were relatively happy and successful years for Jackson, she missed the bustle of city life, especially the company of her old circle of writer friends. She traveled back east in 1879 to celebrate Oliver Wendell Holmes's birthday. While in Boston for the party, Jackson attended a public lecture offered by Chief Standing Bear of the Ponca tribe. She found herself enthralled by Standing Bear's story, and she devoted the rest of her career to working within the burgeoning Indian reform movement.[62]

Jackson's background fit the profile of a nineteenth-century social reformer: born in New England, raised in a Protestant evangelical household, befriended by leading activists. But despite close ties to people like Thomas Wentworth Higginson, Jackson had yet to engage directly with politics. Hearing Standing Bear speak, though, awakened something in her. Three years earlier, the Poncas had rejected the federal government's decision to resettle them in Indian Territory (present-day Oklahoma). Despite their protests, Secretary of the Interior Carl Schurz ruled that they would nevertheless have to be evicted from their homeland in Nebraska. In 1877, the tribe began a long trek to their new reservation, where many of them—including Standing Bear's only living son—died of malnutrition, malaria, and other diseases. A year later, Standing Bear, accompanied by a small group of followers, carried his child's body back to Nebraska, where the Ponca chief hoped to bury his boy. Soon after they arrived, U.S. soldiers arrested them for having left their reservation without permission from federal authorities. While the Poncas waited under guard at Fort Omaha, Thomas Tibbles, an editor at a local newspaper, publicized their case, found them legal representation, and, after they won their freedom at trial, arranged for Standing Bear to embark on a multicity speaking tour in fall 1879. The chief discussed his tribe's history and the federal government's mistreatment of indigenous peoples. The audience at the Boston lecture included the poet Henry Wadsworth Longfellow and Massachusetts Senator Henry Dawes, as well as Jackson, who, after hearing Standing Bear deliver his speech, decided to turn her literary talents to ameliorating the suffering of Native Americans.[63]

Jackson campaigned by writing letters to prominent newspapers, including the *New York Tribune*. Pugnacious and scathing, her first missive damned Secretary of the Interior Schurz, who was also renowned as something of a reformer, for callousness, cruelty, and dereliction of duty. Schurz defended himself, explaining in an open letter that the decision to remove the Poncas predated his administration and that the tribe had acclimated quickly to life in Indian Territory. Early in 1880, as her exchange with Schurz helped keep Standing Bear in the public eye, Jackson turned her attention closer to home, to Colorado, focusing on another episode in which the government had mistreated Native people: the so-called White River War, which resulted in the removal of most Ute peoples from Colorado. The previous fall, Nathan Meeker, federal Indian agent to the Utes, had summoned cavalry support after his conversion efforts enraged the tribe. When the troops arrived, the Utes seized the offensive, holding off the cavalry and killing Meeker and nine of his colleagues. The fight lasted for nearly a week, ending only when the Utes withdrew from the field. In the aftermath of the violence, some outraged Coloradans fondly recalled John Chivington and called for "another Sand Creek" to quiet the Utes forever.[64]

With the "Indian question" and Sand Creek back in the headlines, local sentiment along the Front Range typically favored the men of the 3rd Colorado and their unrepentant commander. One contemporary history of the region, written by W. B. Vickers, contextualized the Ute uprising by referring back to summer and fall 1864. Vickers granted that "the Sand Creek fight" had "evoked a great deal of hostile criticism" and had even in some quarters "been called a massacre." But, he countered, "If so, it was a massacre of assassins, for fresh scalps of white men, women and children were found in the Indian camp after the battle." In another dispatch to the *Tribune*, Jackson refuted such claims, defending the Utes and declaring that Sand Creek had actually been an unwarranted and depraved bloodletting. She insisted that the Arapahos and Cheyennes gathered at Sand Creek had been guaranteed "perfect safety" by white authorities in Colorado, that Black Kettle had flown both the American and a white flag on the day of the attack, that John Chivington's troops had committed atrocities during the mayhem, and that they had returned to Denver as heroes, where the local press had celebrated those brave "Colorado soldiers" who had "covered themselves with glory."[65]

Such claims did not sit well with William Byers, who, as editor of the *Rocky Mountain News* at the time of Sand Creek, had defended Chivington from charges that he had massacred peaceful Indians. Picking up where he had left off a decade and a half earlier, Byers responded to Jackson with a letter of his own. Hewing to a line drawn by Chivington in the aftermath of the bloodshed, Byers claimed that the Colorado volunteers had discovered ironclad evidence that the camp at Sand Creek contained hostile warriors: "scalps of white men" which "had not yet dried"; "an Indian saddle-blanket entirely fringed around the edges with white women's scalps, with the long, fair hair attached"; and the skin of a white woman stretched over the pommel of a saddle. He also denied that Black Kettle's people had been under the protection of the government. He then insisted that corruption had compromised the Sand Creek investigations. Finally, he guessed that if Jackson "had been in Denver in the early part of that summer," as Byers had been, "when the bloated, festering bodies of the Hungate family . . . were drawn through the streets naked in an ox-wagon, cut, mutilated, and scalped—the work of those same red fiends who were so justly punished at Sand Creek," she would have offered a "word of excuse" for the Colorado volunteers. "Sand Creek," he explained, had "saved Colorado, and taught the Indians the most salutary lesson they had ever learned." Jackson could not understand this part of the state's history, Byers concluded, because she had been back east, living in comfort and safety, at the time.[66]

Back and forth they went. Jackson cited chapter and verse from the Sand Creek inquiries. Byers countered that her critique, written so long after the fact, should not be trusted. Byers also expanded his claims to encompass Chivington's most ambitious defense of Sand Creek. The violence, Byers said, had ended the region's Indian problem. "We, who were so unfortunate as to be citizens of Colorado at the time, know that a very great majority of the savage atrocities of that period occurred before the battle of Sand Creek," he began. "We know that the Sand Creek Indian camp was the common rendezvous of the hostile bands who were committing these atrocities, [and] we know that comparatively few occurred afterward." He added, "No amount of special pleading, no reiteration of partial statements, and withholding of more important truths, will change the facts so well known to the earlier settlers of Colorado." For the state's pioneers, memories of Sand Creek, forged in an era of violence, remained immutable even in a time of peace. Jackson rebutted first with figures: the "Indian war" following Sand Creek had cost more than $30 million. If Chivington had intended to pacify the local tribes, he had failed. Then she waved the bloody shirt: fighting Native people on the Plains during that conflict had required "no less than 8,000 troops . . . withdrawn from the effective forces engaged with the Rebellion." Sand Creek not only had been a massacre, she charged, it had also detracted from the Union war effort.[67]

While Helen Hunt Jackson sparred with William Byers in the *Herald*'s pages, she also worked on a longer manuscript examining the federal government's mistreatment of Native Americans. Later titled *Century of Dishonor*, Jackson's book has much in common with Dee Brown's *Bury My Heart at Wounded Knee*. A relentless exposé of double-dealing, *Century of Dishonor*'s chapters detail the bloody consequences of a long series of shattered agreements between whites and tribal peoples, including the Cheyennes. As in Brown's work, Jackson places the violence at Sand Creek in the context of numerous gory conflicts, suggesting that it was hardly unique, a by-product of a single individual's treachery or the poor character of the Colorado troops. Instead, the bloodshed stemmed from misguided federal policy and represented a predictable result of "the robbery, the cruelty which were done under the cloak of this hundred years of treaty-making and treaty-breaking." Jackson writes, "The history of the United States Government's repeated violations of faith with the Indians thus convicts us, as a nation, not only of having outraged the principles of justice, which are the basis of international law; and of having laid ourselves open to the accusation of both cruelty and perfidy; but of having made ourselves liable to all punishments which follow upon such sins." Only by repenting of those sins, by overhauling its treatment of Native American peoples, could the United States avoid being harshly judged by "any civilized nation who might see fit to call us to account, and to that more certain natural punishment which, sooner or later, as surely comes from evil-doing as harvests come from sown seed."[68]

Jackson wrote *Century of Dishonor* as a political brickbat. Upon its publication, in 1881, she sent copies, bound in red and embossed with a quote from Ben Franklin—"Look upon your hands! They are stained with the blood of your relations."—to every member of Congress. Most lawmakers ignored it. But the book nevertheless gained cultural purchase. With the Modoc War, the Red River War, and the Great Sioux

War, including the Battle of the Little Bighorn, having just taken place, some officials in the Department of the Interior acknowledged that federal Indian policy had largely failed. They turned to reform. And though Jackson's arguments about tribal autonomy were out of place during the so-called era of assimilation, many politicians eventually embraced her work. Even Senator Henry Dawes, who later crafted the government's policy of general allotment, a sweeping effort at detribalization, admired Jackson. *Century of Dishonor*'s impact, then, outstripped its sales figures, particularly after Jackson's *Ramona,* a story of California Native people that some observers have called the "Indians' *Uncle Tom's Cabin,*" became a sensation in 1884. Jackson died a year after that, a celebrated figure in American letters and politics. In the time since, her work has shaped popular memories of Sand Creek as a massacre, just as Jerry Russell claimed when he arrived in Jackson's hometown of Colorado Springs more than a century later. Russell hoped that his Order of the Indian Wars would serve as a counterweight to Jackson's and Dee Brown's books, "balancing the way people think about Western history."[69]

At first glance, the OIW's Colorado Springs meeting seemed like a relatively low-key affair, a close approximation of a small scholarly conference: seminar-style papers delivered to a fidgeting audience, followed by question-and-answer periods. But the content was the key. Many of the presenters focused their wrath on what they labeled politically correct histories. As for Sand Creek, they sometimes parroted John Chivington's stories of the violence. Jerry Russell warned of the memorialization effort, "Ben Nighthorse Campbell will make sure the site only deals with the Indian side. And that's just wrong. . . . For years, the Battle of Little Bighorn was called the Custer Massacre. But now, everything's changed. They don't say 'massacre' anymore because it's pejorative, divisive. And yet the National Park Service will call Sand Creek a massacre even though the monument down there says battleground." Mike Koury, a local author and editor who years earlier had fought to keep Sand Creek among the Civil War battles listed on the statue located on the state capitol steps in Denver, next gave a paper titled "I Stand by Sand Creek: A Defense of Colonel Chivington and the Third Colorado." Koury explained that he would speak in the "spirit of reconciliation," trying to "right the wrongs of the past." Still, he continued, he would take care to "not infuse the [Sand Creek] battlefield with a modern meaning untrue to the past" nor "bend it artificially to serve contemporary needs." With that said, he argued: "The 3rd Colorado did their job. Now some of them were overly zealous, and they did more than their job. But that's not to condemn the regiment, the entire group." So it went into the evening.[70]

The event continued the next day, when the OIW traveled to Kiowa County for a tour of "the real Sand Creek battlefield": the Bowen ranch. Months earlier, Jerry Russell had contacted Alexa Roberts, seeking permission to enter the national historic site. Ed Bearss, an expert on the Civil War and World War II who had retired years earlier from his job as the NPS's chief historian, had agreed to lead the excursion. Russell assumed that Bearss's participation would open doors at the NPS. Roberts, though, wrote back to Russell, informing him that the site was private property, owned by Jim Druck, and off limits to the public. Russell, annoyed that he would "have to scramble around now and see if [I] can come up with a solution to the situation," charged that the NPS was more focused on satisfying its Native American patron, Senator Campbell, than on fulfilling its mandate to serve the public. Jeff Broome, the Denver professor who was an OIW member and who had worked with the Bowens in the past, then suggested to Russell that he inquire about going to their land instead. Russell did that, heard the saga of the Sand Creek search from the Bowens' perspective, and, after agreeing to champion their cause, received permission to visit the family ranch.[71]

The tour captivated the OIW members. The Bowens laid out a table, covered with artifacts drawn from their land, in an Eads restaurant. Using a large map, Chuck Bowen pointed out where he had found the displayed materials and shared his view that the NPS had systematically gamed the Sand Creek search so that Bill Dawson's property would become the centerpiece of the historic site. The NPS had done this, he explained, to placate Senator Campbell and the descendants, and also because Dawson would sell out and the Bowen family would not. Indians, in this view, had become the puppet masters of regional collective memory; the NPS was pursuing "a multicultural agenda" and assaulting American heritage. The group then loaded into vans and toured the Bowen ranch, listening to Ed Bearss's version of the Sand Creek story.[72]

Two days later, Russell made good on part of the deal that he had struck with Chuck and Sheri Bowen: he issued a press release, explaining that the NPS had again misplaced the Sand Creek Massacre National Historic Site. The "real Sand Creek site," Russell claimed, could be found on the Bowen ranch. After years of sparring with the NPS over the interpretation of Civil War battlegrounds, Russell had finally exacted his revenge. The Bowen property provided him with a competing narrative to undermine the story that the NPS would tell at the "traditional site," the neighboring Dawson ranch. A month earlier, Alexa Roberts had written to Dwight Pitcaithley, then the NPS's chief historian and a friend of Ed Bearss, hoping that Pitcaithley could convince Bearss to intervene with Russell on her behalf. Roberts suggested that the OIW would "discredit the National Park Service's, Tribes', and Congress's efforts" to that point. "Every such event," she explained to Pitcaithley, "derails much of the progress we have made in the site establishment effort." Finally, she noted that, while the ensuing controversy would "delight the press," it would also deepen preexisting worries among Kiowa County's residents, making her job that much more difficult. Bearss and Jerry Greene, who also had worked with the OIW in the past, reached out to Russell. By then, though, it was too late. Roberts found herself shifting back into damage control mode.[73]

6

You Can't Carve Things in Stone

In September 2003, after the Order of the Indian Wars (OIW) visited Colorado, the Sand Creek memory fight shifted to a new venue: the Internet. The struggle to memorialize the massacre became more public than it had been since the nineteenth and early twentieth centuries, when William Byers, Helen Hunt Jackson, and George Bent had argued over Sand Creek in the pages of books, magazines, and news-papers. In 1999, an Eads resident named Sharon Pearson created a web-site to boost Kiowa County's economic prospects. Against a backdrop of sky blue, Pearson placed images of the open prairie on her home page. Beneath enticements to visitors—"The vast beauty of Kiowa County is . . . only a 2 to 3 hour drive from Denver and Colorado Springs. Visi-ble wildlife and scenic vistas provide welcome relief from the snarl and congestion of crowded cities."—she offered descriptions of local attrac-tions (hunting, fishing, camping), an information clearinghouse (pub-lic notices, business listings, a community calendar), and updates about the status of the Sand Creek site, including a "discussion forum" where people could chat about the massacre. After Jerry Russell strafed the National Park Service (NPS) during his tour of the Bowens' ranch, the Sand Creek forum became an online coffeehouse, with people from throughout the nation weighing in on the memorial's future.[1]

Alexa Roberts worried that attacks on the NPS, growing out of Jerry Russell's dealings with the Bowens, might compromise her partnership with the residents of Kiowa County. Unfortunately, some local people still distrusted federal authorities, including Roberts, even though she had woven herself into the fabric of the community. She had made her home in town. She had attended functions that marked the passage of time in the county, from high school plays to the annual fair. And she had cooperated with local law enforcement, elected officials, and land-owners, trying, at every step of the memorialization process, to ensure that the creation of the historic site would not burden Kiowa County's infrastructure. In short, she had been a good neighbor. And as time had passed, she had harvested the fruits of her outreach efforts. "I think people eventually stopped seeing me as a fed," she recalled, "and started to look at me as part of the local scene." But then the OIW con-troversy cropped up. Bill Dawson's ranch remained in the hands of a casino magnate. The Sand Creek historic site existed on paper only. Its doors were closed to the public; as an engine of economic development, it had stalled. In that context, charges of federal bungling and arro-gance threatened to undermine relationships Roberts had worked hard over time to build in Eads.[2]

Jerry Russell had his own worries. He had agreed, as part of the deal to gain access to the Bowen ranch, to send out a press release in the days leading to the tour. He had promised to explain key elements of Chuck and Sheri Bowen's grievances against the NPS. Fearing the po-tential for public relations fallout, Alexa Roberts had tried to nip the problem in the bud. She had asked Ed Bearss and Jerry Greene, friends of Russell, to explain the NPS's side of the dispute. They had agreed. But Russell had proceeded anyway, reporting that the OIW had visited the Bowens' ranch, "the real Sand Creek site," as opposed to the former Dawson property, a pretender. Reporters ignored the story, leaving the Bowens feeling betrayed again. Russell tried to mend fences with them, thanking the Bowens for their hospitality in an e-mail asking OIW members to post to the Kiowa County website and share experiences from the tour of the family ranch. Russell's gesture doubled as an act of defiance toward the NPS. He pointedly suggested that commenters might want to note that Chuck Bowen had made "a persuasive case for believing that the site of Black Kettle's village was on the Bowen Ranch."[3]

Internet-based discussion fora allow people with a variety of shared interests to congregate in cyberspace, where they can chat about their common passions: cooking, knitting, parenting, politics, and so on. If one looks hard enough, one can turn up sites in dusty corners of the Web devoted to almost any topic under the sun. Assuming they share a common language, cat fanciers or philatelists in Nome, Alaska, can converse, in real time, with like-minded individuals in Harare, Zimbabwe. These sites flirt with fulfilling the Net's promise as a social experiment: by annihilating the space and time separating their users, they create functioning communities. But the results are often less utopian than that. With participants distant from one another, their identities obscured by pseudonyms, the Web can become an echo chamber, amplifying heated discussions. Liberated from the rules of civil discourse, participants often assume bad faith in their interlocutors, hurl epithets, and shout across the digital divide by typing in ALL CAPS. Before the OIW's visit to the Bowen ranch, discussions on the Kiowa County website's Sand Creek forum typically focused on the massacre's details or on the status of the memorial. People inquired about topics like a prospective opening date for the site, the composition of the 3rd Colorado Regiment, or the best available biography of Chief Black Kettle. That all changed after the OIW membership descended, virtually, on Kiowa County for a second time. And though Jerry Russell later maintained that he had not anticipated the controversy that his e-mail request would stir up—protesting, "How could I have known?"—an impish chortle suggested otherwise.[4]

The pixel war that resulted from Russell's pot-stirring ate up time and bandwidth, unsettling NPS officials, Kiowa County residents, and the descendants. The post that touched off the firestorm derided Russell's original request, labeling the OIW's members "racist" and suggesting that they "still think the American Indian is 'the enemy.'" Written by someone posting under the screen name "Ron," the missive explained that Russell had used the site's placement as a stalking horse for reopening an age-old debate over whether the violence should be described as a battle or a massacre. Russell, Ron noted, "has launched another campaign to delete the term 'massacre' from all Park Service material dealing with the Sand Creek site." But, Ron explained, "every credible historian who has written on Sand Creek has concluded it was a massacre." Composing his post on the second anniversary of the 9/11 attacks, Ron claimed the high ground in what he apparently saw as a struggle over the relationship between patriotism and public memory.

Urging people to avoid the Kiowa County website, he asked that they instead "write one of our soldiers currently fighting for our freedom in Afghanistan and/or Iraq."[5]

The next few posts disregarded Ron and followed Russell's script: noting the fine time that the OIW's members had had during their visit to Kiowa County, thanking the Bowens for hosting them, and remarking on the compelling evidence Chuck Bowen had presented to support his claim that the "Sand Creek affair" had taken place on the family ranch. Then Jeff Broome, the Denver-area professor who had made the match between Jerry Russell and the Bowens, engaged with Ron, insisting that people should ignore semantics and focus on the question of historical authenticity borne out by archeology. "The real issue," Broome explained, was "where was the November 29, 1864 village of Black Kettle located and where did the fight/massacre/battle occur?" He reiterated, "That is the question and readers should not be diverted away from THAT issue by getting involved with the emotional issue of whether it was a massacre or a battle." Based on seeing the artifacts, "the village in 1864 was on the Bowen property and not at the traditional site," Broome insisted. "Regardless of how the new National Parks site is managed or what it is named," he concluded, "the question is, do you want it on the real site or a site that had nothing to do with November 29, 1864?" From Broome's point of view, people had a choice to make: between fealty to the past, represented by the Bowens' tireless efforts, or a slapdash treatment of Western history, the interpretation offered by the NPS.[6]

At that juncture, another OIW member, Greg Michno, an independent scholar, weighed in. Yes, Michno agreed, the historic site's proper location mattered. But so, too, did the unresolved question of whether Sand Creek had been a battle or a massacre. Moving forward, the dispute would have multiple fronts: one focused on the placement of the Sand Creek site, another on the proper designation for the violence, and a third on the question of who had the standing to speak authoritatively about such a contested episode from the region's past.[7]

Greg Michno seemed like an improbable culture warrior. A slight man with a soft voice and thoughtful manner, he gathered himself, pausing for several beats, before speaking. Retired from a job in state government, Michno lived north of Denver, in a home with a large li-

brary and a view of the Rockies. The author of books on World War II
and the Indian Wars, he had just completed *Battle at Sand Creek: The
Military Perspective* when the OIW arrived in Colorado. Michno believed
that the NPS, by focusing on the Dawson ranch, had trapped itself in a
web of lies. "They can't admit they've got the wrong place, because it's
going to make them look foolish," he said. As for whether Sand Creek
was a massacre, he framed the question using post-9/11 terms: "These
people [the Arapahos and Cheyennes] were not peaceful. Black Kettle,
he was harboring terrorists." Turning to numbers, Michno elaborated,
"Out of the 1,450 or so fights during the Indian Wars, there were only six
battles in which the soldiers or militia lost more men, took more casualties, than at Sand Creek. So in the context of the Indian wars, it was a
heck of a fight." The NPS's nomenclature did violence to the past, to the
memory of decent soldiers. "It just cements it that it was a massacre,"
Michno observed, "that it was some horrible atrocity committed by U.S.
troops against Native Americans." He concluded by scoffing at "politically correct Native American histories": "They're always victims. They're
always downtrodden, victimized by oppressive power. And there's some
truth to that, yeah. But it's an excuse now. Get over it."[8]

Michno brought an academic bearing and deep wells of frustration to the dispute at the Kiowa County website. "For a century," he
wrote, "Sand Creek has been portrayed as a massacre, and there has
been good cause for the portrayal. There is another side to the issue,
however, which has not gotten equal time, and that is from the military and pioneer perspective." He went on to represent the Chivingtonite viewpoint, established during the federal inquiries following
Sand Creek: "the Indians attacked on Sand Creek were not peaceful";
"they had been raiding and killing for years"; "those particular Indians were not under the protection of the soldiers"; and "there were
white scalps found in the teepees." In the end, Michno explained, all
he wanted was "the preservation of the correct location where the village and fight actually took place, and, even more important, [to] have
the NPS present the story in an even-handed manner." He suggested,
"Both sides need to be given," so that "the visitor [could] form his or
her own opinion." The results would be palliative: "In this way, instead
of aggravating wounds that have been with us for too long, perhaps we
can start to heal them."[9]

News travels fast on the Internet. For some readers of the Kiowa County website, Michno's call for a reappraisal of Sand Creek seemed like moral equivalence. Less than two hours after Michno posted his comment, a man named Smoke Randolph dashed off a reply. He suggested, "wounds cannot heal when posts such as the one by Greg Michno contain such faulty and selective research." After calling Michno "obviously ignorant," Randolph demanded evidence that Black Kettle's people had been hostile. He pointed to Silas Soule's testimony, insisting, "Sand Creek was a massacre, an ambush of innocents, who were betrayed by Colorado authorities." Michno's rejoinder, which indicated that he was "concerned by [Randolph's] anger," did not defuse the tension. Randolph shot back that he still wanted Michno to show his work, to document assertions about the presence of white scalps in Black Kettle's camp. When Michno ignored him, Randolph mocked the historian: "Well, it appears that our friend, Mr. Michno, has declined the invitation to provide sources for his ridiculous claims about Sand Creek." Randolph then wrestled the flag from Michno's grasp by questioning his patriotism: "Or maybe he's just too busy to respond—maybe working on a new book—one that justifies the Japanese attack on Pearl Harbor."[10]

As charges and countercharges bounced around cyberspace, the conflict became still another echo of Sand Creek, this time the rhetorical skirmishes that followed the massacre. Chivington's modern defenders, Greg Michno and Jeff Broome, worked to repair the Fighting Parson's damaged reputation. His latter-day detractors, Ron and his ally, Smoke Randolph, stood opposite, eager to uphold the honor of Silas Soule and the Cheyennes and Arapahos at Sand Creek. The two sides even struggled over the same details that had been at issue in the decades following the massacre: the disposition, measured by the presence of white scalps in their camp, of the Native people butchered at Sand Creek; the reliability of the deponents who had provided eyewitness testimony about the event's particulars; and the existence of a symbol, the American flag, that either had or had not flown over Black Kettle's lodge during the melee. It seemed that this brave new world of online discourse could indeed annihilate space and time, sometimes bringing past and present into uncomfortable proximity.[11]

With their professional credibility and their love of country called into question, Michno and Broome returned to the fray. Michno answered Smoke Randolph's challenge; he toted out sources, quoting from the *Official Records of the War of the Rebellion* and other primary documents. Pointing to testimony offered by members of the 3rd Colorado Regiment, he tried to substantiate the contention that Black Kettle's people had been involved in the depredations visited upon settlers during spring and summer 1864. Thaddeus Bell, for instance, claimed to have seen "a good many white scalps" in the Sand Creek camp. Luther Wilson remembered "one new scalp, a white man's, and two old ones." And Stephen Decatur recalled the horror of stumbling upon "a number of white person's scalps—men's women's and children's," including tresses of "auburn and hung in ringlets." Broome, for his part, kept hammering a familiar theme: that the Dawson ranch "IS NOT CONNECTED TO NOVEMBER 29, 1864 AT ALL." He suggested that anonymous critics like Ron, "who hide their identity," were akin to the enemy "our good people fighting in Iraq are dealing with ... right now." Finally, Broome set the record straight, noting that he had, along with heeding Jerry Russell's earlier call to post on the Kiowa County website, written to "a serviceman, sending him a package, and ... a note telling him of my appreciation of his performance of duty to our country."[12]

Back and forth it went for a month, each new argument receiving a quick rebuttal. With neither side giving an inch regarding the validity of the other's evidence—Smoke Randolph charged that Greg Michno chose for "witnesses" a group of "thugs, lowlifes, criminals," all men implicated in the slaughter at Sand Creek and thus animated by self-interest; Michno expressed qualms about Silas Soule's character and motivations—the dispute turned from a discussion of sources to the more complicated issue of analysis, resting finally on the thorny question of who had the proper training to interpret Sand Creek. Ron repeatedly labeled Michno and Broome "pseudo-historians," suggesting that their views could not be trusted. Randolph piled on, insisting that Michno stood at odds with scholarly consensus because of his "faulty and incomplete" research. Michno, dedicated to his craft, responded with long lists of citations. Broome then asked, "What constitutes a 'Real' historian?" He answered by citing his own book on the Indian

Wars and then reasserting his academic credentials. Randolph just jeered that Broome had a "mail-order PhD." By that time, the light-to-heat ratio had become vanishingly small.[13]

All the while, Alexa Roberts lurked on the sidelines, upset that her neighbors, her superiors, and the descendants could hear the screams emanating from cyberspace. "It was frustrating," Roberts recalled. "We wanted to build trust between the tribes, the Park Service, and the people of the county. And here we had this thing playing out online, with all kinds of people claiming we had the wrong site and that Sand Creek was a battle." After Jeff Broome and Greg Michno preserved their dignity by walking away from the fight at September's end, another OIW member posted a comment, seeing if perhaps the argument might be stricken from the electronic record: "I wonder if the webmaster would consider cleaning the slate on this discussion site." Roberts at the time contemplated asking Sharon Pearson to go a step beyond that and take down the entire website. But after Pearson rejected the call to scrub the offending posts, suggesting that people upset by the discussion should click away from the forum, Roberts decided against it: "It's a danger-ous thing when federal officials try to censor public comments." Never-theless, she readied herself for blowback.[14]

Roberts's bosses were starting to wonder what could go wrong next with a site that seemed like it was doing the NPS's image more harm than good. Meanwhile, the Cheyenne descendants fumed. Laird Com-etsevah saw the Internet scuffle as evidence that some residents of southeastern Colorado, working with the OIW, could not be trusted. "If they can't see that Sand Creek was a massacre," he wondered, "how in the world can we be expected to work with these people?" Pointing to the NPS's *Site Location Study,* the contents of the Treaty of the Little Arkansas, and the national historic site's name, Cometsevah protested: "It's not just Indian people calling Sand Creek a massacre anymore. The government says so too." Jerry Russell, by contrast, delighted at the thought that people were scuffling anew over nomenclature. Con-sidering the substance of Jeff Broome's and Greg Michno's posts on the Kiowa County website, Russell suggested, "If Custer and his men didn't get massacred at the Little Bighorn, then neither did the Indians at Sand Creek. What's good sauce for the goose is good for the gander. And it's refreshing that somebody is finally supporting the troops."[15]

The troops, as it happened, could take care of themselves. Just as the online contretemps settled into a lull, Captain Charles Zakhem and other officers from the Colorado National Guard visited the Sand Creek site on October 24, 2003. The guardsmen were there for a "Staff Ride," an exercise in which army personnel study a significant moment from the nation's military history, travel to its scene, and then "try to replay the event." Civil War battlefields, Gettysburg especially, are common locations for Staff Rides on the East Coast. But in Colorado, Zakhem regretted, "our choice of destinations is pretty limited." Having settled on Sand Creek, he and his colleagues spent months researching the slaughter, learning that "unspeakable things happened there." Because the modern guardsmen identified with troops from the 1st and 3rd Regiments, Zakhem revealed, "It really put a shock into us that this was done by Coloradans. That was really tough for us to swallow." Zakhem "came to the conclusion that it's more a scene of a crime than a battle." The previous day, he and his colleagues had presented the results of their studies during a seminar held at their base at Fort Carson.[16]

Fort Carson is located just south of Colorado Springs. Named for Kit Carson, one of Western history's legendary trappers, scouts, and military commanders, the base hosted approximately 10,000 people at the time, many of them waiting for orders deploying them to one of two war zones. On October 23, though, with bright sunshine flooding the Front Range, Captain Zakhem remarked that Iraq and Afghanistan seemed very far away. Most of the deciduous trees in the area had recently dropped their leaves, but the cottonwoods still retained their foliage. Fort Carson appeared sylvan that morning, beautiful, even welcoming—if you overlooked the armed soldiers patrolling its entrance gates, screening visitors before waving them inside. But even with the guards in place, the base resembled the campus of a midsized state university or an unusually well-fortified suburban subdivision. Clusters of ranch houses, a few community buildings, athletic fields, and playgrounds filled with shouting children sprawled across nearly ten square miles. Posted signs apparently aimed to boost morale: the "word of the month" was "caring." With so many young people wandering around carrying M-16s, that seemed like an excellent choice.[17]

The Sand Creek Staff Ride symposium took place in a squat conference center near a basketball court and a group of small houses labeled, coincidentally, Cheyenne Village. Inside the building, officers from Captain Zakhem's unit shared what they had learned about the massacre. Zakhem himself had first encountered Sand Creek while reading Dee Brown's *Bury My Heart at Wounded Knee* in a class at the University of Colorado. In his presentation, Zakhem contrasted commemorative efforts at the Sand Creek site—"it's empty, there's nothing there"—with the more elaborate memorial at the Murrah Building in Oklahoma City, asking his audience which choice seemed more appropriate. Other officers talked about the cultural conflict that had emerged out of nineteenth-century westward expansion, musing about the nation's ongoing imperial ambitions; about Colonel Chivington's tactics, focusing especially on the rules of engagement; about weapons used by the Colorado volunteers and the Cheyennes and Arapahos at Sand Creek; and about the challenge of studying sources in which "all of the testimony seems to contradict itself." With the preliminaries over, Zakhem and his colleagues prepared to visit the site the next day.[18]

They did not go alone. Captain Zakhem, seeking authorization to visit Sand Creek, had contacted Alexa Roberts months earlier. Roberts had then invited the descendants and Bill Dawson to attend the event as well. Zakhem understood the significance of the gathering. It would be, he said, "the first time that the Colorado National Guard has recognized the activities of the Colorado militia a hundred and some odd years ago. We're going in uniform, so there's no mistake about who we are. It's a big deal to them [the descendants] and a big deal to us." Zakhem anticipated tension. Using passive constructions that obscured the identity of the perpetrators, he noted, "some truly horrible things were done on that battlefield." He then admitted, "It's something that still happens." In the end, he concluded that there likely would be lingering ill will: "In terms of the engagement, there were so many broken promises, before and after, fallacies and fabrications. And we expect to hear about that from the tribes."[19]

At a meet and greet held in a conference room in the Kiowa County courthouse, Laird Cometsevah signaled that Zakhem was right: the day would be devoted not only to remembrance but also to recriminations. Scolding the soldiers for the sins of their forebears, Cometsevah said, "The Cheyennes will not accept an apology for what happened at Sand Creek for the simple reason that Sand Creek is not over. The U.S.

government still owes the descendants of the massacre. We're not going to accept any apology until Article 6 of the Treaty of the Little Arkansas is completed." Zakhem, who nodded as Cometsevah spoke, recalled later that no matter how sorry he personally might have been about Sand Creek, he could not apologize on behalf of the federal government or the army. Then, as the group arrived at the monument overlook, Steve Brady, wearing emblems from his service in Vietnam, explained: "From Sand Creek on, the U.S. military took human remains from the Cheyennes. We, the Cheyenne people, were the scientific specimens that improved the U.S. military's killing efficiency, its ordnance. So whenever you pull the trigger on your weapon, and you see the tight grouping of your round, remember to thank the Cheyenne people." One officer in Zakhem's unit winced; another looked skyward, shook his head, and then lowered his gaze to the ground.[20]

For the most part, though, the gathering was more than amicable; it was a meeting of brothers in arms. Many of the descendants, as well as Bill Dawson, had served in the military. They laughed about unit discipline with the guardsmen or traded tales of tight spots. In their common experiences, Alexa Roberts noted, they found a bridge between cultures. At one point, Captain Zakhem sidled up to Steve Brady, asking, "How does Cheyenne medicine work?" Without missing a beat, Brady replied, "How does the Rosary work?" "Faith," Zakhem answered. Brady just shrugged in response, leaving Zakhem nodding and smiling. Throughout the day, Ray Brady, Steve's uncle, found himself surrounded by soldiers. The elder Brady had served valiantly in World War II, and the assembled troops wanted to hear of his exploits. He obliged them. When it was all over, Alexa Roberts beamed. "Can you believe how great that was?" she asked. Then she wrote a press release, declaring, "The Sand Creek Massacre site is already serving its memorial purpose." Having distracted herself from the bickering on the Kiowa County website, Roberts recalled that she wanted nothing more than to rest for a few weeks before preparing for the next event on her calendar: the ceremony celebrating the transfer of the Dawson ranch to the Cheyenne and Arapaho Tribes.[21]

The Lucky Star Casino was huge when Alexa Roberts arrived there late in 2003. Located off Highway 81 in Clinton, Oklahoma, its stucco and stone bulk seemed especially outsized when juxtaposed with the spareness of the surrounding prairie. An immense archway greeted visitors, who entered a smoke-filled cavern that might just as well have been located in Nevada, Connecticut, New Jersey, or anywhere else that casino gambling was legal. There were no windows; patrons could not inadvertently catch a glimpse of the darkening sky and realize that a day had slipped away. The sound of one-armed bandits—clanking, ringing, whirring—overwhelmed all of the other noise in the building, except for the occasional exclamation of delight accompanying a payout. But those shouts were rare. Most players stared straight at the machines in front of them, reaching down into buckets of coins and dropping them into insatiable slots, gambling metronomes oblivious to the time they were keeping.[22]

On December 19, 2003, Eugene Black Bear, who served his tribe as a master of ceremonies at powwows, climbed atop a podium deep inside the Lucky Star. Thundering over announcements of prize drawings, Black Bear presided over a somber celebration: the Cheyenne and Arapaho Tribes would now own what Laird Cometsevah called "the traditional site." After several descendants spoke, Jim Druck walked to the microphone. He recounted his father's World War II service, the horrors of the Holocaust, and his sorrow about the massacre, before explaining to the crowd that he "understood their pain and what it means to fight for your heritage." Finally, in an odd moment suggesting that the tribes remained divided over acquiring the site, Druck looked uncertain as he searched for someone to accept the deed to the Dawson ranch. With tribal officials suddenly scarce, Druck handed the document to Cometsevah, who took it on behalf of his people.[23]

Alexa Roberts believed that the path from the deed transfer ceremony to the opening of the historic site would be straightforward. Congress had to pass legislation placing the former Dawson ranch into federal trust, and the Cheyenne and Arapaho Tribes had to agree to allow the NPS to manage the property. Roberts thought that the first condition would be no problem. So did Senator Campbell. "I don't anticipate opposition in Congress," Campbell said. But securing the tribes' agreement worried Roberts. "That was a wild card," she recalled. Robert Tabor had recently been deposed as chair of the Cheyenne and Arapaho Business Committee, and the political landscape remained uncertain. Some of the descendants also were not sure they wanted the NPS involved in any way with the memorial. With Bill Dawson's land back in Cheyenne hands, Laird Cometsevah wondered if having the government manage the site served his people's interests or honored their ancestors' memories. Looking back on the search, Cometsevah asked, "Why should we trust the Park Service?" With that question unanswered, other factors threatened to derail the memorialization process.[24]

Just days after the transfer ceremony, author and activist Suzan Shown Harjo penned an exposé for the online edition of *Indian Country Today*, the nation's largest weekly newspaper devoted to covering Native American issues. A headline asked, "Who's Keeping Secrets from the Sand Creek Descendants?" Harjo answered: "There's big talk about a big money deal in the making in the name of the Cheyenne and Arapaho people." The deal, known as the "Cheyenne-Arapaho Homecoming Project," was "the brainchild" of a venture capitalist named Steve Hillard and would be carried out by his company, Council Tree Communications. Harjo reported that the Homecoming Project's prospectus, spread across sixteen pages all stamped with the warning, "Strictly Confidential," identified "10 core objectives," including funding the opening of the historic site and "publicly redress[ing] the crimes committed against Native Americans and the particular atrocity of Sand Creek." How would Council Tree accomplish these goals? By exchanging Cheyenne and Arapaho land claims in Colorado for a small parcel of property, a new reservation to be created on the plains just east of Denver. The catch? The proposed location sat adjacent to Denver International Airport, and on it, Council Tree "would build a full-service casino and hotel, a Plains Indian Cultural and Media Center, and a five-star restaurant in a glass-enclosed rooftop observatory."[25]

Six months earlier, Steve Hillard had called a meeting in Billings, Montana, hoping to sell the Northern Cheyenne government on his plan. Steve Brady attended and warned Hillard that he should steer clear of Sand Creek. Linking memorialization of the massacre with gambling, Brady explained, "was completely unacceptable." Brady next contacted Laird Cometsevah, inquiring about where he stood on the Homecoming Project. Cometsevah responded that he "didn't care at all if there were hundreds of new casinos built in Colorado, so long as Sand Creek isn't dragged into it and Article 6 claims aren't involved." Reassured, Brady thought they should write to Senator Campbell, clarifying the Cheyenne descendants' position: Sand Creek and gaming must remain separate. When news of Hillard's proposal made its way to Suzan Harjo, generating the first trickle of what ultimately would be a flood of bad press suggesting that the Homecoming Project rested on the dubious proposition that the horrors of Sand Creek could be swept away for the affected tribes by waves of corporate profits, the entrepreneur wondered if Brady had leaked the news. Brady acknowledged only that Harjo was "a good friend."[26]

Brady initially dismissed the Homecoming Project as grandiose and very likely doomed. "Steve Hillard made lots of promises," Brady recalled, "but I wasn't sure he'd keep a single one of them." The scheme, as Brady understood it, hinged on the contention that federal authorities had violated the Fort Laramie treaty. The Cheyenenes and Arapahos, Hillard argued, had legal rights to huge swaths of Colorado, perhaps 40 percent of the state. But, Brady countered, such claims had been extinguished when the tribes had settled with the U.S. government in 1965. Brady did not like it, but in his view no room remained for another land claim. As for the idea that Hillard would fund the historic site, Brady muttered, "I'll believe it when I see it." Finally, he responded to Hillard's plan to use the federal government's promise of reparations in Article 6 of the Little Arkansas treaty as leverage to secure a casino outside Denver's massive airport, sneering: "It's disgusting. He really *should* be ashamed of himself. But he's shameless."[27]

Nevertheless, Brady feared that Hillard was dangerous and that his plan might actually scuttle the historic site. Brady's concerns reflected his sense that the lure of easy money could divide the descendants between those people committed to memorializing the massacre and those willing to trade the moral authority associated with Sand Creek for cash. "We had been mostly unified up till then," he remembered, "sticking together because we knew that we needed to protect the site and honor our ancestors." But the lure of a healthy bottom line threatened that rapport, because Hillard had a track record of brokering deals involving communities of color—including helping to finance Telemundo, the successful Spanish-language cable television station. Hillard, in other words, was not just a grifter looking for an easy mark. So when he suggested that the proposed casino would be a "money machine," the Cheyenne and Arapaho Business Committee cooperated with him. Pointing to rampant poverty within the tribes, James Pedro,

Robert Tabor's replacement as tribal chairman, believed that the Homecoming Project "would allow us to return to a presence in our ancestral lands, participate in the economic energy of our home and earn money to meet the basic needs of our people." Brady, Laird Cometsevah, and the other descendants, by contrast, maintained their opposition, insisting, "it is outrageous exploitation that Steve Hillard would propose to use something like the Sand Creek Massacre for a casino proposal."[28]

Beyond just Hillard's financial muscle, Brady also feared the venture capitalist's political connections. Hillard counted several Alaska Native Corporations among his partners in the Homecoming Project. Those groups, in turn, had the ear of Senator Ted Stevens. Notorious for a take-no-prisoners approach to legislating, Stevens chaired the Senate Appropriations Committee, making him one of the most powerful people in the federal bureaucracy. The *Denver Post* reported, "Stevens . . . has immense control over the nearly $800 billion doled out by Congress every year. As a result, he's able to single-handedly push through legislation by attaching it to must-pass spending bills." One corporation backing Hillard reportedly paid Stevens's business partners $6 million in rent annually. And executives at Council Tree had recently hired the senator's brother-in-law as a lobbyist focused on Indian gaming. Brady understood that Stevens's power worried even Senator Campbell, who feared that his colleague might pressure him into supporting the Homecoming Project, complicating his bid for reelection in Colorado, where Indian gaming remained unpopular. Campbell, therefore, struck preemptively. He opposed the deal, attributing his decision to bedrock principals. It was, he said, "sacrilegious to link gambling to the Sand Creek Massacre." Nobody knew how Senator Stevens would react.[29]

News of the Homecoming Project hit NPS officials and Kiowa County residents hard, leaving Janet Frederick scrambling to reassure people that the descendants would not allow a casino at the Sand Creek site: "We've had to say, over and over, 'no casino, no casino.' But everyone's just assuming, 'Yeah, you're telling us that, but once they get the land, then a casino will go in.'" Chuckling at the thought of opening a gambling parlor in sparsely populated Kiowa County, she remarked, "Well, I suppose parking wouldn't be a problem. We have room for the biggest parking lot in the world here." Alexa Roberts appreciated

Frederick's good humor but knew that associating the site with gambling would be a political loser for the NPS. Congress still had to place the Dawson ranch into trust, and Roberts worried, "if the perception exists that the tribes are using Sand Creek as a wedge to open a casino, we're probably sunk."[30]

With the descendants, people in Kiowa County, and the NPS arrayed against him, Steve Hillard faced another problem: the regional press began painting him as the villain in a modern massacre story. Hillard, from this perspective, hoped to capitalize on the memory of Sand Creek by taking advantage of credulous Indians and transforming white guilt into cash. The *Denver Post* noted that it was "ghastly to pretend that such a worthy goal [commemorating the massacre] could be accomplished by building a gambling hall filled with card tables and binging, blinking slot machines. That's not honoring the dead, that's defilement." The story derided Hillard as "smarmy" for trying to "ride the coattails of respected Indian leaders who for years have worked diligently to create an appropriate memorial." A day later, the *Post* asked saracastically, "Why lament this chapter in Colorado history when we can slam chips on the table and try to make a buck off it?" The article jeered, "there's nothing like the ching-ching-ching of slot machines to soothe the haunting memories of genocide," before concluding, of the Indians at Sand Creek, "they slaughtered them under a banner of economic development. And if a few wealthy and powerful people have their way, we shall memorialize their brutal murders in the same vein." So while Jim Druck, who also had linked Sand Creek with casino gambling, remained something of a local hero, Hillard played the part of moustache-twisting heel.[31]

Accused of cultural insensitivity and threatening to despoil critical episodes from Colorado's past, Hillard responded. To the descendants, he insisted that he had the tribes' best interests at heart. To his non-Indian detractors, he made more promises while issuing veiled threats couched in accusations of elitism. Referring to the casino he hoped to build for the Cheyennes and Arapahos, Hillard declared, "The tribes want to escape the cycle of poverty." He also said, "The proposition that Indians should stay poor but noble only comes from those who haven't experienced poverty." He guaranteed that the deal contained something for everyone. The casino, he surmised, would generate massive tax revenue, as much as $1 billion annually, for Coloradans. But if the state obstructed his plans, he would have to litigate: "These claims, if left unresolved, will cloud title to land and water in a large portion of Colorado." Such statements had the ominous ring of a protection racket. "Nice state you've got here," Hillard seemed to be implying, "it would be a shame if something terrible had to happen to it." As for Steve Brady's and Laird Cometsevah's worries, he explained, "Reparations are entirely right. But they have to know it's a tough shot. So let's be real about it, the Homecoming Project could help their entire tribes." In the end, he concluded, his plan might face long odds, but it merited the risk because the payoff would be huge: "Even if there's just a one percent chance, that's significant." And so, despite heavy early losses, Hillard doubled down on red.[32]

But then, after receiving more negative press for linking the Homecoming Project and the memorialization of the massacre, Hillard changed his bet. In a press release apparently designed to win Laird Cometsevah to his side, Hillard untangled the two initiatives, explaining that the Homecoming Project "does not seek reparations for the Sand Creek Massacre"; "does not and will not prejudice the individual claims of the Sand Creek Descendants"; and "will make certain that the federal government is aware of Article 6, and that it is not diminished through the Homecoming Project." Hillard added privately to Cometsevah: "You can be assured that Council Tree Communications and Native American Land Group, including their principals and any affiliates are in agreement with ensuring that Article 6 of the Little Arkansas Treaty of 1865 remains intact and undisturbed by this project." He moved forward with his plan to win a small reservation near Denver's busy international airport. In early spring 2004, the Cheyenne and Arapaho Tribes filed claim for 27 million acres of Colorado property. Pushing to settle, one of the tribes' lawyers let slip that "in similar cases, such claims have made it expensive for landowners to get title insurance, and in the worst cases, they have interfered with land sales." The Cheyennes and Arapahos were dabbling in historical irony, tampering with legal instruments of private property in the state that white settlers had taken from their ancestors.[33]

Even as Hillard retreated from Sand Creek, Alexa Roberts and Steve Brady remained frustrated about the Homecoming Project. Hillard's

play, they feared, could still kill the historic site by dividing the descendants or leaving Congress with the sense that memorializing the massacre had something to do with casinos. At a meeting held just after
Hillard wrote his reassuring note to Laird Cometsevah, the Northern
Cheyenne descendants were wary of their Southern Cheyenne kin. Otto
Braided Hair suggested that the Cheyenne and Arapaho Tribes' status
as a landowner had tilted the playing field: some descendants were
more equal than others in planning the site. Alexa Roberts warned
that Congress would kill the trust legislation if it were "tainted" by
Indian gaming. Cometsevah and Joe Big Medicine replied that Hillard's posture had shifted, that he would distance himself from Sand
Creek and provide support for efforts to secure Article 6 reparations.
Norma Gorneau, another Northern Cheyenne descendant, later bemoaned associating the massacre with gambling: "The casino thing
became a real distraction. It slowed us down from doing our important
work. Every day we talked about gambling was another day that the
massacre site wasn't being protected."[34]

By late May, more Coloradans had wearied of Steve Hillard. Jim
Spencer, a columnist at the *Denver Post*, acknowledged, "there's no question the U.S. mistreated the Cheyenne and Arapaho. But this looks more
like a sweet deal for developers and a few tribal leaders than restitution
for the rank-and-file." Pointing to Hillard's carrot-and-stick strategy,
Spencer warned, "Coloradans are not interested in being pushed around
by people making extravagant threats." Especially with the stakes so
high, he concluded–without acknowledging the painful historical
ironies—"What isn't fun is out-of-state Indians screwing with the title
to your house." Sensing in June that he had public opinion on his side,
Colorado governor Bill Owens announced his opposition to the project.
Members of the Cheyenne and Arapaho Business Committee responded
with a public relations blitz, explaining the economic hardships afflict-
ing their people. Only half of their constituents had jobs, they said,
and per capita income on their reservation hovered around $8,000 an-
nually. So even though approximately 80 percent of the two hundred
tribes with gaming throughout the nation were losing money or barely
breaking even on their ventures, one tribal spokesman explained,
"That's why a casino in Colorado looks like hope."[35]

Rumors circulated throughout August that Senator Stevens would attach a so-called midnight rider to an upcoming appropriations bill, sneaking the Homecoming Project into federal law. Senator Campbell responded by inviting Steve Hillard to Washington to discuss his proposition with the Senate Indian Affairs Committee, which Campbell chaired. It would be a "briefing," a low-key session, Campbell's staff informed Hillard, rather than a formal "hearing." But when Hillard arrived on September 8, he found himself facing off with Governor Owens and Colorado's congressional delegation. The meeting became testy when Owens accused Hillard of "blackmail." The Department of the Interior's lead attorney then explained that the Cheyenne and Arapaho Tribes' land claims had been settled in 1965. Darrell Flyingman, who had just become chairman of the business committee, questioned the fairness of that deal. He snapped at Owens, "Would you sell Colorado to us for 2.75 cents an acre?" Owens replied coolly that no, he would not, but the terms had been approved by the tribes, and he "wouldn't want to second-guess [their] tribal council." After the meeting, Hillard displayed the bravado that had in the past served him well in tense negotiations, observing of Owens's demeanor: "The seeds of settlement are sown in his discomfort." Owens, for his part, seemed more concerned that Senator Stevens might still outflank him, quipping of the Alaska lawmaker, "[He] won't return my phone calls."[36]

Despite Hillard's brave face, Senator Campbell had effectively killed the Homecoming Project. Nevertheless, fallout from the episode would linger for years to come. Part of a national trend in which Indian tribes engaged in "reservation shopping"—the practice of asserting ownership over parcels of land, typically developed property located in a distant state, and promising to relinquish those potentially nettlesome claims in exchange for a new reservation on which a casino could be built—Hillard's deal prompted frenzied discussions among governors and members of Congress. But Alexa Roberts shifted her attention to other issues: the uncertain status of the trust legislation then wending its way through the Senate; morale among the descendants, who struggled to stand united; and some of her neighbors in Kiowa County, who were growing increasingly frustrated as the historic site's gates remained padlocked.[37]

Because the relevant land still lay in private hands, the NPS could not open the Sand Creek site to the public throughout summer and fall 2004. NPS administrators fretted over questions of liability in the event that a trespasser twisted an ankle in a prairie dog burrow or snagged a limb on a piece of stray barbed wire. Both Kiowa County and NPS officials also worried about the prospect of someone starting a blaze that might destroy historic materials before spreading to a neighboring ranch. And absent a management plan, including interpretive guidelines, the proprietors, the Cheyenne and Arapaho Tribes, refused to throw open the front door for tourists, who they feared might use the sacred site in inappropriate ways. Nevertheless, people clamored for a chance to visit Sand Creek, peppering Alexa Roberts with requests for permission. Roberts recalled, "most of the folks who inquired with us were nice enough, but a few just wouldn't take no for an answer." In those cases, she wondered: "Would they vandalize the site? How could we keep the place safe?" The more publicity Sand Creek received, the more unwanted interest became a problem. Roberts hoped the trust legislation would work its way through Congress quickly, making it possible to open the site.[38]

In the meantime, Chuck and Sheri Bowen, apparently frustrated but also emboldened by their experience with the OIW a year earlier, seized an opportunity. With demand for access to a Sand Creek memorial far outstripping supply, the Bowens in June 2004 began offering tours of their family ranch. Advertising online and with fliers, they promised customers "a unique educational experience!" and a detailed recounting of their personal quest to find the Sand Creek site. Participants would "hear all the arguments" and then decide for themselves where the violence had unfolded. A testimonial from NPS archeologist Doug Scott suggested, "the Bowen land contains an incredibly important part of the archeological record related to Sand Creek," while another blurb from Jeff Broome asserted, "artifacts do not lie, and 3,000 battle and village related artifacts remove all doubt about where the village and battle was on November 29, 1864." Broome's endorsement concluded: "For the past 3 years I have brought students to the Bowen property, and without question, it is there that the fight took place." The Bowens still wanted to claim authority over the massacre's geography. If tourists visited their land while the NPS site remained closed, they might seize control of the debate.[39]

With stories about the Homecoming Project splashed on the front pages of the local papers, the Bowens' new business soon began attracting attention from reporters. And though both Chuck and Sheri Bowen promised that they would not "be involved in the controversy" swirling around the site, explaining that their tours would forgo contentious interpretation in favor of just-the-facts-ma'am narration, they nevertheless found themselves at the center of another storm surrounding Sand Creek. The problems started when the Bowens tried to drum up customers on the Kiowa County website. Sharon Pearson, the site administrator, explained that the webpage belonged to her, and that she felt no obligation to allow people to "promote and advertise their personal business" there. She also intimated that she remained skeptical about the Bowens' claim that the massacre had taken place on their property. The Bowens fired back. They noted that their tours were a Kiowa County concern, reiterated that they had found more artifacts on their land than the NPS had discovered within the confines of the Dawson ranch, and promised that when confronted they would "NOT back down." Once again, the Sand Creek discussion forum threatened to devolve into a pixelated shoutfest, a place where disgruntled parties could air their grievances and trade "personal slurs."[40]

The arguments droned on for months, recapitulating many of the issues from the previous summer, when members of the OIW had sparred with their detractors on the Kiowa County website. This time, though, the Bowens made their own case, defending their methodology and good name. One commenter, assuming that the descendants were as interested in properly locating the site as anyone else was, wondered "why the Indian tribes themselves are not on the bandwagon proclaiming [that] Bowen's land is the real site?" He then speculated that the Bowens were driven less by the unrelenting search for historical truth that they identified as their priority than by "the almighty dollar." Only an hour elapsed before Chuck Bowen, whose rapid response suggested that he had taken to bird-dogging the website, posted an angry rebuttal. He fumed that his family had "NEVER ASKED for any money" before complaining about a double standard: "Nobody seems to have a problem with Dawson selling for almost 10 times the appraised value . . . and no one even mentions that the town of Eads and surrounding towns . . . are wanting nothing more than 'to cash in' on the Sand Creek Site." By contrast, he insisted that he and his wife wanted only "the TRUTH to be told." He stated, "We have a majority of the site, which the NPS knows and the Indians know." The Bowens again cast themselves as victims of a cabal organized to rob them of credit that rightfully should have been theirs. Federal authorities, collaborating with Native people, were running roughshod over the West's history and landowners.[41]

Bill Dawson, once among the most pugnacious stakeholders in the memorialization process, had been observing the fray from the comfort of the study in his new home in Colorado Springs. To that point, Dawson had remained silent. But he could not allow Chuck Bowen's charges to stand unchallenged in cyberspace. Suggesting that the Bowens were indeed looking for a payday, Dawson pointed back to his neighbors' offer, years earlier, to sell out for $15 million. "Tired of [the] cheap shots on this forum," he challenged Chuck Bowen to come see him "in person" or to "select a neutral battleground" where the two men apparently could settle their differences once and for all.[42]

At around the same time, Sheri Bowen, simultaneously playing the roles of peacekeeper and provocateur, addressed a cutting reply to Dawson. She and her husband did not "have any problem with [Dawson] selling [his] land for a lot more than any one else in Kiowa County could get. That's the American way." The Bowens would even allow that "some important things happened" in the South Bend, so long as Dawson admitted that "90% of [the massacre] happened" on their land. "It is a little difficult to argue," she suggested, "against all our documented artifacts." Still, she said, she and her husband would comfort themselves with the truth, facts that even the NPS acknowledged in private: "The NPS knows what we have and have chosen not to recognize it for whatever reason." She added: "what we have is VERY important information and it is being suppressed." Despite being robbed of their just due, she concluded: "Chuck will continue metal detecting and mapping the artifacts by GPS and I'll continue to pray that the truth comes out eventually."[43]

Alexa Roberts watched the drama unfolding on the Sand Creek discussion forum with a feeling of déjà vu. Congress was deliberating about placing the Dawson property into federal trust. And the specter of the Homecoming Project still complicated that bill's prospects. Plus, Roberts knew, newspapers serving the Cheyenne and Arapaho Tribes were covering the controversy over the Bowens' tour business. John Sipes, a tribal historian, suggested, "If Eads, Colorado . . . hopes for economic benefits from the historic site, the perspective of Sand Creek descendants needs to be heard." Roberts believed, "if we can just open, the fighting will stop." If people visited the site, she hoped, skepticism surrounding its authenticity would diminish, and the Bowens would not have a platform from which they could criticize the NPS and descendants.[44]

With Roberts frustrated about the slow pace of progress on the site, she looked east. Festivities in Washington, DC, buoyed her spirits, suggesting that some federal-tribal collaborations could eventually succeed. On September 21, 2004, more than 20,000 indigenous people from throughout the Americas gathered in the nation's capital. They met to celebrate the opening of the National Museum of the American Indian (NMAI). Built of wavy limestone blocks, nodding to cliff dwellings in the American West, the five-story NMAI looked unlike anything else in the city, its unique architectural design accentuated by its remarkable location: a spot on the National Mall, one of the most prestigious and symbolically resonant pieces of real estate in the United States. For scores of Native activists, scholars, and political figures, including Ben Nighthorse Campbell, the NMAI's site on the Mall and inclusion in the Smithsonian Institution suggested a ritual claiming of space, a declaration of "survivance" that echoed throughout the building's exhibit halls. So while critics piled on, panning the NMAI's focus on cultural persistence at the expense of rigorous interpretation—a typical reviewer sniffed the "unmistakable air of ethnic boosterism" wafting around the array of artifacts and multimedia presentations that greeted visitors in the galleries—many Native people viewed the museum as a triumph. Wilma Mankiller, former principal chief of the Cherokee Nation, hailed the NMAI as "an important opportunity to show tribal people as participants in a living culture, not something in museums or history books."[45]

The opening of the NMAI also demonstrated how deeply memories of Sand Creek reached into contemporary Native affairs. The museum had traveled a serpentine path to the National Mall. Around the turn of the twentieth century, as the United States became more urban, more industrial, and less white, George Heye, a second-tier oil baron, followed the lead of men like Teddy Roosevelt: he went west, measuring his manhood and allaying his growing racial anxieties by traveling among Native people, who at the time most observers saw as part of a vanishing race. Bitten by the collecting bug during one of his trips, Heye began acquiring vast holdings of indigenous artifacts from throughout the Americas. He eventually put together a collection that numbered, by some counts, in excess of a million pieces. In 1916, Heye crammed his trove into an exhibition and research space in Harlem, New York. He called the repository the Museum of the American Indian. For two decades, Heye's collection thrived in upper Manhattan. But the museum, along with the rest of the United States, fell on hard times during the Great Depression, and fund-raising became more difficult. Heye's death in 1957 exacerbated the museum's financial woes. In the 1960s and 1970s, new leadership struggled to revive the once-proud institution, but a series of high-profile scandals surrounding the sale of treasures from within the collections suggested the need for a revised strategy.[46]

By the early 1980s, fewer than 50,000 people visited the museum annually. Its endowment had sunk below the $5 million mark, and dusty exhibits—including dioramas such as "Chippewa Maple Syrup Camp" and "The Potlatch"—struck even unseasoned onlookers as anachronistic. At that time, Roland Force, only the third director in the museum's history, began negotiating with other institutions (the city's famed American Museum of Natural History), individuals (the Texas oil billionaire H. Ross Perot), and government entities (the New York City Council, the New York State Legislature, the U.S. Congress), playing one off against the next in order to secure the Heye collection's legacy and ongoing autonomy. After initially striking a deal with the Museum of Natural History, Force backed out because of a dispute over space. He next used his flirtations with Perot as a threat, demanding and receiving additional concessions in exchange for a promise to stay in Manhattan. Still Force wavered, until Robert Abrams, attorney general of the State of New York, went to court to block a proposed move to Dallas. Only after New York's U.S. senators, Alfonse D'Amato and Daniel Patrick Moynihan, began bickering over the museum's fate did Senator Daniel Inouye of Hawaii broker a deal to bring the majority of Heye's artifacts to Washington, DC, where they would be housed on the Mall as part of the Smithsonian.[47]

Native people rarely figured in press coverage of the NMAI's history—except as objects on display. But after the museum opened, Suzan Shown Harjo offered a different creation story, linking the NMAI's genesis to the memorialization of Sand Creek. Harjo recalled discussions in 1989 about the Heye collection's future. Those talks nearly broke down when the negotiator for the Smithsonian, which was exempt from the Native American Graves Protection and Repatriation Act, refused to relent on the question of repatriating the remains of tens of thousands of Native people still stored within the institution's archives. Many of those crania and other body parts, collected across more than a century, had figured in the federal government's studies of the impact of military hardware during the Indian Wars. Harjo remembered phoning Robert Adams, secretary of the Smithsonian, and telling him, "we had to have a repatriation agreement," or there would be no deal. As she spoke with Adams, Harjo leafed through documents detailing the Smithsonian's grim holdings: "I was looking at bills of lading . . . showing how the remains of five of the Sand Creek massacre victims wound up in his institution." An emotional Harjo cut the call short, explaining to Adams, "we were out of time." Concerned that the Heye collection might be slipping through his grasp, Adams called back and promised, "we have a deal." Months later, Adams, Harjo, Senator Campbell, and Senator Inouye announced that the Smithsonian would revise its repatriation policies as part of the legislation to create the National Museum of the American Indian.[48]

As for the massacre victims whose remains still gathered dust in the Smithsonian, not long after Harjo's conversation with Adams, the Cheyenne and Arapaho Tribes and Laird Cometsevah's descendants' group put in a repatriation request with the U.S. government. Three years later, a group of Cheyennes arrived in Washington at the Smithsonian's repatriation office. Archivists had removed the remains from the file drawers where they had been stored and arrayed them on a conference table beneath a sheet. As a museum curator pulled back the shroud, several Cheyenne people began sobbing. Women gathered around the cranium of a girl killed at the massacre before she reached her sixteenth birthday. Another skull, taken from a man in his mid-thirties, betrayed the trauma of having been scalped, definitive physical evidence, Cometsevah believed, of atrocities committed by Chivington's men. After praying and placing the bones in small coffins, the Cheyennes loaded the remains into a yellow Ryder truck and drove back to their reservation. Once there, the Sand Creek descendants buried their ancestors, hopeful that the spirits of the massacre's victims might find peace at last. More than a decade later, Harjo, recounting the origins of the NMAI, pointed back to those individuals and suggested, "these people were as much a part of the making of this museum as anyone living."[49]

With the NMAI in the news in September 2004, the Sand Creek site's fate hung in the balance. Months earlier, during the Homecoming Project controversy, Senator Campbell had introduced the Sand Creek Massacre National Historic Site Trust Act of 2004. It seemed like a simple bill; it would place the former Dawson ranch into federal trust so that it could be incorporated into the National Park System. But as James Doyle, Campbell's aide, explained, NPS lands were held by the U.S. government "for the common benefit of the people of the United States," whereas federal authorities "must manage Indian trust lands for the exclusive benefit of the Indian beneficiaries of the trust relationship." Campbell's bill tried to reconcile these competing mandates. The property would be administered by the secretary of the interior "in accordance with the law generally applicable to property held in trust by the United States for the benefit of Indian tribes" and also "in accordance with the Sand Creek Massacre National Historic Site Establishment Act of 2000." "The trust property," the bill went on, "shall be used only for historic, religious, or cultural uses that are compatible with the use of the land as a national historic site." Practically speaking, the implications of such language remained unclear. Politically, though, the bill promised that the Sand Creek historic site would attempt to serve the affected tribes and the American people more broadly.[50]

On September 16, 2004, a week after Steve Hillard's disastrous visit to Capitol Hill, Otto Braided Hair received an oddly muted e-mail from Paul Moorhead, lead staffer on the Senate Indian Affairs Committee. Moorhead informed Braided Hair that the Sand Creek trust bill had passed the Senate the previous day. But, he cautioned, because of ongoing "hysteria" over the Homecoming Project, the legislation might face challenges in the House. It remained important to keep Sand Creek separate from any of Hillard's schemes. Senator Campbell would not issue a celebratory press release and would instead be "playing it low-key." Six months earlier, Campbell had cited health concerns in announcing that he would retire from the Senate. He still hoped that opening the historic site would cap a career devoted, in his words, to "serving the American people and my people, Indian people." Now he had to wait to see if the House would pass a final piece of his signature legislation.[51]

The outcome disappointed the senator and nearly everyone else involved in the memorialization effort. With Congresswoman Marilyn Musgrave, who had sponsored the trust bill in the House of Representatives, still worrying about political fallout from the Homecoming Project, the legislation languished for months before getting bottled up in committee and then dying in mid-December. Despite all the hand wringing, casinos had nothing to do with the bill's fate in the end. Instead, intraparty politics doomed the legislation. A California congressman who for years had nursed a grudge against Campbell would not, even as a courtesy to a retiring colleague, bring the Sand Creek bill up for a vote. A shaken Campbell explained, "House leaders refused to act." Janet Frederick groaned: "It sets us back. And in these small towns, we can't really afford to be set back." And after Alexa Roberts wistfully recalled how "it sailed through the Senate so easily," she wondered how the legislation would fare without Campbell's backing in Washington: "I just don't know how this is going to happen without Ben's help." Otto Braided Hair, though, remained philosophical and focused on the long term: "We got overconfident. We'll just have to lobby harder the next time."[52]

The next time arrived early in the new year, when Colorado's other U.S. senator, Wayne Allard, reintroduced the Sand Creek trust legislation. This time, the people of Kiowa County and the descendants lobbied Marilyn Musgrave relentlessly to stay on top of the issue in the House of Representatives. And when, in mid-April 2005, the House Subcommittee on National Parks held hearings on the legislation,

Steve Brady traveled to Washington, where he described the lingering impact of the massacre and the importance of the historic site for his people. Mike Snyder, at the time deputy director of the NPS, also testified at the hearings. Snyder explained that if Congress placed the former Dawson ranch into trust, "the NPS believes it would have sufficient land for the establishment of the National Historic Site and would forward a recommendation to the Secretary of the Interior to formally establish the park." But until that happened, Snyder warned, the NPS had no authority to enforce federal law within the Sand Creek site's boundaries. The property would have to remain closed to the public, generating no economic activity for Kiowa County.[53]

Even with the reintroduced trust legislation making its way through Congress, the sting of the previous year's disappointment remained fresh in Eads, where some people questioned whether they wanted any part of the historic site. Alexa Roberts recalled, "Walking down the street, people would stop me and ask, 'Is this thing going to happen?' It was a roller coaster for the county, and people were getting sick of the ride." In June, the frustration came to a head when students from the University of Wisconsin, part of a seminar traveling across the West studying cross-cultural encounters, arrived in Eads to learn about the massacre. The course instructor had arranged for a panel of speakers, including Roberts, Laird Cometsevah, Joe Big Medicine, and Lee Pedro, along with Alonzo Sankey, one of the Southern Arapaho delegates to the memorialization project. Roberts had suggested that, if the class wanted a genuinely multicultural event, it would make sense to include Janet Frederick and Rod Brown to represent the local community. On June 15, 2005, the group—minus Cometsevah, who recently had been in a car accident and sent his assistant, Linda DeCarlo, instead—met in the basement of the Kiowa County courthouse.[54]

The event quickly veered toward chaos when Linda DeCarlo claimed that the area around Eads remained a hotbed of neo-Chivingtonites. For proof, she pointed to the "Friends of Chivington Church." DeCarlo would not be deterred, even when members of the audience corrected her, noting that the name of the Quaker congregation in the neighboring town was the Chivington Friends Church. Things went downhill from there. After DeCarlo linked memorializing the massacre with

Article 6 reparations, Lee Pedro concluded his presentation by mumbling something about the 9/11 attacks. Because he spoke into his chest, nearly everyone agreed that his exact words were unintelligible. But Chuck and Sheri Bowen, seated in the audience, later insisted that Pedro had celebrated the 9/11 hijackers, labeling the destruction of the Twin Towers just deserts for a nation responsible for the violence at Sand Creek. Janet Frederick countered that Pedro had only suggested that having experienced the horror of 9/11, white Americans might be able to empathize with the plight of Cheyenne and Arapaho people affected by the massacre. Regardless, as Alexa Roberts prepared to leave at the end of the panel, Chuck Bowen confronted her. He accused Roberts, who had not heard Pedro's comments, of having lied about the potential windfall the historic site would bring to Kiowa County. Bowen then blurted out, "You will be responsible for the next Sand Creek massacre." A puzzled Roberts just walked away.[55]

The event's consequences boomeranged from Kiowa County to Washington, DC, to Lame Deer, Montana, to Clinton, Oklahoma, and back again to southeastern Colorado. The next day, Sheri Bowen called Alexa Roberts, letting her know how appalled she had been at the sight of a federal employee applauding Lee Pedro's remarks. Roberts replied that she had no idea why the Bowens were upset, and that regardless, it was not the government's place to censor its citizens. "We can't tell people they can't exercise free speech," she recalled explaining. As it happened, after the panel discussion, the Bowens apparently had surfed the Internet, where they discovered a website linking Pedro and Ward Churchill, who at the time remained embroiled in a controversy surrounding an essay he wrote in the wake of the September 11 attacks. In that piece, Churchill explained 9/11 in part by pointing to American imperialism, going on to describe some of the victims of the World Trade Center attacks as "little Eichmanns"—technocrats implicated in genocide. Culture warriors nationwide seized on the Churchill case as proof of the American professorate's liberal bias. As late as summer 2005, a seemingly unrepentant Churchill could still be found sitting above the fold in Colorado's newspapers. Now, it appeared to Sheri Bowen, Lee Pedro had made common cause with Churchill, and the NPS had cheered them from the sidelines. She explained that from her family's perspective the Sand Creek project had already done enough damage, and she demanded an audience with the Kiowa County commissioners.[56]

At that meeting, which took place on July 14, Alexa Roberts learned that some of the commissioners agreed with the Bowens: the NPS, they believed, had bent over backward to keep the descendants happy, and the historic site might do their community more harm than good. Roberts left feeling dejected, she said, "[like] this thin crust of tolerance had formed through the years, so that we could all work together, and now the commissioners' anger at the situation had come bubbling through." She also wondered if "maybe there wasn't something to what they were saying." To that point in the memorialization process, the site had hovered in the hazy distance, a mirage, never really an immediate concern for Kiowa County. But as the opening drew nearer, the commissioners confronted the reality of having a unit of the NPS nearby: their county would change forever. Many local people did not want that. Thinking like an anthropologist, Roberts suggested that the county had been "almost like an island, and now we're adding this unknown element into the mix. There's no way of predicting the impact, no way at all." She concluded, "So people got worried. And they decided they needed to express their concerns."[57]

Chuck and Sheri Bowen, meanwhile, believed that their Sand Creek story, hushed up for years, would finally be heard. The Bowens alerted associates from the OIW that while Lee Pedro had denigrated the 9/11 dead, an NPS employee had clapped politely in the background. The Kiowa County website lit up with posts. A man named Curt Neeley related, "Mr. Pedro reportedly said he thought the Twin Tower victims of 9/11 deserved to die because whites had swindled Manhattan Island from the Indians for a few beads." The next day, a local Civil War reenactor sent an e-mail to the Sand Creek site threatening "serious repercussions" for the NPS officials who had applauded Pedro. After explaining that he was "very anti-Indian," he warned that "this latest outrage can not go uncontested" before finally promising that he would "make sure that justice is served." Back on the Kiowa County website, the Bowens asked, of the memorialization project broadly and the Sand Creek descendants specifically, "How is this for your economic development? Why does everyone have to walk on eggshells with these people?"

Then, on August 4, Neeley added more grist to the mill, writing of the "7 white scalps" retrieved from Black Kettle's village after Sand Creek and suggesting that the violence should be memorialized as a battle rather than a massacre.[58]

The same day that Curt Neeley posted his defense of the Colorado volunteers, the Denver press reported that President George W. Bush had signed the Sand Creek trust legislation into law on August 2. The *Rocky Mountain News* hailed the act as "potentially healing" before closing its story with a quote from philosopher Theodor Adorno: "The abundance of real suffering tolerates no forgetting." The *Denver Post*'s tone, by contrast, remained measured, hinting, with an examination of the rhetoric surrounding current discussions of Sand Creek, that healing might be hard to come by. The *Post*'s Diane Carman noted that in a recent press conference Senator Allard had shied away from labeling Sand Creek "a massacre," instead calling the violence "a dispute." Such bloodless language did not sit well with Carman, who scolded: "In the face of all the evidence of treachery and savagery, and the dramatic gesture to acknowledge what really happened, Allard still couldn't bring himself to call it what it was: a massacre." Of course, in her own story's lead, Carman had referred to Sand Creek as "a battle," so perhaps it was a wash. Nevertheless, all of the news coverage agreed that it would only be a matter of time before the NPS finally opened the Sand Creek site to the public.[59]

All eyes returned to the Cheyenne and Arapaho Tribes, which still had to convey the former Dawson property into federal trust before the historic site could be formally established. In order for that to happen, the tribes' business committee had to prepare a resolution and bring it to a vote before the full tribal electorate. Unfortunately, as Alexa Roberts recalled, "they can't get a resolution, because there is no functioning business committee." With the tribal government as divided as it had been during the controversy over Jim Druck's acquisition of the Dawson ranch, the business committee's chairman, Bill Blind, called Roberts and said that Druck would be advising the tribes about the proposed land transfer. Blind asked Roberts to meet with him and the casino magnate.[60]

On August 26, 2005, Alexa Roberts, Bill Blind, Joe Big Medicine, Lee Pedro, Laird Cometsevah, Jim Druck, and several other people gathered at the Cow Palace hotel in Lamar. Blind informed Roberts that they would "negotiate" issues important to the tribes, including special access to the site for the descendants. They would also, Blind said, hash out how the tribes would *"lease"* the land to the NPS. That word brought Roberts up short. There could be no lease, she knew, as the federal trust legislation stated that title to the property had to be conveyed to the U.S. government, which would then manage the land as part of the historic site. Moreover, the NPS leadership, facing a funding crisis, had grown tired of Sand Creek. What had once seemed like a chance to burnish the agency's multicultural credentials while memorializing a national tragedy increasingly looked like a snakebit project. Roberts went to the Cow Palace to explain, "there's only one thing that's left to be done. Either the deed gets transferred and the park gets established, or it doesn't. You don't have to transfer the deed. But then we can't establish the park. That's where we are now."[61]

At the meeting, it became clear that representatives from the Cheyenne and Arapaho Tribes were in a position similar to that of the Kiowa County commissioners. As the site became less of an abstraction, they faced difficult choices. Laird Cometsevah, for example, had to decide whether to convey hard-won property to federal authorities—which is why Cometsevah kept returning to the idea of a lease. A lease, he reasoned, would allow the descendants to forge a management agreement with the NPS while keeping control of the former Dawson ranch. Cometsevah said that he "didn't want to give away tribal land." He asked, given the difficulty of acquiring "the traditional site," how he could "tell [his] people" that they should "now hand it over to the government." Jim Druck then stepped in. He explained that this would be a different trust arrangement than the tribes were used to. Instead of federal authorities managing the land for the tribes' economic benefit, they would protect the tribes' history. He summed up the options for Cometsevah: "You own the land. It's yours. You can choose to convey it. Or you don't have to. If you think doing so will allow you to preserve your heritage, then go ahead. If you don't, then keep it yourself." Roberts reassured the descendants that their concerns could be addressed in the park's general management plan, a document that would take years to produce after the site opened. But in the interim, she said, they could draw up a binding memorandum of understanding that would protect the descendants' interests.[62]

In the days after the meeting, Alexa Roberts took stock of the situation. The descendants at last seemed to agree that there could be no lease. Most of their remaining worries focused on questions of access to the site and the importance of including a tribal cemetery where repatriated human remains could be buried. Although Laird Cometsevah had at one point during the meeting suggested that the secretary of the interior would need to create a list of descendants for the purposes of allotting Article 6 reparations, Roberts had steered clear of the topic. She was confident that constructing a memorandum of understanding would not be difficult. But she still worried about political uncertainty within the Cheyenne and Arapaho Tribes. More and more, Roberts found herself discussing the situation with her confused neighbors. "People come around and ask, 'When's it going to be open?'" She typically responded with a shrug, explaining, "there are some technicalities to take care of first," before admitting, "everything's in limbo at the moment."[63]

It remained that way for more than another year. For every step forward in the memorialization process, either the Cheyenne and Arapaho Tribes or the NPS took a step back. In September 2005, Bill Blind decided that despite the politics hobbling the tribes' business committee he would seek a resolution conveying the former Dawson property into trust. On October 1 of that same year, though, the eligible tribal electorate rejected a referendum on continuing to work with Steve Hillard's Council Tree Communications. Blind had thrown the full weight of his office behind that measure, seeing in it hope for economic development for the tribes. He resolved after the vote to avoid more controversy, including issues surrounding Sand Creek. Then, in mid-December, Alexa Roberts's superiors warned her that fiscal woes throughout the federal apparatus and growing concerns in the NPS about the viability of the historic site threatened her budget for the coming year. When Roberts replied that ample funding from Congress seemed to be available for new memorials to the victims of the September 11 attacks, her bosses noted archly that compared to the divided Sand Creek descendants, the 9/11 widows "always speak with one voice."[64]

After hearing from her superiors, Roberts addressed the Cheyenne descendants. During negotiations over a memorandum of understanding, Laird Cometsevah signaled that he remained uncertain about the land transfer by again raising the possibility of a lease agreement between the tribes and federal authorities. Roberts, who sympathized with Cometsevah's misgivings about turning tribal property over to the U.S. government, remembered that meeting as "a low point. Years of work for the descendants, for Kiowa County, for the NPS, all that work and all that time seemed like it would be wasted." Finally, at yet another consultation meeting, this one held in Cheyenne, Wyoming, on June 28, 2006, Roberts told the group, "With wars going on in Iraq and Afghanistan, every part of the federal budget is being mined. Washington knows that this park, which still doesn't really exist except on paper, has been funded for six years. They aren't willing to do that any more." Pointing to Senator Campbell's retirement and the replacement of Secretary of the Interior Gale Norton, a Coloradan and proponent of the Sand Creek project, who had recently resigned amid allegations that her department had mishandled the government's Native American trust funds, Roberts warned: "Our support has eroded." She believed a moment of truth had arrived; the Cheyenne and Arapaho Tribes would place the former Dawson ranch into trust with the NPS or accept that there would be no historic site.[65]

As though on cue, the situation improved. In a flurry of activity in spring 2006, the Cheyenne and Arapaho Tribes addressed their internal political conflicts. On April 4, the tribes promulgated a new constitution. They would replace their business committee and chairman with a legislature and governor. The first person to occupy the governor's office would be Darrell Flyingman. Although legal challenges immediately swirled around his administration, Flyingman assured Alexa Roberts that he "would convey the tribes' portion of the Sand Creek site into trust as quickly as possible." On August 23, the Cheyenne and Arapaho Tribes' legislature held hearings on Flyingman's trust resolution. Despite tension between the governor and the legislature, Flyingman announced, "I fully support this bill. The day you hand it to me, I will sign it." After a constitutionally mandated thirty-day waiting period, Flyingman would then transfer the tribes' title to the former Dawson ranch to the federal government. Roberts left Oklahoma hopeful that the secretary of the interior might be able to publish a *Federal Register* notice marking formal establishment of the historic site, possibly even in time for the anniversary of the massacre in late November.[66]

On September 9, 2006, the Cheyenne and Arapaho legislature opened its session by asking Laird Cometsevah to offer a prayer. As Cometsevah spoke in the Cheyenne language, a mural covered the wall behind him: images of tribal people wearing regalia, a drum circle, the flags of the United States and the Cheyenne and Arapaho Tribes, mounted chiefs, bison grazing on the prairie, and in the background, looming over everything else, diaphanous elders, the omnipresent memory of the tribes' past. After Cometsevah finished, Darrell Flyingman rose. Exhibiting the bonhomie of a small-town mayor, Flyingman joked, "watching legislative proceedings is like driving through Kansas at night: dull and hard to see what's really happening." He then entertained a motion to bring Tribal Bill 01-08-02 to a final vote. "A bill to authorize the governor to sign the conveyance of the former Dawson ranch to the United States to hold in trust for the Cheyenne and Arapaho Tribes," the legislation noted that "the Sand Creek Massacre and its related history is central to the identity and sovereignty of the Cheyenne and Arapaho Tribes." After receiving a quick second from another representative, Flyingman related that there had not been "a word of opposition" to the measure. He hailed this moment of comity, so unusual for tribes often plagued by factionalism.[67]

Alexa Roberts walked to the microphone. Fighting back tears, she thanked the Cheyennes and Arapahos for their faith in the NPS and asked for their support in clearing any final hurdles on the road to creating the historic site. Joe Big Medicine next recounted the long struggle to memorialize the massacre. Without further ado, the legislature unanimously voted through the bill. As quickly as that, it was over. The tribal officials returned to more prosaic business: establishing a position of legislative clerk and poring over the details of a budget bill. Roberts later joked that she had half expected Steve Hillard to burst through the doors and object. Instead, as people filed out of the legislative chambers at the end of the session, they walked past a bronze bust guarding the entrance: "The Great Cheyenne Peacemaker, Chief Black Kettle, Died November 27 1868, Massacred at the Battle of

Washita." Joe Big Medicine nodded at the memorial. On the way to his car, he remarked, "Well, we got that done." And in the depths of the building, Darrell Flyingman signed the title to the Dawson ranch and handed it to Roberts. It was a beautiful day: sunny and breezy, uncommonly cool for late summer in central Oklahoma. Blue skies stretched to the horizon. Events accelerated from there toward the Sand Creek Massacre National Historic Site's opening ceremony.[68]

At a consultation meeting held in Eads on September 12, less than a week after the deed transfer, the Sand Creek stakeholders gathered again. The Cheyenne descendants remained uneasy about having given up control of their land, and they struggled to gain purchase in the new landscape of memorialization they had created. Eager to leave some imprint on the historic site, some emblem of tribal sovereignty on a federally sponsored public space, Laird Cometsevah insisted that the "Sand Creek Battle Ground" marker that still sat atop the monument overlook should remain in place, but a new edifice, with George Bent's map depicting the geography of the massacre engraved upon it, should be erected nearby. Cometsevah mused that still another plaque might include the names of the "real descendants, the people who actually came from Sand Creek." That nobody else at the meeting engaged with this notion, seemingly an effort to revive dormant animosities with the Northern Arapahos, suggested that the group had grown weary of fighting. The next day, as the descendants walked the site with representatives from the NPS and Kiowa County, Cometsevah seemed to sense that times had changed. He stated that he still did not "trust the Park Service" before acknowledging, "Ben Campbell went with them. That's how he chose to do it. And that's why we're here." Gazing around the South Bend, Cometsevah proclaimed, with posterity on his mind, "Sand Creek is about our Indianness, about our tribal ways." Revisiting the idea of creating a monument to the Bent map, he added: "People always say you can't carve things in stone, but we have to. We have to be sure nobody forgets."[69]

For his part, Joe Big Medicine focused on land-use issues, bemoaning the fact that in the future the NPS would determine who could use the site and for what purposes. For years, the Cheyenne and Arapaho Tribes had enjoyed their status as proprietors, exercising occasional veto power over visitation requests. Big Medicine chuckled: "We've been able to keep white people away from here. For the first time in American history, we've been able to keep white people where we've wanted them." Equally important, the Cheyenne descendants had been able to give orders to federal employees, instructing the NPS about how the site could be used. The previous year, for instance, Alexa Roberts had dealt with Kiowa County officials who viewed ungrazed land as a potential fire hazard. Roberts had asked the Southern Cheyenne descendants for permission to run cattle on the tribes' property. Cometsevah, speaking for the descendants, had agreed to limited grazing in areas far from the creek bed but balked when Roberts broached the topic of killing feral pigs running wild on the site. "No. No more guns," Cometsevah answered. "There's been enough shooting, enough killing there already." If neighboring landowners were frustrated about that, Cometsevah explained, Roberts would just have to explain the significance of the sacred site.[70]

Now the descendants' ability to regulate hunting, grazing, and public access had disappeared. The NPS, balancing its mandated responsibilities to the American people and its role as trustee to the Cheyenne and Arapaho Tribes, would determine who would enter the memorial and what they could do once on site. Considering the case of the Bowens, Joe Big Medicine shook his head at the thought of the upcoming transition. A few months earlier, Chuck and Sheri Bowen had suggested that the opening of the historic site might endanger their family's cattle operation. In a story reported in the *Denver Post*, Chuck Bowen recounted the mysterious demise of two cows recently discovered dead with the skin peeled from their faces. Asked if perhaps aliens had been involved in the strange dissections, Bowen answered in good humor: "You would think they would have something more important to do." Still, some of the descendants remained concerned that the Bowens might sabotage the site in the future. Big Medicine, gazing at the monument overlook, cleared his throat and changed the subject. Addressing the best location for a tribal cemetery, he suggested that a graveyard would provide the descendants with some comfort, perhaps even offering them a modicum of healing. He concluded, "At least that will be ours alone. And that's where our ancestors will finally be able to rest."[71]

From Janet Frederick's perspective, cattle mutilations and the repatriation of human remains seemed somewhat less pressing in that moment than preparing her hometown for the anticipated arrival of tens of thousands of visitors annually once the site opened its doors. The memorialization process had dragged on for so long, with so many twists and turns along the way, that Frederick suspected her neighbors did not fully understand that the milestone of the park's opening might actually be imminent. "We just have to convince the community that this is really happening," she said, as the initial day of the consultation neared its conclusion. With Frederick wringing her hands, Alexa Roberts looked on, bemused at the thought of welcoming an untold number of dignitaries to a ribbon cutting. Over the next several months, Roberts and Frederick, along with scores of NPS staffers and local volunteers, would transform themselves into event planners, poring over details of the ceremony. The descendants, meanwhile, would consider their accomplishments and what to do next.[72]

With the Sand Creek site finally protected, the Ridgely brothers, Ben and Gail, returned to their life's work: educating young people on the Northern Arapahos' Wind River Reservation. As for their Southern Arapaho kin associated with the memorialization effort, both Lee Pedro and Alonzo Sankey had recently passed away. Pedro, not long after igniting controversy in Kiowa County over his alleged remarks about the 9/11 attacks, had died in a car accident. Sankey, for his part, had lost a long battle with cancer. They were among the many descendants who would not live to see the historic site's opening, including Luke Brady, Eugene Ridgely Sr., and Colleen Cometsevah, Laird Cometsevah's wife, who had succumbed to Parkinson's disease a year earlier. Throughout the Sand Creek project, people had grown used to seeing Laird Cometsevah gently towering over Colleen Cometsevah in her wheelchair: handing her documents, bringing her food before eating himself, and bending his long frame into an L to drape a blanket on her legs or whisper in her ear. Without his wife by his side, and with the site under federal protection, Cometsevah, though still impressive, seemed somehow diminished. It was not clear which project, if any, the chief would take on in the coming years, though he insisted, "the United States government owes the Sand Creek descendants the reparations laid out in Article 6 of the Little Arkansas treaty." Cometsevah promised that so long as that guarantee remained unfulfilled, he would not rest.[73]

The two men known affectionately as the Brady boys, Otto Braided Hair and Steve Brady, appeared to be tireless. Braided Hair continued overseeing the Northern Cheyenne Sand Creek Office as well as planning the tribe's annual Healing Run, which coincided each year with the anniversary of the massacre. He also worked with his older brother, Brady, who devoted himself to the repatriation of human remains, the protection of sacred sites, teaching Cheyenne culture at the reservation high school, and serving, in his position as headman of the Crazy Dogs Society, as a leading traditionalist in the tribe. In that role, Brady found himself in legal trouble around the time that the Cheyenne and Arapaho Tribes deeded the Dawson property to the federal government. A year earlier, in summer 2005, Brady had accused a non-Indian doctor, Steven Sonntag of the Indian Health Service, of creating a prayer circle on the Northern Cheyenne Reservation and thus "desecrating sacred tribal symbols." Guarding the Northern Cheyennes' cultural patrimony, Brady asked the tribal council to banish Sonntag from the reservation. When the council failed to act, Brady and several other society men reportedly scooped the doctor into a van, whisked him off Northern Cheyenne land, and informed him that he was not welcome back. Sonntag ignored the warning and pressed charges against Brady. As the historic site readied to open, a judge in Montana considered the case.[74]

Almost three years before that, at one of the Sand Creek consultation meetings held on the Northern Cheyenne Reservation, Brady had seemed to anticipate his future run-in with the law. He offered to take people involved in the memorialization effort on a tour of Lame Deer and the surrounding area, treating the trip as a lesson in Northern Cheyenne history. After climbing to the top of one of the pine-covered mountains that sits between Lame Deer and the neighboring town of Ashland, Brady gestured widely at the open vista spread out before him. He appeared to embrace his tribe's homeland as he spoke of the Cheyennes' fate after Sand Creek, about how the massacre had split the tribe again and again. Some Cheyennes, Brady stated, had traveled to the Powder River country, where they had joined the Oglala Lakota leader Red Cloud in his fight against U.S. cavalry charged with clearing the way for Anglo expansion into the West after the Civil War. Others, including Black Kettle's followers, had headed further south, where, despite lessons learned at Sand Creek, they still hoped to live in peace with whites. But Brady spat that in 1868 "[George Armstrong] Custer's men attacked the Cheyennes camped at the Washita, killing Black Kettle." After that, many remaining Southern Cheyennes were forced to live on a reservation in Indian Territory.[75]

Brady then turned his attention back to the Powder River country. He explained that the Northern Cheyennes, fresh from victories in Red Cloud's war, continued skirmishing with federal troops for years afterward: notably at Summit Springs in 1869 and the Rosebud Battle in 1876, just prior to Custer's undoing at the Little Bighorn. Custer's defeat, Brady suggested, provided the federal government with a pretext to seize more land in the region and visit additional indignities on its indigenous peoples. Still, he noted, the Northern Cheyennes had kept struggling, including Chief Dull Knife's and Chief Little Wolf's epic efforts to keep their people safe and free. In 1877, white authorities insisted that the Northern Cheyennes had to live with their southern relatives on their reservation in Indian Territory. Upon arriving there, Dull Knife and Little Wolf found conditions impossibly bleak and chose to run rather than allow their people to starve on the Southern Plains. Brady recalled that "on the way back home" the Northern Cheyennes had "fought on." For example, Dull Knife's people had broken out of prison at Fort Robinson in northern Nebraska and, in Brady's estimation, left exhausted federal authorities little choice but to provide the Northern Cheyennes with a reservation exactly where they wanted to live: on the Tongue River. "We are the only Indian people who got the land that we demanded," Brady concluded. The subtext was clear: Brady's vision of Northern Cheyenne history suggested that only through fierce vigilance could lasting victory against the federal government finally be secured. Three years later, Brady maintained his militant stance. The presiding judge in his case nevertheless ruled that a tribal court had jurisdiction and thus dismissed the suit. A relieved Brady did not skip a beat; he refocused his energies on a repatriation request already underway at the time.[76]

Meanwhile, Alexa Roberts and her staff continued with the day-to-day work of operating the site: improving the land, working with local authorities, considering questions of interpretation. As time passed, though, and the secretary of the interior seemed to be dawdling over the final arrangements for the national historic site, Roberts's concerns

A stand of young cottonwoods that have taken root in the dry bed of Sand Creek, upstream from the monument overlook. *(Photo by Tom Carr.)*

mounted. Even after the NPS set an opening date, Secretary Dirk Kempthorne still did not sign the documents establishing the Sand Creek site. Officials in the Department of the Interior believed that the Cheyenne and Arapaho Tribes, working under their new constitution, had not legally conveyed the deed to the Dawson property into federal trust. With that issue unresolved, a crisis over title insurance cropped up. Roberts wondered, "Will we ever get this done?" Then, in late fall and early winter 2006–2007, lawyers at the Interior Department determined that the Sand Creek trust had been established properly, and underwriters found a way to insure the property.[77]

On April 23, Secretary of the Interior Kempthorne, along with Mary Bomar, the director of the NPS, and Senator Wayne Allard at his side, signed the paperwork formally establishing the Sand Creek Massacre National Historic Site, the 391st unit of the National Park System. In a statement released to the media, Kempthorne expressed his hope that the site would guarantee that "as a country, we might never forget the events that took place along the banks of Sand Creek." But he carefully avoided using the word "massacre." Bomar added, "The history of this country is not complete without an understanding and respect for the tragedies that affect our national consciousness." Less than a week after that, the site opened to the public. Laird Cometsevah, allowing himself a moment of rest, declared: "Now Sand Creek will never be forgotten."[78]

Early in the morning of April 29, 2007, less than twenty-four hours after the Sand Creek Massacre National Historic Site formally opened it doors, volunteers cleared away evidence of the previous day's furious activity. They loaded chairs onto flatbeds, pulled mobile command centers away behind semitrucks, and carted off loads of trash. At the same time, the Southern Cheyennes and Arapahos, who had camped near the creek bed the previous week, packed up their tents and prepared for the long drive east, back to Oklahoma. By midday, only a few stragglers milled around, taking advantage of the NPS's decision to keep the site open for visitors. Finally, as the sun began setting, the prairie stood open, grass waving in the breeze, the tableau broken only by the low rise of the monument overlook, cottonwood trees beginning to leaf out in the riparian bottoms, and a two-story workshop, the last reminder of Bill Dawson's stewardship of the land (the NPS had torn down his ranch house two years earlier). Although temporary signs led the way to the newest unit of the National Park System, a stout chain stood between the massacre site and the county road, warning away trespassers who might consider entering the property. It seemed, for the moment, that Laird Cometsevah was right: the Sand Creek site would be protected, the events of November 29, 1864, remembered. But it remained to be seen how, exactly, that would happen, how the NPS and the descendants would wrestle with the troubling question of interpretation, and what visitors, once they began arriving in numbers, would make of the memorial.[79]

Epilogue: When Is Enough Enough?

On June 8, 2008, just over a year after the Sand Creek memorial began welcoming visitors to Kiowa County, a small caravan of vehicles made its way westward into the teeth of an unseasonably bitter wind, traveling roughly an hour on Highway 50 across the plains of southeastern Colorado. The group began its journey in the parking lot of Lamar's Cow Palace hotel before heading toward Bent's Old Fort National Historic Site, the location where William Bent (George's father), along with his two partners—his brother, Charles, and a fur trader named Ceran St. Vrain—set up shop along the Santa Fe Trail in the 1830s and 1840s. The National Park Service (NPS) has reconstructed that outpost in its original location: a gentle bend of the Arkansas River, surrounded by towering cottonwood trees, approximately ten miles outside of what today is the small town of La Junta. The historic structure's squat buildings conjoin to form a rectangle that encompasses a dusty central plaza. Stout adobe walls and a formidable guard tower can be seen from miles away across the prairie. The NPS operates the fort as a historic site, and every day of the year except Thanksgiving, Christmas, and New Year's visitors are welcome to take tours guided by "living historians" wearing "period clothing." Bent's Old Fort is meant to look, feel, and even smell like the Old West.[1]

Otto Braided Hair, Steve Brady, Lee Lonebear, and several other descendants spent their early summer morning driving toward Bent's Fort because the remains of six of their ancestors waited there. The

NPS had stored those body parts, all removed from the Sand Creek killing field, in the site's climate-controlled curatorial facility. The remains had previously been scattered across the Great Plains, from Lincoln, Nebraska, to Denver, Colorado, waiting in three museums and a private collection. The process of repatriating them had been long, stretching more than a decade in some cases. The Northern and Southern Cheyenne and Arapaho tribes had worked together, cutting red tape and putting aside rivalries, ensuring that the massacre's victims would no longer be housed in soulless repositories, where they sometimes were subject to academic study or idle curiosity. Now they would be buried in the soil where they had fallen, at a cemetery that the descendants had insisted must be part of the Sand Creek Massacre National Historic Site. This was how the Native American Graves Protection and Repatriation Act (NAGPRA) was supposed to work: by providing Native American communities with an opportunity to reclaim their cultural patrimony, seized from them during the wholesale dispossession and destruction that attended the conquest and colonization of the continent.[2]

Passed by Congress and signed into law by President George H. W. Bush in 1990, NAGPRA mandated that within three years, even reluctant universities, museums, and other federally funded repositories had to catalog their collections of Native American sacred and ceremonial objects. Just two years after that, in 1995, these same institutions had to present a full accounting of the human remains they held, at which point members of "affiliated tribes" who sought the safe return of those items could begin submitting repatriation requests through the NPS. Some estimates suggested that the remains of approximately 1 million Native people were housed within affected organizations throughout the United States at that time, with still more individuals held by private collections, where many of them would remain, beyond NAGPRA's reach, into the future. Prior to the law's passage, the graves of Native people buried on federal property enjoyed few safeguards; the bodies they contained could be treated as "archeological resources" by researchers or removed by robbers and sold on the black market. NAGPRA extended protections already taken for granted by most other U.S. citizens to Native Americans as well—that their ancestors' remains would not be disturbed by looters.[3]

From the beginning, the law generated controversy. Some physical anthropologists hailed the nation's tradition of studying Native bodies for insights into human development, pointing to erstwhile masterpieces of the American intellectual tradition, including Thomas Jefferson's *Notes on the State of Virginia*. Other scholars warned that returning the vast storehouses of human remains to Native communities would cripple ongoing research by robbing scientists of crucial osteological data. Steve Brady, for his part, dismissed such warnings as a smokescreen for intellectual imperialism. The protests, he believed, hid the deeper misgivings of academics loath to cede control of indigenous bodies. Referring to anthropologists, Brady said, "they've had centuries now to desecrate the remains of Indians in the name of 'science.'" He wondered, "When is enough enough?" Although Brady appreciated that NAGPRA provided a mechanism for repatriating artifacts and remains, he nevertheless scorned the law as "one more hoop that tribes must jump through to get their ancestors back." The other descendants agreed with him. But they had no choice. If they wanted to bury the massacre's victims at Sand Creek, they had to comply with NAGPRA's dictates. So they traveled to Bent's Fort.[4]

When the descendants arrived there, they retrieved their ancestors' remains from the secure location where the NPS had temporarily housed them at the tribal delegates' request. After performing a purification ritual in private, the Cheyennes and Arapahos loaded the sacred cargo into their vehicles for the drive back east across Colorado's plains toward Kiowa County. Approximately forty people waited for them at the Sand Creek site, gathered for a burial ceremony in the lee of the monument overlook. The NPS had built a temporary shelter there, providing relief from the sun. The wind, though, whipped across the open ground, stiffening the American and white flags that the descendants flew from a lodge pole over the ceremony. Lee Lonebear offered a prayer in the Cheyenne language before a drum group sang White Antelope's death song. A descendant of Silas Soule read aloud the full text of the letter that the martyred hero of Sand Creek had written to Ned Wynkoop in the days following the massacre. The descendants then lowered their ancestors' remains—interred within coffins fashioned by Karl Zimmerman, an NPS employee, from deadfall left by the cottonwood trees lining the nearby creek bottom—into graves dug deep in the sandy soil. Finally, the observers and participants at the event took turns shoveling dirt onto the coffins until they were safely buried.[5]

The repatriation and funeral ceremonies wove together strands of the descendants' memorialization efforts: asserting their control over that process and the ceremonial space that it had produced, highlighting the efficacy of their traditional ways of understanding history, reiterating their commitment to stewarding connections between the past and present, and proclaiming their ongoing cultural and political sovereignty. At the Sand Creek cemetery, the Arapahos and Cheyennes reclaimed their ancestors' remains and recast stories that had, through the years, attached themselves to those bodies. In one case, Caroline Downing, Major Jacob Downing's widow, had in 1911 donated remains of one of the repatriated individuals to the Colorado Historical Society. For nearly a century, that scalp lock had stayed there, known only by an accession number, E 1748, and a brief description: "Scalp (Cheyenne or Arapaho), Taken from an Indian by a soldier at Sand Creek Massacre, by Jacob Downing Nov. 29, 1864." Downing was one of John Chivington's stalwart supporters at the massacre, and later, through his activities as a member of Denver-area heritage organizations, including the local chapter of the Grand Army of the Republic, a guardian of his former commander's Sand Creek memories. In that capacity, Downing squared off with George Bent early in the twentieth century, disparaging him as a "halfbreed" after Bent's *Frontier* articles appeared in print.[6]

The descendants, for their part, tried at the burial ceremony to erase such slurs by honoring Bent's massacre memories as tribal histories and foundational texts for their commemorative efforts. They did so by siting their cemetery at the foot of the monument overlook. That small hill rose above the creek bend in which the Cheyenne descendants believed that Bent had depicted Black Kettle's village on the maps he had drawn at roughly the same time that Caroline Downing had donated her husband's massacre trophy to the Colorado Historical Society. The thirty-three-star American and white flags flying over the burial ceremony also evoked Bent's recollection of the standards that had topped Black Kettle's lodge on November 29, 1864. Bent used those flags as evidence that the Indians at Sand Creek had been peaceful, that they had believed themselves to be under the protection of the U.S. government, and that they had nevertheless been massacred by federal troops. If the descendants had their way, Bent's Sand Creek stories, not Chivington's, would endure over time.[7]

The treatment of the remains themselves—that they would be accorded long-deferred respect and afforded a peaceful final resting place—also demonstrated the descendants' commitment to memorializing their fallen ancestors and preserving their threatened tribal traditions. The disposition of corpses figured prominently throughout Sand Creek's history: in the months leading to the violence, when the Hungates' ruined bodies moldered in the public eye in Denver; at the massacre itself, when Chivington's troops revenged themselves on the Hungates' purported murderers by hacking apart the Cheyenne and Arapaho dead, removing scalps, genitalia, and other body parts as souvenirs from the blood-soaked field; and in the years afterward, when researchers on and off the federal payroll studied the remains of Sand Creek's victims, using their corpses to improve the U.S. military's weaponry and as data marshaled in support of elaborate pseudoscientific theories about human evolution and the inevitability of white civilization's triumph over Native savagery on the frontier. That the descendants set aside a cemetery within the historic site to house those remains, which they buried following strict tribal protocols, spoke volumes about the persistence of the Cheyennes and Arapahos as well as their ongoing respect for a traditional way of life.[8]

Beyond that, elements of the reburial ceremony underscored the significance of the descendants' contributions during the memorialization process, as well as establishing their exclusive claim to certain areas of the historic site. The decision to place the cemetery near the banks of the so-called Dawson South Bend, for instance, nodded not only to the work of George Bent but also to the leadership of Chief Laird Cometsevah, who had died only a few months earlier. Cometsevah had always suggested that a tribal graveyard should be located near the spot where, he insisted, Bent had diagrammed the massacre on his maps. The cemetery, consequently, reflected the ongoing significance of Bent's cartography for the Cheyenne people, the Sacred Arrow Keeper's consecration of the earth on William Dawson's land early in the 1970s, and the uneasy resolution of the village controversy during the site search. At the same time, regulations governing the use of the cemetery made it clear that the descendants alone controlled that space. In the future, they, and not the NPS, would determine who walked the sacred ground there, in effect privatizing what otherwise had become a public landscape. For the descendants still involved in the site's management, those special privileges helped mitigate the deep misgivings that Laird Cometsevah had expressed years earlier, when he had confronted the prospect of handing recovered tribal land over to the U.S. government.[9]

The descendants' determination to leave an indelible mark on the historic site manifested itself again at another consultation meeting, held just three days after the burial. On June 11, 2008, stakeholders in the Sand Creek project met in familiar surroundings: one of the Cow Palace hotel's conference rooms. The previous evening, the tribal representatives, emotionally spent from interring their ancestors' remains earlier in the week, had sat down with Alexa Roberts and other NPS personnel, including Tom Thomas, the official charged with overseeing the creation of the Sand Creek memorial's general management plan (GMP). That document, intended to serve as a road map for the site's day-to-day operations in the future, would also have to cover the politically charged question of interpretation. But even with that contentious issue looming on the horizon, the evening meeting had been informal and collegial. Everyone there seemed to be looking forward to opening up discussion of how the massacre's history would be recounted for visitors arriving at the site.[10]

The next day, though, proved anything but cordial. Thomas and Roberts, at the urging of the NPS's Intermountain regional director at the time, had invited Patty Limerick, still on faculty at the University of Colorado–Boulder and among the most renowned Western historians in the United States, to serve as a discussion leader and, if necessary, a mediator at the meeting and perhaps occasionally for the rest of the planning process. Limerick had firsthand experience with the politics of memory surrounding Sand Creek. Years earlier, she had found herself mired in ugly controversy after recommending that Nichols Hall, a dormitory on the Boulder campus named for one of Chivington's subordinates, should be rechristened. In the time since, Limerick had directed the Center of the American West, a "forum committed to the civil, respectful, and problem-solving exploration of important and often contentious public issues." In that capacity, she had dedicated herself "to bridging the gap between academics and the general public and to demonstrating the benefits of applying historical perspective to contemporary dilemmas and conflicts." Thomas and Roberts selected Limerick because, "in an era of political polarization and contention," she took pride in "striv[ing] to bring out 'the better angels of our nature' by appealing to our common loyalties and hopes as Westerners." Because of her academic interests and experience uniting traditional antagonists, Limerick seemed like an ideal choice as the NPS began the process of sorting through the historical literature that would be used as a guide in interpreting the Sand Creek site.[11]

Some of the descendants disagreed. From the first, several of the Cheyenne tribal representatives resented Limerick's presence at the meeting. They wondered why a newcomer had been introduced into the memorialization process at the eleventh hour. Limerick, after all, had not earned their trust by working with them on commemorating the massacre. Quite the contrary, years earlier she had inadvertently run afoul of David Halaas, the historian who remained a close friend and advisor to the Cheyenne descendants. Upon hearing word in 2000 of the discovery of Silas Soule's letters, which turned up in a Denver-area attic on the eve of Senator Campbell's Capitol Hill hearings to determine whether the Sand Creek memorial should be established as a national historic site, Limerick initially had expressed ambivalence about the documents' contents. Her muted reaction in the Denver papers had angered Halaas. Even after Limerick had clarified that a reporter had mischaracterized her position, and that she actually had not yet read the correspondence, some bad feelings lingered through the years. Beyond professional friction, though, the Cheyenne descendants were not overawed by Limerick's scholarly credentials. Instead, they viewed her MacArthur "genius grant" and her international reputation as potential challenges to their cultural authority. As Otto Braided Hair explained, "We've got a good handle on our own history. We don't need an outsider to tell us about Sand Creek."[12]

Looking back on that meeting, Alexa Roberts acknowledged: "We [the NPS personnel] made some mistakes." The NPS had "scheduled that consultation for immediately after the burial of human remains, so everyone's emotions were running really hot." Not to mention that "Patty Limerick and Tom Thomas were new to the project and were relatively unknown quantities to the descendants." Roberts had not yet fully explained to Limerick and Thomas "the relationship between the process of putting together the general management plan, including how we would interpret the massacre, and everything that had already happened with the memorialization of Sand Creek." Roberts later recalled, "We eventually wanted to sit down and figure out with a group of people, including the tribal representatives and some independent scholars [in this case, historians unaffiliated with the NPS], to identify a strategy that would allow us to choose some documentary sources over other documentary sources." She remained certain at the time that the tribal oral histories would occupy a central place in the site's interpretation. The issue, then, was that hard experience had taught Roberts, "The public would want to know how we chose our sources." She added, "The meeting with Patty Limerick was intended to lay the groundwork for dealing with that issue in the future. Unfortunately, we dropped the ball by not preparing the descendants for what we were trying to do."[13]

From Roberts's perspective, adding new elements into the mix had destabilized the memorialization process's volatile chemistry. As in the past, tension emerged from a struggle to control the production and distribution of history and memory. The tribal representatives had fought for years for some say in how the NPS would depict the violence, and they were unwilling to let an interloper become an arbiter of ongoing disputes. They rejected having Limerick, in Roberts's words, "choose between conflicting documentary sources and assess the validity of one perspective versus another perspective." Given the long struggles over incommensurable Sand Creek narratives, Otto Braided Hair believed that his people should select from among competing accounts. As he said, the descendants understood their past. They understood, too, that whoever crafted the massacre story related at the Sand Creek site would determine who would be cast as an insider or an outsider, a perpetrator or a victim. For a century and a half after Sand Creek, Arapahos and Cheyennes typically were written out of American history, more often forgotten than remembered. The Sand Creek memorial would provide them with a platform from which they could tell their stories at a national historic site—stories of tragedy and betrayal, of loss and heartbreak, but also of survival and persistence.[14]

After protesting Limerick's involvement, the descendants began questioning exactly how the GMP would be crafted. Did Senator Campbell's Sand Creek legislation not make clear the tribal representatives' prerogatives in the process? Had they not secured for themselves, through a series of negotiations during the site search, a seat at the planning table, including the right to shape how the massacre would be interpreted for the visiting public? The sense of distrust in the conference room ran so deep that Norma Gorneau, one of the Northern Cheyenne Sand Creek delegates and a longtime friend of Alexa Roberts, wondered aloud if the federal government had betrayed the Cheyennes, if the NPS would now insist on recapitulating the fight over nomenclature. Would the bloodshed, Gorneau asked, be presented as a battle rather than a massacre? At its end, the meeting produced more questions than answers. The NPS personnel asked themselves how they could interpret such a politically fraught episode as Sand Creek and if they had irreparably damaged their relationship with the descendants. Some of the descendants, in turn, asked themselves if the NPS had been acting in bad faith all along and if they had mistakenly placed a site sacred to their people in the hands of bureaucrats committed to "protecting their jobs instead of the Cheyennes' and Arapahos' heritage."[15]

Following the consultation at the Cow Palace, NPS personnel, including Alexa Roberts and Tom Thomas, decided to table questions of interpretation temporarily as they continued working on the GMP. Roberts remembered, "After that meeting we reluctantly put interpretation on the back burner." The NPS representatives believed at the time that they did not have any option; they had to rebuild trust with the descendants, again proving their good intentions before broaching discussions of how to present the massacre's history to the public visiting the memorial. The problem, though, was that the NPS relied on what Steve Brady had years earlier dubbed its "sacred playbook," a series of guidelines for systematizing agency tasks, including the planning of new units of the National Park System. Roberts admitted, "[This] was not how we did things in the NPS. And so we found ourselves having to explain, internally, why we didn't have long-range interpretative planning as part of the GMP process. It was sort of uncomfortable in that moment but absolutely necessary over the long term, Tom [Thomas] and I believed." Casting about for subjects that they hoped would not generate more ill will, Roberts and Thomas made what seemed, in light of the history of the site search, a surprising choice. "We turned to mapping," Roberts recalled, "which, ironically, brought us back to questions of interpretation."[16]

The descendants remained wary of the NPS and stepped up their efforts to shape how the massacre would be represented at the site, and how, by extension, it might be remembered collectively by visitors to the memorial. On December 7, 2010, Otto Braided Hair, Joe Big Medicine, and David Halaas arrived at the NPS's Denver offices, where they met with Alexa Roberts and Tom Thomas, as well as other NPS staffers, including representatives from the organization's Geographic Information Systems division. The group planned to talk about an upcoming cartography meeting. Roberts remembered, "It was just supposed to be a technical, nuts-and-bolts discussion." Trying to avoid a repeat of the debacle following the burial ceremony, she hoped to "lay some groundwork for a future mapping workshop we had in mind." Around the noon hour, Roberts introduced Jeff Campbell, a volunteer at the Sand Creek site. Campbell, Roberts explained, had done some cartographic research on his own time, and had generated a hypothesis that might allow competing constituencies to compromise, perhaps finally putting to rest the village controversy. Aware that all eyes in the room were on him, Campbell "worried that [he] was going to be on the stand, facing a hostile cross-examination." He recalled, "But that wasn't what happened." Instead, as he spun out his theory, rooted in an array of primary sources, the response was positive.[17]

Jeff Campbell looked a bit like the Marlboro Man—not the Marlboro Man of the advertisements that last ran in the United States in the 1980s and 1990s, but how that model might have appeared in 2010 (assuming that lung cancer had not long since caught up with him). Campbell often wore a white cowboy hat, a Western shirt tucked into Wrangler jeans, work boots that had seen their share of dusty miles, and a belt featuring a buckle whose size typically fell, on a scale that only ranch hands and Brooklyn hipsters seemed to understand, somewhere between dressy and ironic. He had a full head of graying hair and a bushy mustache. Raised in Phoenix, Arizona, and El Paso, Texas, in a home where history was central—"I was just nursed on the stuff. Growing up, most of our family vacations, usually camping trips, were to historic sites."—Campbell went on to major in the subject, with an emphasis on the American West, at the University of Texas at El Paso. After graduating, he moved to Albuquerque, New Mexico, where he worked for decades as a criminal investigator, eventually serving as a special agent in the state attorney general's office. He focused on cases that had gone cold and grew expert at pulling together intelligence sources, which, he noted, meant, "working the archives." Campbell brought his research skills with him after he retired from law enforcement, moved to Eads, and turned his attention to Sand Creek.[18]

Starting in 2002, Campbell began studying the massacre, poring first over the NPS's *Site Location Study*. The hardened cop in him worried that "there was too much certainty" in the document. "As a criminal investigator" he was "always suspicious of that kind of thing, when an event is so terribly complicated and yet the people recounting it are so completely confident about their stories." He "decided to launch [his] own investigation" into the violence. Campbell learned quickly from the secondary literature that "none of the major authors agreed." Then, like so many others before him "hooked" by the mysteries of Sand Creek, he dove into the primary sources. As he got deeper and deeper into the archives, he eventually produced two book-length document readers of his own, one devoted to the history of the 1st Colorado Regiment, the other to the 3rd Colorado Volunteers. At the time, the NPS wanted to acquire Bill Dawson's property, and the village controversy burned at its brightest. Campbell, consequently, "realized that there was this whole other issue: the site." As he remembered it, "from where I sat, the site was a crime scene and had to be investigated like that."[19]

Using methods that he had mastered while still working at the New Mexico attorney general's office, Campbell tacked a large sheet of butcher's paper to the wall of his home in Eads and began sketching out the massacre, creating what amounted to a chronological map, starting with the moment Chivington's men departed from Fort Lyon, through the slaughter itself, and concluding with the Colorado volunteers bivouacked near the killing field. Campbell planned to "diagram every prominent feature of Sand Creek" and then, as he would have done with a cold case, "line up that drawing with witness statements"—in this instance the primary accounts, drawn from the federal inquiries, and also the various tribal oral histories collected through the years—of the bloodshed, "to determine if the witnesses could have seen what they said they had seen." As Campbell continued sifting through testimony, "sorting the wheat from the chaff," he realized that several eyewitnesses suggested that at the time of the attack, "the stream channel wasn't running at a 90-degree angle. It was more like a 120-degree angle. And then, George Bent's letters also said that the bend was about 120 degrees, rather than 90 degrees, which, of course, is why Laird Cometsevah thought that." Campbell finally suspected that the so-called Big Bend of Sand Creek, known during the site search as the Dawson South Bend or the traditional site, had been shaped differently at the time of the massacre.[20]

In 2008, Campbell completed most of his research and arrived at a working theory. Early in the twentieth century, he learned, the Chivington Canal Company had constructed a large irrigation ditch running between Sand Creek and the nearby town of Brandon, Colorado. When the creek ran high during the wetter winter and spring months, impoundment reservoirs would gather its floodwaters, where they would wait to be used by local ranchers during the dry summer and fall seasons. That canal, Campbell believed, had eventually "shifted the stream's course," moving its bed approximately a mile southward over time, toward the base of what would become the monument overlook, and causing the Dawson South Bend to assume a 90-degree angle.[21]

As Jeff Campbell related his hypothesis at the consultation meeting on December 7, 2010, the NPS personnel and the descendants understood that if fieldwork confirmed Campbell's suppositions, many of the contentious issues plaguing the memorialization process would disappear. Doug Scott and Jerry Greene, who had argued for years that the concentration of artifacts unearthed in 1999 marked the location of Black Kettle's village, could be right. So, too, could Laird Cometsevah, who had insisted that George Bent had accurately mapped the massacre, that the Big Bend had embraced Black Kettle's people's lodges. If the stream had moved since the era of the bloodshed, there might be no discrepancy between those intractable positions or others: between Samuel Bonsall's depiction of the massacre site and Bent's, between firsthand accounts offered by perpetrators and oral histories collected from survivors, between social-scientific methods that had yielded a bounty of relics during the archeological component of the

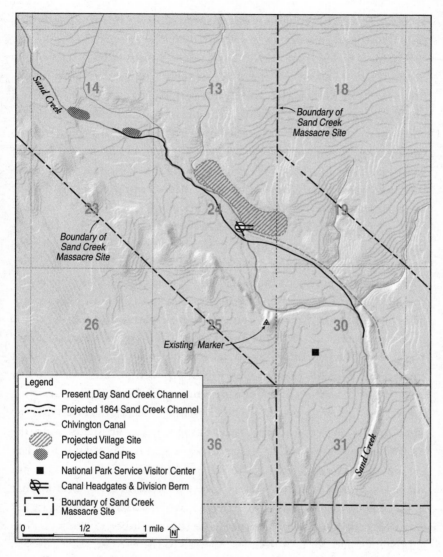

Jeff C. Campbell's theory of the projected course of Sand Creek in 1864.
(*Adapted from a map provided courtesy of Jeff C. Campbell.*)

search and traditional Native ways of understanding the past. The
next day, the descendants traveled to the memorial site with Campbell,
Alexa Roberts, Tom Thomas, and several other NPS officials. They did
not have time to survey the area under suspicion, but Otto Braided
Hair and Joe Big Medicine remarked, taking Campbell's ideas into

account, "everything made so much more sense." The group agreed to return to the site as soon as possible.[22]

Five months later, on May 17, 2011, nearly two decades after fortune hunters had touched off the modern memorialization effort by informing David Halaas that the Sand Creek site had gone missing, and almost a century and a half after the massacre itself, Northern Arapaho descendants and the NPS personnel charged with producing the GMP met in the historic site's conference center, the renovated shell of what had been Bill Dawson's ranch maintenance facility. Alexa Roberts remembered that after Gail Ridgely offered a prayer, "everyone gave opening statements about what had happened to that point in our efforts, focusing on the discrepancies between Bent's maps and the artifact find, and how we couldn't do anything about interpretation because of those differences." Jeff Campbell next recounted his theory, explaining the potential impact of the Chivington Canal. The group then walked the site, talking about how "human activities had modified the landscape over time and conceivably had resulted in a change in the course of the stream channel through the years." The day, Roberts noted, "turned into a fabulous concurrence of different ideas. It turned out that everyone, people who had been at odds for years or even longer than that, had all been right in some important ways."[23]

Over the following two days, the Cheyenne descendants arrived at the site. On May 19, Jeff Campbell stood atop a ridge, upstream from the monument overlook, and explained his research to a rapt audience. David Halaas was delighted: "If the Big Bend of Sand Creek was crescent shaped back then, not the L shape of the Dawson South Bend today, that makes George Bent's map right! There's no more basis for dismissing it!" Gary Roberts then tied up another loose thread. Roberts, who had studied the massacre for four decades, referred to the rite performed in 1978 by the Sacred Arrow Keeper and Laird Cometsevah: "If Jeff [Campbell] is right, they made Cheyenne earth in the correct place, because the spot where the monument is now is the spot where the troops began their attack. The people in the village would have first seen the troops there." In other words, "the making of Cheyenne earth at that spot," which, along with the Bent map, had always informed Cometsevah's understanding of the massacre, "made perfect sense." Finally, late in the afternoon, a hydrologist and geomorphologist allowed that Campbell's theories did not necessarily contradict the surveys completed during the site search.

Earlier geomorphological research had never concluded that the stream had been immobile through the years, only that it had not moved outside the confines of its expansive flood plain. Campbell's theories fit with these assertions and could, the two scientists noted, be tested. But confirmation would have to wait for another day.[24]

In the meantime, the NPS personnel celebrated, albeit, because of past history, tentatively. Alexa Roberts said of Jeff Campbell's methods and background, "This was the biggest mass murder he ever worked." For his part, Campbell seemed surprised by the reception that his theories had received. "All I've done for ten years is put stickers on maps," he said, "letting the evidence guide me. I never thought my research would bring everyone together onto the same page." Still, he counseled caution: "I'd never say I'm 100 percent sure about this. More than 140 years have passed since the massacre, remember."[25]

Campbell's careful perspective was born of a career spent studying violent encounters, an appreciation for the uncertain nature of memory, and an understanding of the massacre's history and the modern effort to commemorate Sand Creek. Years of working with incompatible testimony, recounting crime scenes awash in blood, had taught him to proceed deliberately before reaching conclusions. As for the massacre, Campbell suggested, based on the archival sources and tribal oral histories, that it might be possible to know what had happened on the banks of Sand Creek. But even then, he admitted to lingering doubts: "I think I know what I know. But what I know is still pretty limited." What Campbell meant is that he had only tried to determine some relatively basic information about the massacre, including the site where it took place. Put another way, he was reasonably confident about the question of *where*, but deeper analytical queries—*How* could such a thing have happened? *Who* should be held accountable? *What* were the massacre's lasting implications?—were still, he acknowledged, "a matter of interpretation." And of course there was the rub.[26]

At this writing, the NPS, working with the descendants and the public, still has to interpret the massacre. Jeff Campbell's theory, by staking out terrain on which conflicting accounts can coexist, may simplify that process—but only if further geomorphological and archeological research supports his hypothesis. But in other ways, the idea that the creek shifted course might complicate the work of memorialization, raising questions about one element of the story—the where of Sand

Creek—that John Chivington, Silas Soule, and George Bent initially took for granted; that, late in the twentieth century and early in the twenty-first, became shrouded in mystery; and that may now be known again. After all, if the creek moved in the past, who is to say that it will not move again in the future? Who is to say that even an apparently permanent and ostensibly static feature of Sand Creek's history is not actually as ephemeral as memory and as open to debate and interpretation as history? And if that is the case, then what of the landscape's apparent utility as a commemorative canvas, a vehicle for carrying the lessons of the past into the present and the future? That utility, it appears, is predicated on the misapprehension that place is more permanent, more stable, than narrative. Campbell's theory suggests that perhaps White Antelope, when he sang his death song at Sand Creek, only had it partly right. The earth and mountains may be durable, as the chief suggested while waiting for the Colorado volunteers to cut him down, but not even they will live forever.[27]

At the same time, as the United States celebrates the sesquicentennial of the Civil War, it remains unclear where exactly the massacre fits into the national narrative. Ironically, the NPS's interpretation of Sand Creek will challenge visitors to the site not because federal officials will ask anew whether the violence was a battle or a massacre, but because they have definitively answered that question. Nations rely on origin stories to provide order to their histories and a shared identity for their citizens. The United States boasts two creation narratives: the Revolution and Civil War, tales of birth, death, and rebirth. In popular memory, patriots secured their independence from Great Britain through rebellion, beginning a grand experiment in democracy that changed the world. The Founders, regrettably, also legitimated the institution of slavery, embedding the nation's original sin and the seeds of its undoing in the Constitution. Collective recollections of the Civil War suggest that conflict was the moment when the United States redeemed itself in the eyes of God by liberating the four million African American slaves then living in the South. Out of a paroxysm of violence and bloodshed the nation was reborn, a resurrection story that fits neatly within Christian narratives of catharsis through suffering. In this way, Americans remember the Civil War as a good war, transfiguring a history of violence into one of virtue, of tragedies into triumphs. Such is the power of memory to smooth the past's rough edges.[28]

Sand Creek, depicted as a massacre at the historic site, will buck the redemptive and reconciliationist currents running through most national memorials, including those recalling the Civil War. The massacre emerged out of corruption and malfeasance, race hatred rather than uplift. Its history indicts characters typically cast as heroes in the American imagination—citizen soldiers, rugged pioneers, Union officials— suggesting a darker vision of the Civil War's causes, prosecution, and consequences. Westward expansion touched off the war that destroyed slavery, but also another war with the Plains Tribes, a brutal conflict that lasted decades and left behind no simple lessons for federal commemorators hoping to bend public memory to nationalist ends. With Americans still looking to the Civil War as an origin story, a way to understand who they are, the NPS and descendants must contemplate how to interpret an event like Sand Creek, an irredeemable tragedy that casts doubt on the enduring notion that the United States enjoys a special destiny, that it is an exceptional nation among nations, favored by God. The question of whether visitors to the Sand Creek site are ready to broach such difficult topics, to reassess their homeland's character and fate, remains unsettled.[29]

For in the end, this story of memorializing Sand Creek suggests that history and memory are malleable, that even the land, despite its implied promise of permanence, can change, and that the people of the United States are so various that they should not be expected to share a single tale of a common past. Sometimes their stories complement one another; sometimes they clash. Sometimes they intersect; sometimes they diverge. Depending on who tells it, the story of Sand Creek, for instance, suggests that the Civil War midwifed, in President Lincoln's words, "a new birth of freedom," but also that it delivered the Indian Wars; that it was a moment of national redemption for some Americans, but of dispossession and subjugation for others. NPS officials and the descendants will never concur on every element of Sand Creek's interpretation, but they might agree that the historic site should challenge visitors to grapple with competing narratives of U.S. history, to struggle with ironies embedded in the American past. If that happens, then perhaps the massacre will no longer be misplaced in the landscape of national memory.[30]

NOTES

I. A PERFECT MOB

1. "National Park Service News Release: National Park Service Announces 391st Unit, Sand Creek Massacre National Historic Site," found in uncataloged files of the Sand Creek Massacre National Historic Site (FSCMNHS), currently held by National Park Service, Western Archeological and Conservation Center (NPS-WACC), Tucson, AZ. For population figures and other relevant statistics on the town of Eads and Kiowa County more broadly, see U.S. Census Bureau, "State and County QuickFacts, Kiowa County, Colorado," http://quickfacts.census.gov/qfd /states/08/08061.html.

2. Except where otherwise noted, details of the opening ceremony, including quotes, have been drawn from raw documentary footage of the event in FSCMNHS, now at NPS-WACC. See also Anthony A. Mestas, "A Nation Pays Tribute," *Pueblo Chieftain,* April 29, 2007, in FSCMNHS, now at NPS-WACC; Anthony A. Mestas, "Sand Creek Massacre Site to Be Dedicated Saturday," *Pueblo Chieftain,* April 24, 2007, in FSCMNHS, now at NPS-WACC; Robert Weller, "Memorial Opens at Sand Creek Massacre Site," Associated Press, April 29, 2007, in FSCMNHS, now at NPS-WACC.

3. Quotes from Abraham Lincoln, "First Inaugural Address," in David A. Hollinger and Charles Capper, eds., *The American Intellectual Tradition,* vol. 1: *1630–1865,* 3rd ed. (Oxford: Oxford University Press, 1997), 476. See also Michael Kammen, *Mystic Chords of Memory: Transformations of Tradition in American Culture* (New York: Vintage, 1993), 4, 13; Kenneth E. Foote, *Shadowed Ground: America's Landscapes of Violence and Tragedy*

(Austin: University of Texas Press, 1997), 5–8, 33–35; John Bodnar, *Remaking America: Public Memory, Commemoration, and Patriotism in the Twentieth Century* (Princeton, NJ: Princeton University Press, 1992), x–xii.

4. Edward Tabor Linenthal, *Sacred Ground: Americans and Their Battlefields* (Urbana: University of Illinois Press, 1993), 1, 60; Michael A. Elliot, *Custerology: The Enduring Legacy of the Indian Wars and George Armstrong Custer* (Chicago: University of Chicago Press, 2007), 4–8, 10, 50; David Chidester and Edward T. Linenthal, "Introduction," in David Chidester and Edward T. Linenthal, *American Sacred Space* (Bloomington: Indiana University Press, 1995), 12; James E. Young, *The Texture of Memory: Holocaust Memorials and Meaning* (New Haven, CT: Yale University Press, 1993), 41; Karl Jacoby, *Shadows at Dawn: A Borderlands Massacre and the Violence of History* (New York: Penguin, 2008), 2–5.

5. Quote from Alexa Roberts, superintendent, Sand Creek Massacre National Historic Site, interview by author, April 29, 2003, Denver, CO, tape recording, in author's possession. See also David Blight, *Race and Reunion: The Civil War in American Memory* (Cambridge, MA: Harvard University Press, 2001), 203; Edward Tabor Linenthal, *The Unfinished Bombing: Oklahoma City in American Memory* (Oxford: Oxford University Press, 2001), 94–96; Philip Nobel, *Sixteen Acres: Architecture and the Outrageous Struggle for the Future of Ground Zero* (New York: Metropolitan Books, 2005), 68–70, 81; Elliot, *Custerology*, 129; Foote, *Shadowed Ground*, 6; Kammen, *Mystic Chords of Memory*, 5.

6. "Clash of cultures" from Robert M. Utley, *A Clash of Cultures: Fort Bowie and the Chiricahua Apaches* (Washington, DC: National Park Service, 1977), title; and Elliot, *Custerology*, 135. See also Annie E. Coombes, *Visual Culture and Public Memory in Democratic South Africa* (Durham, NC: Duke University Press, 2003), 6–17, 19–115, 244–287; Steven Conn, *History's Shadow: Native Americans and Historical Consciousness in the Nineteenth Century* (Chicago: University of Chicago Press, 2004), 3–32, 116–197; Jonathan Crewe, "Recalling Adamastor: Literature as Cultural Memory in 'White' South Africa," in Mieke Bal, Jonathan Crewe, and Leo Spitzer, eds., *Acts of Memory: Cultural Recall in the Present* (Hanover, NH: University Press of New England, 1999), 75–86; Bodnar, *Remaking America*, 181; Foote, *Shadowed Ground*, 322, 334; Devon A. Mihesuah, *Repatriation Reader: Who Owns Native American Remains?* (Lincoln: University of Nebraska Press, 2000), 10.

7. Sanford Levinson, *Written in Stone: Public Monuments in Changing Societies* (Durham, NC: Duke University Press, 1998), 10; David Hurst Thomas, *Skull Wars: Kenniwick Man, Archaeology, and the Battle for Native American Identity* (New York: Basic Books, 2000), xxvii; Charles Wilkinson, *Blood Struggle: The Rise of Modern Indian Nations* (New York: W. W. Norton,

2005), xiii, 249; Linenthal, *Sacred Ground,* 1; Foote, *Shadowed Ground,* 33; Edward T. Linenthal, *Preserving Memory: The Struggle to Create America's Holocaust Museum* (New York: Columbia University Press, 1995), 63; Otto Braided Hair, director, Northern Cheyenne Sand Creek Office, interview by author, May 11, 2007, telephone, notes in author's possession.

8. Raw documentary footage of the opening ceremony found in FSCMNHS, now at NPS-WACC; Alexa Roberts, interview by author, July 30, 2005, telephone, notes in author's possession; Linenthal, *Sacred Ground,* 55, 146.

9. "Nobody has . . ." from Rod Brown, Kiowa County commissioner, interview by author, June 17, 2003, Eads, CO, tape recording, in author's possession. "There is . . ." from Janet Frederick, director, Kiowa County Economic Development Corporation, interview by author, June 17, 2003, Eads, CO, tape recording, in author's possession. See also Alexa Roberts, interview by author, January 8, 2007, telephone, notes in author's possession; and U.S. Census Bureau, "State and County QuickFacts, Kiowa County, Colorado."

10. Janet Frederick interview, June 17, 2003; U.S. Census Bureau, "State and County QuickFacts, Kiowa County, Colorado"; Kenneth Johnson, "Demographic Trends in Rural and Small Town America," *Reports on Rural America* 1, no. 1 (2006): 1, 11.

11. Quotes from Janet Frederick interview, June 17, 2003.

12. Marc Bloch, *The Historian's Craft,* trans. Peter Putnam (1954; reprint, Manchester: Manchester University Press, 2004), 84–85; Lauren O'Neill Shermer, Karen C. Rose, and Ashley Hoffman, "Perceptions and Credibility: Understanding the Nuances of Eyewitness Testimony," *Journal of Contemporary Criminal Justice* 27 (May 2011): 183–203; Robert Burkhout, "Eyewitness Testimony," in Ulric Neisser and Ira E. Hyman Jr., eds., *Memory Observed: Remembering in Natural Contexts* (New York: Worth, 1982), 214–222; Sven-Ake Christianson, "Emotional Stress and Eyewitness Memory: A Critical Review," *Psychological Bulletin* 112 (September 1992): 284–309.

13. Colonel John Chivington to Messrs. Beyers and Dailey, *Editors News,* November 29, 1864, *The War of the Rebellion: A Compilation of the Official Records of the Union and Confederate Armies* (Washington, DC: Government Printing Office, 1900) (hereafter *Official Records of the War of the Rebellion*), Series I, XLI, Pt. 1, 951; William M. Thayer, *Marvels of the New West. A Vivid Portrayal of the Stupendous Marvels in the Vast Wonderland West of the Missouri River. Six Books in One Volume, Comprising Marvels of Nature, Marvels of Race, Marvels of Mining, Marvels of Stock-Raising, and Marvels of Agriculture* (Norwich, CT: Henry Hill, 1887), 241–246; Silas Soule to Mother, January 8, 1865, Carey Collection, Box 5, Folder 13, University of Denver Special Collections, Penrose Library, Denver, CO (hereafter

Carey Collection); George Bent, "Forty Years with the Cheyennes," ed. George Hyde, *Frontier: A Magazine of the West* 4 (October 1905): 5–6; George Bent to George Hyde, June 9, 1905, Letter 10, Bent Manuscripts 54, Colorado Historical Society, Denver, CO (hereafter Bent Manuscripts); George Bent to George Hyde, September 26, 1905, Coe Collection, Beinecke Library, Yale University, New Haven, CT (hereafter Coe Collection); George E. Hyde, *Life of George Bent: Written from His Letters,* ed. Savoie Lottinville (Norman: University of Oklahoma Press, 1968), vi–xiv.

14. Quotes from Colonel John Chivington to Major General Samuel Curtis, November 29, 1864, *Official Records of the War of the Rebellion,* Series I, XLI, Pt. 1, 948.

15. Alvin Josephy Jr., *The Civil War in the American West* (New York: Random House, 1991), 61–94; Don E. Alberts, *Battle of Glorieta: Union Victory in the West* (College Station: Texas A&M University Press, 1998), 45–68; David Fridtjof Halaas and Andrew E. Masich, *Halfbreed: The Remarkable True Story of George Bent, Caught between the Worlds of the Indian and the White Man* (New York: Da Capo Press, 2004), 120–125; Reginald S. Craig, *The Fighting Parson: The Biography of Colonel John M. Chivington* (Los Angeles: Westernlore Press, 1959), 9–17.

16. "Bloodless Third" from Report of Lieutenant Colonel Leavitt L. Bowen, Third Colorado Cavalry, November 30, 1864, *Official Records of the War of the Rebellion,* Series I, XLI, Pt. 1, 957; and William Breakenridge, *Helldorado: Bringing Law to the Mesquite* (Boston: Houghton Mifflin, 1928), 32. All other quotes from Chivington to Beyers and Dailey, November 29, 1864, *Official Records of the War of the Rebellion,* Series I, XLI, Pt. 1, 951–952.

17. Quotes from Colonel John Chivington to Major General Samuel Curtis, December 16, 1864, *Official Records of the War of the Rebellion,* Series I, XLI, Pt. 1, 948–950.

18. Ibid.

19. Ibid.

20. *New York Herald,* December 26, 1864; *Washington Daily Star,* December 27, 1864; *Rocky Mountain News,* January 30, 1864; *Congressional Globe,* 38th Cong., 2nd Sess., Part 1, 158, 173, 250–256; Major General Samuel Curtis to Colonel Thomas Moonlight, January 13, 1865, *Official Records of the War of the Rebellion,* Series I, XLVIII, Pt. 1, 511; Gary Leland Roberts, "Sand Creek: Tragedy and Symbol" (unpublished PhD dissertation, University of Oklahoma, 1984), 464.

21. Quotes from "Massacre of Cheyenne Indians," in *Report of the Joint Committee on the Conduct of the War, at the Second Session, Thirty-Eighth Congress* (Washington, DC: Government Printing Office, 1865), 101–102.

22. Ibid., 103–104.

23. Ibid., 104.

24. Ibid., 104–105.

25. Ibid., 104. See also Chivington to Beyers and Dailey, November 29, 1864, *Official Records of the War of the Rebellion,* Series I, XLI, Pt. 1, 951, and Chivington to Curtis, December 16, 1864, 948–950; Samuel George Morton, *Crania Americana; or a Comparative View of the Skulls of Various Aboriginal Nations of North and South America; to Which is Affixed an Essay on the Variety of Human Species . . .* (Philadelphia: J. Pennington, 1839); Stephen Jay Gould, *The Mismeasure of Man* (New York: W. W. Norton, 1996), 82–96; Ann Fabian, *The Skull Collectors: Race, Science, and America's Unburied Dead* (Chicago: University of Chicago Press, 2010), 79–120; Thomas, *Skull Wars,* 38–47.

26. Quotes from "Massacre of Cheyenne Indians," 104.

27. Ibid., 106.

28. Ibid., 106–108; Thayer, *Marvels of the New West,* 244–245; James McPherson, *Battle Cry of Freedom: The Civil War Era* (Oxford: Oxford University Press, 1988), 47–169, 450–453; Nicole Etcheson, *Bleeding Kansas: Contesting Liberty in the Civil War Era* (Lawrence: University Press of Kansas, 2006), 9–49, 89–136, 169–177; Eric Foner, *The Fiery Trial: Abraham Lincoln and American Slavery* (New York: W. W. Norton, 2010), 248–289; Michael Vorenberg, *Final Freedom: The Civil War, the Abolition of Slavery, and the Thirteenth Amendment* (Cambridge: Cambridge University Press, 2004), 53–60, 107–114.

29. "Massacre of Cheyenne Indians," 105–106; Frederick E. Hoxie, *A Final Promise: The Campaign to Assimilate the Indians, 1880–1920* (Lincoln: University of Nebraska Press, 1984), 12–14; Elliot West, "Reconstructing Race," *Western Historical Quarterly* 34 (Spring 2003): 7–26.

30. Quotes from "Massacre of Cheyenne Indians," 104–108. See also Chivington to Beyers and Dailey, November 29, 1864, *Official Records of the War of the Rebellion,* Series I, XLI, Pt. 1, 951; and Chivington to Curtis, December 16, 1864, 948–950; Thayer, *Marvels of the New West,* 241–446; Peter Silver, *Our Savage Neighbors: How Indian War Transformed Early America* (New York: W. W. Norton, 2008), 41–44; Louis Warren, "Buffalo Bill Meets Dracula: William F. Cody, Bram Stoker, and the Frontiers of Racial Decay," *American Historical Review* 107 (October 2002): 1124–1157; Alan Taylor, *The Civil War of 1812: American Citizens, British Subjects, Irish Rebels, and Indian Allies* (New York: Alfred A. Knopf, 2010), 203–233.

31. Quotes from Thayer, *Marvels of the New West,* 241–246; emphasis added. See also *Denver Republican,* October 5, 1894; and Silver, *Our Savage Neighbors,* 57.

32. Quotes from the raw documentary footage of the opening ceremony found in FSCMNHS, now at NPS-WACC. See also Miles Moffeit,

"Profile: Bill Ritter," *Denver Post,* August 31, 2006, online edition, http://www.denverpost.com/news/ci_4113098.

33. Quote from Jerome A. Greene and Douglas D. Scott, *Finding Sand Creek: History, Archeology, and the 1864 Massacre Site* (Norman: University of Oklahoma Press, 2004), title. See also Linenthal, *Sacred Ground,* 60, 90, 216; Levinson, *Written in Stone,* 10, 37; Foote, *Shadowed Ground,* 5–7, 33–35, 322; Linenthal, *Preserving Memory,* 63.

34. Quotes from the raw documentary footage of the opening ceremony found in FSCMNHS, now at NPS-WACC. Italics reflect Bomar's spoken emphasis during her speech.

35. Ibid. See also Matthew Mosk, "Brownback Announces Presidential Bid: Republican Senator from Kansas to Make Appeal to Social Conservatives," *Washington Post,* January 21, 2007, A-8; and Alexa Roberts interview by author, May 1, 2007, telephone, notes in author's possession.

36. Quotes from the raw documentary footage of the opening ceremony found in FSCMNHS, now at NPS-WACC. See also Mike Soraghan, "Massacre Site Plans Stymied," *Denver Post,* December 14, 2004, A-1; and "House Silent on Sand Creek," *Denver Post,* December 15, 2004, B-6.

37. Quote from *Denver Rocky Mountain News,* December 13, 1864. See also Samuel Forster Tappan diary, MSS 617, Colorado Historical Society, Denver, CO; *Denver Rocky Mountain News,* December 8, 1864; Roberts, "Sand Creek: Tragedy and Symbol," 458–459.

38. Virginia Claire Seay, "Pioneers of Freedom: The Story of the Soule Family in Kansas," *Kansas Magazine* (1943): 107–115.

39. Quotes from Gary Leland Roberts and David Fridtjof Halaas, "Written in Blood: The Soule-Cramer Sand Creek Letters," *Colorado Heritage* (Winter 2001): 25.

40. Ibid.

41. Ibid. See also Silas Soule to unknown, July 21, 1861, Carey Collection; Etcheson, *Bleeding Kansas,* 94–129; Edward E. Leslie, *The Devil Knows How to Ride: The True Story of William Clarke Quantrill and His Confederate Raiders* (Cambridge, MA: Da Capo Press, 1998), 3–34, 157–192.

42. Quotes from Roberts and Halaas, "Written in Blood," 25–26.

43. Soule to unknown, July 21, 1861, Carey Collection; Soule to Mother, January 8, 1865, Carey Collection; "Report of the Secretary of War," 39th Cong., 2nd Sess., S. Ex. Doc. 26, 10–11, 13, 16–29; Roberts and Halaas, "Written in Blood," 25–26; Ronald Walters, *American Reformers, 1815–1860* (New York: Hill and Wang, 1997), 87–99.

44. Quotes from Roberts and Halaas, "Written in Blood," 26.

45. "You and mother . . ." and "I think . . ." from Silas Soule to Annie, July 16, 1864, Carey Collection. "We have . . ." from Silas Soule to Annie,

August 15, 1864, Carey Collection. "They are . . . ," "I think Government . . . ," and "if that is the case . . ." from Silas Soule to Annie, October 30, 1864, Carey Collection.

46. "Present at . . . ," "friendly," "not let [his] . . . ," "little Children . . . ," and "their brains . . ." from Silas Soule to Mother, December 18, 1864, Carey Collection. All other quotes from Soule to Mother, January 8, 1865. See also *Official Records of the War of the Rebellion,* Series I, XLI, Pt. 4, 948.

47. Quotes from "Report of the Secretary of War," 39th Cong., 2nd Sess., S. Ex. Doc. 26, 8–9.

48. Ibid., 9–10.

49. Ibid., 10–13.

50. Ibid., 16–29.

51. Ibid., 25–29.

52. Ben Nighthorse Campbell, U.S. senator, interview by author, September 10, 2003, telephone, tape recording, in author's possession; James Doyle, Colorado communications director for Senator Ben Nighthorse Campbell, interview by author, June 10, 2003, Fort Collins, CO, tape recording, in author's possession; M. E. Sprengelmeyer, "A Career Come Full Circle," *Rocky Mountain News,* September 18, 2004, A-25; Herman J. Viola, *Ben Nighthorse Campbell: An American Warrior* (Boulder, CO: Johnson Books, 1993), 17–29, 51–54, 74–86, 109, 144–151, 177, 181, 226–231, 304–310.

53. "World's most . . ." from James Doyle interview, June 10, 2003. "Home" from Ben Nighthorse Campbell interview, September 10, 2003.

54. Quotes from the raw documentary footage of the opening ceremony found in FSCMNHS, now at NPS-WACC. See also Philip J. Deloria, *Indians in Unexpected Places* (Lawrence: University Press of Kansas, 2006), 70–73, 156–167; and Philip J. Deloria, *Playing Indian* (New Haven, CT: Yale University Press, 1999), 74–94.

55. Quote from Abraham Lincoln, "Address Delivered at the Dedication of the Cemetery at Gettysburg," in David A. Hollinger and Charles Capper, eds., *The American Intellectual Tradition,* vol. 1: *1630–1865* (Oxford: Oxford University Press, 1993), 429. See also Gary Wills, *Lincoln at Gettysburg: The Words That Remade America* (New York: Simon and Schuster, 2006), 67–82; Gabor S. Boritt, *The Gettysburg Gospel: The Lincoln Speech That Nobody Knows* (New York: Simon and Schuster, 2006), 37–41, 106–118, 149–158; "Gettysburg Address (1863)," Our Documents, http://www.ourdocuments.gov/doc.php?flash=true&doc=36; John Bodnar, *The Good War in American Memory* (Baltimore, MD: Johns Hopkins University Press, 2010), 3–4; Drew Gilpin Faust, *This Republic of Suffering: Death and the American Civil War* (New York: Vintage, 2009), 5–10, 71–93; David

Blight, *American Oracle: The Civil War in the Civil Rights Era* (Cambridge, MA: Belknap Press of Harvard University Press, 2011), 5–7, 19–24.

56. Kristin Ann Hass, *Carried to the Wall: American Memory and the Vietnam Veterans Memorial* (Berkeley: University of California Press, 1998), 1–32, 103–126; Jeffrey Karl Oschner, "A Space of Loss," *Journal of Architectural Education* 50 (February 1997): 156–171; Karal Ann Marling and Robert Silberman, "The Statue Near the Wall: The Vietnam Veterans Memorial and the Art of Remembering," *Smithsonian Studies in American Art* 1 (Spring 1987): 4–29; Daphne Berdahl, "Voices at the Wall: Discourses of Self, History, and National Identity at the Vietnam Veterans Memorial," *History and Memory* 6 (Fall–Winter 1994): 88–124; Michael S. Sherry, "Patriotic Orthodoxy and American Decline," in Edward T. Linenthal and Tom Engelhardt, eds., *History Wars: The Enola Gay and Other Battles for the American Past* (New York: Holt Paperbacks, 1996), 97–114; Marilyn B. Young, "Dangerous History: Vietnam and the 'Good War,'" in Linenthal and Engelhardt, *History Wars,* 199–209; Max Weber, *The Vocation Lectures: "Science as a Vocation," "Politics as a Vocation,"* ed. David Owen and Tracey B. Strong, trans. Rodney Livingston (Indianapolis, IN: Hackett Publishing Company, 2004), 32–27; Linenthal, *Sacred Ground,* 1; Foote, *Shadowed Ground,* 333–335; Kammen, *Mystic Chords of Memory,* 101–131; Blight, *Race and Reunion,* 204–216.

57. Quotes from the raw documentary footage of the opening ceremony found in FSCMNHS, now at NPS-WACC. See also Montana Census and Economic Information Center, Montana Department of Labor and Industry Research and Analysis Bureau, Montana Governor's Office State Tribal Economic Development Commission, *Demographic and Economic Information for Northern Cheyenne Reservation* (Helena, MT: n.p., 2006), 1–8; and Stephen R. Anderson, Gordon M. Belcourt, Kathryn M. Langwell, "Building Healthy Tribal Nations in Montana and Wyoming through Collaborative Research and Development," *American Journal of Public Health* 95, no. 5 (May 2005): 784–789.

58. Quotes from the raw documentary footage of the opening ceremony found in FSCMNHS, now at NPS-WACC. See also Otto Braided Hair interview, May 11, 2007.

59. Halaas and Masich, *Halfbreed,* xii–xiv, 23–25, 39, 59–72, 86–89.

60. Bent, "Forty Years with the Cheyennes" (October 1905): 6. "Afraid of . . ." from Bent to Hyde, June 9, 1905, Bent Manuscripts 54. See also Hyde, *Life of George Bent,* vii–xiii; Hoxie, *A Final Promise,* 41–81; Halaas and Masich, *Halfbreed,* 1–112; L. G. Moses, *The Indian Man: A Biography of James Mooney* (Lincoln: University of Nebraska Press, 2002), 7–31, 71–86, 130–140; Michael Punke, *Last Stand: George Bird Grinnell, the Battle to Save*

the Buffalo, and the Birth of the New West (Washington, DC: Smithsonian, 2007), 177-204.

61. "Always thought . . ." from George Bent to George Hyde, September 22, 1915, Coe Collection. "Give credit . . ." from Bent to Hyde, January 29, 1913, Coe Collection. All other quotes from Bent, "Forty Years with the Cheyennes" (October 1905): 3. See also Bent to Hyde, January 19, 1905, Coe Collection; Bent to Hyde, January 23, 1905, Coe Collection; Bent to Hyde, June 4, 1909, Coe Collection; Bent to Hyde, February 22, 1912, Coe Collection; Bent to Hyde, November 29, 1912, Coe Collection; Bent to Hyde, February 19, 1913, Coe Collection; Bent to Hyde, January 17, 1914, Coe Collection; Bent to Hyde, October 17, 1916, Coe Collection.

62. Quotes from Bent, "Forty Years with the Cheyennes" (October 1905): 3. See also Bent to Hyde, September 26, 1905, Coe Collection.

63. Quotes from Bent, "Forty Years with the Cheyennes" (October 1905): 3-4. See also Bent to Hyde, March 6, 1905, Coe Collection.

64. "Wynkoop told . . ." and "this was the reason . . ." from Bent to Hyde, April 30, 1906, Coe Collection. "Told Black Kettle . . ." from Bent to Hyde, May 14, 1913, Coe Collection. All other quotes from Bent, "Forty Years with the Cheyennes" (October 1905): 4-6. See also Bent to Hyde, October 15, 1914, Letter 10, Bent Manuscripts 54; Bent to Hyde, March 15, 1905, Coe Collection; Bent to Hyde, February 28, 1906, Coe Collection.

65. Quotes from Bent, "Forty Years with the Cheyennes" (October 1905): 6-7. See also Bent to Hyde, March 15, 1905, Coe Collection; Bent to Hyde, December 21, 1905, Coe Collection; Bent to Hyde, April 14, 1906, Coe Collection; Bent to Hyde, April 25, 1906, Coe Collection.

66. "2 scalps . . ." from Bent to Hyde, March 9, 1905, Coe Collection. "The scalps of White Leaf . . ." from Bent to Hyde, October 12, 1905, Coe Collection. See also Bent to Hyde, May 3, 1906, Coe Collection; and Bent, "Forty Years with the Cheyennes" (October 1905): 6-7.

67. "Still stood . . ." and "most were . . ." from George Bent, "Forty Years with the Cheyennes," ed. George Hyde, *Frontier: A Magazine of the West* 4 (December 1905): 3. See also Bent to Hyde, May 14, 1913, Coe Collection; George Bent, "Forty Years with the Cheyennes," ed. George Hyde, *Frontier: A Magazine of the West* 4 (January 1906): 3-6; George Bent, "Forty Years with the Cheyennes," ed. George Hyde, *Frontier: A Magazine of the West* 4 (February 1906): 3-7.

68. Quotes from Bent to Hyde, June 5, 1906, Coe Collection. See also Bent to Hyde, May 16, 1905, Letter 7, Bent Manuscripts 54; Bent to Hyde, May 7, 1906, Coe Collection; Bent, "Forty Years with the Cheyennes" (December 1905): 4-7; Bent, "Forty Years with the Cheyennes" (January 1906):

3-6; Bent, "Forty Years with the Cheyennes" (February 1906): 3-7; Bent, "Forty Years with the Cheyennes" (March 1906): 3-8.

69. "I don't think . . ." from Bent to Hyde, February 28, 1906, Coe Collection. See also George Bent to George Hyde, January 24, 1906, Coe Collection; Bent to Hyde, March 6, 1913; Bent to Hyde, April 30, 1913; Bent to Hyde, July 14, 1913, Bent Letters, Western History and Genealogy, Denver Public Library, Denver, CO; Bent to Hyde, January 20, 1915, Coe Collection; Bent to Hyde, September 1, 1917, Coe Collection.

70. Quotes from Hyde, *Life of George Bent,* 149-153.

71. Ibid., 149-155.

72. Ibid., 155-163.

73. Bent, "Forty Years with the Cheyennes" (October 1905): 6-7; Bent to Hyde, September 26, 1905, Coe Collection; Hyde, *Life of George Bent,* vii-xiii.

74. Bent to Hyde, September 26, 1905, Coe Collection; Bent to Hyde, March 6, 1905, Coe Collection; Bent to Hyde, March 15, 1905, Coe Collection; Bent to Hyde, February 28, 1906, Coe Collection; Bent to Hyde, April 30, 1906, Coe Collection; Bent to Hyde, May 14, 1913, Coe Collection; Bent to Hyde, October 15, 1914, Coe Collection; Bent, "Forty Years with the Cheyennes" (October 1905): 3-6; Bent, "Forty Years with the Cheyennes" (December 1905): 3; Bent, "Forty Years with the Cheyennes" (January 1906): 3-6; Bent, "Forty Years with the Cheyennes" (February 1906): 3-7; Hyde, *Life of George Bent,* 153-158.

75. Bent, "Forty Years with the Cheyennes" (October 1905): 6; and Hyde, *Life of George Bent,* 150.

76. "Whites never get it straight . . ." from Bent to Hyde, June 9, 1905. See also Donald J. Berthrong, *The Cheyenne and Arapaho Ordeal: Reservation and Agency Life in the Indian Territory, 1875–1907* (Norman: University of Oklahoma Press, 1976), 3-44, 122-171, 214-340; Robert M. Utley, *Frontier Regulars: The United States Army and the Indian, 1866–1891* (Lincoln: University of Nebraska Press, 1973), 114-158, 274-288; Hoxie, *A Final Promise,* 41-81; Donald J. Berthrong, *The Southern Cheyennes* (Norman: University of Oklahoma Press, 1963), 227-381.

77. George Bird Grinnell, *The Fighting Cheyennes* (1915; reprint, Norman: University of Oklahoma Press, 1955), x; Hyde, *Life of George Bent,* xii-xiii; Halaas and Masich, *Halfbreed,* 343-349.

78. Paul Connerton, *How Societies Remember* (Cambridge: Cambridge University Press, 2002), 11-67; Maurice Halbwachs, *On Collective Memory,* ed. and trans. Lewis A. Coser (Chicago: University of Chicago Press, 1992), 46-51, 124-182; Jaques Le Goff, *History and Memory,* trans. Steven Rendell and Elizabeth Claman (New York: Columbia University Press,

1992), 58–67, 81–100; David Lowenthal, *The Past Is a Foreign Country* (Cambridge: Cambridge University Press, 2002), 3–33, 185–236, 327–411; Pierre Nora, ed., *Realms of Memory: The Construction of the French Past,* vol. 1: *Conflicts and Divisions,* trans. Arthur Goldhammer (New York: Columbia University Press, 1996), 1–20; Roy Rosenzweig and David Thelen, *The Presence of the Past: Popular Uses of History in American Life* (New York: Columbia University Press, 1998), 2–7; Michel-Rolph Touillot, *Silencing the Past: Power and the Production of History* (Boston: Beacon Press, 1995), 3–27, 141–152.

79. James Sheehan, "What Is German History? Reflections on the Role of the Nation in German History and Historiography," *Journal of Modern History* 53 (March 1981): 3–5; Linenthal, *Preserving Memory,* 52; Wilkinson, *Blood Struggle,* 249; Kammen, *Mystic Chords of Memory,* 687.

2. LOOTERS

1. "History buffs" from Richard Ellis, chair, Department of Southwest Studies, Fort Lewis College, interview by author, May 25, 2005, Castle Rock, CO, tape recording, in author's possession; "Treasure hunters" from David Halaas, director of publications, library, and archives, John Heinz History Center, interview by author, September 26, 2003, Pittsburgh, PA, tape recording, in author's possession; "Looters" from Susan Collins, Colorado state archeologist, interview by author, September 12, 2003, Denver, CO, tape recording, in author's possession. See also William Dawson, interview by author, June 18, 2003, Kiowa County, CO, tape recording, in author's possession.

2. Quotes from David Halaas interview, September 26, 2003. See also David Fridtjof Halaas and Andrew E. Masich, *Halfbreed: The Remarkable True Story of George Bent, Caught between the Worlds of the Indian and the White Man* (New York: Da Capo Press, 2004), xii–xiv.

3. "It looks . . . ," "an archeological rule . . . ," and "no battle-related . . ." from Andy Masich to All Interested Sand Creek Site Researchers, Memorandum, December 15, 1993, in uncataloged files of the Sand Creek Massacre National Historic Site (FSCMNHS), currently held by National Park Service, Western Archeological and Conservation Center (NPS-WACC), Tucson, AZ. All other quotes from David Halaas interview, September 26, 2003. See also Ann Bond's personal notes, "Sand Creek Reconnaissance," September 1, 1993, in FSCMNHS, now at NPS-WACC; Richard Ellis interview, May 25, 2005.

4. "Demonstrate public . . ." and other information about the Colorado State Historical Fund from http://www.coloradohistory-oahp.org /programareas/shf/shfindex.htm. See also Stuart Davis, "A Million

before the Millennium: Oral History and the Lottery," *Oral History* 28 (Spring 2000): 103-108; David Halaas interview, September 26, 2003; Richard Ellis interview, May 25, 2005; Susan Collins interview, September 12, 2003.

5. David Halaas interview, September 26, 2003; Richard Ellis interview, May 25, 2005; Stan Hoig, *The Sand Creek Massacre* (Norman: University of Oklahoma Press, 1974), vii, 115-127; Gary L. Roberts, "Sand Creek: Tragedy and Symbol" (unpublished PhD dissertation, University of Oklahoma, 1984), 107-119; Robert M. Utley, *Frontier Regulars: The United States Army and the Indian, 1866–1891* (New York: Macmillan, 1973), 63-74, 164-179; Robert M. Utley, *Frontiersmen in Blue: The United States Army and the Indian, 1848–1865* (Lincoln: University of Nebraska Press, 1967), 294-317; Elliot West, *The Contested Plains: Indians, Goldseekers, and the Rush to Colorado* (Lawrence: University Press of Kansas, 2000), 11-17, 281-293.

6. Quotes from Richard Ellis interview, May 25, 2005. See also David Halaas interview, September 26, 2003, and Susan Collins interview, September 12, 2003.

7. Quote from Steve Brady, president, Northern Cheyenne Sand Creek Descendants, interview by author, August 29, 2004, Lame Deer, MT, tape recording, in author's possession. See also Harrison Fletcher, "The Killing Field at Sand Creek: Truth Was the First Casualty," *Westword* 21 (May 28–June 3, 1998): 16; Ray Brady, Northern Cheyenne elder, interview by author, August 15, 2003, Lame Deer, MT, tape recording, in author's possession; Norma Gorneau, member, Northern Cheyenne Tribe Sand Creek Massacre Descendants Committee, interview by author, July 1, 2004, Lame Deer, MT, tape recording, in author's possession; Mildred Red Cherries, member, Northern Cheyenne Sand Creek Massacre Descendants Committee, interview by author, August 13, 2003, Lame Deer, MT, tape recording, in author's possession.

8. "Taught the . . ." from Steve Brady interview, August 29, 2004. "After Sand . . ." from Laird Cometsevah, chief, Southern Cheyenne Tribe, interview by author, May 12, 2003, Denver, CO, tape recording, in author's possession.

9. Steve Brady interview, August 29, 2004; Laird Cometsevah interview, May 12, 2003; Richard Ellis interview, May 25, 2005; David Halaas interview, September 26, 2003.

10. "Thirty or forty descendants" from Richard Ellis interview, May 25, 2005. "Three white guys . . ." from Steve Brady, interview by author, September 12, 2003, tape recording, in author's possession. "We decided . . ." from Mildred Red Cherries interview, August 13, 2003. See also David Halaas interview, September 26, 2003; and Gail Ridgely, Sand Creek representa-

tive, Northern Arapaho Tribe, interview by author, July 29, 2003, Denver, CO, tape recording, in author's possession.

11. Douglas Scott, chief archeologist, National Park Service Midwest Archeological Center, interview by author, October 3, 2003, telephone, tape recording, in author's possession; Douglas D. Scott, "Site Significance and Historical Archaeology—A Scenario and Commentary," *Historical Archaeology* 24 (1990): 52-54; Douglas D. Scott, "Oral Tradition and Archaeology: Conflict and Concordance Examples from Two Indian War Sites," *Historical Archaeology* 37 (2003): 55-65; Steve Brady interview, September 12, 2003; Laird Cometsevah interview, May 12, 2003; Richard Ellis interview, May 25, 2005.

12. Steve Brady interview, September 12, 2003; Laird Cometsevah interview, May 12, 2003; William Dawson interview, June 18, 2003; Richard Ellis interview, May 25, 2005; David Halaas interview, September 26, 2003.

13. Quotes from William Dawson interview, June 18, 2003. See also Steve Brady interview, September 12, 2003; Laird Cometsevah interview, May 12, 2003; Richard Ellis interview, May 25, 2005; David Halaas interview, September 26, 2003; Alexa Roberts, superintendent, Sand Creek Massacre National Historic Site, interview by author, April 29, 2003, Denver, CO, tape recording, in author's possession; Douglas Scott interview, October 3, 2003.

14. Quotes from *Lamar Daily News,* August 2, 1950. See also *Kiowa County Press,* July 28, 1950; *Lamar Daily News,* July 22, 24, 26, August 6, 1950.

15. In an interview conducted in 2005, Modupe Lobode, the Colorado Historical Society's chief historian at the time, described the contents of notes made by Leroy Hafen, chief historian in 1950, accompanying the Historical Society's plans for the obelisk. Hafen alluded to the politics impinging on the memorialization process. Lobode regretted that the notes had been lost. Modupe Lobode, chief historian, Colorado Historical Society, interview by author, June 3, 2005, Denver, CO, tape recording, in author's possession. "Sand Creek: 'Battle' or 'Massacre,' " casualty statistics, and "one of the . . ." all from an image of the obelisk, on which the text is legible, found in File 287, "Sand Creek Massacre," in Colorado Historical Society, Denver, CO. "The actual . . ." from *Kiowa County Press,* August 11, 1950. "A caravan . . ." from *Lamar Daily News,* August 7, 1950. "Battle area" from *Lamar Daily News,* July 22, 1950.

16. Quotes from *Lamar Daily News,* August 2, 1950. See also Modupe Lobode interview, June 3, 2005.

17. Barry Schwartz, *Abraham Lincoln and the Forge of National Memory* (Chicago: University of Chicago Press, 2000), 224-255; David Blight, *Race and Reunion: The Civil War in American Memory* (Cambridge, MA: Belknap

Press of Harvard University Press, 2001), 381; John Bodnar, *The Good War in American Memory* (Baltimore, MD: Johns Hopkins University Press, 2010), 113; Barry Schwartz, *Abraham Lincoln in the Post-Heroic Era: History and Memory in Late Twentieth-Century America* (Chicago: University of Chicago Press, 2009), 59–90; David Blight, *American Oracle: The Civil War in the Civil Rights Era* (Cambridge, MA: Belknap Press of Harvard University Press, 2011), 3–6; Merrill D. Peterson, *Lincoln in American Memory* (Oxford: Oxford University Press, 1995), 198.

18. William Dawson interview, June 18, 2003, and Alexa Roberts, interview by author, August 26, 2004, telephone, notes in author's possession.

19. Quote from William Dawson interview, June 18, 2003.

20. William Dawson interview, June 18, 2003; Elizabeth Mitchell, "Sand Creek Massacre Site: An Environmental History," 2007, 47–73, http://www.nps.gov/sand/naturescience/upload/Sand%20Creek%20-%20An%20Environmental%20History-1.pdf.

21. The sign's text can be found in File 166, "Markers, Sand Creek Massacre," Colorado Historical Society, Denver, CO. "Whole damn . . ." and "Native American . . ." from William Dawson to James Hartmann, vice president, Colorado Historical Society, July 21, 1986, in File 166. "Continue . . ." from James Hartmann, vice president, Colorado Historical Society, to William Dawson, July 28, 1986, in File 166. See also Alexa Roberts interview, April 29, 2003; "News Release: Sand Creek Massacre Marker to Be Dedicated," August 28, 1986, in File 166; William Dawson interview, June 18, 2003.

22. Quotes from William Dawson interview, June 18, 2003. See also Alexa Roberts interview, April 29, 2003.

23. "Walked . . ." from James Amos, "Woman Testified . . ." *Pueblo Chieftain,* April 24, 1997, in FSCMNHS, now at NPS-WACC. "Trespassers" from William Dawson interview, June 18, 2003. See also Alexa Roberts interview, April 29, 2003; Fawn Germer, "Municipal Judge Faces Charges," *Rocky Mountain News,* March 25, 1997, A-8.

24. "Spread like . . ." and "if you . . ." from Germer, "Municipal Judge Faces Charges." "Waste" and "$200 per month . . ." from William Dawson interview, June 18, 2003. See also "Woman Testified That Judge Terrorized Her and Brother," *Pueblo Chieftain,* April 24, 1997, in FSCMNHS, now at NPS-WACC; Janet Frederick, director, Kiowa County Economic Development Corporation, interview by author, June 17, 2003, Eads, CO, tape recording, in author's possession; Dick Foster, "Eads Judge Arrested Again," *Rocky Mountain News,* March 26, 1997, A-8; Dick Foster, "A Judge's Trials," *Rocky Mountain News,* April 14, 1997, A-8; Dick Foster,

"Judge Steps Down in Plea Agreement," *Rocky Mountain News,* December 2, 1997, A-8.

25. Quotes from William Dawson interview, June 18, 2003. See also Elizabeth Cook-Lynn, "Scandal," *Wicazo Sa Review* 22 (Spring 2007): 85–89; Michael Yellow Bird, "On the Justice of Charging Buffalo: 'Who Stole American Indians Studies?,'" *Wicazo Sa Review* 22 (Spring 2007): 91–99; Alexa Roberts interview, April 29, 2003.

26. "I'm the son . . ." and "Not just the . . ." from James Doyle, Colorado communications director for Senator Ben Nighthorse Campbell, interview by author, June 10, 2003, Fort Collins, CO, tape recording, in author's possession. "Hearing . . ." from Ben Nighthorse Campbell, U.S. senator, interview by author, September 10, 2003, telephone, tape recording, in author's possession. See also William Dawson interview, June 18, 2003; Alexa Roberts interview, April 29, 2003; Michael Romano, "Senator Eyes Massacre Site," *Rocky Mountain News,* March 3, 1998, A-8.

27. "Extremely worthy" from Jerry Rogers to Cathy Spude, e-mail, April 29, 1998, in FSCMNHS, now at NPS-WACC. "If Sen. Ben . . ." and "My granddad . . ." from Romano, "Senator Eyes Massacre Site," A-8. Senator Ben Nighthorse Campbell's questionnaire, produced in advance of hearings on S. 1695, and the NPS's responses can be found in FSCMNHS, now at NPS-WACC. See also Adriel Bettelheim, "Sand Creek Acquisition Urged," *Denver Post,* March 3, 1998, B-5.

28. "Conveyed the . . ." from David Halaas interview, September 26, 2003. All other quotes from Adriel Bettelheim, "Historic-Site Ruling Up in the Error," *Denver Post,* March, 6, 1998, A-1. See also Ben Nighthorse Campbell interview, September 10, 2003; James Doyle interview, June 10, 2003.

29. Quotes from C. E. Van Loan, "Veterans of 1864 Revisit Scene of Indian Battle on the Banks of Sand Creek, Colo.," *Denver Post,* July 26, 1908.

30. Ibid.

31. "Where was . . ." and "the place . . ." from Doris Rosalind Wilder, "Indian Battles in Colorado: Sand Creek Battle and Discussion That Followed in Wake of Wiping Out of Indians under Black Kettle and Other Chiefs," *Rocky Mountain News,* July 8, 1923. "Inquire directions . . ." from Works Progress Administration, *Colorado: A Guide to the Highest State* (New York: Hastings House, 1941), 293.

32. "Fill the . . ." from Jerry Rogers to Cathy Spude et al., e-mail, October 16, 1998, in FSCMNHS, now at NPS-WACC. All other quotes from Cathy Spude, National Park Service, interview by author, June 21, 2003, Denver CO, tape recording, in author's possession.

33. Quote from "Charles Pinckney," National Park Service, http://www.nps .gov/chpi/. See also "Charles Pinckney Plantation: Using Archeology to Solve the Mystery," National Park Service, http://www.nps.gov/history /seac/chpi/index.htm.

34. "No more . . ." from Jerry Rogers to Bob Spude, e-mail, March 5, 1998, in FSCMNHS, now at NPS-WACC. All other quotes from Cathy Spude interview, June 21, 2003. See also Steve Brady interview, September 12, 2003; Ben Nighthorse Campbell interview, September 10, 2003; James Doyle interview, June 10, 2003; Barbara Sutteer, interview by author, August 5, 2003, telephone, tape recording, in author's possession; "Charles Pinckney," National Park Service; Committee on Energy and Natural Resources: Subcommittee on National Parks, Historic Preservation, and Recreation, Hearings on S. 1695, to establish the Sand Creek Massacre National Historic Site in the State of Colorado, March 24, 1998, http://www.lib.ncsu.edu/congbibs/senate/105dgst2.html.

35. Richard Ellis interview, May 25, 2005; Douglas Scott interview, October 3, 2003; Douglas D. Scott, Richard A. Fox, Melissa A. Connor, and Dick Harmon, *Archaeological Perspectives on the Battle of Little Bighorn* (Norman: University of Oklahoma Press, 2000); Douglas D. Scott, Peter Bleed, Andrew E. Masich, and Jason Pitsch, "An Inscribed Native American Battle Image from the Little Bighorn Battlefield," *Plains Anthropologist* 42 (August 1997): 287–302; Richard Fox, Douglas D. Scott, John du Mont, John D. McDermott, Robert L. Schuyler, Melburn D. Thurman, and Robert Utley, " 'On Digging Up Custer Battlefield' Some Comments," *Montana: The Magazine of Western History* 36 (Autumn 1986): 83–87.

36. "I don't know . . ." from Douglas Scott interview, October 3, 2003. "Inconclusive . . ." from Douglas D. Scott, Anne Wainstein Bond, Richard Ellis, and William B. Lees, "Archeological Reconnaissance of Two Possible Sites of the Sand Creek Massacre of 1864," (April 1998), 13, in FSCMNHS, now at NPS-WACC. See also Steve Brady interview, September 12, 2003; Gail Ridgely interview, July 29, 2003.

37. "Conducted a . . . ," "without any . . . ," "it was our . . . ," "it was just . . . ," and "white people . . ." from Steve Brady interview, September 12, 2003. "Reclaimed the . . ." and "Cheyenne earth" from Laird Cometsevah interview, May 12, 2003. See also Joe Big Medicine, Sand Creek representative, Southern Cheyenne Tribe, interview by author, July 8, 2003, Lame Deer, MT, tape recording, in author's possession.

38. "Solid physical . . ." from Steve Brady interview, September 12, 2003. "To commemorate . . ." from Statement by Katherine H. Stevenson, associate director, Cultural Resource Stewardship and Partnerships, National Park Service, United States Department of the Interior, Before the

Subcommittee on National Parks, Historic Preservation and Recreation, Senate Energy and Natural Resources Committee, Concerning S. 1695, the Sand Creek Massacre National Historic Site Preservation Act of 1998, in FSCMNHS, now at NPS-WACC. "Traditional tribal . . ." from Laird Cometsevah interview, May 12, 2003. See also Senator Ben Nighthorse Campbell statement in support of S. 1695, unpublished manuscript, in FSCMNHS, now at NPS-WACC; Ben Nighthorse Campbell interview, September 10, 2003; David Halaas interview, September 26, 2003; Public Law 105-243, "An Act to Authorize the Secretary of the Interior to Study the Suitability and Feasibility of Designating the Sand Creek Massacre National Historic Site in the State of Colorado as a Unit of the National Park System, and for Other Purposes"; Deborah Frazier, "Massacre Mystery," *Denver Post,* September 21, 1998, B-6; Michael Romano, "Massacre Remembered," *Rocky Mountain News,* October 7, 1998, A-7; Michael Romano, "Save Site of Massacre, Indians Say," *Rocky Mountain News,* March 25, 1998, A-8; Karen Vigil, "Massacre Site to Be Located, Purchased," *Pueblo Chieftain,* March 25, 1998, in FSCMNHS, now at NPS-WACC; Elliot Zaret, "House OKs Bill for Massacre Site," *Denver Post,* September 19, 1998, B-6.

39. Quote from Steve Brady interview, September 12, 2003.

40. Quotes from *Condition of the Indian Tribes. Report of the Special Joint Committee, Appointed under Joint Resolution of March 3, 1865. With an Appendix* (Washington, DC: Government Printing Office, 1867), 55.

41. George Bent to George Hyde, September 26, 1905, Coe Collection, Beinecke Library, Yale University, New Haven, CT; Colonel John Chivington to Major General Samuel Curtis, August 8, 1864, *The War of the Rebellion: A Compilation of the Official Records of the Union and Confederate Armies* (Washington, DC: Government Printing Office, 1900) (hereafter *Official Records of the War of the Rebellion*), Series I, XLI, Pt. 2, 614; Governor John Evans to Major General Samuel Curtis, July 18, 1864, *Official Records of the War of the Rebellion,* Series I, XLI, Pt. 1, 73; *Condition of the Indian Tribes,* 55; "Massacre of Cheyenne Indians," in *Report of the Joint Committee on Conduct on War, at the Second Session, Thirty-Eighth Congress* (Washington, DC: Government Printing Office, 1865), 31; Leroy W. Hagerty, "Indian Raids along the Platte and Little Blue Rivers, 1865–1865," *Nebraska History* 28 (October–December 1947): 176–186; George Bent, "Forty Years with the Cheyennes," ed. George Hyde, *Frontier: A Magazine of the West* IV (October 1905): 3; George E. Hyde, *Life of George Bent: Written from His Letters,* ed. Savoie Lottinville (Norman: University of Oklahoma Press, 1968), 134–138; Howard Roberts Lamar, *The Far Southwest, 1846–1912: A Territorial History* (Albuquerque: University of New Mexico Press, 2000), 199–217.

42. "Pursue, kill, and destroy . . ." from *Rocky Mountain News,* August 13, 1864. All other quotes from "Proclamation of Governor Evans of Colorado Territory," in "Massacre of Cheyenne Indians," 47. See also Governor John Evans to Secretary of War Edwin M. Stanton, August 23, 1864, in "Massacre of Cheyenne Indians," 65; Governor John Evans to Secretary of War Edwin M. Stanton, August 10, 1864, *Official Records of the War of the Rebellion,* Series I, XLI, Pt. 2, 644; Governor John Evans to Secretary of War Edwin M. Stanton, September 7, 1864, in "Massacre of Cheyenne Indians," 66.

43. Charles Wilkinson, *Blood Struggle: The Rise of Modern Indian Nations* (New York: W. W. Norton, 2005), 304–328, 352–282; Rex Wirth and Stefanie Wickstrom, "Competing Views: Indian Nations and Sovereignty in the Intergovernmental System of the United States," *American Indian Quarterly* 26 (Autumn 2002): 509–525; Gerald Vizenor, "Editorial Comment: Gambling on Sovereignty," *American Indian Quarterly* 16 (Summer 1992): 411–413; Vine Deloria Jr., "Intellectual Self-Determination and Sovereignty: Looking at the Windmills in Our Minds," *Wicazo Sa Review* 13 (Spring 1998): 25–31; Jack D. Forbes, "Intellectual Self-Determination and Sovereignty: Implications for Native Studies and for Native Intellectuals," *Wicazo Sa Review* 13 (Spring 1998): 11–23; Lawrence W. Gross, "Cultural Sovereignty and Native American Hermeneutics in the Interpretation of the Sacred Stories of the Anishinaabe," *Wicazo Sa Review* 18 (Autumn 2003): 127–134; William T. Hagan, "Tribalism Rejuvenated: The Native American since the Era of Termination," *Western Historical Quarterly* 12 (January 1981): 4–16; Austen L. Parrish, "Changing Territoriality, Fading Sovereignty, and the Development of Indigenous Rights," *American Indian Law Review* 31 (2006/2007): 291–313; Duane Champagne, "From Sovereignty to Minority: As American as Apple Pie," *Wicazo Sa Review* 20 (Autumn 2005): 21–36; Wilma P. Mankiller, "'Tribal Sovereignty Is a Sacred Trust': An Open Letter to the Conference," *American Indian Law Review* 23 (1998/1999): 479–480; Robert Allen Warrior, "Intellectual Sovereignty and the Struggle for an American Indian Future. Chapter 3 of Tribal Secrets: Vine Deloria, John Joseph Mathews, and the Recovery of American Indian Intellectual Traditions," *Wicazo Sa Review* 8 (Spring 1992): 1–20; Amanda J. Cobb, "Understanding Tribal Sovereignty: Definitions, Conceptualizations, and Interpretations," *American Studies* 46 (Fall/Winter 2005): 115–132; Henry R. Wagner, "Creation of Rights of Sovereignty through Symbolic Acts," *Pacific Historical Review* 7 (December 1938): 297–326; David Rich Lewis, "Still Native: The Significance of Native Americans in the History of the Twentieth-Century American West," *Western Historical Quarterly* 24 (May 1993): 203–227.

44. Public Law 105-243.

45. Quotes from Public Law 105-243. See also Chuck and Sheri Bowen, interview by author, August 8, 2003, Lamar, CO, tape recording, in author's possession; Rod Brown, Kiowa County commissioner, interview by author, June 17, 2003, Eads, CO, tape recording, in author's possession; Ben Nighthorse Campbell interview, September 10, 2003; William Dawson interview, June 18, 2003; Janet Frederick interview, June 17, 2003; Douglas Scott interview, October 3, 2003.

46. Quote from Cathy Spude interview, June 21, 2003. See also David Lowenthal, *The Heritage Crusade and the Spoils of History* (Cambridge: Cambridge University Press, 1998), 65; Peter V. Schaeffer and Cecily Ahern Millerick, "The Impact of Historic District Designation on Property Values: An Empirical Study," *Economic Development Quarterly* 5 (November 1991): 301–312; N. Edward Coulson and Michael L. Lahr, "Gracing the Land of Elvis and Beale Street: Historic Designation and Property Values in Memphis," *Real Estate Economics* 33 (September 2005): 487–507; Deborah Ann Ford, "The Effect of Historic Designation on Single-Family Home Prices," *Real Estate Economics* 17 (September 1999): 353–362; Douglas S. Noonan, "Finding an Impact of Preservation Policies: Price Effects of Historic Landmarks on Attached Homes in Chicago, 1990–1999," *Economic Development Quarterly* 21 (February 2007): 17–33; William Dawson interview, June 18, 2003.

47. "District Court, County of Kiowa, State of Colorado, Case No. 98, CV 13, William F. Dawson and Jredia A. Dawson, Plaintiffs, v. Homer Flute, Individually and as Trustee of the Sand Creek Massacre Descendants Irrevocable Trust; Robert S. Simpson; Thompson T. Flute; Dorothy Wood; Jimmy G. Antelope; Ricque Richardson; Charlotte Wetselline; John Mack; Dennis Eckart; Dr. John Moore; Dr. Janice Campbell; Larry Derryberry; Justin Whitefield; Hugh Thompson; and All Other Individuals Who Would Trespass Upon Land Owned by Plaintiffs, Defendants," in FSCMNHS, now at NPS-WACC. See also Laird Cometsevah interview, May 12, 2003; William Dawson interview, June 18, 2003; Homer Flute and Robert Simpson, president and vice president, Sand Creek Massacre Descendants Trust, interview by author, December 20, 2004, Anadarko, OK, tape recording, in author's possession; John Hill, "Descendants Gather at Massacre Site," *Lamar Daily News' Tri-State Trader* 29, no. 7 (July 29, 1998): 1; Alexa Roberts interview, April 29, 2003.

48. "Massacre" from Hill, "Descendants Gather at Massacre Site," 1. "Battle" from John Hill, "Wood Emotional Recalling Sand Creek Battle," *Lamar Daily News' Tri-State Trader* 29, no. 7 (July 29, 1998): 1. See also Laird Cometsevah interview, May 12, 2003; William Dawson

interview, June 18, 2003; Homer Flute and Robert Simpson interview, December 20, 2004; Alexa Roberts interview, April 29, 2003.

49. Cathy Spude interview, June 21, 2003.

50. "Because of the connections . . . ," "liaison," "disappointed," and "unsure of where . . ." from Cathy Spude interview, June 21, 2003. "Throw his hat in . . ." from David Halaas interview, September 26, 2003.

51. Daniel Chapman, legislative council staffer, to Dottie Wham, senator, Colorado State Senate, and chair, Capitol Development Committee, May 1, 1998, in File 6-10, "Civil War Monument, 2002," in Colorado Historical Society, Denver, CO; Colorado Legislative Council, *Memorials and Art in and around the Colorado State Capitol* (Denver: Colorado Legislative Council, 1992), 5, found in File 6-10; "Soldier Monument to Be Unveiled at Capitol," *Denver Daily News,* July 24, 1909, 1; David Halaas interview, September 26, 2003; Cathy Spude interview, June 21, 2003; "Shaft for Hero Dead of State," *Rocky Mountain News,* November 10, 1905.

52. Blight, *Race and Reunion,* 1–5; Eric Hobsbawm, "Inventing Traditions," in Eric Hobsbawm and Terence Ranger, eds., *The Invention of Tradition* (Cambridge: Cambridge University Press, 1992), 1–14; Michael Kammen, *Mystic Chords of Memory: Transformations of Tradition in American Society* (New York: Vintage, 1993), 101–139; Gaines M. Foster, *Ghosts of the Confederacy: Defeat, the Lost Cause and the Emergence of the New South, 1865–1913* (Oxford: Oxford University Press, 1988), 4–8, 23–67.

53. Blight, *Race and Reunion,* 2–5; and Kammen, *Mystic Chords of Memory,* 117–132.

54. Quotes from "Shaft to Civil War Martyrs of State Unveiled with Pomp," *Denver Daily News,* July 25, 1909. See also "Hosts Gather to Show Honor to Fallen Heroes," *Denver Post,* July 24, 1909; Colorado Legislative Council, *Memorials and Art in and around the Colorado State Capitol,* 5; "Soldier Monument to Be Unveiled at Capitol," *Denver Daily News,* July 24, 1909.

55. Quotes from Colorado Senate Joint Resolution 98-034, found in File 6-10, "Civil War Monument, 2002"; emphasis added. See also Chapman to Wham, May 1, 1998, in File 6-10; Betty Chronic, vice chair, Capitol Building Advisory Committee, to Dottie Wham, July 31, 1998, in File 6-10; "History of SJR034," in File 6-10; Colorado Legislative Council, *Memorials and Art in and around the Colorado State Capitol,* 5; Wham to Members, Colorado State Senate, May 5, 1998, in File 6-10.

56. Steve Brady interview, August 29, 2004; Laird Cometsevah interview, May 12, 2003; David Halaas interview, September 26, 2003; Modupe Lobode interview, June 3, 2005.

57. Quotes from David F. Halaas, chief historian, Colorado Historical Society, to Georgi Contiguglia, president, Colorado Historical Society, May 29, 1998, in File 6-10, "Civil War Monument, 2002." See also Steve Brady interview, August 29, 2004; Laird Cometsevah interview, May 12, 2003; David Halaas interview, September 26, 2003; Modupe Lobode interview, June 3, 2005.

58. "Assault on Colorado's . . ." and "erasing . . ." from Glenn Morris, member, Leadership Council of the American Indian Movement of Colorado, interview by author, November 29, 2003, Denver, CO, notes in author's possession. "Keep the words . . ." and "if each generation . . ." from Tom Noel, "Don't Erase 'Sand Creek': Leave Record Intact for Future Generations," *Denver Post*, July 5, 1998, G-1. See also Steve Brady, president, Northern Cheyenne Sand Creek Descendants, and Laird Cometsevah, president, Southern Cheyenne Sand Creek Descendants, to Senate and House of Representatives of the State of Colorado, July 25, 1998, in File 6-10, "Civil War Monument, 2002"; David Halaas interview, September 26, 2003; Cathy Spude interview, June 21, 2003.

59. Quotes from Fletcher, "The Killing Field at Sand Creek," 16; and Harrison Fletcher, "History in the Making: The Battle over the Sand Creek Massacre Just Won't End," *Westword* 21 (July 30–August 5, 1998): 6.

60. "Involved in . . . ," "believed the Cheyennes . . . ," and "enlisted Civil War . . ." from David F. Halaas to Georgi Contiguglia, July 28, 1998, in File 6-10, "Civil War Monument, 2002." "Respectfully request[ing] . . ." and "signage be placed . . ." from Brady and Cometsevah to Senate and House of Representatives of the State of Colorado, July 25, 1998. See also Georgianna Contiguglia to Robert Martinez, senator, Colorado State Senate, January 20, 1999, in File 6-10; "Staff Summary of Capital Development Committee, Agenda Item 3, September 15, 1998," in File 6-10; Senate Joint Resolution 99-017, in File 6-10; Dottie Wham to Tony Grampsas, representative, Colorado House of Representatives, and chair, Capitol Building Advisory Committee, September 17, 1998, in File 6-10; "Agenda, State Capitol Building Advisory Committee, House Committee Room 0109, State Capitol, July 31, 1998," in File 6-10; Chronic to Wham, July 31, 1998, in File 6-10; Laird Cometsevah interview, May 12, 2003; David Halaas interview, September 26, 2003; "Summary of Meeting: State Capitol Building Advisory Committee, House Committee Room 0109, State Capitol Building, July 31, 1998," 1–2, in File 6-10.

61. "Spent the . . ." from Steve Brady interview, August 29, 2004. "Oral histories . . ." and "not void . . ." from Cathy Spude to Jerry Rogers, Memorandum, re. meeting of July 25, 1998, at CHS with tribes, August

6, 1998, in FSCMNHS, now at NPS-WACC. "It is not . . ." from Cathy
Spude's personal notes of the meeting (undated), in FSCMNHS, now at
NPS-WACC. See also David Halaas interview, September 26, 2003.

62. "Ground-disturbing" from Cathy Spude interview, June 21, 2003. See
also David Halaas interview, September 26, 2003; Cathy Spude's
personal notes of the meeting (undated), in FSCMNHS, now at NPS-
WACC; Spude to Rogers, July 25, 1998.

63. Quotes from Cathy Spude's personal notes on her meeting with
William Dawson, July 7, 1998, in FSCMNHS, now at NPS-WACC. See
also Cathy Spude's personal notes on her meeting with William
Dawson, July 23, 1998, in FSCMNHS, now at NPS-WACC.

64. "Wanted to . . ." from Cathy Spude interview, June 21, 2003. "Verbatim
copy" from Cathy Spude to Barbara Sutteer, e-mail, August 25, 1998, in
FSCMNHS, now at NPS-WACC; and also William Dawson to Cathy
Spude, e-mail, August 14, 1998, in FSCMNHS, now at NPS-WACC.
"Breach of trust" from William Dawson to Cathy Spude, e-mail, August
14, 1998, in FSCMNHS, now at NPS-WACC. "Problems with . . ." from
William Dawson to John Cook, e-mail, August 17, 1998, in FSCMNHS,
now at NPS-WACC. "As a government . . . ," "A Park Service . . . ," and "If
you want . . ." from William Dawson interview, June 18, 2003. See also
William Dawson to Cathy Spude, e-mail, August 13, 1998, in FSCMNHS,
now at NPS-WACC; and William Dawson to Cathy Spude, e-mail,
August 17, 1998, in FSCMNHS, now at NPS-WACC; Cathy Spude to
John Cook, Mike Snyder, Jerry Rogers, Ernest Ortega, Bob Powers, and
Susan Garland, e-mail, August 24, 1998, in FSCMNHS, now at
NPS-WACC.

65. "Treated as . . ." from Cathy Spude to Ernest Ortega, e-mail, September
30, 1998, in FSCMNHS, now at NPS-WACC. "Devastated," "wasn't
going . . . ," and "I can't . . ." from Cathy Spude interview, June 21, 2003.
"I'll be . . ." from William Dawson interview, June 18, 2003. See also John
Cook to William Dawson, e-mail, September 21, 1998, in FSCMNHS,
now at NPS-WACC; and Cathy Spude to Rick Frost, e-mail, April 10,
1999, in FSCMNHS, now at NPS-WACC.

66. "Bleed green," used in a different context, from Alexa Roberts, interview
by author, October 21, 2005, telephone, notes in author's possession. See
also Rick Frost, associate regional director for communications and
external relations, Intermountain Region, National Park Service,
interview by author, June 11, 2003, Denver, CO, tape recording, in
author's possession.

67. Jerome Greene, research historian, National Park Service, interview by
author, May 27, 2003, Denver, CO, tape recording, in author's posses-

sion; and Jerome A. Greene, *Evidence and the Custer Enigma: A Reconstruction of Indian-Military History* (Kansas City: Kansas City Posse of the Westerners, 1973), 7–46.

68. Quotes from Lysa Wegman-French, historian, Intermountain Region, National Park Service, interview by author, June 9, 2003, Denver, CO, tape recording, in author's possession. See also Roberts, "Sand Creek: Tragedy and Symbol," 1–583; and Christine Whitacre, historian, Intermountain Region, National Park Service, interview by author, May 27, 2003, Denver, CO, tape recording, in author's possession.

69. Quotes from Barbara Sutteer interview, August 5, 2003. See also Alexa Roberts interview, April 29, 2003; Alexa Roberts, interview by author, March 25, 2004, telephone, notes in author's possession; Bob Reece, "The Story of the Indian Memorial," Friends of the Little Bighorn Battlefield, http://www.friendslittlebighorn.com/Indian%20Memorial.htm; "Indian Memorial at the Little Bighorn Battlefield National Monument," http://www.nps.gov/archive/libi/indmem.htm.

70. Alexa Roberts interview, April 29, 2003; Alexa Roberts, "Trust Me, I Work for the Government: Confidentiality and Public Access to Sensitive Information," *American Indian Quarterly* 25 (Winter 2001): 13–17.

71. Barbara Sutteer interview, August 5, 2003; Lysa Wegman-French interview, June 9, 2003; Steve Brady interview, August 29, 2004; Laird Cometsevah interview, May 12, 2003; David Halaas interview, September 26, 2003.

3. THE SMOKING GUN

1. Joyce Oldham Appleby, Lynn Avery Hunt, and Margaret C. Jacob, *Telling the Truth about History* (New York: W. W. Norton, 1995), 15–128, 160–240; Marc Bloch, *The Historian's Craft* (New York: Vintage, 1964), 40–65; Edward Hallett Carr, *What Is History* (New York: Vintage, 1967), 3–35; Richard J. Evans, *In Defense of History* (New York: W. W. Norton, 2000), 13–109; David H. Fischer, *Historians' Fallacies: Toward a Logic of Historical Thought* (New York: Harper Perrenial, 1970), 3–97; Martha C. Howell and Walter Prevenier, *From Reliable Sources: An Introduction to the Historical Method* (Ithaca, NY: Cornell University Press, 2001), 17–42; George Iggers, *Historiography in the Twentieth Century: From Scientific Objectivity to the Postmodern Challenge* (Middletown, CT: Wesleyan University Press, 2005), 1–35, 41–50; Peter Novick, *That Noble Dream: The "Objectivity Question" and the American Historical Profession* (Cambridge: Cambridge University Press, 1998), 1–58, 361–584.

2. Lysa Wegman-French, historian, Intermountain Region, National Park Service, interview by author, June 9, 2003, Denver, CO, tape recording, in author's possession; Christine Whitacre, historian, Intermountain

Region, National Park Service, interview by author, May 27, 2003, Denver, CO, tape recording, in author's possession.

3. Jerome A. Greene and Douglas D. Scott, *Finding Sand Creek: History, Archeology, and the 1864 Massacre Site* (Norman: University of Oklahoma Press, 2004), 30–33; Jerome Greene, research historian, National Park Service, interview by author, May 27, 2003, Denver, CO, tape recording, in author's possession; National Park Service, Intermountain Region, *Sand Creek Massacre Project*, vol. 1: *Site Location Study* (Denver: National Park Service, Intermountain Region, 2000), 34–36 (hereafter *Site Location Study*).

4. "Participant testimony" and "people who were there" from Jerome Greene interview, May 27, 2003. "The Park Service's recognized expert . . ." from Lysa Wegman-French interview, June 9, 2003. See also Quartermaster General of the Army, *U.S. Army Uniforms and Equipment, 1889: Specifications for Clothing, Camp and Garrison Equipage, and Clothing and Equipage Materials* (Lincoln: University of Nebraska Press, 1986), ii–ix; Jerome A. Greene, *Battles and Skirmishes of the Great Sioux War, 1876–1877: The Military View* (Norman: University of Oklahoma Press, 1996), xv–xviii; Richard G. Hardorff, *Lakota Recollections of the Custer Fight: New Sources of Indian-Military History* (Lincoln: University of Nebraska Press, 1997), 1–8; Michael H. Frisch, *A Shared Authority: Essays on the Craft and Meaning of Oral and Public History* (Albany: State University of New York Press, 1990), 1–37, 147–158, 179–190; Alessandro Portelli, *The Death of Luigi Trastulli and Other Stories: Form and Meaning in Oral History* (Albany: State University of New York Press, 1990), 1–79; Donald A. Ritchie, *Doing Oral History* (Oxford: Oxford University Press, 2003), 11–46; Ruth H. Finnegan, *Oral Traditions and the Verbal Arts: A Guide to Research Practices* (London: Routledge, 1992), 1–89, 214–233; Rebecca Sharpless, "The History of Oral History," in Thomas L. Charlton, Lois E. Myers, and Rebecca Sharpless, eds., *History of Oral History: Foundations and Methodology* (Lanham, MD: Altamira Press, 2007), 10–14.

5. Quotes from National Park Service, *Site Location Study*, 35–36. See also pp. 34–40 and 53–70.

6. Lysa Wegman-French interview, June 9, 2003; Patricia Nelson Limerick, *Legacy of Conquest: The Unbroken Past of the American West* (New York: W. W. Norton, 1987), 20–27; Frederick Jackson Turner, *The Frontier in American History* (New York: Henry Holt, 1921), 1–38.

7. "Resurrected a 20-year-old campaign . . ." and "David Nichols" from Kristen Black, "Nichols Hall Report Says New Name Needed," *Colorado Daily*, September 30, 1987, 1. "Open wound . . ." from Kristen Black, "Lt. Governor Joins Dorm Protest," *Colorado Daily*, October 12, 1987, 1. See

also Patricia Nelson Limerick, "What's in a Name? Nichols Hall: A Report" (unpublished manuscript, September 14, 1987), 107.

8. "Ideal topic . . ." from Limerick, "What's in a Name?," 2.

9. Quotes from Limerick, "What's in a Name?," 5, 18, 3, and 2.

10. "To the white participants . . ." from Limerick, "What's in a Name?," 69. All other quotes from Robert M. Utley to Patricia Nelson Limerick, August 2, 1987, in Limerick, "What's in a Name?," appendix.

11. "The University [should] change the name . . ." from Limerick, "What's in a Name?," 107.

12. "Revisionism," "biased," and "The minority students were . . ." from Black, "Nichols Hall Report Says New Name Needed," 1. "Denigrates people," "let the dead bury . . . ," and "If we decide to pull down . . ." from Barry Bortnick, "Regent Says Nichols Report Biased," *Boulder Daily Camera*, September 29, 1987, A-2.

13. "Trying to fight a war . . ." from Kristen Black, "Nichols' Controversy Irks His Descendants," *Colorado Daily*, October 12, 1987, 1. "A great day" from Steve Millard, "Nichols Hall Will Be Renamed," *Boulder Daily Camera*, November 20, 1987, A-1. See also Linda Cornett, "Regents Approve Naming Dorm Cheyenne Arapaho Hall," *Boulder Daily Camera*, April 21, 1989, A-1; Steve Millard, "Regents Postpone Dorm Name Decision," *Boulder Daily Camera*, March 16, 1987, B-1; Renate Robey, "Indian-Fighter's Name to Come Off Dorm at CU," *Denver Post*, November 20, 1997, B-8.

14. Quote from National Park Service, *Site Location Study*, 34; emphasis added. See also Gary L. Roberts, "Sand Creek: Tragedy and Symbol" (unpublished PhD dissertation, University of Oklahoma, 1984), 552; Jerome A. Greene, *Lakota and Cheyenne: Indian Views of the Great Sioux War* (Norman: University of Oklahoma Press, 2000), xiii–xv; Lysa Wegman-French interview, June 9, 2003; Jerome Greene interview, May 27, 2003; Christine Whitacre interview, May 27, 2003.

15. "Folks had complied . . ." and "they weren't fools" from Laird Cometse-vah, chief, Southern Cheyenne Tribe, interview by author, May 12, 2003, Denver, CO, tape recording, in author's possession. See also "Citizenship Act of 1924," Colonial Williamsburg Foundation, http://research.history.org/pf/weThePeople/citizenshipAct.cfm.

16. Quote from Roberts, "Sand Creek: Tragedy and Symbol," 676. See also *Colorado Transcript*, October 10, 1894; *New York Times*, October 14, 1894; *Denver Republican*, October 5, 1894; David Fridtjof Halaas and Andrew E. Masich, *Halfbreed: The Remarkable True Story of George Bent, Caught between the Worlds of the Indian and the White Man* (New York: Da Capo Press, 2004), 327–348; George E. Hyde, *Life of George Bent: Written from His*

Letters, ed. Savoie Lottinville (Norman: University of Oklahoma Press, 1968), v–xvi; George Bird Grinnell, *The Cheyenne Indians: History and Society,* vol. 1 (Lincoln: University of Nebraska Press, 1972), 21, 158; George Bird Grinnell, *The Cheyenne Indians: War, Ceremonies, and Religion,* vol. 2 (Lincoln: University of Nebraska Press, 1972), 271–273; George Bird Grinnell, *The Fighting Cheyennes* (1915; reprint, Norman: University of Oklahoma Press, 1955), 103–201; Roberts, "Sand Creek: Tragedy and Symbol," 676.

17. George Bent map, Folder 1, Bent-Hyde Collection, Western History Collections, University of Colorado Library, Boulder, CO (hereafter Bent-Hyde Collection); and George Bent map, Oklahoma Historical Society, Oklahoma City.

18. Quote from Greene and Scott, *Finding Sand Creek,* 35. See also Jerome Greene interview, May 27, 2003; National Park Service, *Site Location Study,* 43.

19. "Heard people . . ." and "it was actually Hyde . . ." from Lysa Wegman-French to Cathy Spude, e-mail, August 26, 1998, in uncataloged files of the Sand Creek Massacre National Historic Site (FSCMNHS), currently held by National Park Service, Western Archeological and Conservation Center (NPS-WACC), Tucson, AZ. All other quotes from Lysa Wegman-French interview, June 9, 2003. See also Greene and Scott, *Finding Sand Creek,* 43; Jerome Greene interview, May 27, 2003; National Park Service, *Site Location Study,* 43; Christine Whitacre interview, May 27, 2003.

20. "The base map . . ." from Wegman-French to Spude, e-mail, August 26, 1998. All other quotes from Lysa Wegman-French interview, June 9, 2003. See also Bent-Hyde maps, Folders 3 and 10, Bent-Hyde Collection; Greene and Scott, *Finding Sand Creek,* 43; Jerome Greene interview, May 27, 2003; National Park Service, *Site Location Study,* 22, 24, 43; Christine Whitacre interview, May 27, 2003.

21. "Something of an oddity" from Gary Roberts to Jerome Greene, e-mail, August 24, 1998, in FSCMNHS, now at NPS-WACC. All other quotes from Jerome Greene interview, May 27, 2003. Samuel W. Bonsall map, in National Archives, Great Lakes Region, Chicago. See also Greene and Scott, *Finding Sand Creek,* 41–51; David Halaas, director of publications, library, and archives, John Heinz History Center, interview by author, September 26, 2003, Pittsburgh, PA, tape recording, in author's possession; National Park Service, *Site Location Study,* 41–53.

22. "Strip map . . ." from National Park Service, *Site Location Study,* 43. "Commanding officers . . . ," "whose object . . . ," and "every point . . ." from *Revised United States Army Regulations, of 1861, With an Appendix containing the Changes and Laws Affecting Army Regulations and Articles of War*

to June 25, 1863 (Philadelphia: George W. Childs, 1864), 98–103. "Chivington's Massacre" from Samuel W. Bonsall map, National Archives. See also Jerome Greene interview, May 27, 2003; Greene and Scott, *Finding Sand Creek,* 41–51; National Park Service, *Site Location Study,* 41–53.

23. "Chivington's Massacre" from Samuel W. Bonsall map, National Archives. All other quotes from Luke Cahill, "Recollections of a Plainsman," unpublished manuscript, ca. 1915, MSS 99 in Manuscripts Division, Colorado Historical Society, Denver, CO. See also Jerome Greene interview, May 27, 2003; Greene and Scott, *Finding Sand Creek,* 41–51; National Park Service, *Site Location Study,* 41–53.

24. Jerome Greene to Cathy Spude, e-mail, August 13, 1998, in FSCMNHS, now at NPS-WACC.

25. "Eureka moment" from Jerome Greene interview, May 27, 2003. "Chivington's Massacre" from Samuel W. Bonsall map, National Archives. For copies of the Soil Conservation Service photos, see National Park Service, *Site Location Study,* 49–52. See also Amy M. Holmes and Michael McFaul, "Geoarcheological Assessment of the Sand Creek Massacre Site, Kiowa County, Colorado," October 18, 1999, in FSCMNHS, now at NPS-WACC; and Donald Worster, *Dust Bowl: The Southern Plains in the 1930s* (Oxford: Oxford University Press, 1979), 210–226.

26. "Discovery" from Jerome Greene interview, May 27, 2003. "The most directly compelling" from Greene and Scott, *Finding Sand Creek,* 51. See also Lenore Barbian, anatomical collections manager, National Anthropological Archives, Smithsonian Institution, to Gary L. Roberts, National Park Service contract historian, in Gary L. Roberts, "The Sand Creek Massacre Site: A Report on Washington Sources," January 1999 (unpublished manuscript), in FSCMNHS, now at NPS-WACC.

27. Quotes from Chuck and Sheri Bowen, interview by author, August 8, 2003, Lamar, CO, tape recording, in author's possession. See also Jerome Greene interview, May 27, 2003; and National Park Service, Intermountain Region, *Sand Creek Massacre Project,* vol. 2: *Special Resource Study* (Denver: National Park Service, Intermountain Region, 2000), 17 (hereafter *Special Resource Study*).

28. Quotes from Chuck and Sheri Bowen interview, August 8, 2003. The scrapbook, viewed at the time of the interview, is part of the Bowens' extensive archive of Sand Creek materials.

29. Ibid.

30. "We had made . . ." and "three or four . . ." from ibid. "Very significant" from Jerome Greene interview, May 27, 2003.

31. "Suspicious" and "it all came . . ." from Jerome Greene interview, May 27, 2003. See also Lysa Wegman-French interview, June 9, 2003; Douglas

Scott, chief archeologist, National Park Service Midwest Archeological
Center, interview by author, October 3, 2003, telephone, tape recording,
in author's possession; Douglas Scott to Rick Frost, Christine Whitacre,
Lysa Wegman-French, Cathy Spude, Jerome Greene, and Steve De Vore,
e-mail, March 12, 1999, in FSCMNHS, now at NPS-WACC; Christine
Whitacre interview, May 27, 2003.

32. "Evidence gleaned . . ." from Greene and Scott, *Finding Sand Creek,* 60–61.
All other quotes from National Park Service, *Site Location Study,* 63. See
also Lysa Wegman-French interview, June 9, 2003; Jerome Greene inter-
view, May 27, 2003; Greene and Scott, *Finding Sand Creek,* 51–63; National
Park Service, *Site Location Study,* 53–63; Christine Whitacre interview,
May 27, 2003.

33. "Efficiently" from Alexa Roberts, superintendent, Sand Creek Massacre
National Historic Site, interview by author, April 29, 2003, Denver, CO,
tape recording, in author's possession. "The time frame . . ." from Cathy
Spude, National Park Service, interview by author, June 21, 2003,
Denver, CO, tape recording, in author's possession.

34. "Indian people . . ." from Mildred Red Cherries, member, Northern
Cheyenne Sand Creek Massacre Descendants Committee, interview by
author, August 15, 2003, Lame Deer, MT, tape recording, in author's
possession. "Well, there's Indian . . ." from Norma Gorneau, member,
Northern Cheyenne Tribe Sand Creek Massacre Descendants Committee, interview by author, July 1, 2004, Lame Deer, MT, tape recording, in
author's possession. "We've been waiting . . ." from Otto Braided Hair,
director, Northern Cheyenne Sand Creek Office, interview by author,
May 11, 2007, telephone, notes in author's possession. See also National
Park Service, *Site Location Study,* 13, 17.

35. "Bolted without . . ." from Otto Braided Hair interview, May 11, 2007.
"We cannot trust . . ." from Cathy Spude's personal notes of the November 14, 1998 meeting, in FSCMNHS, now at NPS-WACC. See also Steve
Brady, headman, Crazy Dogs Society, Northern Cheyenne Tribe,
interview by author, August 29, 2004, Lame Deer, MT, tape recording, in
author's possession; Laird Cometsevah interview, May 12, 2003; Alexa
Roberts interview, April 29, 2003.

36. "An American project . . ." from Cathy Spude's personal notes of a
subsequent site location meeting, held December 13, 1998, in Lamar,
CO, at which the controversial comment came up again, found in
FSCMNHS, now at NPS-WACC. All other quotes from Rick Frost,
Associate Regional Director for Communications and External
Relations, Intermountain Region, National Park Service, interview by

author, June 11, 2003, Denver, CO, tape recording, in author's possession. See also Steve Brady interview, August 29, 2004; Laird Cometsevah
interview, May 12, 2003; David Halaas interview, September 26, 2003;
Alexa Roberts interview, April 29, 2003.

37. Quote from David Halaas interview, September 26, 2003. See also Steve
Brady interview, August 29, 2004; Laird Cometsevah interview, May 12,
2003; Rick Frost interview, June 11, 2003; Alexa Roberts interview, April
29, 2003.

38. "Park service . . ." from Steve Brady, interview by author, September 12,
2003, Lame Deer, MT, tape recording, in author's possession. "What I
learned . . . ," "was, for them . . . ," "we were talking . . . ," and "if I was . . ."
from Rick Frost interview, June 11, 2003. "I've come to . . ." from Cathy
Spude's personal notes of the November 15, 1998, meeting, in FSCMNHS,
now at NPS-WACC. See also Gail Ridgely, Sand Creek representative,
Northern Arapaho Tribe, interview by author, July 29, 2003, Denver,
CO, tape recording, in author's possession.

39. "Sometimes I had to . . . from Steve Brady interview, September 12, 2003.
All other quotes from Rick Frost interview, June 11, 2003.

40. "Confidentiality . . ." from Steve Chestnut, founding partner, Ziontz,
Chestnut, Varnell, Berley & Slonim, interview by author, February 6,
2004, Seattle, WA, tape recording, in author's possession. "White
scholars . . ." from Conrad Fisher, director, Northern Cheyenne Cultural
Center, interview by author, July 1, 2004, Lame Deer, MT, tape recording, in author's possession. "You know . . ." from Steve Brady, interview
by author, September 16, 2006, telephone, notes in author's possession.
See also Laird Cometsevah interview, May 12, 2003; David Halaas
interview, September 26, 2003; Donald Fixico, "Ethics and Responsibilities in Writing American Indian History," in Devon A. Mihesuah, ed.,
Natives and Academics: Researching and Writing about American Indians
(Lincoln: University of Nebraska Press, 1998), 84–99; Thomas Biolsi and
Larry Zimmerman, "What's Changed, What Hasn't?," in Thomas Biolsi
and Larry Zimmerman, eds., *Indians and Anthropologists: Vine Deloria, Jr.
and the Critique of Anthropology* (Tucson: University of Arizona Press,
1997), 3–24; Angela Cavender Wilson, "Power of the Spoken Word:
Native Oral Traditions in American Indian History," in Donald L.
Fixico, ed., *Rethinking American Indian History* (Albuquerque: University
of New Mexico Press, 1997), 101–116; Cecil King, "Here Come the
Anthros," in Biolsi and Zimmerman, *Indians and Anthropologists*, 116–119;
Linda Tuhiwai Smith, *Decolonizing Methodologies: Research and Indigenous
People* (London: Zed Books, 1999), 1–57; Angela Cavender Wilson,

"American Indian History or Non-Indian Perceptions of American Indian History?," in Devon A. Mihesuah, ed., *Natives and Academics: Researching and Writing about American Indians* (Lincoln: University of Nebraska Press, 1998), 23–26; Randall H. McGuire, "Why Have Archaeologists Thought the Real Indians Were Dead and What Can We Do about It?," in Biolsi and Zimmerman, *Indians and Anthropologists*, 63–91.

41. "Some of us . . . ," "family stories," "as young people . . . ," "Cheyennes never did have . . . ," "today we do . . . ," and "they're afraid . . ." from National Park Service, *Site Location Study*, 137, 139. "*The* traditional method" from Steve Brady interview, September 16, 2006.

42. "Traditional approaches" from Laird Cometsevah interview, May 12, 2003. See also National Park Service, *Site Location Study*, 138.

43. "Agreement . . ." from Steve Chestnut interview, February 6, 2004. All other quotes from Alexa Roberts interview, April 29, 2003.

44. Quote from National Park Service, *Site Location Study*, 145. See also pp. 137–149.

45. For Jackson home prices, see "Jackson, Wyoming," City-Data.com, http://www.city-data.com/city/Jackson-Wyoming.html. Labor statistics for the Wind River Reservation can be found in Garth Massey and Audie Blevins, "Employment and Unemployment on the Wind River Indian Reservation," http://www.doe.state.wy.us/lmi/1199/a2.htm. See also Alexa Roberts interview, April 29, 2003.

46. "Creating a national . . ." from Gail Ridgely interview, July 29, 2003, See also Ben Ridgely, Sand Creek representative, Northern Arapaho Tribe, interview by author, May 25, 2005, Denver, CO, tape recording, in author's possession; Alexa Roberts interview, April 29, 2003.

47. Quotes and other information about Clinton from Clinton Chamber of Commerce, http://www.clintonok.org/.

48. Laird Cometsevah interview, May 12, 2003; National Park Service, *Site Location Study*, 151–153; Alexa Roberts interview, April 29, 2003.

49. Quotes from Otto Braided Hair interview, May 11, 2007. See also National Park Service, *Site Location Study*, 154–155.

50. A list of the state's historic sites can be found at Wyoming State Historical Society, http://www.wyshs.org/histsites.htm. See also Alexa Roberts interview, April 29, 2003.

51. "Familiar, like home" from Alexa Roberts, superintendent, Bent's Old Fort National Historic Site, interview by author, January 27, 2008, telephone, notes in author's possession. For information on the Northern Cheyenne Reservation, see http://www.mnisose.org/profiles /ncheyne.htm. See also Alexa Roberts interview, April 29, 2003.

52. "Earned" from Otto Braided Hair interview, May 11, 2007. "Time allowed . . . ," "a gift commensurate . . . ," "as much time . . . ," "a lack of time . . . ," "traditional protocols . . . ," and "adversely affected . . ." from National Park Service, *Site Location Study,* 157. See also Steve Brady interview, August 29, 2004; National Park Service, *Site Location Study,* 149–160; Alexa Roberts interview, April 29, 2003.

53. Quotes from National Park Service, *Site Location Study,* 159. See also Steve Brady interview, August 29, 2004; Laird Cometsevah interview, May 12, 2003; Otto Braided Hair interview, May 11, 2007; Alexa Roberts interview, April 29, 2003.

54. Quote from National Park Service, *Site Location Study,* 159. See also Steve Brady interview, August 29, 2004; Laird Cometsevah interview, May 12, 2003; Otto Braided Hair interview, May 11, 2007.

55. "Ethnic cleansing," "cultural persistence," and "they represent . . ." from Alexa Roberts interview, April 29, 2003.

56. "Its own symbol . . ." from National Park Service, *Site Location Study,* 188. Because I did not seek permission from the Cheyennes and Arapahos who participated in the ethnographic study to quote from their oral histories, I have not done so. I have relied on summaries provided by the Park Service. See also pp. 158–160, 186–189, and 275–281.

57. Quotes from National Park Service, *Site Location Study,* 277. See also pp. 186–189 and 275–281.

58. Quotes from James Doyle, Colorado communications director for Senator Ben Nighthorse Campbell, interview by author, June 10, 2003, Fort Collins, CO, tape recording, in author's possession.

59. "Hearing one . . ." and "you really . . ." from Barbara Sutteer, interview by author, August 5, 2003, telephone, tape recording, in author's possession. "We have . . ." from Laird Cometsevah interview, May 12, 2003. See also Alexa Roberts interview, April 29, 2003.

60. "Stakeholders" and "remained at . . ." from Rick Frost interview, June 11, 2003. See also National Park Service, *Special Resource Study,* 6.

61. "We didn't . . ." from Joe Big Medicine, Sand Creek representative, Southern Cheyenne Tribe, interview by author, July 8, 2003, Lame Deer, MT, tape recording, in author's possession. "I personally . . ." and "artifacts can . . ." from Hew Hallock, "Battle over Sand Creek Continues," *Lamar Daily News,* April 20, 1999, A-1. See also Holmes and McFaul, "Geoarcheological Assessment of the Sand Creek Massacre Site"; Laird Cometsevah interview, May 12, 2003; Rick Frost interview, June 11, 2003; Mildred Red Cherries interview, August 15, 2003; Alexa Roberts interview, April 29, 2003; Douglas Scott interview, October 3, 2003.

62. Variations on "he buys land; he doesn't sell it" can be found in Chuck and Sheri Bowen interview, August 8, 2003; William Dawson, interview by author, June 18, 2003, Kiowa County, CO, tape recording, in author's possession; Janet Frederick, director, Kiowa County Economic Development Corporation, interview by author, June 17, 2003, Eads, CO, tape recording, in author's possession; Rod Johnson, member, Kiowa Country Economic Development Corporation, interview by author, June 17, 2003, Eads, CO, tape recording, in author's possession. See also Rick Frost interview, June 11, 2003; Douglas Scott interview, October 3, 2003.

63. "A very important item" from Scott to Frost, Whitacre, Wegman-French, Spude, Greene, and De Vore, e-mail, March 12, 1999, in FSCMNHS, now at NPS-WACC. See also Douglas Scott, "Trip Notes, March 10–11, 1999," in FSCMNHS, now at NPS-WACC.

64. "Be condemned," "future lost . . . ," "the history . . . ," "dry land . . . ," and "liking Greene . . ." from Chuck and Sheri Bowen interview, August 8, 2003. "Fair market . . ." from Alexa Roberts, interview by author, August 26, 2004, Denver, CO, tape recording, in author's possession. "Pulled artifacts . . ." from Jerome Greene interview, May 27, 2003.

65. "Are not anti-Indian . . ." and "political correctness" from Chuck and Sheri Bowen interview, August 8, 2003.

66. "True site" from Robert Perry to Laird Cometsevah, March 9, 1999, facsimile, in FSCMNHS, now at NPS-WACC. "Greedy people" from Joe Big Medicine interview, July 8, 2003. See also Chuck and Sheri Bowen interview, August 8, 2003; Laird Cometsevah interview, May 12, 2003; Douglas Scott interview, October 3, 2003; Hew Hallock, "New site on Sand Creek to Be Explored," *Lamar Daily News,* April 21, 1999, A-1.

67. "Visited the . . ." and "walked on . . ." from Laird Cometsevah interview, May 12, 2003. "Little aggradation" and "well within . . ." from Douglas Scott interview, October 3, 2003. "Nearly ideal . . ." from National Park Service, *Site Location Study,* 78. See also Amy Holmes and Michael McFaul, "Geomorphological and Geoarchaeological Assessment of the Possible Sand Creek Massacre Site, Kiowa County, Colorado," 1999, manuscript found in FSCMNHS, now at NPS-WACC; and Greene and Scott, *Finding Sand Creek,* 66–68.

68. Quotes from Douglas Scott interview, October 3, 2003. See also National Park Service, *Site Location Study,* 78–79; Greene and Scott, *Finding Sand Creek,* 71–73; Douglas D. Scott and Melissa Connor, "The Role and Future of Archaeology in Forensic Science," *Historical Archaeology* 35 (2001): 101–104; and Melissa Connor and Douglas D. Scott, "Metal Detector Use in Archaeology: An Introduction," *Historical Archaeology* 32 (1998): 76–85.

69. Douglas Scott interview, October 3, 2003; National Park Service, *Site Location Study*, 78–79; Greene and Scott, *Finding Sand Creek*, 71–73.

70. "Heard the . . ." and "knew that . . ." from Laird Cometsevah interview, May 12, 2003. See also National Park Service, *Site Location Study*, 81–83; Greene and Scott, *Finding Sand Creek*, 72–74.

71. Quote from Greene and Scott, *Finding Sand Creek*, 73. See also National Park Service, *Site Location Study*, 81–83.

72. "Shrapnel from . . ." and "the only recorded . . ." from Deborah Frazier, "Signs of 1864 Massacre Found," *Rocky Mountain News*, May 25, 1999, A-7. See also Greene and Scott, *Finding Sand Creek*, 74–81, appendix A; and National Park Service, *Site Location Study*, 83–111.

73. Quote from Douglas Scott interview, October 3, 2003. See also Jim Hughes, "Land's Secrets Sought," *Denver Post*, May 29, 1999, A-1.

74. "It was fascinating . . ." from Douglas Scott interview, October 3, 2003. "I must have dug up . . . ," "every time Mildred . . . ," "it was stunning . . . ," and "it was hard . . ." from Rick Frost interview, June 11, 2003.

75. "The Park Service . . ." from Laird Cometsevah interview, May 12, 2003. "Archeologists were jumping . . ." from Steve Brady interview, August 29, 2004. "It was emotional . . ." from Mildred Red Cherries interview, August 15, 2003. "The tribes . . ." from Barbara Sutteer interview, August 5, 2003.

76. "Wasn't anything" and "sue if [they] got . . ." from Chuck and Sheri Bowen interview, August 8, 2003. See also Rick Frost interview, June 11, 2003; Mildred Red Cherries interview, August 15, 2003; Douglas Scott interview, October 3, 2003.

77. "For the tribe" from Mildred Red Cherries interview, August 15, 2003. See also Chuck and Sheri Bowen interview, August 8, 2003.

78. "Forbearance will . . ." from *Rocky Mountain News*, June 27, 1860. See also Elliot West, *Contested Plains: Indians, Goldseekers and the Rush to Colorado* (Lawrence: University Press of Kansas, 2000), 280–283.

79. *Rocky Mountain News*, October 17 and 30, 1860; *Western Mountaineer*, October 4, 1860; A. B. Greenwood, Commissioner of Indian Affairs, to J. Thompson, Secretary of the Interior, October 25, 1860, *Report of the Commissioner of Indian Affairs Accompanying the Annual Report of the Secretary of the Interior, for the Year 1860* (Washington, DC: George W. Bowman, 1860), 228–230. See also Roberts, "Sand Creek: Tragedy and Symbol," 91–93; Stan Hoig, *The Sand Creek Massacre* (Norman: University of Oklahoma Press, 1974), 10–11; Donald J. Berthrong, *The Southern Cheyennes* (Norman: University of Oklahoma Press, 1975), 147–150.

80. "Would enter . . ." from Greenwood to Thompson, October 25, 1860, *Report of the Commissioner of Indian Affairs;* emphasis added. See also *Western Mountaineer,* September 20, 1860; Mildred Red Cherries interview, August 15, 2003; Chuck and Sheri Bowen interview, August 8, 2003.

81. Laird Cometsevah interview, May 12, 2003; Rick Frost interview, June 11, 2003; Mildred Red Cherries interview, August 15, 2003; Douglas Scott interview, October 3, 2003.

82. Quotes from Douglas Scott interview, October 3, 2003. See also Rick Frost interview, June 11, 2003; Joe Big Medicine interview, July 8, 2003.

83. "Absolutely unequivocal" from Steve Brady interview, September 12, 2003. "Ballistics research . . ." and "Not everything . . ." from Steve Brady interview, August 29, 2004. "Numbers . . ." and "seemed like he . . ." from Laird Cometsevah interview, May 12, 2003. "But the Park Service . . ." from Barbara Sutteer interview, August 5, 2003.

84. Quote from Douglas Scott interview, October 3, 2003.

85. Quotes from Alexa Roberts interview, April 29, 2003.

4. ACCURATE BUT NOT PRECISE

1. "Caucused" from Otto Braided Hair, director, Northern Cheyenne Sand Creek Office, interview by author, May 11, 2007, telephone, notes in author's possession. "Everyone had reached . . ." from Christine Whitacre, historian, Intermountain Region, National Park Service, interview by author, May 27, 2003, Denver, CO, tape recording, in author's possession. "A map of . . . ," "DRAFT," and "an explosion . . ." from Rick Frost, Associate Regional Director for Communications and External Relations, Intermountain Region, National Park Service, interview by author, June 11, 2003, Denver, CO, tape recording, in author's possession. "Betrayed" from Laird Cometsevah, chief, Southern Cheyenne Tribe, interview by author, May 12, 2003, Denver, CO, tape recording, in author's possession. See also National Park Service, Intermountain Region, *Sand Creek Massacre Project,* vol. 2: *Special Resource Study* (Denver: National Park Service, Intermountain Region, 2000), 16–19 (hereafter *Special Resource Study*).

2. "Not surprised . . . ," "bureaucratic imperialism," and "cultural genocide" from Laird Cometsevah interview, May 12, 2003. "Had made a huge . . ." from Rick Frost interview, June 11, 2003. "Corrected the diagram" from Larry Borowsky, "Where the Truth Lies," *5280* 9 (August–September 2001): 104.

3. "Floored . . ." and "there was such . . ." from Douglas Scott, chief archeologist, National Parks Service Midwest Archeological Center, interview by author, October 3, 2003, telephone, tape recording, in author's posses-

sion. "Found the site" and "maybe this isn't . . ." from Christine Whitacre interview, May 27, 2003. "Not so fast . . ." and "meddling" from Laird Cometsevah interview, May 12, 2003.

4. "Sand Creek assemblage" and "an 1864-era Cheyenne . . ." from National Park Service, Intermountain Region, *Sand Creek Massacre Project*, vol. 1: *Site Location Study* (Denver: National Park Service, Intermountain Region, 2000), 130 (hereafter *Site Location Study*). See also Jerome A. Greene and Douglas D. Scott, *Finding Sand Creek: History, Archeology, and the 1864 Massacre Site* (Norman: University of Oklahoma Press, 2004), 87-98, appendixes A-D; Jerome Greene, research historian, National Park Service, interview by author, May 27, 2003, Denver, CO, tape recording, in author's possession; National Park Service, *Site Location Study*, 126-135, appendixes 1-3; Douglas Scott interview, October 3, 2003; Lysa Wegman-French, historian, Intermountain Region, National Park Service, interview by author, June 9, 2003, Denver, CO, tape recording, in author's possession.

5. "Mute testimony" and "nearly unequivocal" from National Park Service, *Site Location Study*, 132 and 130 respectively. See also Greene and Scott, *Finding Sand Creek*, 87-98, appendixes A-D; Jerome Greene interview, May 27, 2003; Douglas Scott interview, October 3, 2003; Mark Neely, *The Civil War and the Limits of Destruction* (Cambridge, MA: Harvard University Press, 2007), 140-169.

6. "Might have been . . ." from National Park Service, *Site Location Study*, 134. "The absence of definitive . . ." from Greene and Scott, *Finding Sand Creek*, 96. See also Jerome Greene interview, May 27, 2003; Douglas Scott interview, October 3, 2003.

7. For details on the Cheyennes' and Arapahos' Sand Creek stories, see "The Sand Creek Massacre Site Location Study Oral History Project," in National Park Service, *Site Location Study*, 137-285. See also Jerome Greene interview, May 27, 2003; Douglas Scott interview, October 3, 2003.

8. "Accurate but . . . ," "Bent's account . . . ," and "so when . . ." from Jerome Greene interview, May 27, 2003. "I don't . . ." and "taken aback . . ." from Douglas Scott interview, October 3, 2003.

9. "There's this . . ." and "it was . . ." from Rick Frost interview, June 11, 2003. "Archeological evidence . . . ," "heard voices . . . ," and "I don't . . ." from Christine Whitacre interview, May 27, 2003.

10. "Feel where Sand Creek . . ." from Laird Cometsevah interview, May 12, 2003. "The Cheyennes feel . . ." from Mary Jean Porter, "Many Indians Believe the Site Lies on Dawson Land," *Pueblo Chieftain*, March 15, 1999, in uncataloged files of the Sand Creek Massacre National Historic Site (FSCMNHS), currently held by National Park Service, Western

Archeological and Conservation Center (NPS-WACC), Tucson, AZ. "But according to . . ." from Associated Press, "Park Service Searching for Massacre Site," *Colorado Springs Gazette,* February 21, 1999, n.p., in FSCMNHS, now at NPS-WACC. "The Cheyenne have always . . ." from Harrison Fletcher, "Shifting Sands," *Westword,* June 10, 1999, http://www .westword.com/issue/1999-06-10/columns.html. "The digging . . ." and "typically high-handed . . ." from Steve Brady, president, Northern Cheyenne Sand Creek Descendants, interview by author, September 12, 2003, Lame Deer, MT, tape recording, in author's possession.

11. "Dawson South Bend" and "Cheyenne earth" from National Park Service, *Site Location Study,* 10. "Spiritually and religiously . . ." from Fletcher, "Shifting Sands." "The Arrow Keeper wasn't wrong . . ." from Laird Cometsevah interview, May 12, 2003.

12. "Stabbed . . ." from Mildred Red Cherries, member, Northern Cheyenne Sand Creek Massacre Descendants Committee, interview by author, August 13, 2003, Lame Deer, MT, tape recording, in author's possession. "They're calling . . ." from Borowsky, "Where the Truth Lies," 113. "The Park . . ." from Laird Cometsevah interview, May 12, 2003.

13. Steve Brady interview, September 12, 2003; Laird Cometsevah interview, May 12, 2003.

14. "Work in . . ." from "Sand Creek Massacre National Historic Site Study Act of 1998," Public Law 105-243. "Will affect . . ." from "National Historic Preservation Act of 1966, as Amended through 2006 [with Annotations]," 16 U.S.C. 470. See also a discussion of Executive Order No. 13804, "Sand Creek Massacre Site Project Agreement for the Development of a Site Location and Special Resource Study, October 1998," in FSCMNHS, now at NPS-WACC; Senator Ben Nighthorse Campbell's questionnaire, produced in advance of hearings on S. 1695, and the NPS's responses, in FSCMNHS, now at NPS-WACC; National Park Service, *Special Resource Study,* appendixes 1 and 2.

15. "Methods . . ." from "Sand Creek Massacre Site Project Agreement for the Development of a Site Location and Special Resource Study, October 1998," in FSCMNHS, now at NPS-WACC. "Cheyenne and Arapaho . . . ," "work to help . . . ," "best efforts . . . ," and "the project . . ." from "Memorandum of Understanding among National Park Service, Cheyenne and Arapaho Tribes of Oklahoma, Northern Cheyenne Tribe, and Northern Arapaho Tribe for Government-to-Government Relations in the Implementation of P.L. 105-243," in FSCMNHS, now at NPS-WACC. See also "Cooperative Agreement between the National Park Service and the Cheyenne and Arapaho Tribes of Oklahoma," in FSCMNHS, now at NPS-WACC; Steve Brady interview, September 12,

2003; Steve Chestnut, founding member, Ziontz, Chestnut, Varnell, Berley & Slonim, interview by author, Februrary 6, 2004, Seattle, WA, tape recording, in author's possession; Laird Cometsevah interview, May 12, 2003; National Park Service, *Special Resource Study,* appendixes 1 and 2.

16. "Had their oral traditions . . ." from Rick Frost interview, June 11, 2003. All other quotes from Steve Brady, interview by author, August 29, 2004, Lame Deer, MT, tape recording, in author's possession.

17. Steve Brady interview, August 29, 2004; David Fridtjof Halaas and Andrew E. Masich, *Halfbreed: The Remarkable True Story of George Bent, Caught between the Worlds of the Indian and the White Man* (New York: Da Capo Press, 2004), xiv, 124–157, 328–349; George E. Hyde, *Life of George Bent: Written from His Letters,* ed. Savoie Lottinville (Norman: University of Oklahoma Press, 1968), 151–163.

18. Francis B. Heitman, comp., *Historical Register and Dictionary of the United States Army from Its Organization, September 29, 1789, to March 2, 1903,* vol. 1 (Washington, DC: Government Printing Office, 1903), 230; Greene and Scott, *Finding Sand Creek,* 45–51.

19. "He claims . . ." from Steve Brady interview, September 12, 2003.

20. "Rosetta Stone" and "the most compelling . . ." from Gary L. Roberts, "The Sand Creek Massacre Site: A Report on Washington Sources," 11, in FSCMNHS, now at NPS-WACC. All other quotes from Laird Cometsevah interview, May 12, 2003. See also Joe Big Medicine, Sand Creek representative, Southern Cheyenne Tribe, interview by author, July 8, 2003, Lame Deer, MT, tape recording, in author's possession; Steve Brady interview, September 12, 2003; Conrad Fisher, director, Northern Cheyenne Cultural Center, interview by author, July 1, 2004, Lame Deer, MT, tape recording, in author's possession.

21. Quotes from Governor John Evans to Secretary of War Edwin Stanton, December 14, 1863, in *Report of the Commissioner of Indian Affairs for the Year 1864* (Washington, DC: Government Printing Office, 1865), 225–226. See also Gary Clayton Anderson, *Kinsmen of Another Kind: Dakota-White Relations in the Upper Mississippi Valley 1650–1862* (Lincoln: University of Nebraska Press, 1984), 261–280; Gerald S. Henig, "A Neglected Cause of the Sioux Uprising," *Minnesota History* 45 (Fall 1976): 107–110; Priscilla Ann Russo, "The Time to Speak Is Over: The Onset of the Sioux Uprising," *Minnesota History* 45 (Fall 1976): 97–106; Kenneth Carley, "As Red Men Viewed It: Three Indian Accounts of the Uprising," *Minnesota History* 38 (September 1962): 126–149; Governor John Evans to Colonel John Chivington, September 21, 1863, in Indian Letter Book, Colorado State Archives, Denver, CO; Governor John Evans to Colonel John Chivington, November 7, 1863, in Letters Received, Office of

Indian Affairs, Colorado Superintendency, National Archives, Record
Group 75, Washington, DC.

22. Harry Edwards Kelsey Jr., *Frontier Capitalist: The Life of John Evans* (Denver:
State Historical Society of Colorado and Pruett Press, 1969), 142-168;
Gary L. Roberts, "Sand Creek: Tragedy and Symbol" (unpublished PhD
dissertation, University of Oklahoma, 1984), 254-255; Stan Hoig, *The Sand
Creek Massacre* (Norman: University of Oklahoma Press, 1961), 134.

23. Roberts, "Sand Creek: Tragedy and Symbol," 207; Major General Samuel
Curtis to Colonel John Chivington, June 20, 1864, *The War of the Rebel-
lion: A Compilation of the Official Records of the Union and Confederate Armies*
(Washington, DC: Government Printing Office, 1900) (hereafter *Official
Records of the War of the Rebellion*), Series I, XXXIV, Pt. 4, 595; Governor
John Evans to Colonel John Chivington, March 16, 1864, *Official Records
of the War of the Rebellion,* Series I, XXXIV, Pt. 2, 633-634; Major General
Samuel Curtis to Colonel John Chivington, April 8, 1864, *Official Records
of the War of the Rebellion,* Series I, XXXIV, Pt. 2, 85; Lieutenant George
Eayre to Colonel John Chivington, April 18, 1864, *Official Records of the
War of the Rebellion,* Series I, XXXIV, Pt. 1, 880-881.

24. "Very much . . ." from Captain Samuel Cook to Captain George Stilwell,
April 22, 1864, *Official Records of the War of the Rebellion,* Series I, XXXIV,
Pt. 3, 262. "I believe . . ." from Major Jacob Downing to Colonel John
Chivington, May 3, 1864, *Official Records of the War of the Rebellion,* Series
I, XXXIV, Pt. 3, 908. "The fate . . ." appears in Roberts, "Sand Creek:
Tragedy and Symbol," 234. See also Major Jacob Downing to Colonel
John Chivington, April 12, 1864, *Official Records of the War of the Rebellion,*
Series I, XXXIV, Pt. 3, 146; *Black Hawk Mining Journal,* April 14, 1864;
Rocky Mountain News, April 20, 1864; Colonel John Chivington to
Governor John Evans, April 15, 1864, *Official Records of the War of the
Rebellion,* Series I, XXXIV, Pt. 1, 883-884; Governor John Evans to Major
General Samuel Curtis, April 11, 1864, *Annual Reports, Commissioner of
Indian Affairs, 1864* (Washington, DC: Government Printing Office, 1865),
370; Governor John Evans to Major General Samuel Curtis, April 25,
1864, in Indian Letter Book, Colorado State Archives, Denver, CO;
Lieutenant George Eayre to Colonel John Chivington, May 19, 1864,
Official Records of the War of the Rebellion, Series I, XXXVI, Pt. 1, 935;
Colonel John Chivington to Major Edward Wynkoop, May 31, 1864,
Official Records of the War of the Rebellion, Series I, XXXIV, Pt. 4, 151.

25. "In a box . . ." from Henry Littleton Pitzer, *Three Frontiers: Memories and a
Portrait of Henry Littleton Pitzer as Recorded by His Son Robert Claiborne
Pitzer* (Muscatine, IA: Prairie Press, 1938), 162-163. See also Elmer R.
Burkey, "The Site of the Murder of the Hungate Family by Indians in

1864," *Colorado Magazine,* 12 (1935): 135–142; J. S. Brown and Thomas
J. Darrah to Governor John Evans, June 11, 1864, *Official Records of the
War of the Rebellion,* Series I, XXXIV, Pt. 4, 319–320; Alice Polk Hill, *Tales
of Colorado Pioneers* (Denver: Pierson and Gardner, 1884), 79–80; Nathaniel P. Hill, "Nathaniel P. Hill Inspects Colorado, Letters Written in
1864," *Colorado Magazine,* 33–34 (1956–1957): 245–246.

26. "All the . . ." from Hill, "Nathaniel P. Hill Inspects Colorado," 246.
"Every bell . . ." and "men, women . . ." from Hill, *Tales of Colorado
Pioneers,* 80. "Three thousand . . ." from Mollie D. Sanford, *Mollie: The
Journal of Mollie Dorsey Sanford in Nebraska and Colorado Territories,* ed.
Donald F. Daker (Lincoln: University of Nebraska Press, 1959), 187.

27. "Whole regiment" and "murdered and . . ." from Governor John Evans
to Major General Samuel Curtis, in Indian Letter Book, Colorado State
Archives, Denver, CO. See also Senate Executive Doc. 26, 39th Cong.,
2nd Sess., *Report of the Secretary of War, Communicating, in Compliance with
a Resolution of the Senate of February 4, 1867, a Copy of the Evidence Taken at
Denver and Fort Lyon, Colorado Territory, by a Military Commission Ordered
to Inquire into the Sand Creek Massacre, November, 1864* (Washington, DC:
Government Printing Office, 1867), 226; Governor John Evans to
Commissioner of Indian Affairs William Dole, June 15, 1864, Indian
Letter Book, Colorado State Archives, Denver, CO; *Annual Report of the
Commissioner of Indian Affairs, 1863* (Washington, DC: Government
Printing Office, 1864), 240; Governor John Evans to Secretary of War
Edwin P. Stanton, *Official Records of the War of the Rebellion,* Series I,
XXXIV, Pt. 4, 381; Brown and Darrah to Evans, June 11, 1864, 319–320.

28. "Cheyenne scalps . . ." from *Rocky Mountain News,* December 13, 1864.
"Trophies . . ." from *Rocky Mountain News,* December 28, 1864. "The
Battle of Sand Creek" from *Rocky Mountain News,* January 4, 1864.

29. "Ancestors could . . ." from Gail Ridgely, Sand Creek representative,
Northern Arapaho Tribe, interview by author, July 29, 2003, Denver, CO,
tape recording, in author's possession. See also Public Law 101-601,
November 16, 1990, Native American Graves Protection and Repatriation Act, http://www.nps.gov/history/nagpra/; Devon Abbott Mihesuah,
ed., *The Repatriation Reader: Who Owns American Indian Remains?* (Lincoln: University of Nebraska Press, 2000), 19–73, 95–105, 123–168,
180–189, 211–238, 294–306.

30. "Hunt all over . . ." from Luke Cahill, "Recollections of a Plainsman,"
unpublished manuscript ca. 1915, MSS 99, in Manuscripts Division,
Colorado Historical Society, Denver, CO. See also Lenore Barbian,
anatomical collections manager, National Anthropological Archives,
Smithsonian Institution, to Gary L. Roberts, National Park Service

contract historian, in Gary L. Roberts, "The Sand Creek Massacre Site: A Report on Washington Sources," January 1999 (unpublished manuscript), in FSCMNHS, now at NPS-WACC; United States Army Medical Museum Anatomical Section, "Records Relating to Specimens Transferred to the Smithsonian Institution," National Anthropological Archives, Smithsonian Institution, 1990, 7, in FSCMNHS, now at NPS-WACC; Scott Brown, museum technician, National Museum of Natural History and National Museum of Health and Medicine to Tom Killion, case officer, repatriation office, October 21, 1991, in Roberts, "The Sand Creek Massacre Site: A Report on Washington Sources"; War Department, Surgeon General's Office, *A Report of Surgical Cases Treated in the Army of the United States from 1865–1871* (Washington, DC: Government Printing Office, 1871), 15–16.

31. Rick Frost interview, June 11, 2003.

32. "Village controversy," from Norma Gorneau, member, Northern Cheyenne Tribe Sand Creek Massacre Descendants Committee, interview by author, July 1, 2004, Lame Deer, MT, tape recording, in author's possession. "The imperialist . . ." from Conrad Fisher interview, July 1, 2004. "With documents . . ." from Laird Cometsevah interview, May 12, 2003. See also Borowsky, "Where the Truth Lies," 113.

33. National Park Service, *Site Location Study*; National Park Service, *Special Resource Study*.

34. "Cordial" from Alexa Roberts, superintendent, Sand Creek Massacre National Historic Site, interview by author, April 29, 2004, telephone, notes in author's possession.

35. Quotes from Susan Collins, state archeologist and deputy state historic preservation officer, and David Halaas, chief historian, Colorado Historical Society, to Christine Whitacre, team captain, National Park Service, December 29, 1999, in FSCMNHS, now at NPS-WACC.

36. Quotes from David Halaas, director of publications, library, and archives, John Heinz History Center, interview by author, September 26, 2003, Pittsburgh, PA, tape recording, in author's possession. See also Douglas Scott interview, October 3, 2003; Colorado Senate Joint Resolution 99-017, "Draft," October 19, 1998, in File 6-10, "Civil War Monument, 2002," in Colorado Historical Society, Denver, CO; Robert Martinez, senator, Colorado State Senate, to David Halaas, chief historian, Colorado Historical Society, February 2, 1999, in File 6-10, "Civil War Monument, 2002"; David Halaas to Robert Martinez, May 5, 1999, in File 6-10, "Civil War Monument, 2002."

37. Quotes from Susan Collins and David Halaas to Christine Whitacre, March 27, 2000, in FSCMNHS, now at NPS-WACC. See also Rick Frost

to Susan Collins and David Halaas, March 8, 2000, in FSCMNHS, now at NPS-WACC.

38. "The Northern Arapaho Business..." from Ben S. Ridgely, cochairman, Northern Arapaho Business Council, to Rick Frost, National Park Service, Denver, Colorado, November 16, 1999, in FSCMNHS, now at NPS-WACC. "Looked at the data..." and "respected science" from Gail Ridgely interview, July 29, 2003. "You would think..." from James Doyle, Colorado communications director for Senator Ben Nighthorse Campbell, interview by author, June 10, 2003, Fort Collins, CO, tape recording, in author's possession. See also Christine Whitacre interview, May 27, 2003; Rick Frost interview, June 11, 2003.

39. "Sensationalism" from Gail Ridgely interview, July 29, 2003. "Hostility" from Ben Ridgely, Sand Creek representative, Northern Arapaho Tribe, interview by author, May 25, 2005, Denver, CO, tape recording, in author's possession. All other quotes from Laird and Colleen Cometse-vah, Southern Cheyenne Sand Creek descendants, interview by author, May 12, 2003, Denver, CO, tape recording, in author's possession. See also Alexa Roberts interview, April 29, 2003.

40. David Halaas interview, September 26, 2003. See also Tom Meier, "Arapahos at Sand Creek Per Written Record," January 10, 2000, in FSCMNHS, now at NPS-WACC; George Bent to George Hyde, April 30, 1913, Coe Collection, Beinecke Library, Yale University, New Haven, CT (hereafter Coe Collection); Bent to Hyde, October 23, 1914, Coe Collection; Bent to Hyde, January 20, 1915, Coe Collection.

41. "Shame is as big..." from *Report of the Commissioner of Indian Affairs for the Year 1865* (Washington, DC: Government Printing Office, 1865), 521. All other quotes from "Treaty with the Cheyenne and Arapaho, October 14, 1865," in Charles J. Kappler, *Indian Affairs: Laws and Treaties,* vol. 2 (Washington, DC: Government Printing Office, 1904), 887–891.

42. Bliss Kelly, attorney for Sand Creek Descendants, Inc., to Professor Raymond Carey, University of Denver, August 30, 1965, in Carey Collection, Box 2, Folder 10, Special Collections, Penrose Library, University of Denver, Denver, CO (hereafter Carey Collection); James E. Officer, associate commissioner, Bureau of Indian Affairs, U.S. Department of the Interior, to Professor Raymond Carey, University of Denver, January 3, 1966, in Carey Collection, Box 2, Folder 10.

43. Sam Dicke, Sand Creek Descendants, Inc., to Professor Raymond Carey, University of Denver, November 27, 1965, in Carey Collection, Box 2, Folder 10; Bliss Kelly to Professor Raymond Carey, July 30, 1965, in Carey Collection, Box 2, Folder 10; Bliss Kelly, to Professor Raymond Carey,

August 23, 1965, in Carey Collection, Box 2, Folder 10; *Rocky Mountain News,* December 24, 1864; Ethel M. Arnold, "The Blanket of Chief White Antelope," *Art and Archaeology* 28 (August 1929): 46; Roberts, "Sand Creek: Tragedy and Symbol," 711-714.

44. Dicke to Carey, November 27, 1965; Kelly to Carey, July 30, 1965; Kelly to Carey, August 23, 1965; Kelly to Carey, August 30, 1965; Nancy J. Arnold, chief clerk, Committee on Interior and Insular Affairs, to Professor Raymond Carey, University of Denver, July 16, 1965, in Carey Collection, Box 2, Folder 10; John Jarman, member of Congress, to Professor Raymond Carey, University of Denver, July 19, 1965, in Carey Collection, Box 2, Folder 10; Officer to Carey, January 3, 1966; Homer Flute and Robert Simpson, "Organization of Sand Creek Massacre Descendants' Trust," in author's possession; Homer Flute and Robert Simpson, "Analysis of Southern Cheyenne-Arapaho Claims, Sand Creek Massacre," in author's possession; H.R. 1705, 83rd Cong., 1st Sess., 1953; H.R. 6178, 85th Cong., 1st Sess., 1957; H.R. 5513, 89th Cong., 1st Sess., 1965.

45. Quote from Laird and Colleen Cometsevah interview, May 12, 2003. See also Roberts, "Sand Creek: Tragedy and Symbol," 716-719.

46. "Every time the . . ." from Laird and Colleen Cometsevah interview, May 12, 2003. "Our people didn't . . ." from Steve Brady interview, August 29, 2004.

47. Quotes from Steve Brady interview, August 29, 2004. See also Laird and Colleen Cometsevah interview, May 12, 2003.

48. Quotes from Rick Frost, National Park Service project manager, Sand Creek Site Location Study, to the Honorable Ben Nighthorse Campbell, United States Senator, January 13, 2000, in FSCMNHS, now at NPS-WACC. See also Rick Frost to Gail Ridgely, Northern Arapaho Sand Creek representative, January 20, 2000, in FSCMNHS, now at NPS-WACC.

49. Quotes from Ben Nighthorse Campbell, U.S. senator, interview by author, September 10, 2003, telephone, tape recording, in author's possession. See also Alice Murray, *Historical Memories of the Japanese American Internment and the Struggle for Redress* (Palo Alto, CA: Stanford University Press, 2007), 1-13, 333-381, 436-442; Mary Frances Berry, *My Face Is Black Is True: Callie House and the Struggle for Ex-slave Reparations* (New York: Vintage, 2006), 3-74, 173-182, 230-241; Eric K. Yamamoto, "What's Next? Japanese American Redress and African American Reparations," in Michael T. Martin and Marilyn Yaquinto, eds., *Redress for Historical Injustices in the United States: On Reparations for Slavery, Jim Crow, and Their Legacies* (Durham, NC: Duke University Press, 2007), 411-426; Adrienne D. Davis, "The Case for U.S. Reparations for African

Americans," in Martin and Yaquinto, *Redress for Historical Injustices in the United States,* 371–378; Charles P. Henry, "The Politics of Racial Reparations," in Martin and Yaquinto, *Redress for Historical Injustices in the United States,* 353–370; Martha Biondi, "The Rise of the Reparations Movement," in Martin and Yaquinto, *Redress for Historical Injustices in the United States,* 255–274; James Doyle interview, June 10, 2003.

50. Steve Brady interview, August 29, 2004; Laird and Colleen Cometsevah interview, May 12, 2003; National Park Service, *Special Resource Study,* 20.

51. "Fraud" from Laird Cometsevah interview, May 12, 2003. All other quotes from Homer Flute, president, Sand Creek Descendants Trust, interview by author, December 20, 2004, Anadarko, OK, tape recording, in author's possession. See also Flute and Simpson, "Organization of Sand Creek Massacre Descendants' Trust."

52. "So he talked to . . ." from Steve Brady interview, September 12, 2003. See also Homer Flute interview, December 20, 2004.

53. "It was big" and "seemed like . . ." from Steve Chestnut interview, February 6, 2004. "We showed . . ." from Joe Big Medicine interview, July 8, 2003.

54. Quotes from Laird Cometsevah, chief, Southern Cheyenne Tribe, to Rick Frost, project director, Sand Creek Massacre Project, National Park Service, April 25, 2000, in FSCMNHS, now at NPS-WACC. See also National Park Service, *Special Resource Study,* 20.

55. Quote from National Park Service, *Special Resource Study,* 121. See also pp. 117–122.

56. Ibid., 122–127.

57. Ibid., 125–130.

58. Joe Big Medicine interview, July 8, 2003; Alexa Roberts interview, April 29, 2004; National Park Service, *Special Resource Study,* 21.

59. National Park Service, *Site Location Study;* National Park Service, *Special Resource Study.*

60. Christine Whitacre interview, May 27, 2003.

61. Quotes from National Park Service, *Site Location Study,* 287–288 (emphasis added), 291, 291–292.

62. "Throughout this . . . ," "they believe . . . ," "there also are . . . ," and "Consultation associated . . ." from National Park Service, *Special Resource Study,* 14, 16. "I honestly . . ." from Laird Cometsevah interview, May 12, 2003.

63. National Park Service, *Special Resource Study,* 41–132.

64. Ibid., 41–42.

65. Hyde, *Life of George Bent,* 64–67, 168–197; Major Scott J. Anthony to Major B. S. Henning, December 15, 1864, *Official Records of the War of the*

Rebellion, Series I, XLI, Pt. 1, 952; Major B. S. Henning to Lieutenant J. E. Tappan, December 14, 1864, *Official Records of the War of the Rebellion,* Series I, XLI, Pt. 4, 852; George Bird Grinnell, *The Fighting Cheyennes* (Norman: University of Oklahoma Press, 1915), 181–190; Colonel R. R. Livingston to General R. B. Mitchell, January 8, 1865, *Official Records of the War of the Rebellion,* Series I, XLVII, Pt. 1, 463; Eugene F. Ware, *The Indian War of 1864* (Lincoln: University of Nebraska Press, 1960), 340–397; Leroy R. Hafen, *The Overland Mail, 1849–1869* (Glendale, CA: Arthur H. Clark, 1926), 261–267.

66. Quotes from Major General John Pope to Secretary of War Edwin M. Stanton, February 6, 1864, *Official Records of the War of the Rebellion,* Series I, XXXIV, Pt. 2, 259–264. See also Richard N. Ellis, *General Pope and U.S. Indian Policy* (Albuquerque: University of New Mexico Press, 1970), 26–74.

67. Grenville Mellon Dodge, *The Indian Campaign of Winter 1864–1865* (Denver: Colorado Commandery of the Loyal Legion of the United States of America, 1907), 1–20; Stanley P. Hirchson, *Grenville M. Dodge: Soldier, Politician, Railroad Pioneer* (Bloomington: Indiana University Press, 1967), 115–118; Dee Brown, *The Galvanized Yankees* (Lincoln: University of Nebraska Press, 1963), 12–47, 112–155; Donald J. Berthrong, *The Southern Cheyenne* (Norman: University of Oklahoma Press, 1963), 207–240; Robert M. Utley, *Frontiersmen in Blue: The United States Army and the Indian, 1848–1865* (Lincoln: University of Nebraska Press, 1991), 281–340; Bent to Hyde, March 24, 1905, Coe Collection; Bent to Hyde, March 4, 1906, Coe Collection; Bent to Hyde, November 5, 1913, Coe Collection; Hyde, *Life of George Bent,* 192–211.

68. Quote from Senator James Doolittle to Secretary of the Interior James Harlan, May 31, 1865, *Official Records of the War of the Rebellion,* Series I, XLVIII, Pt. 2, 868–869. See also Utley, *Frontiersmen in Blue,* 309–320; General Alexander M. McCook to Major General John Pope, May 31, 1865, *Official Records of the War of the Rebellion,* Series I, XLVIII, Pt. 2, 707.

69. Commissioner of Indian Affairs William Dole to Secretary of the Interior James Harlan, July 6, 1865, Letters Received, Secretary of the Interior, Indian Division, National Archives, Record Group 48, Washington, DC; Secretary of the Interior James Harlan to Major General John Pope, July 6, 1865, *Official Records of the War of the Rebellion,* Series I, XLVIII, Pt. 2, 1056–1057; Secretary of the Interior James Harlan to Commissioner of Indian Affairs Dennis N. Cooley, July 11, 1865, Letters Sent, Secretary of the Interior, Indian Division, Vol. 5, 283, National Archives, Record Group 48.

70. "The history..." from *New York Times,* July 29, 1865. "Rested with..." from Commissioner Samuel Tappan to Senator Charles Sumner, April 10, 1865, Letters Received, Office of Indian Affairs, Colorado Superintendency, National Archives, Record Group 75. See also Senate Ex. Doc. No. 94, 40th Cong., 2nd Sess., *Message from the President of the United States Transmitting Report of the Indian Peace Commission* (Washington, DC: Government Printing Office, 1868), 4–19.

71. National Park Service, *Special Resource Study,* 43.

72. "A little bit..." and "anything to..." from Ben Nighthorse Campbell interview, September 10, 2003. "Let's take..." and "if you..." from Alyssa Fisher, "A Sight Which Can Never Be Forgotten," *Archaeology* (September 16, 2003), http://www.archaeology.org/online/features /massacre/index.html.

73. Gary L. Roberts and David Fridtjof Halaas, "Written in Blood: The Soule-Cramer Sand Creek Massacre Letters," *Colorado Heritage* (Winter 2001): 29; Percy Ednalino, "Sand Creek Letters Go to Senate," *Denver Post,* September 16, 2000, B-9; Dick Kreck, "Historians Skirmishing over Sand Creek Letters," *Denver Post,* September 20, 2000, A-2.

74. Quotes from Roberts and Halaas, "Written in Blood," 29, 25.

75. Quotes from Steve Brady interview, August 29, 2003. See also "Programs," in Sand Creek Massacre Healing Runs, 2001-2008, Northern Cheyenne Sand Creek Office, Lame Deer, MT.

76. Colonel Edward Wynkoop to General James Ford, January 16, 1865, *Official Records of the War of the Rebellion,* Series I, XLI, Pt. 1, 959–962; Colonel Edward Wynkoop to Lieutenant J. E. Tappan, January 15, 1865, *Official Records of the War of the Rebellion,* Series I, XLI, Pt. 1, 959–961; Major General Samuel P. Curtis to Governor John Evans, January 12, 1865, *Official Records of the War of the Rebellion,* Series I, XLVIII, Pt. 1, 504; Major General Samuel P. Curtis to Colonel Thomas Moonlight, January 12, 1865, *Official Records of the War of the Rebellion,* Series I, XLVIII, Pt. 1, 511; Major General Samuel P. Curtis to Major General Henry Halleck, January 12, 1865, *Official Records of the War of the Rebellion,* Series I, XLVIII, Pt. 1, 502; Roberts and Halaas, "Written in Blood," 29–32; Roberts, "Sand Creek: Tragedy and Symbol," 457–459, 471.

77. Quote appears in Roberts, "Sand Creek: Tragedy and Symbol," 492. See also *Rocky Mountain News,* April 24, 25, and 27, 1865.

78. *Rocky Mountain News,* October 11, 25, November 1, 22, December 8, 1865. See also Roberts, "Sand Creek: Tragedy and Symbol," 495–498.

79. Quotes from *Hearing before the Subcommittee on National Parks, Historic Preservation, and Recreation of the Committee on Energy and Natural*

Resources, United States Senate, 106 Congress, 2 Session, September 14, 2000 (Washington, DC: U.S. Government Printing Office, 2001), 3, 5. See also Steve Brady interview, August 29, 2003.

80. Quotes from *Hearing before the Subcommittee on National Parks,* 19. See also pp. 9, 19, and 26 and Bill MacAllister, "Memorial at Sand Creek OK'd," *Denver Post,* October 24, 2000, A-1.

81. "More of a confirmation . . ." from Ednalino, "Sand Creek Letters Go to Senate," B-4. "Everything that came later" and "dazzling" from Kreck, "Historians Skirmishing over Sand Creek Letters," A-2. See also "Dark Side of Sand Creek," *Denver Post,* September 16, 2000, B-7; Bob Scott, "There's More to Sand Creek Letters Than Meets Eye," *Rocky Mountain News,* September 22, 2000, A-54.

82. Quotes from Public Law 106-465. See also Acting Director, National Park Service, to Regional Director, Intermountain Region, National Park Service, November 21, 2000, "Activation: P.L. 106-465, Sand Creek Massacre National Historic Site Establishment Act of 2000," in FSCMNHS, now at NPS-WACC.

83. Quotes from Public Law 106-465. See also Acting Director to Regional Director, November 21, 2000.

5. INDELIBLE INFAMY

1. Details of the powwow at Lame Deer from Norma Gorneau, member, Northern Cheyenne Tribe Sand Creek Massacre Descendants Committee, interview by author, July 1, 2004, Lame Deer, MT, tape recording, in author's possession. "Like we had accomplished . . ." from Otto Braided Hair, director, Northern Cheyenne Sand Creek Office, interview by author, May 11, 2007, telephone, notes in author's possession. "The spirits can finally rest" from Gail Ridgely, Sand Creek representative, Northern Arapaho Tribe, interview by author, July 29, 2003, Denver, CO, tape recording, in author's possession. "Generations will die out . . ." from Laird Cometsevah, chief, Southern Cheyenne Tribe, interview by author, May 12, 2003, Denver, CO, tape recording, in author's possession. See also Jim Hughes, "Tribe Fetes Sand Creek Designation," *Denver Post,* November 12, 2000, A-1.

2. "We now have . . ." from J. Sebastian Sinisi, "Senator: Preserve Sad, Painful Sites," *Denver Post,* February 2, 2001, B-4. "After years . . ." from "Sand Creek Memorial a Go," *Denver Post,* November 10, 2000, B-8. "America's increasing . . ." and "monuments can . . ." from "Sand Creek Now Belongs to All," *Omaha World-Herald,* October 31, 2000, A-14. See also Bill McKallister, "Memorial at Sand Creek OK'd," *Denver Post,* October 24, 2000, A-1.

3. "Delighted" from William Dawson, interview by author, June 18, 2003, Eads, CO, tape recording, in author's possession. See also Public Law 106-465.

4. "I thought . . ." and "fought tooth . . ." from William Dawson interview, June 18, 2003.

5. Quotes from William Dawson interview, June 18, 2003. See also Lysa Wegman-French and Christine Whitacre, "Interim Report No. 2 Historical Research on the Sand Creek Massacre Site," 8–9, 35, in uncataloged files of the Sand Creek Massacre National Historic Site (FSCMNHS), currently held by National Park Service, Western Archeological and Conservation Center (NPS-WACC), Tucson, AZ; Wilbur F. Stone, ed., *History of Colorado,* vol. 4 (Chicago: S. J. Clark, 1918), 239–240.

6. Quotes from Douglas Scott, chief archeologist, National Park Service Midwest Archeological Center, interview by author, October 3, 2003, telephone, tape recording, in author's possession. See also Jerome Greene, research historian, National Park Service, interview by author, May 27, 2003, Denver, CO, tape recording, in author's possession; William Dawson interview, June 18, 2003; Laird Cometsevah interview, May 12, 2003; Steve Brady, headman, Crazy Dogs Society, Northern Cheyenne Tribe, interview by author, August 29, 2004, Lame Deer, MT, tape recording, in author's possession.

7. Quote from William Dawson interview, June 18, 2003. See also National Park Service, Intermountain Region, *Sand Creek Massacre Project,* vol. 2: *Special Resource Study* (Denver: National Park Service, Intermountain Region, 2000), 85, 115; "Briefing Statement, National Park Service, Sand Creek Massacre National Historic Site, February 5, 2001," in FSCMNHS, now at NPS-WACC; "Weekly List of Actions Taken on Properties: September 23, 2001–September 30, 2001," National Register of Historic Places, http://www.nps.gov/history/nr/listings/20011005.htm.

8. "No such thing . . ." from "Notes, National Park Service, Consultation Meeting, Sand Creek Massacre National Historic Site, Las Animas, Colorado, January 24, 2002," in FSCMNHS, now at NPS-WACC. "Inflexibility infuriating" and "negotiating ploy" from William Dawson interview, June 18, 2003. See also Laird Cometsevah, Cheyenne traditional chief, to Robert Tabor, chairman, 33rd Business Committee, Cheyenne-Arapaho Tribes of Oklahoma, March 16, 2002, Clinton, OK, in FSCMNHS, now at NPS-WACC; "Notes, National Park Service, Consultation Meeting, Sand Creek Massacre National Historic Site, Denver, Colorado, February 27, 2001," in FSCMNHS, now at NPS-WACC; "Notes, National Park Service, Consultation Meeting, Sand Creek Massacre National Historic Site, Lame Deer, Montana, June 6,

2001," in FSCMNHS, now at NPS-WACC; "Notes, National Park
Service, Consultation Meeting, Sand Creek Massacre National Historic
Site, Eads, Colorado, February 28, 2001," in FSCMNHS, now at NPS-
WACC; "National Park Service, Director's Order # 25: Land Protection,"
January 19, 2001, http://www.nps.gov/policy/DOrders/DOrder25.html.

9. "Dedicated to advancing . . ." from "Who We Are," Conservation Fund,
http://www.conservationfund.org/who_we_are. "We are pleased . . ."
from "Briefing Statement, National Park Service, Sand Creek Massacre
National Historic Site, October 21, 2002," in FSCMNHS, now at
NPS-WACC. See also Ben Nighthorse Campbell, U.S. senator, to Karen
Wade, regional director, National Park Service, January 7, 2002, in
FSCMNHS, now at NPS-WACC; "Contract Made to Buy 240 Acres for
Sand Creek Massacre Site," *Watonga Republican,* January 16, 2002, B-12;
Kit Miniclier, "Sand Creek Site Parcel on Block," *Denver Post,* March 8,
2002, B-1; Joe Big Medicine, "Sand Creek Massacre Site Land Acquisi-
tion in Progress," *Watonga Republican,* August 8, 2001, n.p., in FSCMNHS,
now at NPS-WACC; "Briefing Statement, National Park Service, Sand
Creek Massacre National Historic Site, March 6, 2002," in FSCMNHS,
now at NPS-WACC; Conservation Fund to Tribal Representatives,
December 14, 2001, in FSCMNHS, now at NPS-WACC; Conservation
Fund, http://www.conservationfund.org/search/node/sand+creek;
William Dawson interview, June 18, 2003.

10. "Collected . . ." and "sand pits" from National Park Service, Intermountain Region, *Sand Creek Massacre Project,* vol. 1: *Site Location Study*
(Denver: National Park Service, Intermountain Region, 2000), 127 and
135, respectively. "We've never had an issue . . ." from Chuck and Sheri
Bowen, interview by author, August 8, 2003, Lamar, CO, tape recording,
in author's possession.

11. "Compromise" from "Ranchers Oppose Historic Site," *Rocky Mountain
News,* May 16, 2000, A-7. All other quotes from Chuck and Sheri Bowen
interview, August 8, 2003. See also Chuck and Sheri Bowen, "Bowens
Undertake Sand Creek Massacre Research," *Watonga Republican,*
January 1, 2003, B-11.

12. Alexa Roberts, superintendent, Sand Creek Massacre National Historic
Site, interview by author, August 26, 2004, telephone, notes in author's
possession.

13. Quotes from Douglas Scott interview, October 3, 2003. See also Douglas
Scott, Great Plains team leader, to Alexa Roberts, site manager, Sand
Creek Massacre National Historic Site, "Trip Report for 9/17/02,"
e-mail, October 7, 2002, in FSCMNHS, now at NPS-WACC.

14. "In what ways . . ." from Chuck Bowen to Alexa Roberts, e-mail, November 4, 2002, in FSCMNHS, now at NPS-WACC. "Our work . . ." from Douglas Scott to Chuck Bowen, e-mail, December 6, 2002, in FSCMNHS, now at NPS-WACC. See also Jefferson Broome to Douglas Scott, e-mail, October 2, 2002, in FSCMNHS, now at NPS-WACC; Douglas Scott interview, October 3, 2003.

15. Quotes from Janet Frederick, director, Kiowa County Economic Development Corporation, interview by author, June 17, 2003, Eads, CO, tape recording, in author's possession. See also Rod Brown, Kiowa County Commissioner, interview by author, June 17, 2003, Eads, CO, tape recording, in author's possession; Rod Johnson, member, Kiowa County Economic Development Corporation, interview by author, June 17, 2003, Eads, CO, tape recording, in author's possession.

16. "We had all traded . . ." from Rod Brown interview, June 17, 2003. "Gateway community," "rubber tomahawk syndrome," and "a lot in common . . ." from Rod Johnson interview, June 17, 2003.

17. "We've got . . ." from Rod Johnson interview, June 17, 2003. "Ranching-type people" from Rod Brown interview, June 17, 2003.

18. Alexa Roberts, handwritten text of an untitled presentation, Fort Lewis College, October 18, 2001, in FSCMNHS, now at NPS-WACC.

19. Rod Johnson interview, June 17, 2003; Rod Brown interview, June 17, 2003.

20. "Identify with . . ." from Janet Frederick interview, June 17, 2003. All other quotes from Ruthanna Jacobs, director, Kiowa County Museum, interview by author, June 18, 2003, Eads, CO, tape recording, in author's possession.

21. Two of the three inquiries have been collected in John M. Carroll, ed., *Sand Creek Massacre: A Documentary History, 1865–1867* (New York: Amereon Limited, 1985).

22. "Letters received . . ." and "Congressional investigation" from *Rocky Mountain News,* December 29, 1864. "Perhaps it was wrong . . ." and "can only . . ." from *Black Hawk Mining Journal,* January 5, 1865. "It is . . ." and "confessed murderers . . ." from *Rocky Mountain News,* January 30, 1865. "Political ambition" and "put money . . ." from *Rocky Mountain News,* January 31, 1865.

23. "On account . . ." from Major Scott J. Anthony to Colonel Thomas Moonlight, January 21, 1865, *Rocky Mountain News,* February 1, 1865. All other quotes from Colonel Edward Wynkoop to General James Ford, January 16, 1865, *The War of the Rebellion: A Compilation of the Official Records of the Union and Confederate Armies* (Washington, DC: Government Printing Office, 1900) (hereafter *Official Records of the War of the*

Rebellion), Series I, XLI, Pt. 1, 959–962. See also *Congressional Globe,* 38th Cong., 2nd Sess., Pt. 1, 158, 173, 250–255; General Henry Halleck to General Samuel R. Curtis, January 11, 1865, in "Massacre of the Cheyenne Indians," in *Report of the Joint Committee on the Conduct of War* (Washington, DC: Government Printing Office, 1865), 74; General Samuel R. Curtis to Colonel Thomas Moonlight, January 13, 1865, *Official Records of the War of the Rebellion,* Series I, XLVIII, Pt. 1, 511.

24. Quotes from Statement of Commissioner Samuel F. Tappan, in "Report of the Secretary of War," 39th Cong., 2nd Sess., Senate Exec. Doc. 26, 8. See also Curtis to Moonlight, January 13, 1865; Colonel Thomas Moonlight to Commissioner Samuel F. Tappan, February 12, 1865, in "Report of the Secretary of War," 39th Cong., 2nd Sess., Senate Exec. Doc. 26, 3–4; *Rocky Mountain News,* February 8, 16, 22, 1865.

25. Moonlight to Tappan, February 12, 1865; *Rocky Mountain News,* February 9, 16, 1865; Testimony of Silas S. Soule, in "Report of the Secretary of War," 39th Cong., 2nd Sess., Senate Exec. Doc., 8–29.

26. Quotes from Report of the Judge Advocate General in the Case of Colonel John M. Chivington, First Colorado Volunteer Cavalry, as quoted in Gary L. Roberts, "Sand Creek: Tragedy and Symbol" (unpublished PhD dissertation, University of Oklahoma, 1984), 497–498. See also T. Harry Williams, *Lincoln and the Radicals* (Madison: University of Wisconsin Press, 1941), 69–72; Hans L. Trefousse, "The Joint Committee on the Conduct of War: A Reassessment," *Civil War History* 10 (1964): 5–19; Deposition of John M. Chivington, in "Report of the Secretary of War," 39th Cong., 2nd Sess., Senate Exec. Doc. 26, 103–108.

27. "Massacre of the Cheyenne Indians," in *Report of the Joint Committee on the Conduct of War,* iii–v.

28. "Bloody offense" from *Washington Chronicle,* July 21, 1865. "An act . . ." from *Chicago Tribune,* August 26, 1865. "Of a few . . ." from *Weekly Rocky Mountain News,* June 7, 1865. "At present . . ." quoted in *Rocky Mountain News,* August 19, 1865. See also *Nebraska City News,* February 1, 1865.

29. Quotes from Miniclier, "Sand Creek Site Parcel on Block," B-1. See also David Melmer, "Owner Stalls Sand Creek Historic Site," *Indian Country Today,* March 20, 2002.

30. "Traditional . . ." from Laird Cometsevah interview, May 12, 2003. See also Cometsevah to Tabor, March 16, 2002; "Jim Druck Travels to Make Case for Extending Gaming Contract," *Watonga Republican,* April 30, 2003, B-4; "Briefing Statement, National Park Service, Sand Creek Massacre National Historic Site, April 30, 2002," in FSCMNHS, now at NPS-WACC; William Dawson interview, June 18, 2003.

31. Quotes from William Dawson interview, June 18, 2003. See also Steve Brady interview, August 29, 2004.

32. Quotes from Jim Druck, president, Southwest Entertainment, interview by author, March 14, 2003, Pine, CO, tape recording, in author's possession. See also "Purchase Agreement Reported for Dawson Land at Sand Creek," *Watonga Republican,* May 1, 2002, B-4.

33. "Win-win" from Kit Miniclier, "Site of Sand Creek Massacre Sold," *Denver Post,* April 26, 2002, B-1. "Sand Creek . . ." from Katie Kerwin McCrimmon, "Sand Creek Healing Can Begin," *Rocky Mountain News,* April 27, 2002, B-2. "Thanks to . . ." from "Honoring Sand Creek," *Denver Post,* April 29, 2002, B-7. "If Ground Zero . . ." from Pablo Mora, "Sacred Soil," *Pueblo Chieftain,* May 2, 2002, B-1. "The Cheyenne . . ." from Clara Bushyhead, "Southern Cheyenne and Arapaho Tribes Acquire Massacre Site in Colorado," *Southern Cheyenne and Arapaho Nation News* no. 1 (May 2002): 1. See also Owen Good, "Sand Creek Massacre Site Returns to Indians," *Rocky Mountain News,* April 29, 2002, A-5; David Phinney, "Indians Celebrate Sand Creek Memorial Purchase," *Pueblo Chieftain,* May 9, 2002, B-1; "Purchase Agreement Reported for Dawson Land at Sand Creek," B-4; Sam Lewin, "Tribe Purchases Massacre Site," *Native American Times,* December 17, 2003, in FSCMNHS, now at NPS-WACC.

34. "Dedicated steward . . ." from Ben Nighthorse Campbell, U.S. senator, interview by author, September 10, 2003, telephone, tape recording, in author's possession. "A friend . . ." from Laird Cometsevah interview, May 12, 2003.

35. Quotes from Chris Leppek, "Sand Creek: A Genocide Finds a Jewish Redeemer," *Intermountain Jewish News,* February 27, 2004, 28–36. See also Jim Druck interview, March 14, 2003; Miniclier, "Site of Sand Creek Massacre Sold," B-1.

36. "We'll just . . ." from Alexa Roberts, interview by author, September 27, 2004, telephone, notes in author's possession. "The sufficiency . . ." from "Briefing Statement, National Park Service, Sand Creek Massacre National Historic Site, February 27, 2003," in FSCMNHS, now at NPS-WACC. "When Jim Druck . . ." from James Doyle, Colorado communications director for Senator Ben Nighthorse Campbell, interview by author, June 10, 2003, Fort Collins, CO, tape recording, in author's possession.

37. "The first thing . . ." from Rod Brown interview, June 17, 2003. "There's more . . ." from James Doyle interview, June 10, 2003.

38. "Less than five . . . ," "Are we going . . . ," "I didn't want . . . ," and "It's far too . . ." from Jim Druck interview, March 14, 2003. "Mr. Druck paid . . ." from William Dawson interview, June 18, 2003.

39. Quotes from "Purchase Agreement Reported for Dawson Land at Sand Creek," B-4. See also "Sand Creek Land Buy Proposal under Study," *Watonga Republican,* April 24, 2002, B-4; "Jim Druck Travels to Make Case for Extending Gaming Contract," B-4; Kit Miniclier, "'Glitch' Delays Sand Creek Land Deal: Purchase for Massacre Memorial on Hold," *Denver Post,* August 7, 2002, B-8.

40. Quotes from Colorado Senate Joint Resolution 99-017 in File 6-10, "Civil War Monument, 2002," in Colorado Historical Society, Denver, CO. See also Robert Martinez, senator, Colorado State Senate, to David F. Halaas, chief historian, Colorado Historical Society, facsimile, Februrary 22, 1999, in File 6-10; David F. Halaas to Robert Martinez, March 15, 1999, in File 6-10; Georgianna Contiguglia, president, Colorado Historical Society, to Robert Martinez, January 20, 1999, in File 6-10. See also "Staff Summary of Capital Development Committee, Agenda Item #3, September 15, 1998," in File 6-10; Dottie Wham, senator, Colorado State Senate, and chair, Capitol Development Committee, to Tony Grampsas, representative, Colorado House of Representatives, and chair, Capitol Building Advisory Committee, September 17, 1998, in File 6-10; Betty Chronic, vice chair, Capitol Building Advisory Committee, to Dottie Wham, July 31, 1998, in File 6-10; "Summary of Meeting: State Capitol Building Advisory Committee, House Committee Room 0109, State Capitol Building, July 31, 1998," 1–2, in File 6-10.

41. Quotes from Joan Johnson, vice chairman, Capitol Building Advisory Committee, State of Colorado, to Terry Phillips, chairman, Capital Development Committee, State of Colorado, October 2, 2002, in File 6-10, "Civil War Monument, 2002." See also Georgianna Contiguglia, president, Colorado Historical Society, to Modupe Lobode, chief historian, Colorado Historical Society, and Brian Shaw, director, Colorado Roadside Interpretation Project, Colorado Historical Society, e-mail, May 22, 2002, in File 6-10; Brian Shaw to Georgianna Contiguglia, e-mail, May 23, 2002, in File 6-10; "Staff Summary of Meeting, Capitol Building Advisory Committee, June 28, 2002," in File 6-10; Modupe Lobode to Brian Shaw, e-mail, July 25, 2002, in File 6-10; Brian Shaw to Modupe Lobode, e-mail, July 30, 2002, in File 6-10; "Proposed Agenda, State Capitol Building Advisory Committee, August 16, 2002," in File 6-10; Georgianna Contiguglia to Steve Tammeus, legislative council staff, Colorado State Legislature; Joan Johnson, vice chairman, Capitol Building Advisory Committee, State of Colorado; Brian Shaw; and Modupe Lobode, e-mail, August 20, 2002, in File 6-10; Steve Tammeus to Modupe Lobode and Brian Shaw, e-mail, September 11,

2002, in File 6-10; Modupe Lobode to Steve Tammeus and Georgianna Contiguglia, e-mail, September 11, 2002, in File 6-10; "Agenda, Capital Development Committee, October 2, 2002," in File 6-10; Steve Tammeus to Georgianna Contiguglia, e-mail, October 3, 2002, in File 6-10.

42. Quotes from Steve Tammeus, legislative council staff, Colorado State Legislature, to Joan Johnson, vice chairman, Capitol Building Advisory Committee, State of Colorado; Karen Wilde-Rogers, director, Colorado Commission of Indian Affairs; Georgianna Contiguglia, president, Colorado Historical Society; Heather Wittwer, deputy legal council, office of the governor, State of Colorado; Modupe Lobode, chief historian, Colorado Historical Society; Brian Shaw, director, Colorado Roadside Interpretation Project, Colorado Historical Society; and Scott Grosscup, Colorado State Capitol Advisory Committee, e-mail, October 24, 2002, in File 6-10, "Civil War Monument, 2002." See also "Text Draft, Sand Creek Massacre Plaque," January 10, April 11, August 16, 2002, in File 6-10.

43. Quotes from Deborah Frazier, "138 Years after Sand Creek, 'Our People Are Still Here,'" *Rocky Mountain News,* November 30, 2002, A-1. See also Robert Tabor, "Sand Creek Trip Culminates in Druck's Purchase of Land," *Watonga Republican,* December 4, 2002, B-4; Kit Miniclier, "Sand Creek History Corrected," *Denver Post,* December 1, 2002, B-1; Robert Weller, "History Is Corrected at State Capitol," *Pueblo Chieftain,* November 30, 2002, A-1; Deborah Frazier, "Honoring Hallowed Ground," *Rocky Mountain News,* November 28, 2002, A-34; "Dedication Ceremony for the Sand Creek Interpretive Plaque, West Steps, State Capitol, November 29, 2002," in File 6-10, "Civil War Monument, 2002"; "Sand Creek Ceremony, Program Presenters," in File 6-10; Otto Braided Hair interview, May 11, 2007.

44. Quotes from "Civil War Memorial," in File 6-10, "Civil War Monument, 2002"; emphasis added. See also Modupe Lobode, chief historian, Colorado Historical Society, interview by author, June 3, 2005, Denver, CO, tape recording, in author's possession.

45. "Colorado and . . . ," "a mob of 700 . . . ," and "The effort . . ." from "Anniversary of a Massacre," *Denver Post,* November 29, 2002, B-7. All other quotes from Laird Cometsevah interview, May 12, 2003.

46. Roberts, "Sand Creek: Tragedy and Symbol," xi–xii, 453; *Black Hawk Mining Journal,* December 20, 1864, and January 4, February 18 and 24, 1865; "Anniversary of a Massacre," B-7.

47. Quotes from Laird and Colleen Cometsevah, Southern Cheyenne Sand Creek descendants, interview by author, May 12, 2003, Denver, CO, tape recording, in author's possession.

48. Quote from Jim Druck interview, March 14, 2003. See also "Jim Druck Travels to Make Case for Extending Gaming Contract," B-4.

49. Quote from Alexa Roberts interview, September 27, 2004. See also Jim Druck interview, March 14, 2003.

50. "Did you see . . ." from author's notes, Annual Assembly of the Order of the Indian Wars, Colorado Springs, CO, September 4, 2003, in author's possession. "Twenty-Fourth Annual Assembly of the Order of the Indian Wars, September 4–6, 2003," conference program, in FSCMNHS, now at NPS-WACC.

51. Quotes from Jerry Russell, CEO, Order of the Indian Wars, interview by author, September 12, 2003, telephone, tape recording, in author's possession. See also Order of the Indian Wars, http://www.indianwars .com/; "An Arkansas Original," *Arkansas Democrat-Gazette,* December 11, 2003, 20; "Jerry L. Russell: His Jingles Left Mark on Political Contests," *Arkansas Democrat-Gazette,* December 6, 2003, 14.

52. "It's tedious . . . ," "the Sand Creek Battlefield," "decision to . . . ," and "When did . . ." from Jerry Russell interview, September 12, 2003. All other quotes from Jerry L. Russell, "Refighting the Civil War: Park Service Wants to Talk about the Causes," *Arkansas Democrat-Gazette,* October 20, 2002, 92.

53. Quote from Jerry Russell interview, September 12, 2003. See also Stephen Deere, "Historian Dee Brown Dead at 94," *Arkansas Democrat-Gazette,* December 13, 2002, 20; Douglas Martin, "Dee Brown, 94, Author Who Revised Image of West," *New York Times,* December 14, 2002, A-27; "Dee Brown: Bury His Spirit at Wounded Knee," *Arkansas Democrat-Gazette,* December 17, 2002, 12; T. Louise Freeman-Toole, "Dee Brown's Legacy Lives On," *Arkansas Democrat-Gazette,* December 14, 2003, 100.

54. "Permanent Indian . . . ," "the culture . . . ," and "it was . . ." from Dee Brown, *Bury My Heart at Wounded Knee: An Indian History of the American West* (New York: Henry Holt, 1970), 7, xvii, 445. "I'm a very old Indian . . ." from Martin, "Dee Brown, 94," A-27.

55. Quotes from Brown, *Bury My Heart at Wounded Knee,* 86, 90.

56. "Polemic" from Thomas F. Schilz, "The Indian Frontier of the American West: An Indian History of the American West, by Robert F. Utley," *American Indian Quarterly* 8 (Autumn 1984): 351. "Believing that . . ." from Tom Philips, "Bury My Heart at Wounded Knee: An Indian History of the American West, by Dee Brown," *Wisconsin Magazine of History* 55 (Spring 1972): 250. "Committed errors" and "distorted . . ." from Henry E. Fritz, "Bury My Heart at Wounded Knee: An Indian History of the American West, by Dee Brown," *Pacific Historical Review* 41 (November

1972): 539. All other quotes from Francis Paul Prucha, "Bury My Heart at Wounded Knee: An Indian History of the American West, by Dee Brown," *American Historical Review,* 77 (April 1972): 589.

57. "Original . . ." and "it is a book . . ." from Thomas Lask, "'A People's Dream Died There,'" *New York Times,* February 2, 1971, BR-35. "The first accurate . . . ," "this is a book . . . ," and "White people . . ." from Phyllis Pearson, "Bury My Heart at Wounded Knee, by Dee Brown," *Montana: The Magazine of Western History* 22 (Winter 1972): 69. See also "Best Seller List," *New York Times,* March 14, 1971, BR-45; "Best Seller List," *New York Times,* April 9, 1972, BR-45; Deere, "Historian Dee Brown Dead at 94," 20; Martin, "Dee Brown, 94," A-27; "Dee Brown: Bury His Spirit at Wounded Knee," 12.

58. Quote from Philips, "Bury My Heart at Wounded Knee," 249. See also Charles Wilkinson, *Blood Struggle: The Rise of Modern Indian Nations* (New York: W. W. Norton, 2005), 136–149; Richard DeLuca, "'We Hold the Rock!': The Indian Attempt to Reclaim Alcatraz Island," *California History* 62 (Spring 1983): 2–22; Jack D. Forbes, "Alcatraz: Symbol and Reality," *California History* 62 (Spring 1983): 24–25; Carolyn Strange and Tina Loo, "Holding the Rock: The 'Indianization' of Alcatraz Island, 1969–1999," *Public Historian* 23 (Winter 2001): 55–74; Dean J. Kotlowski, "Alcatraz, Wounded Knee, and Beyond: The Nixon and Ford Administrations Respond to Native American Protest," *Pacific Historical Review* 72 (May 2003): 201–227; Troy Johnson, "The Occupation of Alcatraz Island: Roots of American Indian Activism," *Wicazo Sa Review* 10 (Autumn 1994): 63–79; James S. Olson and Randy Roberts, *My Lai: A Brief History with Documents* (New York: Bedford Books, 1998), 2–35; Kendrick Oliver, *The My Lai Massacre in American History and Memory* (Manchester: Manchester University Press, 2007), 11–52; Steven Sutcliffe, *Children of the New Age: A History of Alternative Spirituality* (New York: Routledge, 2003), 1–30.

59. Quotes from Freeman-Toole, "Dee Brown's Legacy Lives On," 100. See also Donald L. Fixico, "Rise of American Indian Studies," in *The American Indian Mind in a Linear World: American Indian Studies and Traditional Knowledge* (New York: Routledge, 2003), 105–124; Peter Farb, "Indian Corn," *New York Review of Books* 17 (December 16, 1971), http://www.nybooks.com/articles/10348; Patricia Nelson Limerick, *Something in the Soil: Legacies and Reckonings in the New West* (New York: W. W. Norton, 2001), 66.

60. Quotes from Jerry Russell interview, September 12, 2003. See also Michael S. Sherry, "Patriotic Orthodoxy and American Decline," in Tom Engelhardt and Edward T. Linenthal, eds., *History Wars: The Enola Gay*

and Other Battles for the American Past (New York: Holt Paperbacks, 1996), 97-114; Paul Boyer, "Whose History Is It Anyway: Memory, Politics, and Historical Scholarship," in Engelhardt and Linenthal, *History Wars,* 115-139; Mike Wallace, "Culture War, History Front," in Engelhardt and Linenthal, *History Wars,* 171-198; Marilyn B. Young, "Dangerous History: Vietnam and the 'Good War,'" in Engelhardt and Linenthal, *History Wars,* 199-209.

61. Valerie Sherer Mathes, *Helen Hunt Jackson and Her Indian Reform Legacy* (Norman: University of Oklahoma Press, 1997), 21-22; Siobhan Senier, *Voices of American Indian Assimilation and Resistance: Helen Hunt Jackson, Sarah Winnemucca, and Victoria Howland* (Norman: University of Oklahoma Press, 2001), 29; Kate Phillips, *Helen Hunt Jackson: A Literary Life* (Berkeley: University of California Press, 2003), 11, 14-18; Valerie Sherer Mathes, "Helen Hunt Jackson and the Ponca Controversy," *Montana: The Magazine of Western History* 39 (Winter 1989): 42-53; John R. Byers Jr., "Helen Hunt Jackson (1830-1885)," *American Literary Realism, 1870-1910* 2 (Summer 1969): 143-148; John R. Byers Jr., "The Indian Matter of Helen Hunt Jackson's 'Ramona': From Fact to Fiction," *American Indian Quarterly* 2 (Winter 1975-1976), 331-346; John M. Gonzalez, "The Warp of Whiteness: Domesticity and Empire in Helen Hunt Jackson's 'Ramona,'" *American Literary History* 16 (Autumn 2004): 437-465; Michael T. Marsden, "A Dedication to the Memory of Helen Hunt Jackson: 1830-1885," *Arizona and the West* 21 (Summer 1979): 109-112.

62. Mathes, *Helen Hunt Jackson and Her Indian Reform Legacy,* 21-22; Phillips, *Helen Hunt Jackson,* 23-26; Senier, *Voices of American Indian Assimilation and Resistance,* 43.

63. Valerie Sherer Mathes and Richard Lowitt, *The Standing Bear Controversy: Prelude to Indian Reform* (Urbana: University of Illinois Press, 2003), 9-104.

64. "Another Sand Creek" from *Gunnison Democrat,* October 20, 1880. The exchange between Jackson and Schurz can be found in Helen Hunt Jackson, *Century of Dishonor: A Sketch of the United States Government's Dealings with Some of the Indian Tribes* (New York: Harper and Brothers, 1881), appendix, 359-374. See also David Rich Lewis and William Wash, "Reservation Leadership and the Progressive-Traditional Dichotomy: William Wash and the Northern Utes, 1865-1928," *Ethnohistory* 38 (Spring 1991): 124-148; Mathes, "Helen Hunt Jackson and the Ponca Controversy"; Ned Blackhawk, *Violence over the Land: Indians and Empires in the Early American West* (Cambridge, MA: Harvard University Press, 2008), 176-225.

65. "The Sand Creek . . .," "evoked a . . .," "been called . . .," and "if so . . ." from W. B. Vickers, *History of Clear Creek and Boulder valleys, Colorado: containing a brief history of the state of Colorado from its earliest settlement to the present time, embracing its geological, physical and climatic features, its agricultural, stockgrowing, railroad and mining interests, an account of the Ute trouble, a history of Gilpin, Clear Creek, Boulder, and Jefferson Counties, and biographical sketches* (Chicago: O. L. Baskin, 1880), 42. "Perfect safety," "Colorado soldiers," and "covered themselves . . ." from Jackson's first letter regarding Sand Creek, in Jackson, *Century of Dishonor,* appendix, 343–345.

66. Quotes from Byers to Jackson, in *Century of Dishonor,* appendix, 346–350.

67. The Byers-Jackson exchange can be found in ibid., appendix, 343–358. Quotes from pp. 357–358.

68. Ibid., 27, 29.

69. "Look upon . . ." from Mathes, *Helen Hunt Jackson and Her Indian Reform Legacy,* 36. "Indians' *Uncle Tom's Cabin*" from Senier, *Voices of American Indian Assimilation and Resistance,* ix. "Balancing the . . ." from Jerry Russell interview, September 12, 2003. See also Frederick Hoxie, *A Final Promise: The Campaign to Assimilate the Indians, 1880–1920* (Lincoln: University of Nebraska Press, 2001), 3–29, 36–40, 87–104, 130–136, 159–181, 239–244; Donald J. Berthrong, "Legacies of the Dawes Act: Bureaucrats and Land Thieves at the Cheyenne-Arapaho Agencies of Oklahoma," *Arizona and the West* 21 (Winter 1979): 335–354; Francis Paul Prucha, "American Indian Policy in the Twentieth Century," *Western Historical Quarterly* 15 (January 1984): 4–18.

70. Quotes from author's notes, Annual Assembly of the Order of the Indian Wars, Colorado Springs, CO, September 4, 2003, in author's possession.

71. "The real Sand Creek . . ." from Jerry Russell interview, September 12, 2003. "Have to scramble . . ." from Jerry Russell to Alexa Roberts, e-mail, June 23, 2003, in FSCMNHS, now at NPS-WACC. See also Alexa Roberts to Jerry Russell, e-mail, June 19, 2003, in FSCMNHS, now at NPS-WACC; Jerry Russell to Alexa Roberts, e-mail, June 19, 2003, in FSCMNHS, now at NPS-WACC; Jerry Russell to Ed Bearss, e-mail, September 5, 2002, in FSCMNHS, now at NPS-WACC.

72. Quote from Jerry Russell interview, September 12, 2003. See also Alexa Roberts interview, August 26, 2004.

73. "Real Sand Creek . . ." and "traditional site" from "Order of the Indian Wars, Press Release, September 6, 2003," in FSCMNHS, now at NPS-WACC. "Discredit the . . . ," "every such . . . ," and "delight the press" from Alexa Roberts to Dwight Pitcaithley, chief historian, National

Park Service, e-mail, August 6, 2003, in FSCMNHS, now at NPS-WACC. See also Jerry Russell interview, September 12, 2003.

6. YOU CAN'T CARVE THINGS IN STONE

1. Quotes from Kiowa County, Colorado, http://www.kiowacountycolo.com/.
2. Quote from Alexa Roberts, superintendent, Sand Creek Massacre National Historic Site, interview by author, August 26, 2004, telephone, notes in author's possession.
3. "The real . . ." from "Press Release, the Order of the Indian Wars, September 6, 2003," in uncataloged files of the Sand Creek Massacre National Historic Site (FSCMNHS), currently held by National Park Service, Western Archeological and Conservation Center (NPS-WACC), Tucson, AZ. "A persuasive . . ." from Jerry Russell to Order of the Indian Wars members, e-mail, September 12, 2003, copy in author's possession. See also Alexa Roberts, superintendent, Sand Creek Massacre National Historic Site, to Dwight Pitcaithley, chief historian, National Park Service, e-mail, August 6, 2003, in FSCMNHS, now at NPS-WACC; "Press Release: Indian Wars Study Group Visits the 'Real' Sand Creek Site, September 6, 2003," in FSCMNHS, now at NPS-WACC; Jerry Russell to Order of the Indian Wars members, e-mail, September 13, 2003, copy in author's possession.
4. Quote from Jerry Russell, CEO, Order of the Indian Wars, interview by author, September 30, 2003, telephone, tape recording, in author's possession. See also Greg Michno, independent scholar, interview by author, June 30, 2006, telephone, notes in author's possession; Alexa Roberts interview, August 26, 2004; Kiowa County, Colorado, http://www.kiowacountycolo.com/.
5. Quotes from Ron, September 11, 2003, Sand Creek Massacre Discussion Forum, Kiowa County, Colorado, http://www.kiowacountycolo.com /signKiowaCounty.htm.
6. "Sand Creek . . ." from Greg Michno, September 11, 2003, Sand Creek Massacre Discussion Forum. "The real issue . . . ," "that is the question . . . ," "the village in 1864 was . . . ," and "regardless of how the new . . ." from Jeff Broome, September 12, 2003, Sand Creek Massacre Discussion Forum. See also Greg Michno, September 19, 2003, Sand Creek Massacre Discussion Forum.
7. Greg Michno, September 19, 2003, Sand Creek Massacre Discussion Forum.
8. Quotes from Greg Michno interview, June 30, 2006. See also Gregory F. Michno, *Battle at Sand Creek: The Military Perspective* (El Segundo, CA: Upton and Sons, 2004), 1–4.

9. Greg Michno, September 19, 2003, Sand Creek Massacre Discussion Forum.

10. "Wounds . . . ," "obviously ignorant," and "Sand Creek . . ." from Smoke Randolph, September 19, 2003, Sand Creek Massacre Discussion Forum. "Concerned . . ." from Greg Michno, September 19, 2003, Sand Creek Massacre Discussion Forum. "Well it . . ." and "Maybe he's . . ." from Smoke Randolph, September 22, 2003, Sand Creek Massacre Discussion Forum.

11. See scattered posts by Jeff Barnes, Jeff Broome, Randy Garlipp, Greg Michno, Curt Neeley, Smoke Randolph, and Ron between September 11 and October 3, 2003, Sand Creek Massacre Discussion Forum.

12. "A good many . . . ," "one new . . . ," "a number . . . ," and "auburn and . . ." from Greg Michno, September 28, 2003, Sand Creek Massacre Discussion Forum. "Traditional site," "IS NOT CONNECTED . . . ," "who hide . . . ," "our good people . . . ," and "a serviceman . . ." from Jeff Broome, September 28, 2003, Sand Creek Massacre Discussion Forum.

13. "Pseudo-historians" from Ron, September 11 and 23, 2003, Sand Creek Massacre Discussion Forum. "Research," "faulty," and "incomplete" from Smoke Randolph, September 28, 2003, Sand Creek Massacre Discussion Forum. "What constitutes . . ." from Jeff Broome, September 28, 2003, Sand Creek Massacre Discussion Forum. "Mail-order PhD" from Smoke Randolph, October 1, 2003, Sand Creek Massacre Discussion Forum.

14. "It was . . . ," "We wanted . . . ," and "It's a . . ." from Alexa Roberts interview, August 26, 2004. "I wonder . . ." from Jeff Barnes, October 1, 2003, Sand Creek Massacre Discussion Forum. See also Webmaster, October 1, 2003, and scattered posts by Jeff Broome, Greg Michno, Curt Neeley, Smoke Randolph, and Ron between September 11 and October 3, 2003, Sand Creek Massacre Discussion Forum.

15. "If Custer . . ." from Jerry Russell, interview by author, September 12, 2003, telephone, tape recording, in author's possession. "If they . . ." and "It's not just . . ." from Laird Cometsevah, chief, Southern Cheyenne Tribe, interview by author, May 12, 2003, Denver, CO, tape recording, in author's possession. See also "Controversy on Sand Creek Raging Now on Internet Site," *Watonga Republican,* October 27, 2003, n.p., in FSCMNHS, now at NPS-WACC; John Sipes, "Tribal Historian Enters Colorado Internet Site Fray," *Watonga Republican,* November 3, 2003, n.p., in FSCMNHS, now at NPS-WACC; Jerry Russell interview, September 30, 2003; Alexa Roberts interview, August 26, 2004; Steve Brady, head-man, Crazy Dogs Society, Northern Cheyenne Tribe, interview by author, October 24, 2004, Denver, CO, notes in author's possession.

16. Quotes from Charles Zakhem, captain, Colorado National Guard, interview by author, October 12, 2003, telephone, tape recording, in author's possession. See also author's notes, Colorado National Guard Staff Ride, October 23–24, 2003, in author's possession.

17. Quotes from author's notes, Colorado National Guard Staff Ride, October 23–24, 2003.

18. Ibid.

19. Quotes from Charles Zakhem interview, October 12, 2003.

20. Quotes from author's notes, Colorado National Guard Staff Ride, October 23–24, 2003. See also "Spiritual Run Schedule Postponed and Changed," *Watonga Republican,* November 19, 2003, B-4.

21. "How does . . ." from author's notes, Colorado National Guard Staff Ride, October 23–24, 2003. "Can you believe . . ." from Alexa Roberts interview, August 26, 2004. "The Sand Creek . . ." from "Briefing Statement, National Park Service, Sand Creek Massacre National Historic Site, October 24, 2003," in FSCMNHS, now at NPS-WACC. See also Alexa Roberts, "Tribal Representatives Meet Colorado National Guardsmen," *Kiowa County Press,* October 31, 2003, http://www.kiowacountypress.com/2003-10/10-31/Tribal %20Representatives%20meet%20Colorado%20National%20Guards men.htm.

22. Lucky Star Casino, http://www.luckystarcasino.org/.

23. "The traditional . . ." from Laird Cometsevah interview, May 12, 2003. "Understood their . . ." from Kit Miniclier, "Casino Operator Gives Massacre Site to Indians," *Denver Post,* December 30, 2003, B-1. See also Emogene Bevitt, deputy chief, American Indian Liason Office, National Park Service, to Alexa Roberts, superintendent, Sand Creek Massacre National Historic Site, e-mail, December 18, 2003, in FSCMNHS, now at NPS-WACC; Sam Lewin, "Tribe Purchases Massacre Site," *Native American Times,* December 17, 2003, in FSCMNHS, now at NPS-WACC; Deborah Frazier, "Massacre Site Given to Tribes," *Rocky Mountain News,* December 29, 2003, B-1; "Press Release, December 16, 2003: Concho, OK—The Cheyenne and Arapaho Tribes . . . ," in FSCMNHS, now at NPS-WACC.

24. "I don't . . ." from Miniclier, "Casino Operator Gives Massacre Site to Indians," B-1. "That was . . ." from Alexa Roberts, interview by author, September 27, 2004, telephone, notes in author's possession. "Why should . . ." from Laird Cometsevah interview, May 12, 2003.

25. Quotes from Suzan Shown Harjo, "Strictly Confidential: Who's Keeping Secrets from the Sand Creek Descendants?," *Indian Country Today,* December 22, 2003, http://IndianCountry.com/?1072109373.

26. "Was completely..." and "is a..." from Steve Brady interview, October 24, 2004. "Didn't care..." from Laird Cometsevah, interview by author, October 24, 2004, Denver, CO, notes in author's possession. See also Steve Hillard, president, Council Tree Communications, interview by author, January 12, 2004, telephone, tape recording, in author's possession; Gerald Vizenor, "Editorial Comment: Gambling on Sovereignty," *American Indian Quarterly* 16 (Summer 1992): 411–413; Jessica R. Cattelino, "Tribal Gaming and Indigenous Sovereignty, with Notes from Seminole Country," *American Studies* 46 (Fall–Winter 2005): 187–204; Franke Wilmer, "Indian Gaming: Players and Stakes," *Wicazo Sa Review* 12 (Spring 1997): 89–114; Mary Lawlor, "Identity in Mashantucket," *American Quarterly* 57 (March 2005): 153–177; Gary Sokolow, "The Future of Gambling in Indian Country," *American Indian Law Review* 15 (1990–1991): 151–183; Gerald Vizenor, "Casino Coups," *Wicazo Sa Review* 9 (Autumn 1993): 80–84.

27. Quotes from Steve Brady interview, October 24, 2004. See also Deborah Frazier, "Indians File Huge Land Claim," *Rocky Mountain News*, April 15, 2004, A-5.

28. "We had..." and "fast cash" from Steve Brady interview, October 24, 2004. "Would allow..." from Deborah Frazier, "Gambling Supporter Says Towns Clamoring," *Rocky Mountain News*, January 15, 2004, A-6. "It is outrageous..." from Mike McPhee and Kit Miniclier, "Casino Project Raises Outcry," *Denver Post*, December 31, 2003, A-4.

29. Quotes from Mike Soraghan, "Senator Tied to Backers of Casino Plan," *Denver Post*, January 14, 2004, B-1. See also Mike Soraghan, "Okla. Tribes Push for Controversial Casino near Denver," *Denver Post*, January 15, 2004, A-1.

30. "We've had..." and "Well, I suppose..." from Janet Frederick, director, Kiowa County Economic Development Corporation, interview by author, November 24, 2004, Eads, CO, notes in author's possession. "If they..." from Alexa Roberts interview, August 26, 2004.

31. "Ghastly..." from "Casino Plan Insensitive," *Denver Post*, January 3, 2004, C-15. "Why lament..." from Al Lewis, "Plan Bets on Odd Idea to Heal Past," *Denver Post*, January 4, 2004, K-1. See also "An Indian Casino on the Plains?," *Rocky Mountain News*, January 1, 2004, A-41; Peter Blake, "The Deck Is Stacked against Indian Casino on Plains," *Rocky Mountain News*, January 3, 2004, C-12; Mike Soraghan, "Casino 'Crossfire' Infuriates Campbell," *Denver Post*, January 16, 2004, A-1; Kit Miniclier, "Indian Casino Not a Sure Bet," *Denver Post*, February 4, 2004, A-1; "Indian Casino Plan Is a Bad Bargain," *Denver Post*, May 17, 2004, B-7; Jim Spencer, "Land Claim Has Feel of Extortion," *Denver Post*, May 19, 2004, C-1.

32. "The tribes . . ." from Frazier, "Gambling Supporter Says Towns Clamoring," A-6. "The proposition . . ." from Mike Soraghan, "Indians' Leveraged Efforts for Casinos Reach beyond Colorado," *Denver Post,* August 16, 2004, A-1. "These claims . . ." from Soraghan, "Okla. Tribes Push for Controversial Casino Near Denver," A-1. "Reparations are entirely right . . ." from Steve Hillard interview, January 12, 2004. See also Deborah Frazier, "Casino Plan Stirs Opposition," *Rocky Mountain News,* January 1, 2004, A-26; Karen Rouse, "Casino Group Offers Schools $1 Billion to Get State Support," *Denver Post,* July 8, 2004, A-1; David Harsanyi, "Luck May Be on Casino Backers' Side," *Denver Post,* June 26, 2004, C-1; "Indian Casino Plan Is a Bad Bargain," B-7.

33. "Does not . . ." from "Press Release, Council Tree Communications, March 16, 2004, in FSCMNHS, now at NPS-WACC. "You can . . ." from Steve Hillard, CEO, Native American Land Group, to Laird Cometsevah, president, Traditional Sand Creek Cheyenne Descendants, March 16, 2004, in FSCMNHS, now at NPS-WACC. "In similar . . ." from Arthur Kane, "Okla. Tribes Seek 27 Million Acres in Eastern Colo.," *Denver Post,* April 15, 2004, B-1. See also Deborah Frazier, "Beauprez Opposed to Casino," *Rocky Mountain News,* January 3, 2004, A-15; Soraghan, "Casino 'Crossfire' Infuriates Campbell," A-1; "Don't Let Gambling Expand," *Denver Post,* January 17, 2004, C-15; Mike Soraghan, "Tribes to Pursue Colorado Casino," *Denver Post,* April 14, 2004, B-1; Frazier, "Indians File Huge Land Claim," A-5; Andy Vuong, "Tribes Put Title Firms on Notice," *Denver Post,* May 4, 2004, C-1; "Owens Right to Reject Tribes' Offer," *Denver Post,* June 21, 2004, B-7.

34. "Tainted" from Alexa Roberts, interview by author, March 25, 2004, telephone, notes in author's possession. "The casino . . ." from Norma Gorneau, member, Northern Cheyenne Tribe Sand Creek Massacre Descendants Committee, interview by author, July 1, 2004, Lame Deer, MT, tape recording, in author's possession. See also Otto Braided Hair, director, Northern Cheyenne Sand Creek Office, interview by author, May 11, 2007, telephone, notes in author's possession; "Notes, Consultation Meeting, Sand Creek Massacre National Historic Site, March 17–18, 2004," in FSCMNHS, now at NPS-WACC; Mildred Red Cherries, member, Northern Cheyenne Sand Creek Massacre Descendants Committee, interview by author, August 13, 2003, Lame Deer, MT, tape recording, in author's possession.

35. "That's why . . ." from Deborah Frazier, "Tribes Hope to Take a Gamble," *Rocky Mountain News,* May 8, 2004, A-28. "There's no question . . ."

from Spencer, "Land Claim Has Feel of Extortion," C-1. See also Julia Martinez, "Campbell Weighs Hearings on Plan for Tribal Casino," *Denver Post,* April 23, 2004, A-25; Jason Blevins, "Casino Numbers Debated," *Denver Post,* May 21, 2004, C-1; Andy Vuong, "Owens Rejects Pact with Tribes for Casino," *Denver Post,* June 18, 2004, C-1; "Tribes Stalk Casino Bid," *Pueblo Chieftain,* June 16, 2004, B-4.

36. "Briefing" and "hearing" from Mike Soraghan, "Tribal Casino's Backers to Speak at D.C. Briefing," *Denver Post,* August 13, 2004, A-4. All other quotes from Mike Soraghan, "Indian Casino Quashed," *Denver Post,* September 9, 2004, A-1. See also Peter Blake, "Delegation on the Lookout for Midnight Casino Riders," *Rocky Mountain News,* June 19, 2004, C-12; Soraghan, "Tribal Casino's Backers to Speak at D.C. Briefing," A-4; Mike Soraghan, "Owens to Denounce Casino," *Denver Post,* August 29, 2004, C-1; Al Lewis, "Bet on Casino Backer's Doggedness," *Denver Post,* September 12, 2004, K-1.

37. "Reservation shopping" from Soraghan, "Indians' Leveraged Efforts for Casinos Reach beyond Colorado," A-1. See also Electa Draper, "Indian Gaming's Future Eyed," *Denver Post,* March 30, 2005, F-1; "Tribal Proposals to Acquire Land-in-Trust for Gaming across State Lines and How Such Proposals Are Affected by the Off-Reservation Discussion Draft Bill," oversight hearing before Committee on Resources, U.S. House of Representatives, 109th Cong., 1st Sess., April 27, 2005, http://www.access.gpo.gov/congress/house; Justin Neel Baucom, "Bringing Down the House: As States Attempt to Curtail Indian Gaming, Have We Forgotten the Foundational Principles of Tribal Sovereignty," *American Indian Law Review* 30 (2005–2006): 423–442.

38. Quotes from Alexa Roberts interview, September 27, 2004.

39. "A unique . . ." from "Bowen Tours," in FSCMNHS, now at NPS-WACC. All other quotes from Sand Creek Tours, http://www.sandcreektours.com/.

40. "Promote and . . ." and "personal slurs" from Sharon Pearson, July 6, 2004, Sand Creek Massacre Discussion Forum. "NOT back down" from Chuck and Sheri Bowen, July 6, 2004, Sand Creek Massacre Discussion Forum. See also Cindy Buxton, "Bowens Offer Tour of Historic Sand Creek Area," *Lamar Daily News,* June 16, 2004, A-1; "Controversy on Sand Creek Now Raging on Internet Site," *Watonga Republican,* October 27, 2004, B-4; Sand Creek Tours, http://www.sandcreektours.com/.

41. "Why the Indian . . ." and "the almighty . . ." from Parker Holden, November 14, 2004, Sand Creek Massacre Discussion Forum. All other

quotes from Chuck Bowen, November 14, 2004, Sand Creek Massacre Discussion Forum.

42. Quotes from Bill Dawson, November 28, 2004, Sand Creek Massacre Discussion Forum.

43. Quotes from Sheri Bowen, December 1, 2004, Sand Creek Massacre Discussion Forum.

44. "If Eads . . ." from Sipes, "Tribal Historian Enters Internet Site Fray," n.p. "If we can . . ." from Alexa Roberts, interview by author, December 3, 2004, telephone, notes in author's possession. See also Cindy Buxton, "Bowens Giving Sand Creek Tours," *Watonga Republican,* July 7, 2004, n.p.

45. "Survivance" from Amanda Cobb, "The National Museum of the American Indian: Sharing the Gift," *American Indian Quarterly* 29 (Summer–Fall 2005): 362; Amanda Cobb, "Interview with W. Richard West, Director, National Museum of the American Indian," *American Indian Quarterly* 29 (Summer–Fall 2005): 521, 536. "Unmistakable air . . ." from Jerry Reynolds, "National Museum of the American Indian Review: Ceremonies Were Nice but Critics Pan Content," *Indian Country Today,* October 8, 2004. "An important opportunity . . ." from Elizabeth Olson, "A Museum of Indians That Is Also for Them," *New York Times,* August 19, 2004, E-1. See also James Dao, "Drums and Bells Open Indian Museum," *New York Times,* September 22, 2004, A-14; Steven Conn, "Heritage vs. History at the National Museum of the American Indian," *Public Historian* 28 (Spring 2006): 69–74; Ann McMullen, "Reinventing George Heye: Nationalizing the Museum of the American Indian and Its Collections," in Susan Sleeper-Smith, ed., *Contesting Knowledge: Museums and Indigenous Perspectives* (Lincoln: University of Nebraska Press, 2009), 65–105.

46. Olson, "A Museum of Indians That Is Also for Them," E-1; McMullen, "Reinventing George Heye"; Ira Jacknis, "A New Thing? The NMAI in Historical and Institutional Perspective," *American Indian Quarterly* 29 (Summer–Fall 2005): 511–542; William Grimes, "The Indian Museum's Last Stand," *New York Times Sunday Magazine,* November 27, 1988, 46–52.

47. Francis X. Clines, "Smithsonian Making Room for Indian Museum," *New York Times,* September 29, 1999, A-14; Irvin Molotsky, "Federal Panel Approves Indian Museum on Mall," *New York Times,* June 18, 1999, E-35; Ashley Dunn, "A Heritage Reclaimed: From Old Artifacts, American Indians Shape a New Museum," *New York Times,* October 9, 1994, A-45; Barbara Gamarekian, "Senate Passes Indian Museum Bill," *New York Times,* November 15, 1989, B-4; Irvin Molotsky, "Smithsonian Votes Plan

for an American Indian Museum," *New York Times,* January 31, 1989, B-3; Irvin Molotsky, "Indian Museum Plan Favors Smithsonian over New York Site," *New York Times,* January 25, 1989, A-1; Grimes, "The Indian Museum's Last Stand"; Irvin Molotsky, "Compromise Is Reached to Keep Indian Museum in New York City," *New York Times,* April 13, 1988, A-1; Irvin Molotsky, "New York Officials Reach Indian Museum Agreement," *New York Times,* November 10, 1987, B-2; Robert D. McFadden, "Koch Offers Inducement to Keep Museum in City," *New York Times,* October 10, 1987, A-34; Irvin Molotsky, "Inouye Seeks to Move Indian Museum to Capital," *New York Times,* September 30, 1987, B-3; Thomas Morgan, "Fast Action Urged for Indian Museum," *New York Times,* July 17, 1987, B-1; Irvin Molotsky, "Smithsonian Pushes Its Plan to Move the Indian Museum," *New York Times,* July 16, 1987, B-3; Douglas Martin, "Fight Builds over New Site for Museum," *New York Times,* May 21, 1987, B-1; Irvin Molotsky, "Plan to Move Indian Museum Is Under Attack," *New York Times,* May 13, 1987, B-36; Douglas McGill, "Perot Backs Museum's Plan," *New York Times,* January 28, 1987, C-23; David Dunlap, "A Museum Turns to Congress for Help," *New York Times,* January 5, 1987, B-1.

48. Quotes from Jim Adams, "Museum Opening on National Mall Signals End to Years of Horror," *Indian Country Today,* September 18, 2004.

49. Ibid. See also Thomas W. Killion, Scott Brown, and J. Stuart Speaker, "Naevahoo'ohtseme: Cheyenne Repatriation," Repatriation Office, National Museum of Natural History, Smithsonian Institution, May 10, 1992; Thomas W. Killion, "A View from the Trenches: Memories of Repatriation at the National Museum of Natural History, Smithsonian Institution," in Thomas W. Killion, ed., *Opening Archaeology: Repatriation's Impact on Contemporary Research and Practice* (Santa Fe, NM: School for Advanced Research Press, 2007), 134–138; *The Long Journey Home,* Human Studies Film Archive, Smithsonian Institution, Washington, DC, 93.10.1.

50. "For the common . . ." and "must manage . . ." from James Doyle, Colorado communications director for Senator Ben Nighthorse Campbell, to Sand Creek Massacre National Historic Site Stakeholders, December 13, 2002, in FSCMNHS, now at NPS-WACC. All other quotes from Senate 2173, "Sand Creek Massacre National Historic Site Trust Act of 2004," 108th Cong., 2nd Sess., March 8, 2004.

51. "Hysteria" and "playing it low-key" from Otto Braided Hair, director, Northern Cheyenne Sand Creek Office, to Ari Kelman, e-mail, September 16, 2004, in author's possession. "Serving the American people . . ."

from Ben Nighthorse Campbell, U.S. senator, interview by author, September 10, 2003, telephone, tape recording, in author's possession. See also John Aloysius Farrell and Mike Soraghan, "Senate Slot Up for Grabs: Recent Weeks Brought Health, Ethics Issues," *Denver Post*, March 4, 2004, A-1; Anne C. Mulkern, "Health Issue, Stress Faded Campaign Enthusiasm," *Denver Post*, March 4, 2004, A-21; Electa Draper, "It's Time to Walk Away . . . Get a Life Again," *Denver Post*, March 4, 2004, A-1.

52. "House leaders . . ." and "it sets us back . . ." from Mike Soraghan, "Massacre Site Plans Stymied," *Denver Post*, December 14, 2004, A-1. "It sailed . . ." and "I just don't know . . ." from Alexa Roberts interview, December 3, 2004. "We got overconfident . . ." from Otto Braided Hair, interview by author, December 13, 2004, telephone, tape recording, in author's possession. See also "House Silent on Sand Creek," *Denver Post*, December 15, 2004, B-6.

53. "The NPS believe . . ." from "Statement of Michael D. Snyder, Acting Deputy Director, National Park Service, U.S. Department of the Interior, Before the House Subcommittee on National Parks of the Committee on Resources, Concerning H.R. 481, the Sand Creek Massacre National Historic Site Trust Act of 2005, April 14, 2005," in FSCMNHS, now at NPS-WACC. See also Joe Hanel, "Sand Creek Massacre Bill Moves Forward," *Longmont Times-Call*, April 15, 2005, A-1; Mike Soraghan, "Sand Creek Bill to Be Reintroduced," *Denver Post*, January 23, 2005, C-4; "Allard Seeks Historic Status for Sand Creek," *Rocky Mountain News*, January 22, 2005, A-22; "Statement of Steve Brady, Sr., Co Chair of the Northern Cheyenne Sand Creek Massacre National Historic Site Project Committee and President of the Northern Band of Cheyenne Sand Creek Massacre Descendants, Before the House Subcommittee on National Park of the Committee on Resources, Concerning H.R. 481, the Sand Creek Massacre National Historic Site Trust Act of 2005, April 14, 2005," in FSCMNHS, now at NPS-WACC; Alexa Roberts, interview by author, April 29, 2005, telephone, tape recording, in author's possession.

54. Quote from Alexa Roberts, interview by author, July 30, 2005, telephone, tape recording, in author's possession.

55. Quotes from Alexa Roberts interview, July 30, 2005. See also Greg Michno interview, June 30, 2006.

56. "We can't . . ." from Alexa Roberts interview, July 30, 2005. "Little Eichmanns" from Ward Churchill, " 'Some People Push Back': On the Justice of Roosting Chickens," (2005), http://www.kersplebedeb.com /mystuff/s11/churchill.html. See also Ward Churchill, *On the Justice of*

Roosting Chickens (Oakland, CA: AK Press, 2003), 1–38; Amy Herdy and Arthury Kane, "Churchill Claims Proof He's Indian," *Denver Post,* May 18, 2005, A-1; Amy Herdy, "Tribe Says Prof's Membership Rescinded in '94," *Denver Post,* May 19, 2005, B-1; Amy Herdy, "Tribe Shifts Stand, Acknowledges Churchill's Alleged Cherokee Ancestry," *Denver Post,* May 20, 2005, B-1; Arthur Kane and Amy Herdy, "Churchill: Heritage Undisputed," *Denver Post,* May 25, 2005, B-1; Jim Hughes and Amy Herdy, "Churchill Says He's Ghostwriter," *Denver Post,* May 26, 2005, B-1; Amy Herdy, "CU Students' Vote Favors Churchill, but Award Withheld," *Denver Post,* May 27, 2005, B-1; Kim McGuire, "Churchill Talks to Supportive Group in Salida," *Denver Post,* June 6, 2005, B-1; Kevin Simpson and Alicia Caldwell, "The Battle over Tenure," Part 1, *Denver Post,* June 12, 2005, A-1; Kevin Simpson and Alicia Caldwell, "The Battle over Tenure," Part 2, *Denver Post,* June 13, 2005, A-1; Jim Kerksey and Amy Herdy, "Prof Defends Military Remarks," *Denver Post,* June 30, 2005, A-1; "Escort Churchill to the Door," *Denver Post,* July 1, 2005, B-1; Amy Herdy, "Opinions Split over CU Prof's War Comments," *Denver Post,* July 1, 2005, A-1; Jennifer Brown, "CU Panel Queries Churchill about Plagiarism Allegations," *Denver Post,* August 11, 2005, B-8; Amy Herdy and Jennifer Brown, "Churchill Plans Spring Sabbatical," *Denver Post,* August 17, 2005, A-1; Arthur Kane and Jennifer Brown, "Panel Gets Findings on Prof," *Denver Post,* August 21, 2005, C-1; Jennifer Brown, "Tentative Victory for Prof," *Denver Post,* August 23, 2005, A-1; Amy Herdy, "CU Panel Drops Three Allegations against Churchill," *Denver Post,* September 7, 2005, B-1; Jennifer Brown and Amy Herdy, "Full-Blown Investigation for Churchill," *Denver Post,* September 11, 2005, A-1; Arthur Kane, "Prof Decries CU Statement," *Denver Post,* September 13, 2005, B-2; Aldo Svaldi, "CU, Accountants to Examine Tenure," *Denver Post,* September 30, 2005, C-3.

57. Quotes from Alexa Roberts interview, July 30, 2005.

58. "Mr. Pedro reportedly . . ." from Curt Neeley, July 31, 2005, Sand Creek Massacre Discussion Forum. "I am very . . . ," "this latest . . . ," and "make sure . . ." from Butch Kelley to Alexa Roberts, superintendent, Sand Creek Massacre National Historic Site, e-mail, August 1, 2005, in FSCMNHS, now at NPS-WACC. "How is this . . ." from Chuck and Sheri Bowen, August 3, 2005, Sand Creek Massacre Discussion Forum. "7 white . . ." from Curt Neeley, August 4, 2005, Sand Creek Massacre Discussion Forum.

59. "The abundance . . ." from "Sand Creek Is Finally a Historic Site," *Rocky Mountain News,* August 4, 2005, A-48. All other quotes from Diane

Carman, "Even Today, Sand Creek's Bloody Reality Is Hard to Face,"
Denver Post, August 4, 2005, B-5. See also Mike Soraghan, "Sand Creek
Massacre Legislation on to Bush," *Denver Post,* July 27, 2005, A-8; M. E.
Sprengelmeyer, "Sand Creek Nears Final Hurdle to Become Protected
Historic Site," *Rocky Mountain News,* August 2, 2005, A-23; "Sand Creek
Massacre Area Now a National Historic Site," *Denver Post,* August 3,
2005, B-2; "President Signs Bill Clearing Way for Sand Creek Site," *Rocky
Mountain News,* August 3, 2005, A-13.

60. Quotes from Alexa Roberts, interview by author, August 17, 2005,
    telephone, tape recording, in author's possession.

61. Ibid.

62. Quotes from Alexa Roberts, interview by author, September 5, 2005,
    telephone, tape recording, in author's possession.

63. Ibid.

64. Quote from Alexa Roberts, interview by author, December 15, 2005,
    telephone, tape recording, in author's possession. See also Alexa
    Roberts, interview by author, October 21, 2005, telephone, tape record-
    ing, in author's possession.

65. "A low point" from Alexa Roberts interview, December 15, 2005. All
    other quotes from "Notes, National Park Service, Consultation Meet-
    ing, Sand Creek Massacre National Historic Site, Cheyenne Wyoming,
    June 28, 2006," in FSCMNHS, now at NPS-WACC. See also Alexa
    Roberts interview, October 21, 2005.

66. "Assured" and "would convey . . ." from Alexa Roberts, interview by
    author, June 16, 2006, telephone, tape recording, in author's possession.
    "I fully support . . ." from Alexa Roberts, interview by author, August 25,
    2006, telephone, tape recording, in author's possession. See also "C & A
    Reps Meet to Plan Sand Creek Massacre National Historic Site,"
    Cheyenne-Arapaho News, April 1, 2006; "Constitution of the Cheyenne
    and Arapaho Tribes," http://www.c-a-tribes.org/cheyenne-arapaho
    -tribes-constitution; Kyme McGaw, partner, Morriset, Schlosser,
    Jozwiak and McGaw, interview by author, June 28, 2006, Cheyenne, WY,
    tape recording, in author's possession.

67. "Watching legislative . . ." and "a word of . . ." from author's notes,
    meeting of the Cheyenne and Arapaho Nation of Oklahoma's Legisla-
    ture, Clinton, OK, September 9, 2006, in author's possession. "A bill
    to . . ." and "the Sand Creek . . ." from "Legislative Proceedings of the
    Cheyenne and Arapaho Tribe of Oklahoma, Bill No: 01-08-02, Septem-
    ber 9, 2006," in FSCMNHS, now at NPS-WACC.

68. Quotes from author's notes, meeting of the Cheyenne and Arapaho
    Nation of Oklahoma's Legislature, Clinton, OK, September 9, 2006.

69. Quotes from author's notes, National Park Service, consultation meeting, Sand Creek Massacre National Historic Site, Kiowa County, CO, September 12–14, 2006, in author's possession.

70. Ibid.

71. "You would . . ." from Rich Tosches, "Theories on Recent Cattle Mutilations Sort of Alien," *Denver Post,* May 24, 2006, B-1. "This will . . ." from author's notes, consultation meeting, September 12–14, 2006.

72. Ibid.

73. Ibid.

74. Quote from Clark Johnson, "Judge Drops Charges in Assault Case," *Billings Gazette,* October 10, 2006, L-1.

75. Quote from author's notes, National Park Service, consultation meeting, Sand Creek Massacre National Historic Site, Lame Deer, MT, July 9, 2003, in author's possession. See also Jerome A. Greene, *Washita: The U.S. Army and the Southern Cheyennes, 1867–1869* (Norman: University of Oklahoma Press, 2008), 3–41, 77–182; George Bird Grinnell, *The Fighting Cheyennes* (Norman: University of Oklahoma Press, 1983), 181–317; Stan Hoig, *The Battle of the Washita: The Sheridan-Custer Indian Campaign of 1867–69* (Lincoln, NE: Bison Books, 1979), 1–38, 112–195; Robert M. Utley, *Frontier Regulars: The United States Army and the Indian, 1866–1891* (Lincoln, NE: Bison Books, 1984), 142–162.

76. Quotes from author's notes, consultation meeting, July 9, 2003. See also Donald J. Berthrong, *The Cheyenne and Arapaho Ordeal: Reservation and Agency Life in the Indian Territory, 1875–1907* (Norman: University of Oklahoma Press, 1992), 3–117; Jerome A. Greene, *Morning Star Dawn: The Powder River Expedition and the Northern Cheyennes, 1876* (Norman: University of Oklahoma Press, 2003), 17–67, 90–206; Stan Hoig, *Tribal Wars of the Southern Plains* (Norman: University of Oklahoma Press, 1993), 244–268, 286–304; John H. Monnett, *Tell Them We Are Going Home: The Odyssey of the Northern Cheyennes* (Norman: University of Oklahoma Press, 2001), 9–43, 78–137, 160–172, 191–208; Utley, *Frontier Regulars,* 267–295; Thomas Powers, *The Killing of Crazy Horse* (New York: Vintage Books, 2011), 6–13, 27–30; Jeffrey Ostler, *The Lakotas and the Black Hills: The Struggle for Sacred Ground* (New York: Penguin, 2011), 31–47, 50–75.

77. Quote from Alexa Roberts, interview by author, January 8, 2007, telephone, tape recording, in author's possession.

78. "As a country . . ." and "the history . . ." from "Office of the Secretary, for Immediate Release, April 23, 2007, Secretary Kempthorne Creates Sand Creek Massacre National Historic Site," in FSCMNHS, now at NPS-WACC. "Now Sand Creek . . ." from Alexa Roberts, interview by author,

April 30, 2007, telephone, tape recording, in author's possession. See also Alexa Roberts interview, January 8, 2007.

79. Alexa Roberts interview, April 30, 2007.

1. Quotes from "Bent's Old Fort," National Park Service, http://www.nps.gov/beol/index.htm. See also Douglas C. Comer, *Ritual Ground: Bent's Old Fort, World Formation, and the Annexation of the Southwest* (Berkeley: University of California Press, 1996), 3–29; Harold H. Dunham, "Ceran St. Vrain," in LeRoy R. Hafen, ed., *Mountain Men and Fur Traders of the Far West: Eighteen Biographical Sketches* (Lincoln: University of Nebraska Press, 1982), 146–165; Lincoln B. Faller and George Bent, "Making Medicine against 'White Man's Side of Story': George Bent's Letters to George Hyde," *American Indian Quarterly* 24 (Winter 2000): 64–90.

2. "Consultation Concerns Sand Creek Repatriation," *Watonga Republican,* May 21, 2003, A-10; Deborah Frazier, "The Echoes of Sand Creek," *Rocky Mountain News,* December 3, 1995, A-32; Jim Hughes, "Burials at Sand Creek," *Denver Post,* August 7, 2005, C-1; Otto Braided Hair, director, Northern Cheyenne Sand Creek Office, to Ari Kelman, e-mail, August 7, 2008, in uncataloged files of the Sand Creek Massacre National Historic Site (FSCMNHS), currently held by National Park Service, Western Archeological and Conservation Center (NPS-WACC), Tucson, AZ; "Introduction to NAGPRA for the Sand Creek Massacre National Historic Site," attached to "Meeting Notes, March 18–21, 2002, Denver, Colorado," in FSCMNHS, now at NPS-WACC; Public Law 101-601; "National NAGPRA," National Park Service, http://www.nps.gov/nagpra/; "Meeting Notes, December 13–14, 2002, Denver, Colorado," in FSCMNHS, now at NPS-WACC; Laird Cometsevah, chief, Southern Cheyenne Tribe, interview by author, May 12, 2003, Denver, CO, tape recording, in author's possession; Steve Brady, president, Northern Cheyenne Sand Creek Descendants, interview by author, August 29, 2004, Lame Deer, MT, tape recording, in author's possession; Joe Big Medicine, Sand Creek representative, Southern Cheyenne Tribe, interview by author, July 8, 2003, Lame Deer, MT, tape recording, in author's possession.

3. Quotes from David Hurst Thomas, *Skull Wars: Kennewick Man, Archaeology, and the Battle for Native American Identity* (New York: Basic Books, 2000), 214–215. See also Devon A. Mihesuah, "Introduction," in Devon A. Mihesuah, ed., *Repatriation Reader: Who Owns Native American Remains?* (Lincoln: University of Nebraska Press, 2000), 1–6; Jack F. Trope and Walter Echo-Hawk, "The Native American Graves Protection

and Repatriation Act: Background and Legislative History," in Mihe-
suah, *Repatriation Reader,* 123–145; Charles Wilkinson, *Blood Struggle: The
Rise of Modern Indian Nations* (New York: W. W. Norton, 2005), 263–274;
Julia A. Cryne, "NAGPRA Revisited: A Twenty-Year Review of Repatria-
tion Efforts," *American Indian Law Review* 34 (2009–2010): 99–122; Susan
B. Bruning, "Complex Legal Legacies: The Native American Graves
Protection and Repatriation Act, Scientific Study, and Kennewick
Man," *American Antiquity* 71 (July 2006): 501–521; Michelle Hibbert,
"Galileos or Grave Robbers? Science, the Native American Graves
Protection and Repatriation Act, and the First Amendment," *American
Indian Law Review* 23 (1998–1999): 425–458; June Camille Bush Raines,
"One Is Missing: Native American Graves Protection and Repatriation
Act: An Overview and Analysis," *American Indian Law Review* 17 (1992):
639–664; James Riding In, Cal Seciwa, Suzan Shown Harjo, and Walter
Echo-Hawk, "Protecting Native American Human Remains, Burial
Grounds, and Sacred Places: Panel Discussion," *Wicazo Sa Review* 19
(Autumn 2004): 169–183; Pamela D'Innocenzo, " 'Not in My Backyard!'
Protecting Archaeological Sites on Private Lands," *American Indian Law
Review* 21 (1997): 131–155; Joe E. Watkins, "Beyond the Margin: American
Indians, First Nations, and Archaeology in North America," *American
Antiquity* 68 (April 2003): 273–285.

4. "They've had centuries . . ." from Steve Brady interview, August 29, 2004.
    "One more hoop . . ." from "Meeting Notes, March 18–20, 2002, Denver,
    Colorado," in FSCMNHS, now at NPS-WACC. See also "Meeting Notes,
    December 12–14, 2002, Denver, Colorado," in FSCMNHS, now at
    NPS-WACC; "Meeting Notes, March 6–8, 2003, Clinton, Oklahoma," in
    FSCMNHS, now at NPS-WACC; "Meeting Notes, July 9, 2003, Lame
    Deer, Montana," in FSCMNHS, now at NPS-WACC; "Meeting Notes,
    November 26, 2003, Eads, Colorado," in FSCMNHS, now at NPS-
    WACC; "Meeting Notes, March 17–18, 2004, Denver, Colorado," in
    FSCMNHS, now at NPS-WACC; Andrew Gulliford, "Bones of Conten-
    tion: The Repatriation of Native American Human Remains," *Public
    Historian* 18 (Autumn 1996): 119–143; T. J. Ferguson, "Native Americans
    and the Practice of Archaeology," *Annual Review of Anthropology* 25
    (1996): 63–79; Jerome C. Rose, Thomas J. Green, and Victoria D. Green,
    "NAGPRA Is Forever: Osteology and the Repatriation of Skeletons,"
    Annual Review of Anthropology 25 (1996): 81–103; Renee M. Kosslak, "The
    Native American Graves Protection and Repatriation Act: The Death
    Knell for Scientific Study?," *American Indian Law Review* 24 (1999–2000):
    129–151; Alexa Roberts, "Trust Me, I Work for the Government: Confi-
    dentiality and Public Access to Sensitive Information," *American Indian*

Quarterly 25 (Winter 2001): 13–17; Clayton W. Dumont Jr., "The Politics of Scientific Objections to Repatriation," *Wicazo Sa Review* 18 (Spring 2003): 109–128; Moira G. Simpson, "A Grave Dilemma: Native Americans and Museums in the USA," *Journal of Museum Ethnography* 6 (October 1994): 25–37.

5. Except where otherwise noted, details of the ceremony have been drawn from photographs of the event, taken by an independent scholar named Tom Meier, found in FSCMNHS, now at NPS-WACC. See also "Reburial Notes, June 8, 2008, Eads, Colorado," in FSCMNHS, now at NPS-WACC; Alexa Roberts, superintendent, Bent's Old Fort National Historic Site, interview by author, July 21, 2008, telephone, notes in author's possession; Otto Braided Hair, director, Northern Cheyenne Sand Creek Office, to Ari Kelman, e-mail, June 24, 2008, in author's possession; Karl Zimmerman, chief of operations, Sand Creek Massacre National Historic Site, to Ari Kelman, e-mail, September 19, 2011, in author's possession.

6. "Halfbreed" from *Denver Times,* November 5, 1905. "E 1748, Scalp (Cheyenne or Arapaho), Taken from an Indian by a soldier at Sand Creek Massacre, by Jacob Downing Nov. 29, 1864," from "Report on Museum Related Materials for the Sand Creek Massacre Site," in FSCMNHS, now at NPS-WACC. See also Grand Army of the Republic, *The National Memorial Day: A Record of Ceremonies over the Graves of the Union Soldiers, May 29 and 30, 1869* (Washington, DC: Headquarters of the Grand Army of the Republic, 1870), 61; George Bent, "Forty Years with the Cheyennes," ed. George Hyde, *Frontier: A Magazine of the West* 4 (October 1905): 6; George Bent, "Forty Years with the Cheyennes," ed. George Hyde, *Frontier: A Magazine of the West* 4 (December 1905): 2; George Bent, "Forty Years with the Cheyennes," ed. George Hyde, *Frontier: A Magazine of the West* 4 (January 1906): 4; George Bent, "Forty Years with the Cheyennes," ed. George Hyde, *Frontier: A Magazine of the West* 4 (February 1906): 6; George Bent, "Forty Years with the Cheyennes," ed. George Hyde, *Frontier: A Magazine of the West* 4 (March 1906): 7; David Fridtjof Halaas and Andrew E. Masich, *Halfbreed: The Remarkable True Story of George Bent, Caught between the Worlds of the Indian and the White Man* (New York: Da Capo Press, 2004), 337–339.

7. "Reburial Notes, June 8, 2008, Eads, Colorado," in FSCMNHS, now at NPS-WACC; Bent, "Forty Years with the Cheyennes," (October 1905): 6–7; George E. Hyde, *Life of George Bent: Written from His Letters,* ed. Savoie Lottinville, (Norman: University of Oklahoma Press, 1968), 149–155.

8. "Massacre of Cheyenne Indians," in *Report of the Joint Committee on the Conduct of the War, at the Second Session, Thirty-Eighth Congress* (Washington, DC: Government Printing Office, 1865), 107–108; Henry Littleton

Pitzer, *Three Frontiers: Memories and a Portrait of Henry Littleton Pitzer as Recorded by His Son Robert Claiborne Pitzer* (Muscatine, IA: Prairie Press, 1938), 162–163; Elmer R. Burkey, "The Site of the Murder of the Hungate Family by Indians in 1864," *Colorado Magazine* 12 (1935): 135–142; J. S. Brown and Thomas J. Darrah to Governor John Evans, June 11, 1864, *The War of the Rebellion: A Compilation of the Official Records of the Union and Confederate Armies* (Washington, DC: Government Printing Office, 1900), Series I, XXXIV, Pt. 4, 319–320; Alice Polk Hill, *Tales of Colorado Pioneers* (Denver: Pierson and Gardner, 1884), 79–80; Nathaniel P. Hill, "Nathaniel P. Hill Inspects Colorado, Letters Written in 1864," *Colorado Magazine* 33–34 (1956–1957): 245–246; Lenore Barbian, anatomical collections manager, National Anthropological Archives, Smithsonian Institution, to Gary L. Roberts, National Park Service contract historian, in Gary L. Roberts, "The Sand Creek Massacre Site: A Report on Washington Sources," January 1999 (unpublished manuscript), in FSCMNHS, now at NPS-WACC; United States Army Medical Museum Anatomical Section, "Records Relating to Specimens Transferred to the Smithsonian Institution," National Anthropological Archives, Smithsonian Institution, 1990, 7, in FSCMNHS, now at NPS-WACC; Scott Brown, museum technician, National Museum of Natural History and National Museum of Health and Medicine, to Tom Killion, case officer, repatriation office, October 21, 1991, in Roberts, "The Sand Creek Massacre Site"; War Department, Surgeon General's Office, *A Report of Surgical Cases Treated in the Army of the United States from 1865–1871* (Washington, DC: Government Printing Office, 1871), 15–16; Thomas, *Skull Wars*, 37–56, 100–107.

9. Associated Press, "U.S. to Return Human Remains to Tribes," *Rocky Mountain News*, October 12, 1992, 16; "Meeting Notes, March 18–21, 2002, Denver, Colorado," in FSCMNHS, now at NPS-WACC; "Meeting Notes, March 17, 2004, Denver, Colorado," in FSCMNHS, now at NPS-WACC; Wilkinson, *Blood Struggle*, 207.

10. Alexa Roberts interview, July 21, 2008; Braided Hair to Kelman, e-mail, June 24, 2008; Alexa Roberts to Ari Kelman, e-mail, September 20, 2011, in author's possession.

11. Quotes from "About the Center," Center of the American West, http://centerwest.org/about/ and http://centerwest.org/about/patty/. See also Alexa Roberts interview, July 21, 2008; Braided Hair to Kelman, e-mail, June 24, 2008; Roberts to Kelman, e-mail, September 20, 2011.

12. Quote from Braided Hair to Kelman, e-mail, June 24, 2008. See also Percy Ednalino, "Sand Creek Letters Go to Senate," *Denver Post*, September 16, 2000, B-4; Dick Kreck, "Historians Skirmishing over Sand Creek Letters," *Denver Post*, September 20, 2000, A-2; "Dark Side

of Sand Creek," *Denver Post,* September 16, 2000, B-7; Bob Scott, "There's More to Sand Creek Letters Than Meets Eye," *Rocky Mountain News,* September 22, 2000, A-54; Alexa Roberts interview, July 21, 2008; "MacArthur Fellows Program," MacArthur Foundation, http://www .macfound.org/site/c.lkLXJ8MQKrH/b.959463/k.9D7D/Fellows _Program.htm.

13. Quotes from Alexa Roberts interview, July 21, 2008.

14. Ibid. See also Braided Hair to Kelman, e-mail, June 24, 2008; Sanford Levinson, *Written in Stone: Public Monuments in Changing Societies* (Durham, NC: Duke University Press, 1998), 10; Jenny Edkins, *Trauma and the Memory of Politics* (Cambridge: Cambridge University Press, 2003), 10–19.

15. "Protecting their ..." from Braided Hair to Kelman, e-mail, June 24, 2008. See also Alexa Roberts interview, July 21, 2008.

16. "Sacred playbook" from Steve Brady, interview by author, September 12, 2003, telephone, tape recording, in author's possession. All other quotes from Alexa Roberts, interview by author, September 15, 2011, telephone, tape recording, in author's possession.

17. "It was just ..." and "lay some ..." from Alexa Roberts, interview by author, September 2, 2011, telephone, tape recording, in author's possession. All other quotes from Jeff Campbell, volunteer interpreter, Sand Creek Massacre National Historic Site, interview by author, September 13, 2011, telephone, notes in author's possession.

18. Quotes from Jeff Campbell interview, September 13, 2011.

19. Ibid. See also Jeff C. Campbell, "Sand Creek Massacre, Background Booklet #1, 1st Regiment Cavalry, Colorado Volunteers, [United States Army Volunteers], Formerly Known as: 1st Regiment Infantry, Colorado Volunteers, 1861–1865, Alphabetical Roll of Regiment and Alphabetical Roll of Regiment by Company," May 2006, in FSCMNHS, now at NPS-WACC; Jeff C. Campbell, "Sand Creek Massacre Background Booklet #2, 3rd Regiment Cavalry, Colorado Volunteers, [United States Army Volunteers], a One Hundred Days Regiment], August to December 1865, Alphabetical Roll of Regiment and Alphabetical Roll of Regiment by Company," May 2006, in FSCMNHS, now at NPS-WACC; Jeff C. Campbell, "Sand Creek Massacre, Background Booklet #3, the John Milton Chivington Record, June 02, 1813–October 04, 1894," May 2006, in FSCMNHS, now at NPS-WACC; Roberts to Kelman, e-mail, September 20, 2011.

20. Quotes from Jeff Campbell interview, September 13, 2011. See also Testimony of Private Alexander F. Safely in "Report of the Secretary of War," 39th Cong., 2nd Sess., S. Ex. Doc. 26, 221–221; Andrew Jackson Templeton papers, Starsmore Research Center, Pioneer Museum of

Colorado Springs, Colorado Springs, CO; Irving Howbert, *Memories of a Lifetime in the Pike's Peak Region* (New York: G. P. Putnam's Sons, 1925), 11-142; George Bent to George Hyde, April 30, 1906, Coe Collection, Beinecke Library, Yale University, New Haven, CT; George Bent to George Hyde, October 15, 1914, Letter 10, George Bent Manuscript Collection 54, Colorado Historical Society, Denver, CO; George Bent to George Hyde, March 15, 1905, Coe Collection.

21. Quote from Jeff Campbell interview, September 13, 2011. See also "Big Sandy Rises," *Brandon Bell*, August 2, 1912; "Headgates Near Completion," *Colorado Farm and Ranch*, October 18, 1912; "Brandon Paragraphs," *Brandon Bell*, December 20, 1912; "Brandon Paragraphs," *Brandon Bell*, June 13, 1913; "Brandon Paragraphs," *Brandon Bell*, February 7, 1913; "The Irrigation Reservoir," *Brandon Bell*, February 28, 1913; "Chivington Canal Election," *Brandon Bell*, December 5, 1913; "Brandon," *Brandon Bell*, December 12, 1913; "Some Contracts Let," *Colorado Farm and Ranch*, January 17, 1913; "Work Begins on Canal Outlet," *Brandon Bell*, February 13, 1914; "Big Reservoirs Filling," *Colorado Farm and Ranch*, May 8, 1914; "Brandon," *Brandon Bell*, May 8, 1914; "Brandon," *Colorado Farm and Ranch*, August 18, 1916; "Chivington Canal Near Brandon to Be Repaired," *Kiowa County Press*, February 16, 1917; "Eads Locals," *Kiowa County Press*, August 6, 1920; "Locals," *Kiowa County Press*, May 8, 1925.

22. Quote from Jeff Campbell interview, September 13, 2011.

23. Quotes from Alexa Roberts, interview by author, May 20, 2011, telephone, notes in author's possession. See also Jeff Campbell interview, September 13, 2011.

24. Quotes from Alexa Roberts interview, May 20, 2011. See also Amy M. Holmes and Michael McFaul, "Geoarcheological Assessment of the Sand Creek Massacre Site, Kiowa County, Colorado," October 18, 1999, 3-11, in FSCMNHS, now at NPS-WACC; National Park Service, Intermountain Region, *Sand Creek Massacre Project*, vol. 1: *Site Location Study* (Denver: National Park Service, Intermountain Region, 2000), 1, 4, 9-10, 15-16, 26, 31-32, 35-36, 76-78, 188; National Park Service, Intermountain Region, *Sand Creek Massacre Project*, vol. 2: *Special Resource Study* (Denver: National Park Service, Intermountain Region, 2000), 14, 17-19, 46; Laird Cometsevah, interview, May 12, 2003; Jeff Campbell interview, September 13, 2011.

25. "All I've been doing . . ." and "I'd never say I'm 100 percent . . ." from Jeff Campbell interview, September 13, 2011. All other quotes from Alexa Roberts interview, May 20, 2011.

26. Quotes from Jeff Campbell interview, September 13, 2011.

27. Kenneth E. Foote, *Shadowed Ground: America's Landscapes of Violence and Tragedy* (Austin: University of Texas Press, 1997), 5-8, 33-35; Hyde, *Life of George Bent*, 149-155; Jeff Campbell interview, September 13, 2011.

28. John Bodnar, *The Good War in American Memory* (Baltimore, MD: Johns Hopkins University Press, 2010), 2–4, 11; Drew Gilpin Faust, *This Republic of Suffering: Death and the American Civil War* (New York: Vintage, 2009), 4–11, 66–97; Stephanie McCurry, *Confederate Reckoning: Power and Politics in the Civil War South* (Cambridge, MA: Harvard University Press, 2010), 2–9, 219–360; Edward T. Linenthal, *Preserving Memory: The Struggle to Create America's Holocaust Museum* (New York: Columbia University Press, 1995), xv, 61–64.

29. David Blight, *American Oracle: The Civil War in the Civil Rights Era* (Cambridge, MA: Belknap Press of Harvard University Press, 2011), 6, 22; Michael A. Elliot, *Custerology: The Enduring Legacy of the Indian Wars and George Armstrong Custer* (Chicago: University of Chicago Press, 2007), 7, 47–49; Michael Kammen, *Mystic Chords of Memory: Transformations of Tradition in American Culture* (New York: Vintage, 1993), 191; Richard Slotkin, *Gunfighter Nation: The Myth of the Frontier in the Twentieth Century* (New York: Harper, 1992), 6; Eric Rauchway, *Blessed among Nations: How the World Made America* (New York: Hill and Wang, 2007), 9–14.

30. Quote from Abraham Lincoln, "Address Delivered at the Dedication of the Cemetery at Gettysburg," in David A. Hollinger and Charles Capper, eds., *The American Intellectual Tradition: 1630–1865* (Oxford: Oxford University Press, 1993), 429. See also Gary Wills, *Lincoln at Gettysburg: The Words That Remade America* (New York: Simon and Schuster, 2006), 63–89; Gabor S. Boritt, *The Gettysburg Gospel: The Lincoln Speech That Nobody Knows* (New York: Simon and Schuster, 2006), 31–47, 96–121, 144–160; "Gettysburg Address (1863)," OurDocuments.gov, http://www.ourdocuments.gov/doc.php?flash=true&doc=36; Avishai Margalit, *The Ethics of Memory* (Cambridge, MA: Harvard University Press, 2002), 77–85; Karl Jacoby, *Shadows at Dawn: A Borderlands Massacre and the Violence of History* (New York: Penguin, 2008), 1–7.

Index

Note: Page numbers in *italics* indicate maps and illustrations.